changing the way the world learns

To get extra value from this book for no additional cost, go to:

http://www.thomson.com/wadsworth.html

thomson.com is the World Wide Web site for Wadsworth/ITP
and is your direct source to dozens of on-line resources.
thomson.com helps you find out about supplements,
experiment with demonstration software, search for a job,
and send e-mail to many of our authors. You can even
preview new publications and exciting new technologies.

thomson.com: *It's where you'll find us in the future.*

From the Wadsworth Series in Television and Film

Broadcast Selling, Advertising, and Programming

Broadcast and Cable Selling, Updated 2nd Ed., Charles Warner/Joseph Buchman

Broadcast/Cable Programming: Strategies and Practices, 5th Ed., Susan T. Eastman/Douglas Ferguson

Writing for Broadcast and Film

Scriptwriting for High-Impact Videos, John Morley

Copywriting for the Electronic Media, 2nd Ed., Milan D. Meeske/R. C. Norris

Writing for Television and Radio, 6th Ed., Robert L. Hilliard

Writing the Screenplay: TV and Film, 2nd Ed., Alan A. Armer

Production for Broadcast, Video, and Film

Video Basics, Herbert Zettl

Television Production Handbook, 6th Ed., Herbert Zettl

Crafting News for the Electronic Media: Writing, Reporting, and Production, Carl Hausman

Lighting for Film and Electronic Cinematography, Dave Viera

Institutional Video: Planning, Budgeting, Production, and Evaluation, Carl Hausman

Video Communication: Structuring Content for Maximum Program Effectiveness, David L. Smith

Sight-Sound-Motion: Applied Media Aesthetics, 2nd Ed., Herbert Zettl

Electronic Cinematography: Achieving Photographic Control Over the Video Image, Harry Mathias/Richard Patterson

Directing TV and Film, 2nd Ed., Alan A. Armer

Audio in Media, 4th Ed., Stanley R. Alten

Modern Radio Production, 4th Ed., Carl Hausman/Philip Benoit/Lewis B. O'Donnell

Other Broadcast Titles

Management of Electronic Media, Alan B. Albarran

Announcing: Broadcast Communicating Today, 3rd Ed., Lewis B. O'Donnell/Carl Hausman/Philip Benoit

Radio Station Operations: Management and Employee Perspectives, Lewis B. O'Donnell/Carl Hausman/Philip Benoit

Stay Tuned: A Concise History of American Broadcasting, 2nd Ed., Christopher H. Sterling/John M. Kitross

World Broadcasting Systems: A Comparative Analysis, Sydney W. Head

Electronic Moviemaking third edition

Lynne S. Gross

Pepperdine University

Larry W. Ward

California State University, Fullerton

Wadsworth Publishing Company

I(T)P® An International Thomson Publishing Company

Belmont, CA • Albany, NY • Bonn • Boston • Cincinnati • Detroit • Johannesburg • London • Madrid • Melbourne
Mexico City • New York • Paris • San Francisco • Singapore • Tokyo • Toronto • Washington

Communications & Media Studies Editor: *Todd R. Armstrong*
Editorial Assistant: *Michael Gillespie*
Production: *Hal Lockwood*
Copy editing: *Jean Mann*
Composition: *Thompson Type*
Print Buyer: *Barbara Britton*
Interior Design: *Ellen Pettengell*
Cover Design: *Cuttriss and Hambleton*
Printer: *Courier, Kendallville*

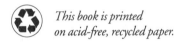
For more information, contact Wadsworth Publishing Company, 10 Davis Drive, Belmont, CA 94002, or electronically at http://www.thomson.com/wadsworth.html.

International Thomson Publishing Europe
Berkshire House 168-173
High Holborn
London, WC1V 7AA, England

Thomas Nelson Australia
102 Dodds Street
South Melbourne 3205
Victoria, Australia

Nelson Canada
1120 Birchmount Road
Scarborough, Ontario
Canada M1K 5G4

International Thomson Editores
Campos Eliseos 385, Piso 7
Col. Polanco
11560 México D.F. México

International Thomson Publishing GmbH
Königswinterer Strasse 418
53227 Bonn, Germany

International Thomson Publishing Asia
221 Henderson Road
#05-10 Henderson Building
Singapore 0315

International Thomson Publishing Japan
Hirakawacho Kyowa Building, 3F
2-2-1 Hirakawacho
Chiyoda-ku, Tokyo 102, Japan

International Thomson Publishing Southern Africa
Building 18, Constantia Park
240 Old Pretoria Road
Halfway House, 1685 South Africa

Library of Congress Cataloging-in-Publication Data

Gross, Lynne S.
    Electronic moviemaking / Lynne S. Gross, Larry W. Ward. — 3rd ed.
        p.   cm. — (Wadsworth series in television and film)
    Includes bibliographical references and index.
    ISBN 0-534-50747-6
    1. Video recording.   2. Electronic cameras.   3. Cinematography.
4. Motion pictures—Production and direction.   5. Video recordings—Production and direction.
I. Ward, Larry Wayne.   II. Title.   III. Series.
TR850.G76   1997
778.5'23—dc20   96-27201

About the Authors

LYNNE GROSS teaches television production at Pepperdine University in Malibu, California. In the past she has taught full-time at California State University, Fullerton, Loyola Marymount University, and Long Beach City College.

She has worked in the television business as program director for Valley Cable TV and as producer for several hundred television programs, including the series "From Chant to Chance," "Effective Living," and "Surveying the Universe."

Her consulting work includes projects for RKO, KCET, CBS, the Olympics, Visa, and the Iowa State Board of Regents. It has also taken her to Malaysia, Swaziland, Estonia, Australia, and Guyana, where she has taught radio and television production.

She is active in many professional organizations, serving as a governor of the Academy of Television Arts and Sciences and president of the Broadcast Education Association. She is the author of ten other books and numerous journal and magazine articles.

LARRY WARD is a professor of communications at California State University, Fullerton, where he teaches primarily film and television production and film history and aesthetics.

He has worked professionally as a film editor on the "Lowell Thomas Remembers" series for PBS and has produced hundreds of hours of sports and public affairs programming broadcast and cablecast in the Los Angeles–Orange County area.

In 1983 he was producer-director for "The Science Report," a series of educational tapes for sixth-grade students funded by Union Oil and the Placentia School District. Before that he was director-editor for "The Moving Picture Boys in the Great War," a documentary film for Post-Newsweek Television Productions.

He has published a number of articles and papers and one other book, *The Motion Picture Goes to War*. He has also served as the western regional coordinator for the Motion Picture Academy's Nicholl Fellowships in Screenwriting Contest.

Preface

Electronic Moviemaking, which emphasizes the combination of film and video, has become more valid as the years progress. The use of electronic equipment in conjunction with traditional film techniques is becoming increasingly widespread, academically and professionally. This edition, like its predecessor, is intended to meet the needs of professionals and academics who are combining film and video and want to emphasize the directorial and storytelling functions of the media.

This third edition of *Electronic Moviemaking* follows the same basic preproduction, production, postproduction structure as the first edition. However, at the suggestion of reviewers and students, we have repositioned and rewritten chapters so that readers now are introduced to an overview of these subjects before being presented with in-depth material. We have also updated a number of chapters, particularly those that deal with equipment operation. The chapters that deal with approaches to handling moviemaking have changed the least. The aesthetic principles remain fairly constant, regardless of changes in technology.

- Preproduction, which is frequently short-changed, is given special emphasis in this book in two chapters. One deals with developing the original concept, and the other covers the various tasks involved in preproduction and the organizational skills and planning concepts needed to ensure a smooth production.
- The first chapter in the production section gives an overview of each activity likely to take place during a typical production. The rest of the chapters in this section are paired. The first chapter in each pair deals with the technical aspects of the subject and the second with the aesthetic concepts. Cameras and lenses, lights and filters, and micro-

phones and recorders are all handled in this way.
- The postproduction section also starts with an overview chapter and is then arranged in pairs. We discuss image editing and sound editing in terms of techniques and creative approaches.

Throughout the book we discuss various levels of equipment, from consumer-grade to professional equipment that is still evolving. We do this because the type of equipment available varies greatly from school to school or company to company and because we feel students should know not only about the equipment they are currently using but about the equipment they may be using in the future. Our emphasis is on electronic equipment, but we also give some attention to film equipment, in part because film and video are often used together and in part because numerous techniques discussed in the book have evolved from film.

The book's focus is on what a student needs to know to develop a successful narrative moving picture, but many of these principles are useful for other forms, such as documentaries, educational programs, commercials, and music videos. Our overall emphasis is on the forethought and care that must go into all aspects of production. A book like this cannot avoid the "techno-speak" associated with film and video, so we have included the technical information that we feel anyone engaged in production in this area should know. However, our main emphasis is on the creative process, the kinds of decisions that are made, and the strategies that are developed.

We have included a number of special features that we hope will aid the reader. The glossary defines all the words that appear in the text in boldface print. The selected readings at the end of the book and the references cited in the notes should lead those who desire more information to appropriate sources. Many notes also contain additional content for those who want to understand a subject more deeply. The many drawings and photographs should be especially helpful in understanding the concepts discussed.

In previous editions of this book we included an introduction that gave a rationale for the combining of film and video. This merging idea, which was rather revolutionary in the late 1980s when we were writing the first edition, has now been so widely adopted that we have eliminated this introductory section. Similarly, previous editions included a final chapter in which we predicted future happenings in the merging of film and video. Sometimes we were wrong, but more often we were simply out of date by the time the book was published. While the ink was drying the future had become the present. Therefore, we have eliminated the future chapter and have incorporated ideas on the horizon within the chapters to which they relate. Electronic moviemaking has become well enough established that we feel it can stand on

its own without the bookends of rationale and future predictions.

We appreciate the help of the many professionals and academicians who made suggestions for this revision. In particular, we wish to acknowledge the following reviewers:

Zaki Lisha, De Anza College
William Neff, Montana State University
Phil Miller, Boston University
Michael Zingale, Pasadena City College

We also thank the reviewers of previous editions as well:

Steve Gilliland, West Virginia State College
Margot Starr Kernan, Maryland Institute College of Art
Jay Korinek, Henry Ford Community College
Philip Miller, Boston University
John W. Newhouse, Southwestern College
Kenny Suit, Baylor University
Gordon Webb, Ithaca College

Brief Contents

Contents

part three
Postproduction 177

part one
Preproduction

chapter one
Developing the Script

William Goldman, a two-time Academy Award winner and the author of screenplays for such films as *Harper, Butch Cassidy and the Sundance Kid, Marathon Man,* and *All the President's Men,* has expressed an obvious but fundamental axiom about moviemaking—"There is no picture without a script."[1]

The script is the crucial element that drives preproduction (planning), production (shooting), and postproduction (editing). Each of these phases is crucial to the phase that follows. Inadequate preproduction almost guarantees poor production, and poor production is seldom "saved" in editing. However, none of these phases is even possible without a script.

The Writer's Role

The idea for a movie may be initiated by the **writer,*** or a **producer** may initiate the idea and find a writer willing to turn the idea into a script. Sometimes scriptwriting begins with the writer verbally presenting the basic story idea or concept to a producer. If the producer buys the idea, the writer may be commissioned to develop it into a completed script. Regardless of who initiates the idea (the writer, the producer, or the director) or where the idea comes from (an original story or an adaptation of a novel or play), someone ultimately must put words on the page and prepare a completed script. That someone is the writer.

The writer's major contribution comes before and during preproduction. As a screenplay evolves from a rough idea to a polished script, it will go through many stages of writing and rewriting. Different writers may be brought in at any stage to turn the story in a new direction, to solve plot problems, or to punch up the dialogue. Although it may be possible to sell an idea and initiate a project based entirely on a verbal presentation, until a complete screenplay actually exists on paper, proceeding with meaningful preproduction is difficult.

The writer's role during shooting is far more limited and often the source of great frustration.[2] The writer may be called on to rewrite dialogue or to make small changes in some area of the script but often has little say about how the screenplay is modified or rewritten during production by the director, producer, actors, agents, or anyone else with the power to make changes. This frustration has sent some writers into directing as the surest way to bring a script to the screen in the way they originally visualized it on paper.

Many excellent books focus on the art and craft of screenwriting.[3] Typically, such books provide guidance on how to develop a story and plot, create characters, write dialogue, and use the proper screenplay format. This book is not a screenwriting text, and for that reason we assume that the student moviemaker will have a completed script in hand before electronic moviemaking begins. Nevertheless, students must be familiar with certain screenwriting terms and concepts. These are discussed in the next section.

Screenplay Terminology

A **shot** begins when the camera and/or videotape recorder starts recording and ends when it stops. It may be short or long, require a complex camera movement, or be totally static. The **scene** is the basic dramatic building block of the screenplay. A scene is usually defined as a unified action occurring in a single time and place. It may be composed of a single shot but normally is made up of a group of shots. A **sequence** is a somewhat more arbitrary concept. It consists of a group of scenes linked together or unified by some common theme, time, idea, location, or action. A sequence might consist of a character coming of age in a series of related scenes. Elaborate car chase scenes are often sequences. In

*Boldfaced terms are defined in the glossary at the end of the book.

```
                        CONCEPT

                    OLD MOTHER WITCH


     Old Mother Witch is a film adapted from the popular
children's book of the same name by Carol Carrick.  It is a story
about understanding, empathy, and the need to bridge the
generation gap.
     A young boy and his rambunctious friends have a running
quarrel with a cranky old woman in their neighborhood.  She is so
mean that they begin calling her the "Old Mother Witch."  During
a dark and eerie Halloween night a "really" frightening event
occurs.  This teaches the young boy and his friends a dramatic
lesson about appreciating and helping other people.
```

Figure 1.1
A sample concept for Old Mother Witch.

Forrest Gump the cross-country running sequence compresses Forrest's three-year, two-month, fourteen-day run back and forth across America into six minutes of screen time. The series of mob murders during the christening scene near the end of *The Godfather* is an example of a far more complex sequence, one that juxtaposes the rituals of religious ceremony and Michael Corleone's consolidation of power through the ritualistic killings of his gangland rivals.

A screenplay is constructed from scenes and sequences. Like any narrative—a novel, short story, or fairy tale—a screenplay has a beginning, middle, and end. But a motion picture narrative is not really complete on paper. Until the screenplay is brought to life by the sounds and images in the completed picture, it is more of a blueprint, a movie in waiting.

Scripting Stages

A narrative screenplay usually goes through many different stages of writing. Sometimes a particular stage will be skipped or combined with another stage. At other times a stage will be repeated again and again, perhaps with a new writer brought in, either to do a complete rewrite or to make minor changes.

The Concept. The **concept**, also called the *story idea, premise,* or *synopsis,* is a brief written account describing the basic idea for the story.

It presents a thumbnail sketch of the story and is often used to provide a busy producer or story editor with a quick means of evaluating the overall scope of a motion picture. It is short (usually only a paragraph or two), simple, and to the point. Some screenwriters believe that a good concept can be expressed in a single sentence, one line that describes who does what and where this takes place. The argument for beginning the screenwriting process with a brief story idea is that if a short concept can't catch and hold a reader's interest, it hardly makes sense to develop that idea into a full-length 120-page screenplay.

Reducing a story to a few sentences or paragraphs is difficult. Professional screenwriters often see this as an effective way to distill the central ideas and to provide direction for writing the entire screenplay. A well-written concept or premise can offer an overview or unifying thread for the entire production; it is a way to keep the screenplay focused on the basic concept.

Figure 1.1 presents an example of a brief concept for a movie script written by Mark Chodzko, based on a children's book by Carol Carrick. This script was made into a twenty-eight-minute movie distributed by Phoenix Films. We will refer to this script from time to time to illustrate the various steps and stages in electronic moviemaking.[4]

The Scene Outline. The **scene outline** is a list in numerical order of all the scenes in a

Figure 1.2

Part of the scene outline for Old Mother Witch.

SCENE OUTLINE

OLD MOTHER WITCH

1. Introduction of the main characters in the film: David Martinez, age 10, and his friends Scottie, Mary Ellen, and Eric-- the so-called neighborhood "wild bunch." They have a brief but noisy confrontation with their neighborhood rivals, the bullies Eddie Malone and Don MacDonald. This disturbs David's next door neighbor, Mrs. Oliver, an old widow who hates the loud noises and disturbances the children frequently cause. She asks them to keep down the racket.

2. David and his friends complain to David's father about Mrs. Oliver's constant nagging. Then they decide to play football.

3. During a spirited football game the ball is accidentally thrown into Mrs. Oliver's yard, almost breaking her window. She decides to keep the football to punish them.

4. David and his parents discuss the need to empathize with the old woman. She is alone and in poor health. David's parents suggest that he go over and apologize to her.

5. Mrs. Oliver explains her difficulties with the neighborhood children to a friend.

6. David, acting on his parents' suggestion, nervously approaches Mrs. Oliver's house. He rings the doorbell.

7. At first, Mrs. Oliver does not hear the bell. When she finally does she hesitates to answer it.

8. By the time she reaches the door and opens it, David has already left in disgust.

9. It's Halloween night, and groups of kids in costumes are trick or treating in the neighborhood. A newly cut jack-o-lantern glows on David's front porch.

10. David and Scottie meet at David's house to plan their evening's trick or treating and to compare costumes.

11. On the sidewalk outside of David's house, David and Scottie discuss the "old witch," Mrs. Oliver. David draws a picture of an old witch on the sidewalk with chalk and adds an arrow pointing toward Mrs. Oliver's front door.

12. The two boys go to the Bridwell's house. The Bridwell's take Halloween seriously, dressing in scary costumes and trying to frighten the would-be trick or treaters. As they are taking candy from a bowl, the boys are given a good scare by Mrs. Bridwell.

screenplay, with a brief description of what occurs in each scene. A scene outline does not use dialogue or elaborate descriptions. Its purpose is to help the writer expand the basic elements suggested in the concept and develop them into a workable structure. This is done by listing, scene by scene, what happens in each setting. The first page of the scene outline for *Old Mother Witch* is shown in Figure 1.2 and photos illustrating some of the scenes are shown in Figures 1.3 and 1.4.

A scene outline is an excellent tool for testing the plot, the way the story will be presented in the screenplay and eventually in the completed film. This is not necessarily the same thing as the story, the chronological telling of events from beginning to end.[5] The same story, for example, might be presented with a variety of different plot structures. One plot presentation might focus on a single day in a character's life with the rest of the story fleshed out by dialogue and voice-over remembrances. Plotted in a different way, the story might begin with a character's death and go back to show the events leading up to the moment at which the film began. Some films, such as Quentin Tarantino's *Pulp Fiction*, have a plot presentation that purposely jumbles the order of the story events, forcing the viewer to mentally reconstruct the story chronology.

Bernardo Bertolucci's Academy Award–winning film, *The Last Emperor* (1987), is a good example of the differences between story and plot. This film tells the story of China's last emperor, a man whose life spanned a period of incredible change from the early 1900s to the late 1960s. He becomes emperor as a small child and grows to manhood a virtual prisoner behind the walls of the Imperial Palace within the Forbidden City. During World War II he cooperates with the Japanese and heads a puppet government in exile in Manchuria. After the war he is thrown in prison by the communist government. His final days are spent as a humble gardener at a time when the Red Guards and the Cultural Revolution are beginning to sweep across China.

The order in which these events are presented on the screen is not chronological. The film begins with a scene in 1950: the emperor attempts to commit suicide at the train station as he is being sent to prison. He is saved but remembers in flashback the day in 1908 when he was crowned emperor of all China. This pattern of plot presentation is repeated throughout *The Last Emperor*, moving back and forth in time from the emperor's life in prison to his memories of various incidents. The flashbacks move consistently forward in time, until the story catches up with the emperor's imprisonment. At that point the story and plot move together to the film's conclusion.

A scene outline can be an invaluable tool for analyzing plot development and for experimenting with the relationships between scenes or between scenes and the screenplay as a whole. It can help the writer see whether a scene is help-

Figure 1.3
The neighborhood kids have a run-in with Mrs. Oliver in Old Mother Witch. *(Photo courtesy of Phoenix Films, Mark Chodzko, and Carol Carrick)*

Figure 1.4
Scottie, David, Eric, and Mary Ellen meet on the street on Halloween night in a scene from Old Mother Witch. *(Photo courtesy of Phoenix Films, Mark Chodzko, and Carol Carrick)*

ing to advance the story or whether it is contributing primarily to character development. Professional screenwriters frequently advocate putting each scene on an index card, a procedure that makes it easy to insert or eliminate scenes or try scenes in a different order.

One of the best-known screenwriting books, Syd Field's *Screenplay*,[6] stresses the importance of having each scene advance the action and move the story forward. Field places special emphasis on what he calls *plot points,* especially important scenes that occur near the end of the screenplay's opening movement and again just before the motion picture's climax and resolution. Plot points help grab the audience's interest and turn the story in a different direction, driving the story to a more powerful and dramatic conclusion.

Most screenwriting books, Field's included, focus on the type of screenplay written for commercial, feature-length motion pictures. This is a highly conventional (or traditional) means of storytelling—what some scholars have referred to as the "classical Hollywood narrative."[7] This style evolved in Hollywood filmmaking over a period of approximately eighty years and became the dominant mode of motion picture storytelling throughout the world. Although there are as many ways to tell a story as there are storytellers, this style of motion picture does have some common patterns or traditions. Typically, such stories are centered on a single character (the protagonist) who has some need or desire that drives the story forward. The basic conflict in the story springs from some character (the antagonist) who blocks or opposes that need or desire. Because of time constraints (normally 90 to 120 minutes), the plot presents only the events that advance the story to resolution of the basic conflict. Finally, this style of narrative almost always has a conclusion that ties up the loose ends. By the time the final credits roll, the conflict is resolved, all our questions are answered, and we usually have a good idea of what will happen to each character. Many films today have two protagonists (the cop and a buddy, Thelma and Louise, the prince and the princess), but the basic narrative structure of such screenplays is similar to the classic Hollywood model.

The student moviemaker often has difficulty applying many of these narrative principles and patterns to a screenplay that is only twenty to thirty pages long (twenty to thirty minutes' running time). The screenplay must have a beginning, a middle, and an end, but such a short script provides far less time for developing characters, creating an elaborate plot, or providing a complete resolution of the conflict. The budget and the lack of equipment and editing may impose additional constraints. The only answer is to keep things simple. Reduce the number of characters and settings, eliminate as much on-screen **backstory** (the background material needed to set up the narrative) as possible, and write a script that can be produced within the many limitations the student moviemaker typically faces. Keep the script short, simple, and focused.

The Treatment.   The **treatment,** one of the most important stages in scriptwriting, is a prose description of the story. It reads like a short story, describing the action in detail (see Figure 1.5). A well-written treatment provides precisely the kind of visual imagery and atmosphere the writer must have to develop a finished screenplay. It gives the first indications of where dialogue will be needed and builds on and amplifies the characters, settings, action, and motivation suggested in the scene outline.

Treatments vary in length. Some writers advocate a full dialogue treatment as the final step before writing the screenplay; such a treatment is much longer than the scene outline. Treatments often are used to sell a project to a network or to raise money. They are excellent for these purposes because they provide a full, readable description of the movie. A treatment developed as a sales tool will be rather short (usually no more than five pages) because that is all a busy executive will take the time to read. A verbal pitch of the story to an executive or potential backer often occurs in conjunction with delivery of the treatment.

The Master Scene Script.   The **master scene script** is a translation of the treatment into script form (see Figure 1.6). It is based on general scenes (like a stage play) rather than on specific shots, a step that takes place at a later stage of scripting. Using the treatment as a guide, a writer creates a master scene script, which includes a heading for each location or scene (for example, INT. GRAND BALLROOM— LATE EVENING). In some cases scenes are numbered, although this is not a requirement. Beneath the scene heading is descriptive material that provides detailed information about the scene and the characters' action. The dialogue

TREATMENT

OLD MOTHER WITCH

The film begins on a beautiful autumn day. Walking down the
sidewalk, carrying the Halloween pumpkins that they have just
purchased at the local pumpkin patch, are the members of the
neighborhood "wild bunch." Their unofficial leader is David
Martinez, a bright dark-haired boy of 10. He is accompanied by
his friends Scottie, a pudgy kid who is always eating something;
Mary Ellen, a black girl with long legs who is very athletic; and
Eric, the "brain" of the group. It is Halloween day and they are
in high spirits as they plan the evening's trick or treating and
refine some new one-liners about Scottie's eating habits and
Eric's intelligence. Their kibitzing is abruptly ended by the
arrival of the long-time neighborhood bullies, Eddie Malone and
Don MacDonald. The two groups exchange putdowns on the sidewalk.
Eddie and Don are out of their league in a game of words, so they
turn to their specialty--threatening to get even with the "wild
bunch" in the dark streets on Halloween night. Laughing, they
speed away on their skateboards. This sidewalk confrontation has
caught the attention of Mrs. Oliver, David's 70-year-old
neighbor. Leaning over her garden fence, Mrs. Oliver delivers an
all too familiar lecture about making noise and causing a
disturbance in her quiet neighborhood.

David's father is washing the family car in the driveway as
David and his friends arrive at David's house. After their
confrontations with Don and Eddie and Mrs. Oliver, the "wild
bunch" is not feeling so wild. Mrs. Oliver, they decide, is
simply a "nag." Mary Ellen suggests they forget their troubles
with a game of touch football.

The football field is the front yard of David's house. Two
trees and some sweatshirts mark the boundaries. Sides are
chosen. Mary Ellen and David are on one team, and Scottie and
Eric are on the other. These teams are not fairly matched. Mary
Ellen is by far the best quarterback, and David is the best
receiver. It is going to be a mercifully quick slaughter. Mary
Ellen and David decide to strike quickly with a "bomb." David
heads for the end zone as Mary Ellen throws a beautiful spiral
toward him. Unfortunately the ball sails far over David's head,
over the fence beyond the end zone and into Mrs. Oliver's yard.
It hits her house with a loud thud, nearly breaking a window.
Everyone freezes. Suddenly Mrs. Oliver storms out the door and
down the steps. She picks up the football and angrily castigates
the children for nearly breaking her window and for making such
an infernal racket. To teach them a lesson, she tells them she
is going to keep their football for a while. After she goes back
in the house, the former football players agree that she is
indeed an "old witch." Mary Ellen suggests that she might have

1

Figure 1.5

Excerpt from the treatment for Old Mother Witch. *The entire treatment runs seven pages.*

spoken by each character and any appropriate
stage directions follow the descriptive material.
There are no camera instructions or detailed
shot descriptions.

At this stage a master scene script is considered a finished product, the final screenplay
commonly shown to producers, directors, studios, and agents. The master scene script contains as many ideas from the treatment as is
feasible, rounding out and filling in details of
location, action, and characterization as needed.
Rewriting or even omitting a few scenes described in the scene outline or the treatment
may be necessary, but these changes are minimal

Figure 1.6
Excerpt from the master scene script of Old Mother Witch, *written by Mark Chodzko and based on the book by Carol Carrick.*

MASTER SCENE SCRIPT

OLD MOTHER WITCH

SCENE 1

EXT. NEIGHBORHOOD STREET - DAY

It's a beautiful autumn day as 10-year-old DAVID MARTINEZ
and his friends, SCOTTIE, a pudgy little kid who is always
eating something; MARY ELLEN, a black girl with long legs
who is very athletic; and ERIC, the "brain" of the group,
walk down the street carrying pumpkins that each of them has
just picked from the local pumpkin patch. They are laughing
and having a good time. Eric tries to balance his on top of
his head. OPENING TITLES and MUSIC play over the scene.

                    DAVID
                  (beaming)
          Now this is what I call a pumpkin!

David's is perfectly shaped.

                    ERIC
          Hey Scottie! Your pumpkin kind of
          reminds me of you. It's a wide body!

Mary Ellen and David laugh.

                    SCOTTIE
          Watch it "slide rule" or you're going
          to be wearing it for a hat!

Everybody laughs as they near Mrs. Oliver's house, which is
next door to David's. MRS. OLIVER, an old cantankerous
woman in her 70s, is out raking leaves in her garden. Just
then Mary Ellen notices EDDIE MALONE, age 12, and his friend DON
MACDONALD drive up with Eddie's brother FRANK, age 16. Frank
just got his driver's license and with it an old junky Fiat
convertible. Frank thinks it's a great car even though it's
not. And Eddie and Don think they are pretty cool riding
around with the top down.

                    MARY ELLEN
          Oh no. Look at the sludge that just
          creeped in.

David groans.

                    DAVID
          Not Eddie and Don.

                                        (CONTINUED)

if the treatment is well developed. The completed master scene script represents the screenwriter's final attempt to visualize the story on the page. Additional changes will be made during production, but in many cases the screenwriter's task ends when the master scene script is finished.

The Shooting Script.   The **shooting script** is the final stage of scriptwriting. Although the director may have collaborated with the screenwriter in the earlier stages of writing, the shooting script is usually the director's responsibility. Different directors have different ways of working, but a shooting script basically consists of

<u>**SHOOTING SCRIPT**</u>

OLD MOTHER WITCH

SCENE 1

EXT. NEIGHBORHOOD STREET - DAY

FADE IN:

1. L.S., <u>HIGH ANGLE</u> of the street on a beautiful autumn
    day. We see four neighborhood kids: 10-year-old DAVID
    MARTINEZ; SCOTTIE, a pudgy little kid who is always
    eating something; MARY ELLEN, a black girl with long
    legs who is very athletic; and ERIC, the "brain" of the
    group. The <u>CAMERA TRACKS</u> with them as they walk down
    the sidewalk. They are each carrying pumpkins that
    they have just picked at the local pumpkin patch. We
    <u>TILT DOWN</u> and <u>MOVE CLOSER</u> as Eric tries to balance a
    pumpkin on top of his head. OPENING TITLES and MUSIC
    play over the scene.

                                          DISSOLVE TO:

2. TWO SHOT David and Eric:

                    DAVID
                  (beaming)
        Now this is what I call a pumpkin!

                    ERIC
        Hey Scottie! Your pumpkin kind of
        reminds me of you. It's a wide body!

3. C.U. of Mary Ellen laughing at Eric's joke.

4. C.U. of Scottie:

                    SCOTTIE
        Watch it "slide rule" or you're going
        to be wearing it for a hat.

5. M.S. as everybody laughs. The <u>CAMERA PANS</u> over to MRS.
    OLIVER'S house. Mrs. Oliver, an old cantankerous woman
    in her 70s is out raking leaves in her garden beside
    the house. The <u>CAMERA MOVES UP CLOSER</u> to register the
    look of irritation on Mrs. Oliver's face as she
    observes the kids on the sidewalk.

6. M.S. of Mary Ellen who turns abruptly and looks toward
    the street at the <u>SOUNDS</u> of an old car <u>SPUTTERING TO A</u>
    <u>STOP</u>.

                                          (CONTINUED)

Figure 1.7
The same scene from Old Mother Witch *in a shooting script format.*

the settings, characters, dialogue, and action in the master scene script broken into individual shots with a particular camera angle, movement, or position. (Figure 1.7 shows part of the shooting script for *Old Mother Witch*.) Some shots may be suggested by the dialogue or scene descriptions, but the kind of technical information in a shooting script is considered, at least in modern filmmaking, a decision to be made by the director, not the screenwriter.

In some respects a shooting script is one of the final steps of preproduction. A detailed shooting script can provide an additional level of control and predictability, supplying the di-

Figure 1.8

*Even people who do not
know how to draw can
use software such as
StoryBoard Quick™
that features predrawn
characters, props, and
locations. Clicking the
mouse on the appropri-
ate tool (a) can change
perspective, size, screen
direction, or other fea-
tures; (b) six frames and
captions from a story-
board created with this
software. (Graphics
courtesy of Power-
Production Software)*

a

Conery's car screeches to a stop in front of the
warehouse...

He runs up the dark staircase.

Conery kicks the door open and it's
Eva...She's been found!

Eva: "I can't believe you, what are you
doing--" Conery slams his hand over her
mouth.

The evil Vance's footsteps echo through the
building as he advances on our hero.

Conery turns to listen as we move in closer on
his face...

b

rector and production crew with the technical information they need to set up each shot of the movie. A shooting script can also save time and money by helping to create a realistic schedule (and budget). For example, an especially long and complex shot (one with much complicated camera movement) might take an entire morning to execute—with obvious ramifications for the budget and the shooting schedule.

The shots in the shooting script are numbered consecutively. In addition to the scene headings, descriptive material, and dialogue from the master scene script, the shooting script includes specific instructions about camera angles, positions, and movements. The shooting script also contains information about the transitions between shots or scenes (for example, FADE IN, CUT TO, DISSOLVE TO). Sometimes this information is suggested in the master scene script and is refined further in the final shooting script.

Some directors supplement the shooting script with drawings known as **storyboards** or with diagrams of the set and camera placements. A storyboard represents the director's initial idea for the composition of each shot. A detailed storyboard can provide valuable guidance for the art director, set designer, or camera crew. The director may hire an artist to draw the storyboard or may use a computer program to develop it. Dedicated computer storyboard programs or paint programs that link graphics and text make it easy to render high-quality storyboards (see Figure 1.8).[8]

Even if the director has a complete shooting script and a storyboard in hand, it is easy to change a shot (or decide to try a new one) when the director arrives on the set and begins working with the actors and crew on location. Changing something that is only on paper is always easier (and less costly) than changing something that has already been shot. Revisions to the shooting script may be made throughout production if the script is too long, if the production is taking too much time and running over budget, or if scenes that read well on paper do not play as well during rehearsals. Nevertheless, a good shooting script creates a kind of safety net for the production. For the beginning moviemaker especially, succumbing to the urge to improvise is far less risky if a shooting script provides a basic foundation.

Other Script Forms

Writing a script for a television documentary, a corporate video, a training program, an educational CD-ROM, or any other of the many forms of film, video, or **multimedia** projects involves many of the same steps we have just discussed in the creation and development of a dramatic screenplay. As was the case with theatrical screenwriting, many textbooks detail the development of scripts for news, features, variety shows, commercials, music videos, multimedia projects, and corporate videos.[9]

Some of these script forms are less likely to require the kind of full-blown development we have been discussing. Many modern documentaries, for example, rely heavily on interviews or actuality shooting, material that is virtually impossible to prescript. As a result, an outline might be the final scripting stage.

Music videos also tend to work more from outlines than fully developed scripts. The outline in Figure 1.9 is one example. The lyrics to the song already exist. They are a given. This outline sets up the basic parameters for the shoot. There will be four different locations, and in two the performer (Brian) will lip-sync the song's lyrics. The third location will feature children who will sing a refrain, and the fourth location will wind up as a nonsync vignette based on specific lyrics from the song. Obviously, this kind of scripting is much looser and more open. It relies on the editor (and director) to select and juxtapose the images and lyrics in postproduction. In reality, the final stage of writing (or rewriting) for most music videos occurs in the editing room.

Other types of script do require full development. Look at the excerpt from the script for *DUII: The Price Is Too High,*[10] shown in Figure 1.10. This movie, used in schools for traffic offenders, is sponsored by departments of motor vehicles around the country. It conveys a strong message about driving under the influence of intoxicants. The script is in standard screenplay form and uses an actor/narrator to set up a variety of dramatic scenes that illustrate the basic message. Documentary and instructional materials give the facts and figures that underscore the anti-intoxicant theme.

Figure 1.9

An example of a music video outline. (Script courtesy of Brian Gross)

MUSIC VIDEO FOR
"I LOOK SO GOOD IN YELLOW'
BRIAN

The video will consist of four different set-ups:
    1. Brian, dressed in a variety of yellow clothes, lip
syncing in a nightclub setting.
    2. A chorus of children dressed in yellow singing the "Oo la
la la la la" refrain.
    3. Brian, dressed in a yellow shirt and lip syncing, walking
a dog dressed in a yellow dog jacket.
    4. The three back-up singers in a department store trying on
ugly colored shirts and finally finding yellow ones they like.

We will build two sets in the studio, one for the nightclub scene
and the other for the children's chorus. The nightclub scene
will have a 1940s look to it and will consist of a sequined
curtain and a floor stand microphone. The audience will not be
shown. An intense spotlight will highlight Brian's yellow
clothing.

The children's chorus (about twenty 8 to 10 year olds) will be on
risers against background flats that are painted with geometric
shapes in primary colors.

The dog walking scene will be shot on an eastern street in the
autumn so that several trees with colorful leaves can be shown in
the background.

The scene with the back-up singers will be shot in the men's
clothing store late at night when the store is closed.

As the track begins, we see Brian in the nightclub scene dressed
in yellow pants and a black shirt. As the first verse
progresses, he adds (in jump cut fashion) additional yellow
clothing--a shirt, shoes, a jacket, and finally a large floppy
hat.

At the first "Oo la la" chorus, we cut to a long shot of the
children singing.

Next, Brian is seen walking the dog. At first the dog is not
seen, but it is obvious from the leash and the way Brian is being
pulled that a dog is present. When the next "Oo la la" section
comes, the dog and its yellow jacket will be revealed. Both the
children and Brian will be heard for this "Oo la la," but the
children will not be seen.

The video returns to the nightclub lip syncing until the words "I
hardly know anyone who wears yellow shirts" at which point the
back-up singers are seen rummaging through shirts on a "sale"
counter in the men's clothing store.

page 1

2.

NARRATOR (cont'd)
And I sure didn't know what a DUII arrest
could do to my life. I want to tell you
what happened to me, but first let me tell
you about some other people who made the
same mistake I did...

DISSOLVE TO:

INT. - CROWDED BAR -NIGHT

Four young women in their early twenties are seated in a booth at
a bar. They are making a toast and laughing uproariously.

NARRATOR (V.O.)
Like Jennifer. It was her birthday. Was
it her fault that everyone from work wanted
to buy her a drink?

GIRL ONE
Happy birthday dear Jennifer...

JENNIFER
(slurring slightly)
Stop it you guys. My poor dumb sister is
waiting with a whole big party she thinks
is going to surprise me and I can't just
not show up. I gotta go.

Jennifer stands up abrubtly, grabs her purse and car keys off the
table and turns to leave.

JENNIFER
Goodnight.

GIRL ONE
Jennifer are you sure you're able to drive?

JENNIFER
Yeah..this is nothing. I've driven in far
worse shape than this before. Nothing is
going to happen to Jennifer.

Jennifer turns and walks away with her girlfriends saying goodbye
in the background.

EXT. - URBAN STREET - NIGHT

Jennifer drives through an intersection and a police car pulls in
behind her, lights flashing. Jennifer glances up at her rear
view mirror and starts to pull over.

JENNIFER
Damn!

Figure 1.10
Scenes from the educational film DUII: The Price Is Too High. *(Script courtesy of AIMS Media, Inc., Chatsworth, CA)*

Figure 1.11
Excerpt from a script in the split-page format.

```
Women at Work                                      page 8
          VIDEO                        AUDIO        TIME
Roof shingler sequence    SOUND ON FILM.  Starts 0:50
from the film "Other      seconds in with "I remember
Women, Other Work"        my father" and runs 2:55
                          ending with "You are the
                          best darn shingler in this
                          country."                  9:15

     HOST                 Psychological ideas have also
                          played a part in the division
                          of labor between men and women.
                          One idea that has existed in
                          the past is that women are
                          frivolous by nature.  This is
                          reflected in the old popular
                          show tune "I Enjoy Being a
                          Girl."                      9:45

Slide 19 - woman in white  RECORD 2 - "I Enjoy Being a
                           Girl."  Start at beginning and
                           go 2:05.  "I'm a girl and by me
                           that's only great.

Slide 20 - woman in black  I am proud that my silhouette is
                           curvy

Slide 21 - woman and       That I walk with a sweet and
     umbrella              girlish gate
```

The key to this kind of scriptwriting is its focus on a message. The script has a definable objective and a client or sponsor who wants to teach, persuade, or inform the viewer about something. Combining narrative and nonnarrative elements is not uncommon. Charts, graphs, and interviews may be interspersed with dramatic illustrations.

This type of scriptwriting tends to place greater emphasis on research, since the entire project is being developed to meet the specific needs and objectives of the client or sponsor. In some instances the writer may need to obtain the client's approval at each stage of the writing process. Before writing begins, surveys may be used to gauge the intended audience's knowledge of a subject, or they may be used after the script is completed to test its effectiveness. Once a basic strategy has been devised (and agreed on), scriptwriting proceeds through as many stages as the particular subject requires.

Many nonnarrative scripts employ a **split-page** format (see Figure 1.11). The video information is written down one side of the page, and audio information (often voice-over narration) is placed opposite it. This two-column format is especially useful for scripts in which the audio comments on or clarifies the visuals.

In a short, highly visual form like a commercial, the best script might actually be a storyboard containing the copy (dialogue or voice-over) and a drawing for each shot.

The newer **interactive media**—CD-ROMs, computer games, and educational programs— often require complex programs that "branch." People are not expected to watch these materials from beginning to end. They skip around viewing the materials they need or want to see. The script material must be written in such a way that it makes sense even though people are making choices, leaving out some of the information. For example, the CD-ROM *Myst* combines elements of a narrative motion picture with a mystery game, allowing the viewer to interact with the story.[11]

Computer Programs for Scriptwriting

Computer scriptwriting programs greatly facilitate the scriptwriting process. As we have already seen, writing a screenplay from concept to outline, treatment, and master scene script is a process of constant revision and rewriting. Computer software makes this task much easier.

Obviously, any of the excellent word-processing programs available for the two most popular computer systems, the Apple Macintosh or the IBM (or IBM-compatible) computer can be used for scriptwriting. Sophisticated word-processing programs, such as *Microsoft Word, WordPerfect,* and *MacWrite,* are easy to use for screenwriting. You can use the program to set the correct margins, to check the spelling, and usually to set a style sheet, a sort of template for your screenplay

format. Many professionals have made screenwriting with their word processor even easier by using macros (a key or keys programmed to execute a series of time-saving keystrokes—most helpful when centering a character's name or changing the margins for the dialogue).

The main advantage of scriptwriting with a word processor is that you probably already are familiar with a program and will not need to spend time learning a new one. The primary disadvantage of screenwriting with your word processor is that such programs have difficulty conforming to the labyrinth of rules surrounding correct screenplay format, such as the proper placement of *continued* or *more* at the top or bottom of the page. If you drop a scene or a few lines of dialogue, you would need to manually correct *continued* and *more* throughout the script.

One way to overcome these problems is to use a scriptwriting program that understands the peculiarities of the screenwriting form. Some scriptwriting software programs perform only formatting functions. These are not word-processing programs. They require you to use a word-processing program such as *Microsoft Word* or *WordPerfect* to actually write the text. Then you use one of these formatting programs to convert that text to the correct screenplay format with margins, page breaks, and transitions. With such a program you can number scenes and shots, insert *continued* at the top and bottom of the page, and print out individual pages or scenes or an entire screenplay. Some formatting programs can also be adapted to different screenplay formats, such as split-page.[12]

The advantage of text-formatting programs is obvious. You don't have to learn a new word-processing program, and you can take advantage of many of the powerful functions already available in your word-processing program. One weakness of some text-formatting programs is that you usually do not see what you have in terms of format until you actually print out your script.

An offshoot of this kind of text-formatting software is a program that employs templates within a standard word-processing program. One example of such an add-on is *ScriptWright.* This inexpensive software turns *Word* (for Macintosh or Windows) into a full-blown screenwriting program. Using a suite of styles and

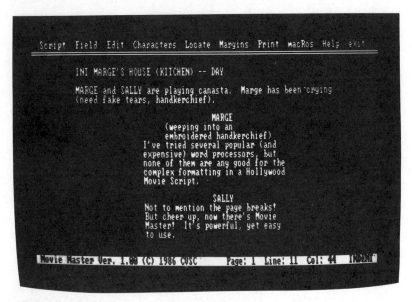

Figure 1.12

A script written with Movie Master *software as it appears on a computer screen. (Photo courtesy of Comprehensive Video Supply Company)*

macros, *ScriptWright* formats as you type, producing a script that conforms to Writers Guild standards.[13]

The other basic approach to screenwriting software is to combine word-processing and formatting in a single program. In dedicated, stand-alone scriptwriting programs (such as that shown in Figure 1.12), a built-in word processor is used to write the text in proper screenplay format. What the screenplay looks like on the computer screen is what it will look like on the printed page. Typically, the word-processing capability of stand-alone scriptwriting programs is not as powerful or sophisticated as the dedicated word-processing programs (such as *WordPerfect* or *Microsoft Word*). You do see what the script will look like on the screen before it is printed out, but you may not have as many text-writing features (high-quality spell checking, grammar analysis, and so on).[14]

Finally, one of the more interesting developments in screenwriting software is the creation of computer programs to help writers analyze their plots, characters, and storylines. Such programs typically are interactive, prompting the writer to answer questions about story structure, character development, and plot conflicts. Beginning writers may find these programs helpful for generating ideas and exploring story structure and character development.[15]

New screenwriting programs undoubtedly will continue to be developed. A computer does not do the writing for you, but it does make it much easier to rewrite and revise while maintaining the correct screenplay format.[16]

Copyright and Clearances

Writers typically **copyright** their work to protect it. One way to do this is to obtain a copyright registration form from the Registrar of Copyrights at the Library of Congress in Washington, D.C.[17] A copyright can be secured for a full treatment or for a completed screenplay.

Another possibility is to register your script with the Writers Guild of America (WGA). The Writers Guild will accept story ideas, synopses, treatments, outlines, and full scripts from members and nonmembers (for a nominal fee). If you live west of the Mississippi River, you register your material with the Writers Guild of America, West; if you live east of the Mississippi, you register with the Writers Guild of America, East.[18]

Perhaps the simplest method of providing proof of authorship is to mail your script to yourself in a sealed envelope by certified mail. Do not open the envelope. The postmark on the envelope establishes a specific date of creation. This kind of self-copyrighting may be difficult to sustain in court and is probably not the best means of protecting your script. The more

```
                  COPYRIGHT AGREEMENT
     I,_____ grant to
                (the copyright holder)

     _____ the
                    (the producer)

     non-exclusive right to produce a motion picture based upon the

     work entitled _____

     written by _____
     and to exhibit, distribute, publicize, and otherwise exploit the
     picture in all media, by any title, in perpetuity, and throughout
     the world.  I hereby grant to the producer any further rights
     that the producer may need to carry out the above-made grant,
     including all rights necessary to adapt the work for the picture
     and to use the name of the author in connection with the picture.
     The producer shall have the right to copyright the picture in
     his/her/its own name.

     I further warrant that I am sole owner of all rights of copyright
     and that I have full authority to convey these; that the work is
     wholly original and that neither any incident contained in the
     work nor any part thereof was taken from or based upon any other
     dramatic, literary, or musical material; that the exercise or use
     of any rights herein granted will not in any way infringe upon or
     violate any rights of any person, corporation, or firm
     whatsoever, including without limitation rights of privacy and
     publicity, and that no part of the rights herein granted have in
     any way been used, limited, or impaired and that they are free
     and clear of any and all claims or liens whatsoever, and that
     there are no claims or litigation outstanding, pending, or
     threatened, which may in any way prejudice the producer's rights
     in the work.

     I warrant that, except as expressly provided herein, neither the
     producer no any of the producer's assigns shall have any
     obligation to pay any monies in respect to this work.


     Signed_____

     Position_____

     Date_____
```

Figure 1.13
Sample copyright agreement form.

completely your idea is developed on paper (a master scene script compared to an outline, for example), the easier it is to prove ownership based on specific details within the work. Trying to sustain a court claim to a basic idea can be almost impossible.

If your script uses or adapts copyrighted material (such as a novel, magazine article, or short story), you must obtain a release from the owner of that original material (see Figure 1.13). This release should contain statements that verify the copyright holder's ownership of the material and warrant that the owner has the right to grant use of the material (that it has not been previously sold). Obtaining the right to use copyrighted material often can be quite expensive.

Material can be used without copyright release if it is old enough to be in the **public domain.** Assuming that a work is in the public domain or out of copyright can be dangerous. A work created before 1978 has an original copyright term of twenty-eight years, which can be extended (or renewed) for twenty-eight to forty-seven years. A work created after 1978 can be protected for the author's lifetime plus fifty years. Even if an author has been dead for a century, a particular edition, translation, or version of a work may still be under copyright protection. If you intend to use material in your screenplay that you suspect may be owned by someone else, you should undertake a full-fledged copyright search.

For a fee the Copyright Office at the Library of Congress can conduct a search for the current copyright holder.[19] A good library with access to the *Catalog of Copyright Entries* may be able to provide this information for you as well. To initiate a search you will need to know the title of the work, the name of the author (or authors), the type of work, and any other information you can gather concerning the original copyright date (or registration number), the date of publication, and the name or names of people who might own the copyright.

Notes

1. Quoted in Jason Squire, *The Movie Business Book* (Englewood Cliffs, NJ: Prentice-Hall, 1983), p. 52.
2. For a funny and insightful view of this problem, see William Goldman, *Adventures in the Screen Trade: A Personal View of Hollywood and Screenwriting* (New York: Warner Books, 1983).
3. See, for example, Richard A. Blum, *Television and Screen Writing* (Stoneham, MA: Focal Press, 1995); Ron Dyas, *Screenwriting for Television and Film* (Madison, WI: Brown and Benchmark, 1993); Linda Seeger and Edward Jay Whetmore, *From Script to Screen* (Stoneham, MA: Focal Press, 1994); Jurgen Wolff and Kerry Cox, *Top Secrets: Screenwriting* (Los Angeles: Lone Eagle, 1992); Margaret Mehring, *The Screenplay* (Stoneham, MA: Focal Press, 1990); Syd Field, *Screenplay: The Foundations of Screenwriting,* (New York: Dell, 1982); and Viki King, *How to Write a Movie in 21 Days: The Inner Movie Method* (New York: Harper & Row, 1988). For a classic text on dramatic structure, see Lajos Egri, *The Art of Dramatic Writing* (New York: Simon & Schuster, 1946).
4. We would like to express our deep appreciation to filmmaker/screenwriter Mark Chodzko, to author Carol Carrick, and to Phoenix Films for making this material available to us.
5. David Bordwell and Kristin Thompson, *Film Art: An Introduction* (New York: McGraw-Hill, 1993), pp. 65–68.
6. Field, pp. 7–13 and pp. 110–152.
7. Bordwell and Thompson, *Film Art,* pp. 82–84 and pp. 471–474. See also Thomas Schatz, *Hollywood Genres* (New York: Random House, 1981), pp. 4–11 and Chapter 2, "Film Genres and the Genre Film."
8. One example of a traditional storyboard program for computers is a program called *Storyboard Quick* from Power Training, Inc., Hermosa Beach, CA; (310) 937-4411. One such example for IBM (or IBM-compatible) computers is *Storyboard Live.* See F. D. Miller, "IBM Storyboard Live!" *AV Video,* October 1991, pp. 62–69. For excellent descriptions of many of the graphics and animation programs for the Mac II computer, see Lon Poole, "Mac TV Tools," *MacWorld,* September 1989, pp. 209–216.
9. See, for example, Edgar E. Willis and Camille D'Arienzo, *Writing Scripts for Television, Radio and Film* (New York: Holt, Rinehart & Winston, 1993); Alan Rosenthal, *Writing Docudrama* (Stoneham, MA: Focal Press, 1994); Dwight V. Swain and Joye R. Swain, *Scriptwriting for New AV Technologies* (Stoneham, MA: Focal Press, 1991); and Ray Di Zazzo, *Corporate Scriptwriting* (Stoneham, MA: Focal Press, 1992).
10. This film is distributed by AIMS Media, 9710 De Soto Ave., Chatsworth, CA 91311–4409. It was written by Renne Leatto, directed by Dan Sandler, and produced by Sandler Films, Inc.
11. David Coller, "Lots of Mouses Will be Stirring," *Los Angeles Times,* 23 November 1995, p. F-1; and Charles Platt, "Interactive Entertainment: Who Writes It? Who Reads it? Who Needs it?" *Wired,* September 1995, pp. 145–150. Also, the computer program *Storyvision* for Windows is a utility for interactive scriptwriting that can be used to structure and branch links in an interactive script.
12. One of the best-known formatting programs is *Scriptor* from Screenplay Systems, 150 East Olive Ave., Suite 305, Burbank, CA 91502; (818) 843–6557. Versions are available for Macintosh and IBM systems. *AVScripter* is another text formatter designed to import files from many word-processing programs and to format the text to a two-

column script. For more information contact Tom Schroeppel, 4705 Bay View Ave., Tampa, FL 33611.

13. *ScriptWright* can be purchased from Indelible Ink, 156 Fifth Avenue, #228, New York, NY 10010. To order call (212) 255-1956, ext. 306. Indelible Ink may offer student discounts and site licenses. It is available for both Mac and Windows. A similar add-on, *Script Wizard* for Windows, provides a large number of script formats. *Side by Side* for Windows and Macintosh offers ten different formats for multicolumn scripts, and *Scriptwriting Tools* has both screenplay and split-column formats.

14. One of the better-known stand-alone scriptwriting programs is *Movie Master* for DOS. Other DOS-based scriptwriting programs include *Scriptware* and *The Script Thing. Final Draft* for Macintosh is one of the most popular Mac-based programs. *Scriptwriter* is a stand-alone program for both the Mac and Windows. It includes a storyboard creation function in addition to screenplay and split-column script formats. It can be purchased from MBC Images in Coopersville, Michigan; (616) 837-9441.

15. Examples of this kind of software are *Collaborator* (Windows and Mac), a script development program based on Aristotle's *Six Elements of Drama; StoryLine,* a story guidance and structure program; *Plots Unlimited* (IBM or Mac), a program that helps generate plots, story ideas, and outlines; *Dramatica* (IBM or Mac), a story creation and analysis tool; and *Idea Fisher* (Mac), an idea-association tool. Other software is designed to help organize and/or outline script ideas in an index-card style. Two examples are *Three By Five* (Mac) and *Writer's Blocks* (Windows).

16. The explosion of scriptwriting and production-related software has been so great that keeping up with it is nearly impossible. One way to do this might be to subscribe to the *Journal of the Writers Guild of America, West* (8955 Beverly Blvd., Los Angeles, CA 90048) or *Screenwriter: The Newsletter for Screenwriters* (Screenwriters International, 9016 Wilshire Blvd., Suite 755, Beverly Hills, CA 90211; (310) 285-6779).

Another way to try to stay abreast of this ever-changing area is via the World Wide Web. The Internet Screenwriters Network provides links to a wide variety of services including screenwriting chat rooms, legal issues, newsletters, and software. In addition to using one of the Web searchers such as Yahoo, you might try a site at http://www.screenwriters.com.

Another good sources of information is The Writer's Computer Store. It has offices in both Hollywood and Sausalito, CA. In Los Angeles their phone number is (310) 479-7774; in Sausalito (415) 332-7005. The Writer's Computer Store sells scriptwriting and production-related software as well as books, scripts, tapes, and supplies. They have a website at http://www.hollywoodnetwork, com/writerscomputer.

Script City is an excellent source for purchasing scripts of current and classic films. The mail order address is 8033 Sunset Boulevard, Suite 1500, Hollywood, CA 90046 (toll-free number for orders is (800) 676-2522; inquiries (213) 871-0707). Script City also sells a wide range of screenwriting software and instructional software, books, and videotapes about screenwriting and screenplay marketing.

Screenwriting software and screenwriting specialty stores are likely to experience a great deal of turnover. By the time this book reaches print, some of these companies undoubtedly will be gone and new ones will have replaced them.

17. The address is Registrar of Copyrights, Library of Congress, Washington, DC 20559. See *Copyright Registration for Motion Pictures, Including Video Recordings* (Washington, DC: Copyright Office, Library of Congress, 1980), p. 6.

18. In the West, Writers Guild of America, West, 8955 Beverly Blvd., Los Angeles, CA 90048. In the East, Writers Guild of America, East, 555 West 57th Street, New York, NY 10019.

19. The address is Reference and Bibliography Section, Copyright Office, Library of Congress, Washington, DC 20559.

chapter two
The Process of Preproduction

Preproduction is one of the most important stages of moviemaking. Unfortunately, students often overlook it. **Preproduction** is the least expensive part of the production chain; thorough planning during this stage will help to avoid unnecessary costs during the **production** and **postproduction** stages. Mistakes made at this "paper" stage can be more easily corrected than mistakes made during shooting.

Elements of preproduction are interdependent. The inability to find a certain type of location may necessitate changes in the script. The signing of a busy actor for a small part may necessitate changes in the shooting schedule. The amount of money that can be raised for the project can affect every element.

Students usually do not have to handle the financial reality that professionals encounter. Equipment is provided by the school, and the crew probably consists of class members who are not paid and who have to be there to receive class credit. Nevertheless, preproduction planning is as important for student productions as for professional productions. The lack of a prop can ruin a whole day's shooting, as can arriving at a local park and learning you can't shoot because you never asked for a permit. Even fellow students do not like to go on a location shoot where there is no time or place to eat.

Students who aspire to become professionals should learn the intricacies of preproduction. Most professional producers say they wish they had learned more about budgeting in school. Script breakdowns, shooting schedules, budgets, location scouting reports, set and costume designs, catering arrangements, releases, and insurance are all important to a production and should be taken care of before shooting begins. This is true not only for full-blown movies but also for music videos, commercials, corporate tapes, and other forms of productions.

Preproduction Planning

One reason that people (especially students) often skimp on preproduction is that it is boring. Much of it involves poring over paper, making sure that small details will not be forgotten. Although attending to such paperwork may not feel creative, it is what allows for creativity during production. If production necessities are not organized and available, proper shooting cannot occur.

The **producer** plays the major role in preproduction. At the height of the studio system (1930–1945), the producer was the chief financial officer—the person who controlled the budget, managed the writer and director, and organized the entire production. As the studio production system began to unravel in the 1960s, the role of the producer began to change. The modern independent producer is responsible not only for basic preproduction planning but also for developing the idea and, more important, for gathering the financing necessary to produce it. Unless the producer is adept at deal making, project packaging, and other financial negotiations, a movie project may die for lack of money. This means that an independent producer is usually deeply involved in scriptwriting, either by purchasing a script or by working closely with a writer to develop the kind of script that the producer can sell.

Independent producers also tend to work more closely with a director during preproduction than their studio predecessors did. Together, the producer and the director make decisions about the script, the cast, and the crew needed to create a specific motion picture. Not surprisingly, many producers (often called *hyphenate producers*) combine the roles of producer and director or of writer and producer. By controlling the money the independent producer can exert creative control at every level of the production, from scripting and casting to choosing the director, production crew, editor, and composer.

Script Breakdown

Once the script is finished (see Chapter 1), it must be broken down into various elements so that preproduction and production can progress smoothly and efficiently. Usually, the producer hires a **production manager** to handle this chore and other phases of preproduction. The production manager reads through the script, marking the important elements of each scene, such as main characters, extras, props, set, costumes, and special effects. Not all scripts have the same elements. A movie set in the Old West will probably have a category for animals; a set with vampires and ghosts might have a category for special makeup; a 1930s gangster plot might have a category for antique cars.

Most production managers develop their own method of lining the script. Some circle characters needed for a scene, underline sets, put stars by special effects, and write a list of props in the margin. Others use different colored pens to highlight each category. (Figure 2.1 shows a page of a script as marked by a production manager doing a breakdown.) Although many elements needed for a **script breakdown** (characters, set) are written in the script, many are not. For example, a scene may take place in a restaurant and mention that the main character is eating lobster. But the script will not detail the dishes, utensils, and glasses that will be needed in the scene. The production manager must recognize these needs and make sure such props are listed.

The information from the breakdown is used to prepare **script breakdown sheets.** (See Figure 2.2 for a sample.) These are among the most important organizational documents generated for production. Breakdown sheets list all the pertinent elements needed at each location. Usually, all scenes at one location are shot at one time, even though some scenes may appear at the beginning of the movie and others may appear in the middle or at the end. In other words, the movie is shot out of sequence. Shooting in this manner saves setup and transportation time, both of which can be costly.

The script breakdown sheet is used to ensure that all people and things needed at a particular location will be available and in place. Most breakdown sheets contain the title of the production, the location, whether the scene is interior or exterior, the time of day the scene is supposed to take place, the scene numbers (taken from the script) to be shot at that location, the number of pages of script for each scene (the importance of this is discussed in the section on shooting schedules), and a brief synopsis of each scene.

Sometimes the actors needed are broken down into **principal actors** (the stars and supporting cast), **bit players** (people with only a few lines of dialogue), and **extras** (people needed for atmosphere but who don't have distinguishable lines). On the student level, one column for cast may suffice. Frequently, for simplicity actors are listed by number rather than by name.

A separate category for props is almost always necessary. Special effects should be indicated if the film contains a large number of them (for example, scenes that are supposed to look like they were shot in the fog). Students often list the equipment and crew members on the breakdown sheet. This is less likely on a professional sheet because a different sheet detailing technical needs is drawn up for each location.

The breakdown sheets are used to generate various lists of what is needed for the production. For example, a list of sets could go to the set designer and/or location scout, a list of costumes to the costume designer, the props list to the propmaster. A list of scenes in which each actor appears can be used for casting purposes. Figure 2.3 shows samples of three different lists generated from the breakdown sheets.

Several computer programs are available to assist with breakdown sheets and the lists generated from them. Professionals use them regularly to keep track of the huge number of elements needed for a two-hour movie. Student films are usually fairly short, so the value of these computer programs is less obvious. However, students who have access to these programs should learn to use them. Doing so will make you more valuable in the job market.

Computer programs make it easy to manipulate everything. Obviously, the computer programs cannot determine what props will be needed. Production managers must go through

Figure 2.1

A page from the Old Mother Witch script as marked by the production manager doing the script breakdown. Note the production manager's marking system: characters circled, locations underlined, costumes in parentheses, and props and effects organized into separate lists.

14.

(CONTINUED)

SCENE 12

EXT.   BRIDWELL'S HOUSE - FRONT PORCH - NIGHT

props
Jack-o-lanterns
Halloween decorations
bowl of candy
skeleton

The Bridwell's house is a big old one like Mrs. Oliver's. *(David as cat)*
It's lit eerily and there are big jack-o-lanterns on the
porch. The front door is ajar. Spooky organ music plays *(Scott as tramp)*
within and a madman's laugh can be heard inside. The boys
know the Bridwells play the holidays to the hilt, but they
are still getting a little scared. When David and Scott go
up on the porch they hear a terrible cackle. It's MRS. *(Mrs. Bridwell as witch with green face)*
BRIDWELL dressed as an ugly witch.

MRS. BRIDWELL
Come in, sonny. Why don't any of you
boys want my candy?

SFX
organ music
mad laugh
scream
thunder

The boys reach for some out of a big bowl when Mrs. Bridwell
lets out a shrieking laugh. The boys stand back afraid.
Then there is a horrible scream from behind them. The boys
whirl around wide-eyed, and a skeleton drops in front of
them. There is a sudden flash of lightning from an
approaching storm, and the boys scream in terror. They back
away from the skeleton, and Mrs. Bridwell's bony fingers
touch their shoulders. They whirl back around toward her.
Her green face is laughing at them. They shriek in terror
and run off the porch. Mrs. Bridwell watches them go,
laughing in her own voice now. She enjoyed that one.

FX
lightning

SCENE 13

EXT. STREET IN FRONT OF BRIDWELL'S HOUSE - NIGHT

(Mary Ellen as Indian scout)
Mary Ellen and Eric are coming down the walk toward them.
David and Scottie are desperately trying to regain their *(Eric as scientist)*
composure. They don't want it to be known that they were *(David as cat)*
scared. Eric is dressed as a scientist, and Mary Ellen is *(Scott as tramp)*
an Indian Scout.

ERIC
Who was screaming?

David and Scottie look at each other and shrug.

DAVID
I didn't hear any screams. Did you?

(CONTINUED)

SCRIPT BREAKDOWN SHEET

Title Old Mother Witch   Prod. No. 1

Director Mark Chodzko   Page No. 1

Location Bridwell's House

Script Page Numbers   14

Day	Night X	Season Fall	Period Modern

Scene Numbers and Synopsis

12 - David and Scottie
go trick or treating
at Mrs. Bridwell's
house and are scared
by her elaborate
decorations and noises.

Cast and Costumes

David - cat costume
Scottie - tramp costume
Mrs. Bridwell - witch costume

Bits
None

Props

Jack-o-lanterns
Halloween decorations
Bowl of candy
Skeleton

Extras
None

Miscellaneous

Decide if sound effects will
be done during production or
post
Special lighting needed for
lightning

Figure 2.2
A script breakdown sheet for scene 12 of Old Mother Witch.

Figure 2.3

*Three different lists
generated from script
breakdown sheets.*

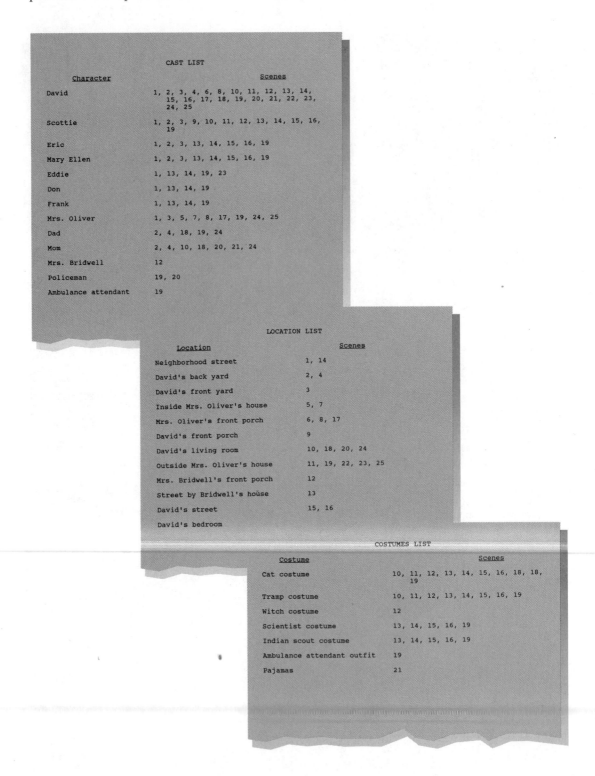

```
                        CAST LIST

        Character                        Scenes

David                       1, 2, 3, 4, 6, 8, 10, 11, 12, 13, 14,
                            15, 16, 17, 18, 19, 20, 21, 22, 23,
                            24, 25

Scottie                     1, 2, 3, 9, 10, 11, 12, 13, 14, 15, 16,
                            19

Eric                        1, 2, 3, 13, 14, 15, 16, 19

Mary Ellen                  1, 2, 3, 13, 14, 15, 16, 19

Eddie                       1, 13, 14, 19, 23

Don                         1, 13, 14, 19

Frank                       1, 13, 14, 19

Mrs. Oliver                 1, 3, 5, 7, 8, 17, 19, 24, 25

Dad                         2, 4, 18, 19, 24

Mom                         2, 4, 10, 18, 20, 21, 24

Mrs. Bridwell               12

Policeman                   19, 20

Ambulance attendant         19
```

```
                      LOCATION LIST

        Location                         Scenes

Neighborhood street           1, 14

David's back yard             2, 4

David's front yard            3

Inside Mrs. Oliver's house    5, 7

Mrs. Oliver's front porch     6, 8, 17

David's front porch           9

David's living room           10, 18, 20, 24

Outside Mrs. Oliver's house   11, 19, 22, 23, 25

Mrs. Bridwell's front porch   12

Street by Bridwell's house    13

David's street                15, 16

David's bedroom
```

```
                           COSTUMES LIST

        Costume                              Scenes

Cat costume                     10, 11, 12, 13, 14, 15, 16, 18, 18,
                                19

Tramp costume                   10, 11, 12, 13, 14, 15, 16, 19

Witch costume                   12

Scientist costume               13, 14, 15, 16, 19

Indian scout costume            13, 14, 15, 16, 19

Ambulance attendant outfit      19

Pajamas                         21
```

scripts and list the initial breakdown data. This is usually accomplished by using simple codes or keystrokes for each category. (Figure 2.4 presents an example of a computer-generated breakdown sheet with its codes.) Once these major elements are listed, the computer can generate separate lists, catch errors, and allow changes made in one area to be recorded in other areas. For example, if a character's name changes from Maribelle to Mary, the production manager can make the change in one place and it will automatically be changed everywhere else.

a

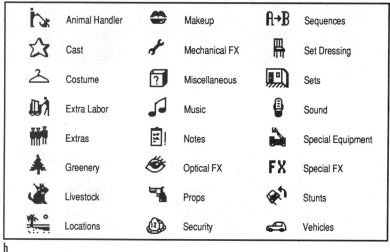

b

Figure 2.4

Screenplay Systems' Movie Magic Script Breakdown and Scheduling, *a program that uses handy icons to denote frequently used breakdown categories. (a) The icons at the bottom left of the breakdown sheet, and (b) the categories for the various icons. A mouse makes it easy to point and click on different elements needed for the breakdown sheet. (Courtesy of Screenplay Systems)*

SHOOTING SCHEDULE

TITLE Old Mother Witch

DIRECTOR Mark Chodzko

Date	Time	Scene	No. of Pages	Description	Location	Cast	Props, etc.
10/6	3:00 p.m.	7	1/8	Mrs. Oliver hides behind curtain	Inside Mrs. Oliver's house	Mrs. Oliver	Curtain
10/6	4:00 p.m.	5	1	Mrs. Oliver's voice over to Vera	Inside Mrs. Oliver's house	Mrs. Oliver	Photographs Clock Writing paper and pen
10/6	7:00 p.m.	21	1-1/2	David and his mother talk about Mrs. Oliver	David's bedroom	David Mom	Pajamas
10/6	8:30 p.m.	12	1/2	Mrs. Bridwell scares the boys	Bridwell's house	Mrs. Bridwell David Scottie	Jack-o-lanterns Halloween decorations Bowl of candy Skeleton Cat costume Tramp costume Witch costume Special lighting for lightning

Figure 2.5
A sample shooting schedule.

Shooting Schedule

The breakdown serves another major function: developing **shooting schedules** (see Figure 2.5). These specify what is to be accomplished each day of production.

Because all scenes at a particular location are usually shot together, the script breakdown sheet for each location is used to devise the shooting schedule. However, location is not always the main factor determining schedule. The availability of a particular actor or place can be a determinant. If an actor needed in three different locations is available for only two days of the shooting schedule, all other cast and crew might be moved to three locations in two days to accommodate the actor's schedule. Or, if a department store can be used for location only on Wednesday night when inventory is in prog-

ress, the cast and crew might shoot in the park Wednesday afternoon, move to the department store for Wednesday night, and go back to the park on Thursday.

Likewise, scheduling might be determined by an expensive piece of equipment. If a helicopter must be rented to shoot two scenes, these (and only these) will be shot in one day, even though they are in different locations.

Generally, however, shooting schedules are set up according to location. Outdoor shoots are often scheduled before indoor shoots because indoor shoots often require sets that can be built while outdoor shooting is underway. Also, if the weather does not cooperate, the schedule can be rearranged to handle indoor shoots. If all the indoor scenes had already been shot, the only option would be to cancel until the weather cleared.

One of the most difficult aspects of formulating a shooting schedule is determining how much time each scene will take. This must take into account many factors, the most significant of which is the length of the scene. A scene that runs three pages will usually take longer to shoot than one that is half a page. This is why the number of pages for each scene should be listed on the script breakdown sheet. Production managers can develop a formula for calculating shooting time for movies that consist primarily of talk (for example, eight pages a day). If this is possible, developing the shooting schedule is fairly easy.

However, many productions contain scenes or circumstances that do not fit into an all-purpose formula. A scene with complicated special effects or stunts can take much longer to shoot than one with straightforward dialogue. Scenes with exotic lighting, large crowds, or elaborate camera movement also take longer than average. Often, scenes shot at the beginning of the production process, when everyone is becoming accustomed to one another, take longer than those shot later, after the crew has developed a working rapport. This is especially true of student productions in which crew members are learning a great deal at the beginning.

In determining the number of pages that can be shot in a day, the production manager must also consider the director's style. Some directors spend a great deal of time on setup so that everything will be perfect for shooting; others retake scenes from many different angles; still others pride themselves on setting up and shooting quickly.

Nevertheless, production managers become quite adept at estimating how long each scene will take. Accurate estimates are important for budgeting and for the preparations that must be made for the entire production. Shooting schedules are often modified during production, but they provide the blueprint for how the production can be shot most efficiently.

Some people organizing shooting schedules like to include everything on the script breakdown sheet. But this usually makes for unwieldy schedules. A better schedule is one that includes date and time, scene numbers, location, a brief description, and one or two of the more crucial elements, such as props or cast members needed.

Of course, with computer programs all elements can be stored in the computer and the essential ones printed out as needed.

Stripboards

Many production managers use **stripboards** to aid them in controlling the overall shooting plans. These large boards hold long cardboard strips that list the locations and characters needed for each scene. They are helpful because an entire production can be laid out on one board and changed easily. If, for example, you discover you can't shoot at the airport on Tuesday afternoon as planned, you can remove the Tuesday afternoon strip, place it at some other time, and juggle other strips to readjust the schedule.

Computer programs are especially valuable for shuffling stripboards (see Figure 2.6). When a shooting time must be changed, the computer can indicate the ramifications and make the necessary adjustments quickly. The computer program can also be used to print out strips for a conventional stripboard. Some programs even bar code the strips so that if they are changed on the stripboard, a light pen attached to the computer can read the changes and resort the electronic data quickly.[1]

Production Schedule

Another important form, the **production schedule** (see Figure 2.7), delineates the length of time allotted for the entire production cycle—preproduction, production, and post-production. Again, the amount of time needed for each phase varies with the complexity of the movie and the amount of time and money available. In student moviemaking preproduction, production, and postproduction time must be allocated to meet the due date specified by the professor. Television projects must be completed by their contracted air dates. Films made to be shown in theaters often need to be finished for certain release times—Christmas or at the beginning of summer when audiences are likely to be biggest. Corporate videos need to be finished to accommodate the schedule of the client.

The three elements of moviemaking may overlap. Some elements of preproduction, such as set construction, may be in the final stages

Figure 2.6

A computer-generated stripboard using the Movie Magic Script Breakdown and Scheduling software. (Courtesy of Screenplay Systems)

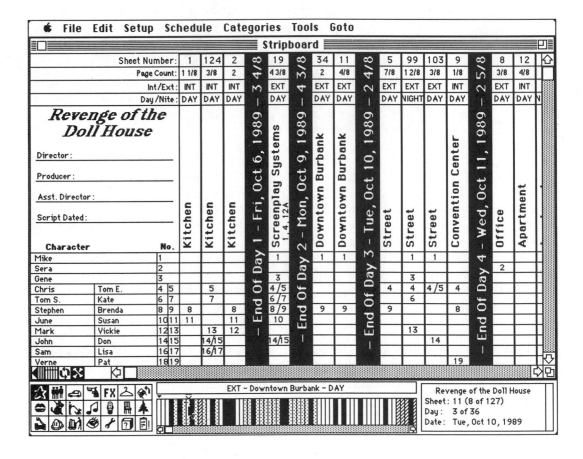

when production begins. With **nonlinear** editing systems, some scenes can be edited while others are still being shot. These overlaps should be delineated on the production schedule. For this reason, one of the forms commonly used for this schedule is a time line.

A major flaw of student productions is not allowing enough time for postproduction. More often than not this is because production runs longer than anticipated. And the main reason production runs long is that preproduction planning was not thorough enough. At the end of the semester students wind up fighting each other for access to the editing equipment during the wee hours of the morning. The wise student, who thinks everything through thoroughly during the preproduction stage, can finish early and avoid this fray.

The Budget

Within the professional world the budget is the governing force of all movies. Estimations of what the picture will cost must be accurate. Di-

rectors who complete a picture on budget or under budget are valued. Those who habitually run over budget are likely to find themselves in unemployment lines.

Financing. The financial arrangements for pictures vary greatly, in part because the business is so risky. For one thing, the money for preproduction, production, postproduction, and distribution must be spent before anyone knows whether the movie will be profitable. Although some movies make huge profits, others never recover their costs. As a result, conventional money-lending organizations such as banks rarely fund individual movies. Rather, the money comes from individual investors and from deals that can be made for advances from distributors, cable and broadcast networks, foreign systems, and companies wishing to sell ancillary products such as T-shirts or toys based on some character in the picture.

Sometimes money can be raised on the merits of an idea or a best-selling book, especially if a few well-known stars are guaranteed. But

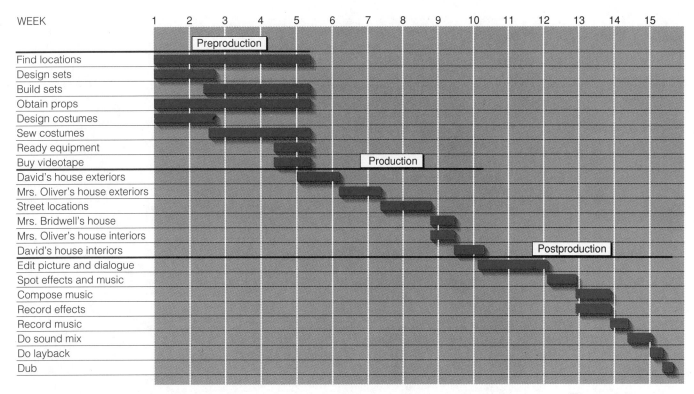

WEEK	1	2	3	4	5	6	7	8	9	10	11	12	13	14	15

Preproduction

Find locations
Design sets
Build sets
Obtain props
Design costumes
Sew costumes
Ready equipment
Buy videotape

Production

David's house exteriors
Mrs. Oliver's house exteriors
Street locations
Mrs. Bridwell's house
Mrs. Oliver's house interiors
David's house interiors

Postproduction

Edit picture and dialogue
Spot effects and music
Compose music
Record effects
Record music
Do sound mix
Do layback
Dub

Figure 2.7
A sample production schedule.

more often the money is raised after the script is completed. Even with a completed script in hand, the budget can change. For example, three scenes of the script may take place in Kenya. If the script is budgeted so that the scenes are actually shot in Kenya, a lot of money will be needed to transport cast and crew to Africa. If the total amount needed for the film cannot be raised, the Kenya scenes might be rewritten so that they can use stock footage of Kenya and other shots, such as close-ups, that do not need the specific location.

If preproduction is progressing on the assumption that a wealthy person is ready to contribute the last $200,000 needed for the production and that investor backs out, breakdowns, shooting schedules, and production schedules will change.

Budgeting Procedures. Although the size of the budget can affect the script, the usual procedure is for the budget to be derived from the script. This means someone must go through the script carefully, figuring the cost of all the elements. Script breakdown sheets and shooting schedules are extremely important in this process. Computer programs are also helpful, especially spreadsheets that can calculate how much

the overall budget will change under varying circumstances.[2]

Budgets for movies are broken down into **above-the-line** and **below-the-line** expenses. Above-the-line expenses are those related to a specific film and are creative in nature. They include the costs of writing and acquiring the script, the costs associated with the producer and director, and the salaries and fringe benefits for the actors. Below-the-line costs are those that could be associated with any picture and are more likely to be in the crafts area. They include the pay for crew and the money needed for equipment, sets, props, costumes, makeup, transportation, food, sound effects, music, and editing.

The organization of a budget can vary from movie to movie. Sometimes all the costs associated with one function, such as lighting, are lumped together, including the salaries of the people who plug in the lights, the cost of renting the lights, and the electricity bill. Similarly, costs for sound, sets, and wardrobe would be together. For other budgets, categories such as crew salaries, utilities, transportation, and insurance serve as the organizing thread. The organization is not nearly as important as the accuracy with which the budget is figured.

Figure 2.8
A budget front sheet (a) presents an overview of the entire budget. Each budget category can be broken down into greater detail; (b) shows some of the typical cost categories associated with the producer and staff; (c) shows the same for props.

```
                              BUDGET


      Title_____

      Date Prepared_____

      Account
      Number           Description               Total
       01        Story and Writers
       02        Producer and Staff
       03        Director and Staff
       04        Cast
                             Total Above-the-Line
      ====================================================

       12        Camera
       13        Sound
       14        Script Supervision
       17        Electrical
       20        Set Construction
       21        Set Dressing
       22        Props
       23        Wardrobe
       24        Makeup and Hair
       30        Special Effects
       40        Transportation
       41        Location Expenses
       45        Stock Footage
       50        Licenses
       51        Insurance
       52        Legal Fees
       60        Editing
       61        Postproduction Sound
       62        Graphics
       63        Music
       70        Dubbing
       75        Publicity
                             Total Below-the-Line
      ====================================================

                   Total Above- and Below-Line
                                      Overhead
                                   Contingency
                                  GRAND TOTALS
```

a

(Continued)

Budgets for complicated productions usually contain a front sheet that summarizes the various costs (see Figure 2.8a). Behind it are more detailed breakdowns for each specific area (see Figure 2.8b and c).

The single factor that can have the greatest effect on a budget is the cost of the above-the-line people, particularly the actors and the director. In Figure 2.8a the above-the-line costs—for writer, producer, director, and cast—consist primarily of salaries and fringe benefits. The latter is always a significant expense that cannot be overlooked if indeed people are going to receive medical benefits, retirement contributions, and

BUDGET SPECIFICS

Title_____

Date Prepared_____

Budget Category_____Producer and Staff_____

Account Number____02_____

Account Number	Description	Days, Hours, or Quantity	Rate	Total
02.10	Producer			
02.12	Production Manager			
02.15	Secretary			
02.20	Fringe Benefits			
02.25	Telephone			
02.26	Postage			
02.27	Copy Costs			
02.30	Entertainment			

_____Grand Total_____

Figure 2.8
(Continued)

b

BUDGET SPECIFICS

Title_____

Date Prepared_____

Budget Category_____Props_____

Account Number____22_____

Account Number	Description	Days, Hours, or Quantity	Rate	Total
22.10	Propmaster			
22,12	Assistant Propmaster			
22.20	Fringe Benefits			
22 25	Prop Purchase			
22.26	Prop Rental			
22.30	Insurance			
22.32	Pickup and Return			

_____Grand Total_____

c

other fringe benefits. Some production companies hire nonunion freelancers for each picture and do not pay fringe benefits.

The below-the-line part of this budget is organized primarily by function—sound, set construction, wardrobe, and so forth. Insurance, legal fees, and licenses are easy to overlook but can add up to substantial numbers.[3]

Overhead includes such items as rent and utilities and is generally figured as a percentage of other costs—usually about 15 percent of the total budget. Movie budgets should usually set aside about 20 percent for contingencies. This not only will take care of overlooked items but also will be needed when the production inevitably falls behind schedule. During the production phase regular reports are made to indicate how much of the budget has been spent.

Budgeting a Student Production. Budgeting for a student movie is quite different from budgeting for a professional movie. Student producers or directors can be less concerned about money. Their classmates work for free, the school may provide equipment and stock, the dorm or campus can be used for locations, and the props can be borrowed from someone's home.

Student productions can accumulate costs if they are period pieces that require costumes, if the director decides to rent special equipment such as a dolly in order to capture certain shots, or if professional actors are hired. Under these circumstances the producer may want to draw up an actual budget and keep track of the expenses.

Even if a production costs very little, students should calculate what it would cost if it were being produced by a professional company that had to rent equipment. This is good practice for future jobs, and it can show how much the college is contributing to the production budget.

Costs vary greatly from one part of the country to another, from one equipment rental house to another, and from one circumstance to another, so students should check out current prices in their area. However, for purposes of the sample student budget shown in Figure 2.9, the following average rental costs from a large metropolitan area were used:[4]

Consumer camcorders (such as S-VHS and Hi-8)	$12 per hour
3/4-inch recorders and 3-chip cameras	$45 per hour
Professional-grade camcorders (such as Betacam)	$120 per hour
Mics and fishpoles (usually rented by the day for $24 per day)	$3 per hour
Cuts-only off-line editing	$50 per hour
On-line editing	$150 per hour
Creating graphics	$60 per hour
Audio services such as mixing	$80 per hour

Costs for cast and crew are negotiable if the production is shot with a nonunion crew. Unionized cast and crew must be paid wages that at least meet union minimums. Of course, people who are well known or successful can demand much more than the minimum rate. Union contracts are complicated, but some general minimum figures that should be helpful in developing budgets follow.

Writers are paid about $35,000 for a feature-length screenplay with a treatment and $22,000 for a screenplay without a treatment. They are paid $4,000 for a TV program of less than 15 minutes; $8,000 for 30 minutes; $15,000 for 60 minutes; and $21,000 for 90 minutes.

Directors' minimums are rather complicated, often pegged to the type and length of the work and sometimes including a guarantee of a certain number of weeks of work. Some minimums are based on days, others on weeks, and still others on total projects. For a very short project, such as a music video, a director's minimum would be about $1,200 a day. A director's fee for a low-budget movie or a 30-minute TV show would be approximately $6,000 a week. Movies with a higher budget would allocate a minimum of $9,000 a week for a director, and a director's fee for a 2-hour TV pilot could run $68,000 for the project.

Producers usually earn about the same or a little more than directors. Feature performers' minimums are $500 per day, and extras should work for about $10 an hour. The minimum hourly fee for a director of photography is about

```
              SAMPLE STUDENT BUDGET FOR A TEN MINUTE SHOW


Above the Line
     Story and Writers                          $4000
     Producer and Staff                          6000
     Director and Staff                          6000
       (5 days at $1200 a day)
     Cast                                        2800
       2 Principals (2 days each at $500 a
          day) - $2000
       5 Extras (16 hours each at $10 an
          hour) - $800


                          Total Above-the-Line  $18,800


Below the Line
     Camera                                      2420
         Director of photography (16 hours at
            $64 per hour) - $1024
         Camera operator (16 hours at $40 per
            hour) - $640
         *Equipment rental (16 hours at $45
            per hour) - $720
         Tape  (2 reels at $18 each) - $36
     Sound                                       1056
         Mixer (16 hours at $33 per hour) -
            $528
         Boom operator (16 hours at $30 per
            hour) - $480
         *Equipment rental (2 days at $24 per
            day) - $48
     Script Supervision                           336
         Script supervisor (16 hours at $21 per
            hour) - $336
     Electrical                                     0
     Set Construction                               0
     Set Dressing                                   0
     Props                                         20
     Wardrobe                                       0
     Make-Up and Hair                             10
     Special Effects                                0
     Transportation (gas money)                   30
     Location Expenses (2 meals)                  75
     Stock Footage                                  0
     Licenses                                     20
     Insurance                                      0
     Legal Fees                                     0


                            1
```

Figure 2.9

A sample budget for a ten-minute student movie.

(Continued)

Figure 2.9
(Continued)

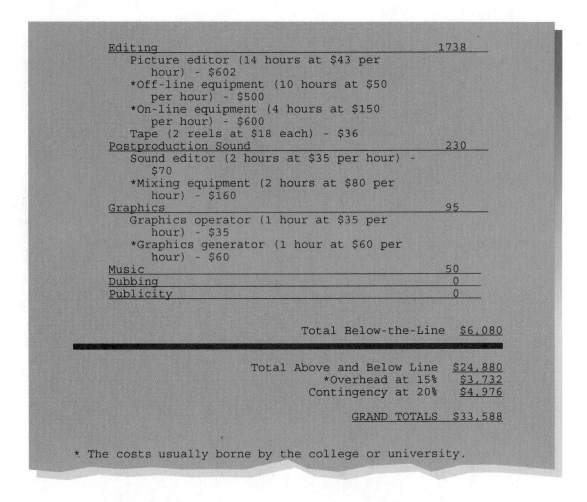

```
       Editing                                              1738
             Picture editor (14 hours at $43 per
                hour) - $602
             *Off-line equipment (10 hours at $50
                per hour) - $500
             *On-line equipment (4 hours at $150
                per hour) - $600
             Tape (2 reels at $18 each) - $36
       Postproduction Sound                                  230
             Sound editor (2 hours at $35 per hour) -
                $70
             *Mixing equipment (2 hours at $80 per
                hour) - $160
       Graphics                                               95
             Graphics operator (1 hour at $35 per
                hour) - $35
             *Graphics generator (1 hour at $60 per
                hour) - $60
       Music                                                  50
       Dubbing                                                 0
       Publicity                                               0


                               Total Below-the-Line    $6,080


                        Total Above and Below Line    $24,880
                               *Overhead at 15%         $3,732
                               Contingency at 20%       $4,976

                                      GRAND TOTALS     $33,588


       * The costs usually borne by the college or university.
```

$64 per hour, camera operator $40, sound mixer $33, boom operator $30, script supervisor $21, art director $45, carpenter $24, propmaster $25, costume designer $26, seamstress $23, makeup artist $21, graphic artist $35, picture editor $43, and sound editor $35. The pay for other crew positions is comparable, at about $25 to $30 an hour.[5]

Given all this, the actual budget for a simple ten-minute student production that is set in modern times, uses only two principal actors, rents middle-of-the-road TV equipment, and employs cast and crew willing to work for minimum rates might look something like the one shown in Figure 2.9. In actual practice the college or university bears the costs of the equipment for a student production, and there are no personnel costs above the line or below the line. Therefore, out-of-pocket costs can be as low as several hundred dollars.

Budgeting usually does not seem important to students because so little actual money is involved. But the professional world places a high value on the ability to read a script, estimate quickly how much it will cost to produce, and determine how to cut costs without cutting content or creativity. For this reason students should take advantage of every opportunity they have to learn how to budget a movie.

Daily Call Sheets

Daily **call sheets** are posted during production to let people know when and where they should report each day (see Figure 2.10). Formal sheets often are not needed for student productions because much of the shooting occurs during one set time, such as a weekend.

However, call sheets are helpful for student productions that require multiple shoots and certainly are necessary for professional shoots. Simple call sheets list all the members of the cast needed for the day and the times they should report for various functions, such as makeup and appearance on the set. More complicated call sheets also specify when caterers are to have

CALL SHEET

Title __Old Mother Witch__   Date __October 16__

Director __Mark Chodzko__   Production No. __1__

Location __1526 Main Street and 1723 Main Street__

SET	SCENES	CAST	PAGES
Inside Mrs. Oliver's house	7	Mrs. Oliver	1/8
Inside Mrs. Oliver's house	5	Mrs. Oliver	1
David's bedroom	21	David Mom	1-1/2
Mrs. Bridwell's front porch	12	Mrs. Bridwell David Scottie	1/2

CAST	PART OF	MAKEUP	SET
Grace Ridgley	Mrs. Oliver	2:00	3:00
Tommy Mays	David	6:00	7:00
Cynthia Thomas	Mom	6:00	7:00
Loreen Washington	Mrs. Bridwell	7:00	8:30
Steve McLean	Scottie	7:30	8:30

ATMOSPHERE AND STAND-INS   REPORT TIME

None

CREW	REPORT TIME
Camera operator	2:00
Boom operator	2:00
Audio/video operator	2:00
Makeup person	2:00
Wardrobe person	6:00
Script supervisor	2:00
Electrician	1:30
Grips	1:30
Prop person	2:00
Caterers	5:00

Figure 2.10
A sample daily call sheet.

meals prepared, when drivers will be needed to move equipment, and when special vehicles or effects must be available. They may also include special instructions for makeup, costumes, or props.

Although call sheets are used during production, they can be at least partially prepared during preproduction. Changes in the shooting schedule can necessitate changes in call sheets, but if the basics have been compiled ahead of time, these alterations can be made fairly quickly, especially if computer programs are used.

Although script breakdown sheets, shooting schedules, stripboards, production schedules, budgets, and call sheets are the primary forms prepared during preproduction, other forms can be generated if needed. For example, work orders list the equipment and supplies needed for each day, and worksheets detail the special working conditions to which the production must adhere because of certain provisions in a star's contract. Most colleges have checkout forms that students must fill out ahead of time to reserve equipment.[6]

Preproduction Responsibilities

Preproduction involves much more than creating schedules. In fact, the schedules are used extensively to accomplish all the chores needed before actual production begins. These chores include hiring behind-the-scenes personnel, casting, finding locations, obtaining permits, designing and building sets, sewing costumes, buying props and other supplies, arranging transportation and catering, obtaining stock footage and music, buying insurance, and checking the equipment.

Hiring Behind-the-Scenes Personnel

By the time a script is approved, several people are usually already involved in the production. The producer, for example, has probably been trying to sell the script. A director may have been hired, and several actors may have been signed in order to sell the script.

If the producer was the only person involved in selling the initial concept, he or she will hire a **director** quickly so that plans for preproduction and production can proceed with the director's participation. The director's primary responsibility is to interpret the script (and to guide the writer in reworking parts that are weak). During preproduction the director will read and reread the script, deciding how best to match the particular character and tone of the screenplay with the appropriate actors, locations, sets, and costumes. This requires the ability to visualize and the ability to communicate that vision to others.

For complicated productions the producer or director will also hire a production manager to handle the details of preproduction. In simpler movies, such as student productions, the same person often serves as producer, production manager, and director.

The director usually makes the hiring decisions, although the producer may participate. In the early stages of preproduction the director may hire a **production designer** or **art director**[7] to develop the overall look of the film, a **set designer** to begin planning sets, and a **costume designer** to plan wardrobe. When these people have their concepts fairly well in mind, they begin hiring others—carpenters, painters, seamstresses, and so on—to execute the work. Directors also make early hires of people in the areas of special effects or animation because this type of work is time consuming.

Some directors like to hire the **director of photography** (also called the **cinematographer**) early in the preproduction stage so that he or she can help decide colors and other aspects of the overall look. Directors who become involved in preproduction often hire an **associate** or **assistant director** to help handle details.[8]

As the preproduction process proceeds, people will be hired to handle properties, set decoration, makeup, and hairstyling. They will begin making plans and buying supplies for their respective areas and will eventually hire assistants who will work during the production phase. Shortly before production begins, members of the production crew—camera operators, audio operators, a script supervisor—will be hired. For complicated productions the number and types of people hired can seem almost infinite—handlers for animals, teachers for child actors, truck drivers, and so on. For smaller productions a few generalists called **production assistants** can be hired to handle various miscellaneous jobs.

Because of their scaled-down nature, student productions usually do not require extensive crews. However, although people are not actually hired, students' abilities must be matched with the jobs that need to be accomplished.

Casting

Choosing people to act in a narrative movie is important because it is the actors who convey the story. In fact, **casting** is one of the director's most crucial decisions. Casting errors inevitably hurt the final product. Behind-the-scenes people who cannot handle their jobs can be replaced in the middle of a production, albeit with some disruption, but people in front of the camera are essentially irreplaceable.

Some directors feel that casting is 90 percent of directing. As a result, they often write rather elaborate descriptions of the personality traits of the main characters and discuss these traits with the auditioning actors to determine who will fit the role most effectively.

Stilted, unnatural performers detract greatly from a story and sometimes even make dramatic moments inappropriately humorous. Student productions are especially vulnerable to poor acting, some of which cannot be helped because of budget and scheduling limitations. However, in both student and professional movies every effort should be made to cast people who fit the parts and can be counted on to perform well.

In the professional realm casting companies are often hired to screen actors. These companies have close contact with agents and can gather quickly any category needed—pudgy men in their fifties, red-headed teenagers, Abraham Lincoln look-alikes. The production manager supplies the casting company with character breakdowns (prepared from the script breakdown), and the company then sends out a call

to agents for actors to fill the various roles. Often these companies will winnow candidates down to four or five for each major role. The director then makes the final selections.

Other directors like to be more involved in casting, to the point of finding their own actors. They watch movies and television shows to check out people who might fit into the movie. They attend community theaters for the same reason. Sometimes they place ads for **open casting** in trade journals. This means anyone can try out for parts. The main difficulty with this is that so many people show up that selection becomes quite time consuming. Open casting often works well for student films, however. An ad in the school newspaper can draw talented people to fill the parts.

Generally, casting involves a short interview with the actors to determine if they appear to be right for the part. Then they read some of the lines with other actors who are trying out or with people who have already been selected for the other parts. Often these short acting scenes are videotaped so they can be reviewed. These videotaped scenes can serve as a **screen test**—a demonstration of how the person will look and sound on video or film. The major roles are cast first, then other people are cast to fit in with the stars.

Student movies usually do not have the luxury or financing to engage in elaborate casting procedures, but every effort should be made to find the best person available for each role. Using your friends and relatives is an accepted but not particularly advisable practice. Generally, directing someone you do not deal with regularly is easier than directing someone you are close to.

One casting problem that student productions often have to a greater degree than professional productions is reliability—making sure that all people cast will be reliable throughout the entire production period. If cast members are not paid, they may have little incentive to stay with the project as it becomes more difficult and time consuming. The person who is doing casting for a student production should be honest with actors about the amount of time and commitment the production will require. Using people in the production class as actors is the best way to ensure reliability, but often they do not fit the roles or they are more interested in behind-the-scenes jobs.

Preproduction also involves working out contracts for the people cast. Lawyers, agents, and personal managers are usually involved in this for well-known stars. The contract stipulates the salary, the working conditions, the placement of credits, the size of the dressing room, and anything else that needs to be negotiated.

Student producers are wise to have actors sign releases, such as that shown in Figure 2.11, so that they do not come back at a later time, demanding pay or some other type of recognition.

Finding Locations

One of the primary functions of the script breakdown sheet is to detail the various locations needed for shooting. Once these are determined, someone must find or build the appropriate locale. Scouting for the proper location is another province of the director.

There are professional companies that will find locations, and many cities and states that want to encourage filmmaking have offices with photographs of various sites. Eastman Kodak has an experimental on-line image service comprised of digitized still photographs from some of these state film commissions. Images of possible locations can be researched using key words and phrases, and then they can be printed so they can be studied.[9]

The assistant director, production manager, or art director often does the initial scouting. But most directors want to see where they will be shooting so that they can anticipate problems and see whether the location fits their conception of the movie. Locations are important to the overall look of a picture. A chase scene can take place just about anywhere, but a director who wants to give scenes a closed-in feeling will want to look for a certain combination of streets and buildings that can be shot at the appropriate angles. Of course, budget must be considered. The ideal street might be in Rome, but cast and crew cannot be transported there economically. A street in Burbank will have to do.

The director (and often the production designer and director of photography) should carefully survey the locales selected to ensure that shooting will go smoothly. The director should note the name of the person in charge of the facility as well as the name of someone to turn to if unexpected problems arise. If the shoot is outdoors or if natural light is going to be used indoors, the director should look at the facility at the same time of day as when the shooting is planned. In this way problems can be noted that might be caused by shadows or the position of the sun. Polaroid pictures with compass directions marked on them are helpful.

Many other important factors must be considered. Where should vehicles be parked? Where can cameras, lights, and mics be placed? How much power is available? Can cables be strung safely? Are there likely to be any interruptions such as a ringing phone? Will any noises such as air conditioning interfere with the audio? Do any large items (telephone poles, billboards) block the camera's view? The best way to cover all the important points while investigating a location is to develop and follow a location survey form such as that shown in Figure 2.12.

Someone must obtain permission, preferably in writing, for shooting at any location. (See Figure 2.13 for a sample location release.) This is true for student productions as well as for professional ones. Releases should be obtained for use of people's homes, stores, or other commercial buildings.

Many cities require movie producers to pay for permits in order to shoot in the city. The money is used to help defray any extra costs the city may incur for directing traffic around the production area or adding security. If permits are required, they should be obtained during preproduction so that production is not delayed.[10]

Designing and Building Sets

Determining what sets to build is closely associated with location scouting. Theoretically, any movie can be shot totally on location or totally in the studio. During the 1920s, for example, the Germans used the massive studios of UFA (Universum Film A.G.) for all scenes in their films—even those that depicted masses of people in city streets or forests (complete with concrete trees). By doing that they were able to control the lighting, the tonalities that would

PERFORMANCE RELEASE

In consideration of my appearing in the movie

_____
                    (title or subject)
and for no subsequent remuneration, I do hereby on behalf of
myself, my heirs, executors, and administrators authorize

_____
                (producer or production company)
to use live or recorded on tape, film, or otherwise my name,
voice, likeness, and performance for television or film
distribution throughout the world and for audiovisual and general
education purposes in perpetuity.

      I further agree on behalf of myself and others as above
stated that my name, likeness, and biography may be used for
promotion purposes and other uses. Further, I agree to
indemnify, defend, and hold the producer (or production company)
harmless for any and all claims, suits, or liabilities arising
from my appearance and the use of any of my materials, name,
likeness, or biography.

Conditions:

Signature_____

Printed Name_____

Street Address_____

City and Zip Code_____

Phone Number_____

Date_____

Figure 2.11

An example of a performance release form.

Figure 2.12

An example of a form that covers some of the primary points to consider when surveying a location.

LOCATION SURVEY CHECKLIST

Type of material being shot _____

Time of shooting _____

Potential location of shooting _____

    Principal contact person _____

    Address _____

    Phone number _____

Camera:

    Where can the camera be placed?
    What, if anything, is needed in the way of camera mounting devices or platforms?
    What, if anything, is needed in the way of special lenses?
    Will any objects interfere with the camera shots? If so, how can this situation be corrected?

Lighting:

    What types of lights will be needed?
    Where can the lights be placed?
    What light stands or particular light holders will be needed?
    What, if any, special lighting accessories will be needed?
    How can any problems regarding mixing indoor and outdoor lighting be solved?
    In what ways will the sun's position at different times of day affect the shooting?
    What kinds of problems are shadows likely to cause?

Power:

    Is enough power available or will a generator be needed?
    Where is the circuit breaker box?
    Who can be contacted if a circuit blows?
    Which circuits can be used and how many watts can be run on them?
    How many, if any, extension cords will be needed?
    What power outlets can be used?

Sound:

    Are there background noises that may interfere with audio? If so, how can they be corrected?
    Where can the microphones and cable be placed?
    Are any particular microphone holders or stands needed?
    What types of microphones should be used?
    How much microphone cable will be needed?

General:

    Where is parking available?
    Where is the nearest telephone?
    If passes are needed to enter the premises, how can they be obtained?

LOCATION RELEASE

I hereby grant_____

permission to use the property located at_____

_____

for the purpose of photographing and recording scenes for the

movie entitled_____.

This permission includes, but is not limited to, the right to

bring cast, crew, equipment, props, and temporary sets onto the

premises. I understand that all things brought onto the premises

will be removed at the end of the production period.

Conditions:

Signature_____

Printed Name_____

Title_____

Street Address_____

City and Zip Code_____

Phone Number_____

Date_____

Figure 2.13

A sample permission form for shooting at a location.

show on the black-and-white film, the shape of all the architectural structures, and the relationship of all other elements of art design.

Control is a primary reason for building a set and shooting in a studio. You do not need to worry about the position of the sun. You can shoot long shots at 9 a.m. and close-ups at 4 p.m. without worrying that when you intercut them they won't match. You can place trees where you want them and not where they happen to be growing. You do not need to worry about airplanes flying overhead and ruining the audio of your Civil War picture. You don't have to hurry to finish a shot because classes will be changing and a horde of unwanted students will appear in the background.

A studio set can also be more convenient if you can leave the set up and plan to shoot in the same place for a number of days. Under these circumstances you can leave everything in place and do not need to set up and break down every day as you might at a remote location.

Another reason for building a set is that you cannot find what you want in the "real world." A "Star Trek" control room does not actually exist anywhere, so you need to build it.

Cost can be another consideration. For student productions sets are usually more expensive than locations because the material for the sets must be purchased, whereas the locations are usually local and free. On professional features this may not be the case, mainly because the wages of crew and cast are such a large percentage of the budget. The extra time needed on location and the costs that may be associated with transportation and lodging can greatly exceed the cost of a set in a studio.

Sometimes a scene requires a combination of location and set. For example, a TV studio control room might serve as the basis for a futuristic space control lab but be augmented by peripheral flats that show additional complicated instruments.

Someone—usually the director, producer, production designer, and/or production manager—must decide which scenes need sets and which need locations. These decisions are usually made tentatively after the script is broken down. The director may look at city photos for available Victorian dining rooms while the art director is planning and determining costs for

what it would take to build one. What to do would be decided after they have both completed their research.

Once the decision to build a set has been made, the set designer draws up the plans, keeping in mind the overall feel of the picture decided on by the director and art director and the lighting and shooting requirements that the cinematographer might impose. (See Figure 2.14 for a drawing and photo of a set design.) Computer programs can help with set designing. For example, one program allows a set designer to "build" a set with computer graphics. Then the set designer, director, and others can "walk through" the computerized drawing as though they were looking through a camera. Aspect ratios or lens focal length can be changed with the click of a mouse.[11]

Once the director approves the set design, it can be built. Construction must be started well in advance of the shooting date because building a set can be a long, multistep process. Flats must be built before they can be painted, must be painted before pictures can be hung on them, and must be erected before major pieces of furniture can be placed in front of them. The sturdiness of the set must be considered. A door that is not used can be rather flimsily built, but one that is going to have characters using it must be sturdy and well braced so that it looks real.

Set decorations must also be considered as part of the set design. These are items that add atmosphere, such as flowerpots, ashtrays, pillows, and lamps.

A set can be expensive if everything is bought new. Students rarely need to do this; they can raid the dorm (with permission!) or their own bedrooms. Even professionals usually deal with secondhand or rental stores or find flats and set pieces among those stored at the studio.

Digital technologies are beginning to provide an alternative to traditional set building. Increasingly, computers are being used to create the sets, themselves, so that they do not need to be constructed. These "virtual sets" are basically a computer-generated graphic that is placed behind the actors, who, while they are performing, do not have an actual set surrounding them. Computerized sets, or parts of them, can be reused in different films. Elements of a set can be modified and reshaped. New elements can be

a

added, cut, and repositioned. Perspective can
be changed and objects can be resized. In a period piece, for example, contemporary buildings
intruding on what is basically a 1920s street setting can be erased and replaced with more
appropriate buildings that are either generated
in the computer or copied from another scene
or film. The digital skyline and sets designed for
Batman Forever can be reused in commercials,
television shows, and other movies. By the time
these sets are digitally repainted, reshaped, repositioned, and composited with other elements
in the new film, we will probably not recognize
them as Gotham City.

However, whether the set is made of pixels or
plywood, a great deal of time, thought, skill, and
hard work goes into it. The whole process must
be considered carefully because the set can be
the major element in creating the atmosphere
for the scene.[12]

Planning Costumes, Wardrobe, Makeup, and Hairstyling

The extent to which costumes, wardrobe, makeup,
and hairstyling need to be considered during the
preproduction phase depends on the nature and
scope of the picture.

b

Figure 2.14

*Emmy Award-winning production designer Jan Scott did the set drawing (a) for the
motion picture* Grandview, U.S.A. *The photo (b) shows the set as it was actually constructed. (Courtesy of Jan Scott, production designer)*

Many student directors give little thought to
these elements. Actors wear their own clothes
and handle their own hairstyling and makeup,
if any. The main consideration is making sure
actors wear the same clothes and makeup in all
scenes that supposedly occur close to each other
in time. Actors should also keep the same general hairstyle. One student actor decided to
shave his beard about three fourths of the way

through a production. Shooting had to be halted for two weeks while he grew his beard back. If a student production is set in a different era, period costumes will be necessary; special makeup will be needed if some characters have an unusual look or are much older than the actors actually portraying them.

Professional productions pay more attention to these elements. Even if a movie is set in modern times, the wardrobe of the stars is usually specially designed so that it flatters the stars and fits the overall mood of the picture. Period pieces require a large staff of people fitting and sewing costumes for many months before production begins. People involved with period hairstyling also can be busy during these weeks, researching the styles of the period and buying and styling wigs. Unusual makeup, such as a hand with six fingers or a burned face, must be considered in advance so that all the necessary supplies are available.

For movies that do not require anything unusual, makeup artists and hairstylists do most of their work during production. They are there to enhance the actors and to make sure face and hair look the same from one day to the next if that is what the shooting schedule requires.[13]

Preparing Props, Effects, and Supplies

A list of essential props can be culled from the script breakdown, but someone, such as the production manager, must make sure all are obtained and fit the director's overall vision of the movie. The person buying or borrowing props can often look for set decorations as well.

Props are usually thought of as items required by the plot (for example, the flowers the hero gives to the heroine to win her heart). **Set decorations** add to the overall feel of the scene but are not integral to the plot (for example, the vase of flowers sitting on the coffee table). The line between the two often becomes blurred. If a scene is shot in a garden in September, but the plot is set in May, someone may need to buy artificial spring flowers.

Special effects can fall into a number of areas: a blood packet that explodes in the mouth of someone who has been socked in the jaw could be considered makeup, a sleeve that rips off could be part of a costume, a chair that breaks in half could be designed into the set, mashed potatoes made to look like ice cream might be considered a prop, and a fog machine might fall in the province of the cinematographer.

It is important that someone makes sure all items needed for special effects are ordered and in place for production. Of course, special effects can also be created on film or tape and then intermingled with the live footage. This work is usually done in a studio and involves the use of models. It must be carefully coordinated with the live shots so that all elements look alike. For example, tiny models of the main characters must wear the same color clothes as the people in the live action scene.

Most supplies that will be needed during production should be purchased during preproduction. This includes all supplies for makeup, hairstyling, special effects, and other elements, as well as such items as masking tape, cleansers, sponges, and a first aid kit. Most important, someone must make sure that the raw stock (tape or film) is purchased or obtained.

Acquiring and Checking Equipment

All equipment should be purchased, rented, or obtained in some other way during the preproduction period. It should then be carefully checked out to make sure it will work properly. Before equipment is taken to a location, it should be connected and operated somewhere close to a maintenance facility so that any problems can be corrected.

Batteries should be checked to make sure they are fully charged. Lenses should be examined for scratches or focus imperfections. Tripods should be lubricated, if necessary, so that they operate smoothly. Lights should focus properly; extra lamps and extension cables should be readily available. The viewfinder should be checked for picture accuracy by framing something with it and making sure the framing is the same when the image is recorded. Camera tests should be run to make sure calibration is correct. Microphones should be tested for proper pickup. The headsets should work. Connectors and cables should be carefully checked both visually and in operation because they are likely to cause trouble.

All in all, a great deal needs to be done before shooting occurs. The individuals involved in the project must be diligent about accomplishing the chores of preproduction so that production and postproduction have a chance of moving smoothly.

Obtaining Rights

Some movies contain elements that involve rights clearance. For example, if the plot calls for a radio to play or one of the characters to sing "I Want to Hold Your Hand," rights to that Beatles song must be cleared. Clearing music is not easy. The first step is to find out what company published the music and ask that publisher for a synchronization license, which usually costs money. The publisher may also require that you receive permission from the performer, the record company, and/or the composer. Gaining all these permissions can be time consuming.[14]

It is easier to use copyright-cleared music from one of the many stock libraries that exist solely for this purpose. The music is not distinctive, but it often can fill the need.[15] Using music that is so old that it is in the public domain is another solution. Music can also be specially written for the scene, but this often costs more than obtaining the rights. Students can sometimes obtain original music economically by talking to friends in the music department who are eager to experiment with music for movies.

Film or tape footage is another item that often needs clearance. One example would be a news story that is an integral part of the plot. You cannot simply tape Dan Rather off the air and include that in a production. Permission must be sought from CBS. Sometimes, rather than shooting at a location, a movie will incorporate a few shots that establish the location; for example, shots of an airplane taking off will establish the location as an airport. Many movies contain shots of airplanes taking off that could be used, but rights again must be cleared. A number of companies supply copyright-cleared

stock footage, including news clips. They charge for the footage, but using them is usually cheaper and more convenient than trying to clear rights.[16]

Photographs, artwork, pictures from books, and sometimes even sound effects must also be cleared through the appropriate contact(s)—publisher, artist, author, photographer, museum, or record company. (Figure 2.15 shows a sample letter requesting permission to use a copyrighted work.) Usually, finding the address of the appropriate contact requires some research. Books such as *Writer's Market* and *Literary Marketplace* can assist you in this search. Other books such as *Backstage, Blu-Book,* and *Motion Picture, TV, and Theatre Directory* can lead you to music libraries, stock footage houses, and other sources of copyright-cleared material.[17]

Arranging Transportation, Lodging, and Meals

Someone must attend to the creature comforts for members of the cast and crew. For any shoot that will last more than four or five hours, someone should locate in advance the nearest restaurant and restrooms. At a more complex level are arrangements for air travel, ground transportation, overnight accommodations, and meals in some exotic country. If the travel is to be extensive, perhaps to several different countries, the production manager can enlist a travel agent to make the arrangements. However, the plans cannot be handled like a simple tourist travel plan. Such a shoot often involves shipping an extensive amount of expensive equipment, and stars may require extra security. If the movie falls behind schedule during production, many of the transportation arrangements made during preproduction may need to be changed.

Usually, someone goes to the location ahead of time to check on whether equipment can be rented and to try to line up some crew members and extras. This will cut down on transportation costs. This person can also check out local hotels, restaurants, and catering services so that cast and crew can be adequately cared for within the limits of the budget.

If the film is shot locally, lodging is not a problem because everyone can go home at night.

Figure 2.15

A sample letter asking for permission to use a copyrighted work.

Date

Name
Licensing Department
Music Publishing Company
Street Address
City, State, and Zip Code

Dear Person's Name:

I am producing a movie entitled <u>Name of Movie</u> for which I would like to have one of the characters sing the song "Name of Song" composed by Name of Composer. I would like to acquire a non-exclusive synchronization license for this musical composition.

I would like permission to use this material for broadcast, cablecast, or other means of exhibition throughout the world as often as deemed appropriate for this movie and for any future revisions of this movie. Your permission granting me the right to use this material in no way restricts your use for any other purposes.

For your convenience, a release form is provided below and a copy of this letter is attached for your files.

Sincerely yours,

Your Name

I (We) grant permission for the use requested in this letter.

Signature_____

Printed Name_____

Title_____

Phone Number_____

Date_____

But transportation for people and equipment still is a consideration. A student producer must make sure enough cars are available to transport everyone and everything to the location site. Maps and phone numbers for the location should be provided for everyone.

For shoots that last all day, at least one meal should be provided. One way to handle this is through caterers. In cities that host a great deal of video and film production, companies specialize in catering to casts and crews at location sites. The production manager hires the catering company and makes sure it is kept up-to-date on when and where the cast and crew will be for lunch. Catering has definite advantages, especially if the shooting is occurring at a remote location. People can get back to work more quickly if the food comes to them than if they have to drive a long distance to a restaurant.

A variation on catering often used by students is sending one of the crew members to the nearest fast-food place to buy lunch for everyone and bring it back to the location.

On the professional level many union regulations govern meal breaks. The production company must follow them strictly or face fines and legal grievances. Requirements vary according to the particular working arrangements for cast and crew, but generally no one can work for more than five hours without at least a thirty-minute meal break. Some contracts stipulate the quality of the food that must be provided—a soft drink and a bag of potato chips won't do. Students are not encumbered with union regulations, but a student producer should still make sure people have time to eat. An empty stomach makes for a grouchy disposition.

Obtaining Insurance

Moviemaking is subject to a great deal of risk. During the preproduction phase the producer or production manager should make sure that adequate insurance is purchased to cover any mishaps.

One risk is that the movie will not be completed because the money runs out. To cover this Hollywood has developed a special type of insurance, called a **completion guarantee.** Of course, like any insurance, a completion guarantee costs the production company money in terms of a premium, usually a percentage of the estimated cost of the picture. The company that provides the money for the completion guarantee usually states that if its money is needed to finish the movie, it can take over the production, which usually means firing the director and hiring someone who can finish the job economically.

Liability insurance is a must, especially if the picture is to be shot on location. This insurance covers damage to people's homes or other sites used as locations, as well as harm to people. Someone on the production crew should be assigned to take before and after pictures of a location in case a damage claim is filed by the owner of the location.

Insurance is also needed to cover theft or breakage of equipment, props, set pieces, and the like. This insurance is often quite expensive or else it doesn't cover much. The producer and production manager must decide on the breadth and depth of the insurance coverage in relation to its cost.

Vehicle insurance is a must for all cars and trucks that will be moving equipment or people during a production. Many other specialized forms of insurance exist—for example, a particular star or a particular prop can be insured. Insurance can even be taken out against inclement weather, but these special insurance plans are expensive and usually not worth the cost. Nothing is fail-safe.

Notes

1. Preproduction software includes *Movie Magic Breakdown and Scheduling* (Mac and DOS), a program that interfaces with *Movie Magic Budgeting* and scriptwriting software. *Movie Magic* is available from Screenplay Systems, 150 East Olive Ave., Suite 305, Burbank, CA 91502; (818) 843-6557. *MacToolkit Script Breakdown and Scheduling* and *MacToolkit Budgeting* are programs that include a complete preproduction program (scheduling, breakdowns, call sheets, and so on) and a comprehensive budgeting program. Quantum Films has budgeting and scheduling software called *Turbo AD,* which is available for DOS and Windows. *Turbo AD* is the breakdown/scheduling software, but other programs are integrated with it: *Script Scan* allows breakdowns to be done within an imported script; *Turbo Report* manages crew and cast lists; *Turbo Budget* and *Cost Tracking* help in budget preparation and analysis and track expenses during the production. These programs are available from Quantum Films Software Division, 8230 Beverly Blvd., Suite 17, Los Angeles, CA 90048; (213) 852-9661.

   Birns and Sawyer, the equipment rental house, sells many of these software packages. It is located at 1026 N. Highland Ave., Hollywood, CA 90038; (213) 466-8211. Another company that sells a variety of film/television preproduction/production software is The Writer's Computer Store at (800) 272-8927 or http://www.hollywoodnetwork.com/writerscomputer.

2. Such programs include *Movie Magic Budgeting* (Mac or DOS) and *Turbo Budget* for DOS and

Windows, both noted above. Programs such as these can usually be linked to libraries containing current union labor rates, overtime, and fringe benefits.

3. Sometimes insurance, legal fees, and licenses are considered to be above-the-line rather than below-the-line costs.

4. These rates are based on a number of rate cards, including those of Yale Video, Anaheim, CA; Alpha Studios, Burbank, CA; Skylight Productions, Inc., Los Angeles, CA; Videomedia Rentals, Sunnyvale, CA; and Audio Services Corp., North Hollywood, CA.

5. These figures were taken from *Paymaster 95-96* (Los Angeles: Entertainment Partners, 1995). This book can be purchased from The Stanley J. Brooks Co., 1487 Glendon Avenue, Los Angeles, CA 90024; (310) 475-2555.

6. For a variety of forms, see Richard Gates, *Production Management for Film and Video* (Stoneham, MA: Focal Press, 1995); Eve Light Honthaner, *The Complete Film Production Handbook* (Los Angeles: Lone Eagle, 1992); Bastian Cleve, *Film Production Management* (Stoneham, MA: Focal Press, 1994); and *Producer's Masterguide* (New York: Producer's Masterguide, 1995).

7. *Production designer* is a fairly new term, popularized by the elaborate science fiction films of the 1970s, such as *Star Wars,* that needed a great deal of design coordination. During the studio era an art director developed the overall look of a film, but now that task is often given to a production designer, who then oversees one or more art directors. As a result, many people who used to be art directors have become production designers, a term that has more stature than art director. Some current movies have a production designer and no art director, some have both, and some still have only art directors.

8. Generally in television production the term used is *associate director* while in film production the term used is *assistant director.*

9. For more information you might contact the Eastman Exchange Business Office at (800) 816-2233; additional information is also available at Kodak's website: http://www.kodak.com. Similar on-line databases have been or are in the process of being developed for talent, props, equipment rental, technical data, and variety of other preproduction and production services. Although web sites seem to change almost daily, several current sites of this kind are: http://www.hollywoodnetwork.com; or http://www.hollywoodshopping.com.

10. See Robert Maier, *Location Scouting and Management Handbook* (Stoneham, MA: Focal Press, 1994).

11. "Making Virtue of Necessity," *Variety,* 26 May 1992, p. 3.

12. For more on set design, see Peter Utz, "The Joy of Sets," *AV Video,* May 1995, pp. 90-93; and "Welcome to Digital Backlot," *Variety,* 22 March 1996, p. A14.

13. For more on costumes, makeup, and hairstyling, see Virginia J-R Kehoe, *The Technique of the Professional Make-Up Artist* (Stoneham, MA: Focal Press, 1995); Rosemary Ingham, *The Costumer's Handbook: How to Make All Kinds of Costumes* (New York: Prentice-Hall, 1987); and James Stevens Cox, *Hairdressing and Wig Making* (London: Batsford Academic, 1984).

14. For more information on copyrights, see John D. Zelezny, *Communications Law* (Belmont, CA: Wadsworth, 1993), pp. 287-323.

15. A list of music libraries can be found in "Production Music Libraries on Audio CDs," *Mix,* September 1995, pp. 127-129.

16. A list of stock footage providers can be found in "UnCommon Stock," *AV Video,* March 1995, pp. 159-172.

17. *Writer's Market* is published by Writer's Digest, 9933 Alliance Rd., Cincinnati, OH 45343. *Literary Marketplace* is published by R.R. Bowker Co., 121 Chanlon Rd., New Providence, NJ 07974. Both are available in most libraries. *Backstage* is published by Backstage Publications, Inc., 5670 Wilshire Blvd., Hollywood, CA 90036; *Blu-Book* is published by The Hollywood Reporter, 6715 Sunset Blvd., Hollywood, CA 90028; and *Motion Picture, TV, and Theatre Directory* is published by Motion Picture Enterprises Publications, Inc., Tarrytown, NY 10591.

part two
Production

chapter three
The Process of Production

The production stage of moviemaking involves a large number of people and complicated logistics. In fact, it has been said that in order to create art, a poet needs a paper and a pencil, an artist needs a canvas and paint, a photographer needs a camera and film, and a moviemaker needs a bank and an army.[1]

Production is the most exciting, high-profile part of the movie business. The various elements needed to make the movie—people, equipment, sets, supplies—come together during production. The individuals involved interact in many ways and usually build personal bonds. Production is also the most expensive and most potentially explosive phase of moviemaking—the one during which Murphy's law (*Anything that can go wrong will go wrong*) is likely to be in full swing.

Production Responsibilities

The major tasks connected with the production stage of moviemaking involve directing, acting, organizing and record keeping, lighting and camera operation, sound and picture recording, and supporting the production. The details of these functions and the people who undertake them vary greatly from one situation to another.

For example, a production with a union crew differs from a production with a nonunion crew. In a union situation the people needed and the specific duties each will perform are often spelled out in the union regulations and cannot be controlled by an individual director. An electricians' union can specify that only its members can handle lights. Someone trying to be helpful by moving a light can cause a grievance to be filed. Union regulations help define the tasks that need to be accomplished and keep people from being exploited, however. In a nonunion situation the assignment of specific tasks is more flexible. Duties can be assigned according to

people's particular talents and the needs of the particular movie. However, movies produced with nonunion crews usually have lower budgets, and people can be called on to work long (sometimes unreasonable) hours for scant remuneration.

Student films present yet another variation. Many of the same tasks need to be performed for student films, but students are in a learning situation. As a result, individual students often undertake a variety of tasks in order to gain experience. In some instances they cannot effectively perform the particular jobs they are assigned, but the school environment is for experimentation and learning individual strengths and weaknesses. Sometimes the final product suffers in the name of learning, but students who work hard and produce an acceptable movie can experience the same excitement professionals do.

The nature of the movie also determines what needs to be done and who should do it. Shooting a documentary in a desert for *National Geographic* is quite different from shooting a narrative movie such as *Independence Day*. The documentary crew would be smaller, with people doubling up on jobs.

The merging of film and video techniques has further complicated the delineation of what needs to be done and who should do it. Technologically, film and video require different tasks. Someone must load film into a separate container called a **magazine** for a film shoot, but this job does not exist for a video shoot.

The tasks to be performed during the production are in a constant state of evolution. No hard and fast rules can be made for every movie about what should be done and by whom. We will therefore discuss, in rather broad terms, the various functions that need to be undertaken and describe some of the variations that exist within professional and student productions.

Directing

The tasks to be performed in relation to directing are multifaceted and to some extent defy definition. They involve developing the overall vision and keeping it alive throughout the production process, getting the strongest performance possible from the actors, making sure that the movie is shot correctly, both technically and aesthetically, and maintaining morale so that people work well toward a common goal.

For the most part these tasks are handled by the **director,** who is the "boss" during production. Directors are part artist, part technician, part psychiatrist, and part judge. They establish the overall creative tone of the motion picture that others follow as they light, frame shots, act, set up props, and attend to the other details of the movie. Directors have the final say regarding all aspects of the picture, so they must be well versed in both the technical and aesthetic principles of moviemaking. They provide the controlling vision that translates the story into images and sound. Before shooting, most directors will have decided what kinds of shots they think they will need and how these shots might be edited in postproduction. Some directors will even develop a complete storyboard or shot list to help them visualize how each shot will fit into the whole.

Directors must also be able to deal well with people. They give specific instructions to actors, in terms of both the emotional content of the script and the physical needs of the shooting environment. They may, for example, tell an actor to be more low-key or to change the expression on his or her face. Actors have more confidence in directors' advice if they sense the directors have done the homework needed in terms of analyzing the characters they are to portray and understanding the actors' methods by having observed some of the actors' past performances.

One of the most important functions of directors is **blocking.** This involves placing the actors in particular spots and telling them where and when to move. Blocking is crucial in terms of making sure the camera can frame the action appropriately. It also must be comfortable for the actors. If the leading lady must contort her body to glance at the leading man, the result may not only be uncomfortable but ludicrous. Some directors make sketches of the action (see Figure 3.1) to help them envision the moves the actors will make.

Directors also deal with the crew. They must be able to communicate their desires effectively so that the various crew members do not waste time setting something up incorrectly.

For some types of productions directors must deal with outsiders. When a commercial is being produced, executives from the ad agency or the advertising company may appear on the set. The client for a corporate video may do likewise. Directors must handle these people (and their ideas) with tact but still maintain control of the creative process. Directors should never allow one of these people to give instructions to cast or crew members.

The atmosphere on a movie set can be emotionally charged. Egos abound, and cast and crew members have their own creative ideas about how the movie should be shot. Directors must be able to handle the conflicts that arise, compromising as needed, cajoling as appropriate, but remaining firmly in control. Directors can certainly take advice from others, but they must be able to reject ideas (preferably in a diplomatic manner) if they will not enhance the final product.

At the beginning of any production there usually is a honeymoon period when everyone is enthusiastic and willing to get along well with everyone else. However, as the work grinds on and perhaps falls a bit behind schedule, people's nerves tend to fray, and morale begins to drop. Directors must solve the interpersonal problems (even though they may be the cause of some of them) and keep the production process on track.

There are as many different styles of directing as there are directors. Some act like generals; others act like buddies. Some interact with all cast and crew members; others interact with only a few and expect them to interact with the rest. Some block all talent and camera angles on paper ahead of time; others improvise on the set. Some rehearse for long periods before shooting; others shoot the first rehearsal. Some give actors specific instructions about how to play a character; others prefer that the actor make character determinations.

Directors sometimes have one or more **assistant directors** to help them with directorial chores. Exactly which aspects of directing these assistant directors undertake depends on what the director wants them to do.

In some instances assistant directors oversee the lighting of one scene while the director is rehearsing another scene—or vice versa. An assistant director may also direct a **second unit,** a group of production people who are in a separate location, shooting scenes that do not require the principal actors. Some assistant di-

Figure 3.1
This blocking sketch is typical of what a director might draw in preparation for a scene that involves four people sitting at a restaurant table, one of whom gets up and leaves. The angles with numbers by them are camera setups. For example, camera setup 2 is a pan shot of the girl as she gets up from the table and goes to the door.

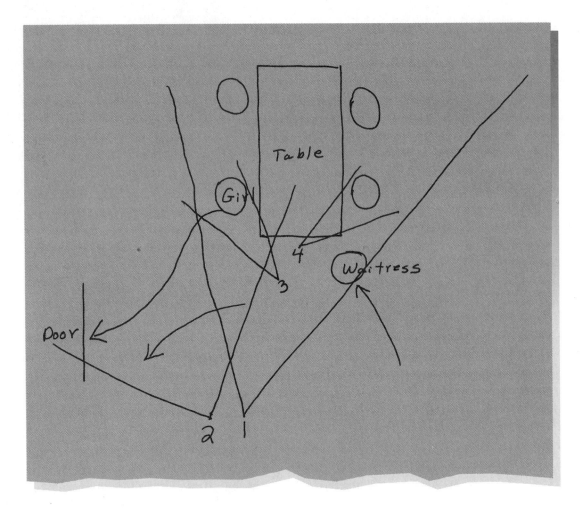

rectors are asked to handle all extras so that the director can concentrate on directing the principal actors. Assistant directors often keep people quiet on the set or handle crowd control if the shooting is taking place in a public area. Or the director may ask an assistant director to handle the problems associated with some particularly cantankerous cast or crew member. In general, assistant directors should be flexible and prepared for the unexpected.[2]

Acting

Principal actors (those who have the main speaking parts) usually come to the production situation trained in their art. They have studied the character and have ideas about how the person should be played. They work with the director and other actors to develop their character. Some people are, of course, much better actors than others. Truly fine actors can leave their real selves behind and "become" the people they are portraying.[3] Although many people aspire to be actors, few can actually do it well.

Acting in a movie is difficult because scenes are shot out of order. Actors have no time to build up to a particular emotion, as they do during a stage play where everything happens in sequence. For example, movie actors may have to react to the death of a loved one days before the recording of the scene in which the loved one dies. They must be able to switch their emotions off and on at the convenience of the schedule. A good director will review with the actors the emotional level of scenes before and after the one being shot. If some of these scenes have already been shot, actors can ask to watch them on videotape so that they can better recall their actions.

Lines are shot out of order even within a single scene. When actors' close-ups are shot, they often deliver their lines out of context. Sometimes the characters they are supposed to be talking to are not even on the set. They must profess mad, passionate love—to a camera.

Bit players and **extras** are also involved in the acting process. Bit players have only a few lines—usually five or fewer. Extras have no speaking lines; mainly they stand in the background and move as they are told. Bit players and extras should remain fairly inconspicuous and not distract attention from the principal actors.

Stand-ins are also part of the acting process. These are people who play the parts of principal actors so that the equipment can be properly set. They stand and move as the actor should so that the crew can adjust lights and plan camera angles. This relieves the actors from tedious and rather unproductive work so that they can memorize lines or prepare emotionally for the upcoming shoot.

Sometimes the actors in movies, particularly student movies, are not professionals. They are friends or relatives of the director or other crew members, or they are people who were recruited through an ad in a newspaper. Getting a good performance from these people may be difficult. For one thing, they are likely to be unreliable, especially if they are not being paid. If the male lead drops out in the middle of a shoot, all his scenes have to be reshot. The director should somehow determine the commitment level of all nonprofessional actors and, if possible, find some way to pay them.

People who have not been trained in acting are often self-conscious and feel awkward doing something they would never consider doing in real life. The best solution to this problem is to cast people who are, in temperament and style, similar to the characters they are to portray.

People who have been trained to act on the stage can usually overcome self-consciousness, but they do not necessarily make good movie actors. They are so used to projecting their voices and using broad gestures—much needed when the audience is yards away—that they cannot give the intimate type of performance needed for most movies.

Organizing and Record Keeping

Movie production is so complicated that someone must keep records of all details. Scenes shot on Friday have to be shot in such a way that they can be intercut with scenes shot on Tuesday. A shot missed the first week of taping has to be rescheduled for the third week. Someone must log and tally spending so that the production does not run over budget. Almost everyone involved in the production process has some paperwork to do, but the main organizing and record-keeping chores fall to the producer, script

Figure 3.2

Continuity would be an important element in the pumpkin-cutting scene from Old Mother Witch. *Someone should carefully keep track of how much of the pumpkin is cut in each shot, how items are arranged on the table, and where each person's hands are during each shot. (Photo courtesy of Phoenix Films, Mark Chodzko, and Carol Carrick)*

supervisor, production manager, and assistant director.

Although they are the chief executives of the picture, many movie producers spend little time on the set. Others, especially those on small independent productions, make their presence felt and oversee the director fairly closely. Generally, however, the production phase is the domain of the director. When producers do come on the set, they are usually there to see that money is not being wasted and the movie will be finished on time. Some producers appoint **line producers** to represent them on the set. These people handle organizational details, try to speed up shooting, and keep an eye on the money. Sometimes **executive producers** oversee a number of TV series or movies. Again, they are not active on the set, but they help solve problems and make sure the production is under control.

Script supervisors (sometimes referred to as **script clerks**)[4] deal primarily with continuity. During rehearsals they take Polaroid and/or camcorder shots or make diagrams detailing where the camera, lights, and actors are placed so that everything can be duplicated during the shoot. They also keep continuity notes on such things as where props were located, whether doors were ajar, unusual filters that were used on the camera, where actors' hands were when they were saying certain words, the direction people walked, the amount of food on a plate, and the color of someone's tie (see Figure 3.2).

Figure 3.3
(a) A page of script and (b) the corresponding notes made by the script supervisor. Note that the script supervisor has listed a few minor dialogue changes and has drawn lines that show how much of the script each shot covered. The sheet of notes lists each shot and all its takes, how long the shot was, whether the shot was completed in its entirety (C for complete) or stopped midway (I for incomplete), uses NG for takes that are definitely no good, and includes other pertinent comments.

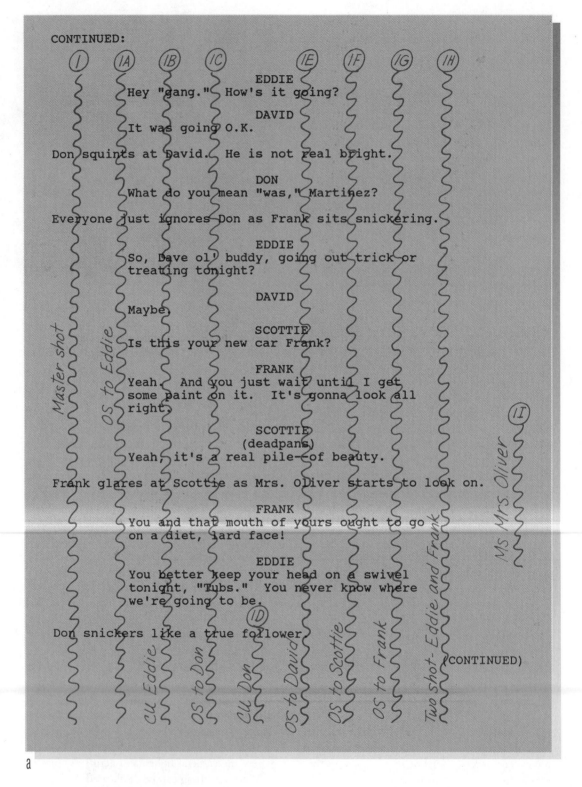

CONTINUED:

① ①A ①B ①C ①E ①F ①G ①H

> EDDIE
> Hey "gang." How's it going?

> DAVID
> It was going O.K.

Don squints at David. He is not real bright.

> DON
> What do you mean "was," Martinez?

Everyone just ignores Don as Frank sits snickering.

> EDDIE
> So, Dave ol' buddy, going out trick or treating tonight?

> DAVID
> Maybe.

> SCOTTIE
> Is this your new car Frank?

> FRANK
> Yeah. And you just wait until I get some paint on it. It's gonna look all right.

> SCOTTIE
> (deadpans)
> Yeah, it's a real pile of beauty.

Frank glares at Scottie as Mrs. Oliver starts to look on.

> FRANK
> You and that mouth of yours ought to go on a diet, lard face!

> EDDIE
> You better keep your head on a swivel tonight, "Tubs." You never know where we're going to be.

①D

Don snickers like a true follower.

(CONTINUED)

(handwritten annotations on shot lines:) Master shot, OS to Eddie, CU Eddie, OS to Don, CU Don, OS to David, OS to Scottie, OS to Frank, Two shot- Eddie and Frank, Ms Mrs. Oliver ①I

a

Script supervisors usually stay close to the director so that they can communicate all the information needed. They also make sure that the director actually shoots all the lines of script dialogue at least once. Script supervisors are extremely important to directors because, if they do their job well, they eliminate the need to bring an entire cast and crew back for a reshoot because shots did not match during editing. Many directors feel that the script supervisor is the most valuable person in the crew; without a competent supervisor the production will flounder.

1		Master shot	10/11	1D	CU Don	10/11

1	Master shot		10/11
1	:44 C NG Hair blend with sky		
2	:33 C NG camera jerked		
3	:35 C good		
1A	OS to Eddie	10/11	
1	:20 I NG Don moves in front of lens		
2	:36 C good		
1B	CU Eddie	10/11	
1	:33 C looks too close to camera		
2	:35 C OK		
3	:34 C best		
1C	OS to Don	10/11	
1	:37 C sun in and out of clouds		
2	:10 I Don said "Marcus"		
3	:34 C OK		

1D	CU Don	10/11
1	:15 C good	
1E	OS to David	10/11
1	:10 I NG boom shadow	
2	:33 C	
1F	OS to Scottie	10/11
1	:33 C good	
1G	OS to Frank	10/11
1	:10 I NG car noise	
2	:35 C	
1H	2-shot Eddie + Frank	10/11
1	:26 I NG Frank laughed	
2	:27 I NG Frank laughed again	
3	:33 C good	
1I	MS Mrs Oliver	10/11
1	:15 C	

Script supervisors also prepare an **editor's script.** On this script they note any changes, such as dialogue rewording, that were made during production. They also mark all takes on the script so that the editor will know how much of the scene each take covers. On the page opposite each page of script they list all the shots and give pertinent information about each (see Figure 3.3).

Production managers (also called **unit managers** or **unit production managers**)[5] are responsible for seeing that all the elements needed

Figure 3.4

An example of how a daily production report might be filled out.

DAILY PRODUCTION REPORT

Title Old Mother Witch   Date October 16

Director Mark Chodzko   Production No. 1

Script Supervisor Susan Stribling   Day 18 of 25

First Call 1:30 p.m.   First Shot 3:07 p.m.   Meal 5:15 p.m. for some of cast. 6:00 for crew

First Shot 7:30   Meal ----   First Shot ----

Wrap 11:38 p.m.   Finish 12:42 a.m.

	Scenes	Pages	Minutes	Setups
Total in Script	24	28	20	138
Taken Previously	16	20-5/8	13	92
Taken Today	4	3-1/8	3	24
Total to Date	20	23-6/8	16	116
To Be Taken	4	4-2/8	4	22

Cast Member	Makeup	Report on Set	Dismiss on Set	Meals Out	In
Grace Ridgley	2:00	3:00	5:45	5:45	6:45
Tommy Mays	6:00	7:00	11:38	5:15	6:00
Cynthia Thomas	6:00	7:00	8:37	5:15	6:00
Loreen Washington	7:00	8:30	11:38	----	----
Steve McLean	7:30	8:30	11:38	----	----

Scenes Shot Today 7, 5, 21, 12

Scheduled Finish Date 10/24   Estimated Finish Date 10/23

COMMENTS (Explanation of Delays, Cast and Crew Absences, Etc.)

30-minute delay on Scene 21 because of need to get extra extension cords.
Grip (Tom Coates) had to leave at 10:30 because of a family emergency. This made wrap time extra long.

for a particular day's shooting (people, equipment, sets, permits, props, makeup) are available and functioning. Their job begins early in preproduction (see Chapter 2) and continues through production. Their duties are primarily logistical. For example, production managers make sure that the smoke machine ordered for day 4 is actually delivered. Or, if the production falls behind schedule, they reschedule the smoke machine for day 5. They constantly check and alter the lists made during preproduction and communicate production needs to the appropriate people. Sometimes production managers keep ledgers detailing what they spend each day.

CALL SHEET

Title Old Mother Witch   Date October 16

Director Mark Chodzko   Production No. 1

Location 1526 Main Street and 1723 Main Street

SET	SCENES	CAST	PAGES
Inside Mrs. Oliver's house	7	Mrs. Oliver	1/8
Inside Mrs. Oliver's house	5	Mrs. Oliver	1
David's bedroom	21	David Mom	1-1/2
Mrs. Bridwell's front porch	12	Mrs. Bridwell David Scottie	1/2

CAST	PART OF	MAKEUP	SET
Grace Ridgley	Mrs. Oliver	2:00	3:00
Tommy Mays	David	6:00	7:00
Cynthia Thomas	Mom	6:00	7:00
Loreen Washington	Mrs. Bridwell	7:00	8:30
Steve McLean	Scottie	7:30	8:30

ATMOSPHERE AND STAND-INS	REPORT TIME
None	

CREW	REPORT TIME
Camera operator	2:00
Boom operator	2:00
Audio/video operator	2:00
Makeup person	2:00
Wardrobe person	6:00
Script supervisor	2:00
Electrician	1:30
Grips	1:30
Prop person	2:00
Caterers	5:00

Figure 3.5
A call sheet for a day when four different scenes are scheduled for shooting.

They also prepare the **daily production report** (see Figure 3.4), a form that goes to the producer listing what has been accomplished each day.[6] It details such points as the number of scenes shot, the number of pages of the script covered, the minutes of footage shot, the time taken for setups, the people who worked and how much time they worked, and the amount of time taken for meals. The form also summarizes what has been accomplished to date and states whether the production is on schedule.

In addition to helping with directing functions assistant directors often undertake organizational and record-keeping duties. For example,

Figure 3.6
An assistant director's log sheet.

PRODUCTION LOG

Title *Old Mother Witch*   Page *5* of *5*

Director *Mark Chodzko*   Date *10/22*

Reel	Scene	Take	Counter	Description and Comments
9	23D	1	126	CU bag and note - bad angle
9	23D	2	132	CU bag and note
9	23E	1	140	CU football
9	23F	1	152	CU chocolate chips
9	23F	2	167	CU chocolate chips - better light
9	23F	3	176	CU chocolate chips - best light
9	23G	1	189	MS note
9	23G	2	197	CU note - hand in way
9	23G	3	209	CU note

an assistant director is often the one who prepares and posts the daily **call sheets** (see Figure 3.5), which tell all cast and crew members when they should report to work. (Refer to Chapter 2 for more information on call sheets.)

Assistant directors sometimes keep **logs.** These list all the shots that were taken in the order that they appear on the tape. They give the tape reel number, the location on the tape, a description of the shot, and comments about the shot (see Figure 3.6). The editor uses log sheets to locate shots. If the sound for a movie is shot on one recorder and the picture is shot on another, the assistant director will keep two separate log sheets, one for picture and one for sound. As with many other aspects of movie-making, generating the log is often made easier by a computer program (see Figure 3.7). A note-book computer used on the set can be connected to the VCR so that time code numbers automatically transfer to the log.[7]

Assistant directors are not always the people who keep log sheets. In a nonunion shoot the person operating the camera, VCR, or audiotape recorder sometimes handles this chore. The specific jobs that particular crew members undertake are fairly well delineated if the movie is shot under union contracts. However, in a nonunion or student shoot various people might handle different organizational and record-keeping tasks. On one production the director may do the call sheets, a script supervisor will prepare continuity notes and an editor's script, the videotape operator will keep the log, and no one will do a daily production report. For another production the assistant director may prepare the call sheets, the camera operator will keep the log, the production manager will make the production report, and no one will prepare a script for the editor.

Lighting and Camera Operation

Historically, the types of jobs related to lighting and camera operation have differed greatly between film and video. In film, lighting and camera operation have been closely aligned and have been considered primarily artistic functions. A **director of photography (DP),** or **cinematographer,** has overall responsibility for creating the image. This includes seeing that the set is lit properly and that the pictures are framed and shot properly. Cinematographers like to think of themselves as artists who paint with light. They work closely with the director because cinematographers establish the look that the director wants the movie to have. Often a director will select the same director of photography for film after film because the two establish such a close relationship that the cinematographer can anticipate the director. This reduces the amount

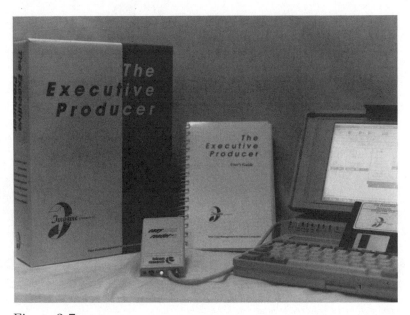

Figure 3.7
The Executive Producer, *time code management software and hardware. (Photo courtesy of Imagine Products, Inc.)*

of time the director needs to spend explaining concepts to the DP.[8]

Usually, cinematographers do not touch either the lights or the camera. They decide what types of lights to use, where the lights should be set, how much light should enter the camera, and some details of shot composition, but they do not actually set up lights, change the settings on the camera, or operate the camera. Electricians position and plug in lights. If the film is complex, it may require a head electrician (also known as a head **gaffer**) who will direct others in setting lights.

A **camera operator** actually sets up and runs the camera. Often the camera operator is aided by one or more **camera assistants.** For a film shoot, these people load film into magazines so that it can be placed on the camera quickly when the old magazine of film is finished. They also measure the distance from the camera to the object to be filmed so that the camera operator can set the focus accurately (see Figure 3.8), and they change the focus setting while the camera is moving so that the picture remains sharp and clear (pulling focus). They hold the slate in front of the camera at the beginning of a take so that pertinent information about the shot is recorded on the film, and they sometimes keep logs.

Figure 3.8
The camera assistant is measuring the distance from the camera to the subject so that focus can be set properly. (Photo courtesy of John Fedel)

The lighting and camera operations in video have traditionally been handled very differently, mainly because video's roots are in live studio production. Lighting has not had nearly the importance in video that it has had in film because a three-camera studio setup requires that all angles be lit equally well. With no stopping between shots, one lighting setup has to work for an entire show. Film, on the other hand, from early in its history was a start-and-stop process that allowed for lighting of individual shots.

As a result, the director made the lighting decisions in television. Each program needed only one lighting setup, and for most comedy series, game shows, news programs, and talk shows this lighting was the same for subsequent shows. The person in charge of setting the lights was the **lighting director,** who usually oversaw a **lighting crew**—people who climbed the ladders and positioned the lights on the grid. Lighting directors used light meters to help set the lights. Sometimes this aided in creating particular aesthetic effects, but more often the meter ensured the light was falling evenly across the whole set.

Historically, TV camera operators have functioned separately from the lighting crew. They, like their film counterparts, were responsible for running the camera. However, they did not usually have assistants, although for shows that required a great deal of camera movement they had **grips** to hold and move the cable as the camera moved around the studio or to push dollies or cranes from place to place.

As film and video are merging, the functions that need to be performed are changing. The TV studio functions are similar to what they have always been, although because cameras are smaller and more maneuverable, grips are not needed as often. Movies shot on film still use much the same crew structure that they have always used.

Movies shot on video are edging toward film techniques in that one person makes lighting and camera decisions for video in much the same way the cinematographer does for film. Some video productions opt for the term **videographer,** although nothing in the term *cinematographer* excludes video. The term *cinematography* literally means "to write in motion." This is appropriate for film and video. The main difference between film and video shoots is that video does not require as many camera assistants. Unlike loading a magazine, loading a videocassette is a simple operation that the camera operator can handle.

Recording the Picture and Sound

Who handles recording varies greatly and according to the equipment that is used. In film, the recording of the picture is inherent in the operation of the camera. This is also the case in video if the equipment used is a **camcorder,** which, as its name implies, is a combination camera and recorder. If the camera and videocassette recorder are separate, someone must operate the VCR. If sound is recorded on the same piece of film or tape as the picture (a process known as **single system**), it is tied closely to camera operation. For video, the VCR that is recording the picture can also record sound. In this case, one person can be responsible for recording both picture and sound, or two people can be involved—one making sure that the picture is recorded and the other listening on headphones to control the audio. If sound is recorded separately from picture (**double system**), either for film or video, someone must operate a separate audiotape recorder.

In any of these configurations someone must make sure the mic is properly positioned. Usually this person is referred to as a **boom operator** because the most common thing he or she does is position and move the mic while it is on some sort of microphone support, often called a **boom.** However, sometimes the boom operator pins mics on people's clothing or places mics on stands.

Someone other than the boom operator must adjust the controls on the sound recorder, be it VCR or audiotape recorder. This person is responsible for making sure the sound is clear and consistent through different setups. In film, this person is called a **mixer.**

In TV, people who deal with any aspect of audio are referred to as **audio technicians** (or *audio mixers* or *mixers*), and the people who operate videotape recorders (even if they control sound as well as picture) are referred to as **VCR operators.**

Large-scale productions are likely to have *sound assistants,* who carry and position cables, carry equipment, and sometimes keep logs.

As in other areas, picture and sound recording is evolving, mainly because of the confluence of film and video and the changing nature of sound recording in relation to picture recording.

Supporting the Production

Shooting a movie involves a vast number of tasks in addition to those connected with directing, acting, organizing and record keeping, lighting and camera operation, and sound and picture recording. These include putting on makeup, fitting wardrobes, hairdressing, placing props in their proper positions, executing special effects, painting, hammering, keeping plants and flowers alive and fresh looking, handling animals, teaching child actors, attending to minor injuries, preparing and serving food, driving trucks, and carrying things.

For a big feature movie separate individuals usually handle each chore—a makeup artist applies makeup, a greensperson keeps plants alive, caterers prepare food, grips carry and move things such as set pieces and cables. Other times jobs are combined, and general purpose people, usually called **production assistants** or **utility persons,** perform them on an as-needed basis. These people may also perform other unassigned jobs in the record-keeping or technical areas, such as holding the slate, keeping logs, or plugging in lights.

The people who undertake the many tasks associated with moviemaking become proficient by working on a multitude of movies. They rarely are bored, however, because each movie has its unique challenges.

The Stages of Production

Some aspects of production (such as putting up sets on a soundstage) can actually begin during preproduction, but production is generally thought of as the time during which the movie is shot. A typical production day includes setting up, rehearsing, shooting, and striking.

Setting Up

Production days usually begin quite early, especially if the day's shooting is to occur outside. Every hour of sunlight must be used to its best advantage. Therefore, it is not unusual for actors and for makeup, hairdressing, and wardrobe people to report to the set at 5 A.M. so that the actors can be in costume and ready to perform by 6:30 or 7. Actors usually practice lines whenever they have time to themselves during setup time.

The early morning hours also are the time for set preparation. If the set is elaborate, truck drivers bring flats, bushes, paintings, and other large items to the location. Grips carry and erect what is needed, painters touch up nail holes, and people dress the set and place props in their correct positions. Even if the set is a natural location, such as a park, there are always minor changes that need to be made to accommodate the script.

Once the set is prepared, or almost prepared, the director of photography and electricians work on the lights. If they are using a generator to supply power, they fire it up. If they are using batteries, they attach them to the lights. If household current is to provide the power, someone should check to see if anything else is operating on the circuits that are to be used for lights so that the lights do not overload and blow out the circuit.

The DP no doubt has thought about the lighting requirements ahead of time and has a sketch—either on paper or in his or her mind—of how the lights should be set. This includes ideas about the overall lighting effect needed for the scene and the types of lights that will be needed.

Light meter in hand, the DP oversees the electricians as they set up and activate the lights according to the plan. The DP cannot fine-tune until the actors arrive on the set but can establish general positions of the lights and use stand-ins to determine more precise lighting requirements. Proper lighting takes a long time, so as much as possible should be done during the setup period.

Once the light positions are fairly firm, the electricians should place sandbags on stands or in other ways secure all lights, tape cords so that actors and crew members do not trip over them, and in general make sure the whole lighting setup is safe. They should not overdo the taping and securing of lights and cords, however, because lights will be moved during and after rehearsal.[9]

Meanwhile, the camera and sound crews should be making their preparations. They, too, must secure power through the generator, batteries, or house current. The camera should be placed on its **tripod** or other support (see Chapter 4). The camera operator should check all the settings to make sure they are correct. The status report that appears in the viewfinder of many cameras is helpful for checking all these functions.

The operator of the videotape recorder should make certain that all connectors coming into it are secure. He or she should also make sure that the day's supply of tape is readily available but in some safe, relatively cool place. If a separate portable **time code generator** is to be used, this should be connected to the appropriate equipment. The VCR operator should decide, in conjunction with the director, what type of time code is going to be used throughout the production (see Chapters 4 and 11 for more about time codes).

During the setup time the camera and VCR operators can record leader material on the tape. The ideal leader consists of about one minute of **color bars, time code,** and audio **tone** (see Chapter 10); however, the equipment to generate this often is not available on the production set. Something should be recorded at the begin-

ning of the tape, though, to identify it and to keep the beginning of the tape (which is somewhat subject to stretching and damage) from being used for important production footage. With consumer-grade cameras it is possible to program some identifying graphics with the character generator built into the camera and record them at the beginning of the tape.

The sound crew should select the proper mic(s) for the scene that is to be shot and should attach the mic to the boom or to whatever type of stand is being used. They should decide the general positioning of the mic.

The person operating audio, like the person operating video, should check to make sure all dials and switches available and related to audio are in the right position (see Chapters 8 and 9). The mic should be firmly connected to the mic input on the recorder, and the whole audio system should be checked to make sure it is operating correctly. It is embarrassing to have the whole cast and crew standing around because the audio operator put the mic battery in backward and did not bother to make sure the mic was actually working.

The director might oversee the whole setup process, or the director may be off planning the blocking for the day's shots or viewing the footage from the day before. In this case, an assistant director or the production manager may be in charge of the overall setup.

Rehearsing

A movie requires two types of rehearsals, one that involves the cast and one that involves the cast and the crew. For the former, the director works with the cast to determine blocking and to build the proper emotional feeling.[10] If a scene doesn't work, a writer may be brought to the set to undertake a minor rewrite. Extras may or may not be part of the cast rehearsals, depending on the specific roles they play.

Once the actors are sure of their lines and the blocking has been worked out, the director holds a rehearsal, sometimes referred to as a **technical rehearsal,** mainly for the benefit of the crew. All cast and crew are present, and all sets, props, lights, and equipment are at least tentatively set up. The actors usually do not give their all during this rehearsal. They just run through their moves and lines so that the crew can determine camera angles, fine-tune lights, and position the mic for best pickup. The director makes any decisions that need to be made about the shooting setup. He or she must always be thinking about the final edited movie and ways to underscore the narrative (see Chapter 5).

This technical rehearsal gives all crew members an opportunity to check details in their areas of responsibility. If something is wrong and the changes can be made quickly, the crew makes them during the rehearsal period. If the changes will take a fair amount of experimentation (such as resetting lights to get rid of undesirable shadows), the crew member in charge makes notes and corrects the problem after rehearsal when doing so will not tie up the whole cast and crew.

The cinematographer pays careful attention to how the light falls on the actors and how it reflects into the camera: Are there undesirable shadows? Are there hot spots? (see Chapter 7). The camera operator frames and focuses the shots according to what the director and cinematographer want. The director may look through the camera viewfinder or may use a monitor to make sure the shot is what is actually desired.

The boom operator should position the mic for best pickup. Undesirable background noises that might still be present when recording begins should be noted so that they can be eliminated. If other shots have been taped that will be intercut with what is being rehearsed, the audio operator should think in terms of continuity to make sure the audio signals will match. A check with the script supervisor may help in this regard.

During rehearsal the script supervisor makes notes related to continuity. Some script supervisors bring a consumer camcorder to work and shoot various angles of the set so that the footage can be used later if continuity questions arise.[11]

Prop, set, costume, and makeup people need to make changes if something doesn't work in the overall scheme. In general, the technical rehearsal is the time when the individual elements of the production must be made to work together.

Once the technical rehearsal is complete, people make the more complicated changes

noted during the rehearsal, usually with the help of stand-ins. The cinematographer and electricians are likely to have the most work to do because of all the fine-tuning that the lights will require. Once they have finished, they must once again check to make sure the set is safe.

During the period between the technical rehearsal and the recording, the director must be totally in control because, although many of the changes crew members desire are justified, others are not worth the time it will take to complete them. Spending endless hours after rehearsal in fiddling with equipment is a major contributor to overbudget movies.

Shooting

The exact procedure for shooting can differ from one situation to another according to the personal style of the director and the needs of the movie. Sometimes directors will rehearse one shot at a time and then shoot it. Other times they will rehearse an entire scene and then shoot all the shots in that scene. In other circumstances they may feel it is more logical to rehearse everything that will be done at a particular location before starting to shoot.

Shortly before shooting begins, the TV camera operator should make sure the camera is **white balanced** for the final lighting setup for the shot. Generally, someone (perhaps a production assistant) holds something white near where the action will take place to white balance the camera. The camera operator then fills the screen with the white, focuses, and presses the white-balance control on the camera (see Chapter 4).

Once this is done, the camera operator should frame the shot as it is going to be recorded. Meanwhile, the person in charge of audio should take a level reading by having the actors talk as they will when the recording begins. The mixer (or audio technician) then sets the volume controls for optimum pickup (see Chapters 8 and 9).

When all this has been accomplished and all people are in their proper places, the director says, "Stand by." The next command is "roll tape." If the production is being shot on videotape, the person operating the VCR places the machine into record. The tape should run for about ten seconds before any crucial material is

Figure 3.9
A slate with a clapper and an electronic time code.
(Photo courtesy of Denecke, Inc.)

recorded. This extra time will be needed later, during the editing process.

If the production is being produced on film, "roll tape" is the command to begin the audio-tape recorder. After that recorder is up to speed, the director says, "Roll camera," and the camera operator starts filming.

After tape or film is rolling, the director says, "Slate." At this point someone (a camera assistant, a production assistant) holds a slate in front of the camera. This slate contains information about the shot that is to be recorded: the director's name, the date, the production title, a short description of the shot, and the scene and take number. The **scene number** should correspond to what is on the **master scene script** (see Chapter 1). Most scene numbers have letters after them (*A, B, C*) to indicate particular shots in the scene. For example, when scene 11 of *Old Mother Witch* was being recorded, scene 11 was a master shot showing the whole set; scene 11A was a close-up of David; scene 11B was a close-up of Scottie; scene 11C was the picture of Mrs. Oliver on the sidewalk; and scene 11D was the final action of the two boys. These are the scene numbers that go on the slate before each shot. **Take** numbers indicate how many times that particular shot has been recorded. The first time the shot is recorded, the take number is 1. If people are not satisfied with the shot and it needs to be done over, the take number on the slate changes to 2. If the close-up of Scottie needs to be recorded for the fourth time, the slate should read "scene 11B, take 4."

Slates are made of virtually anything that can

be written on. Professional slates are usually made of an erasable material so that they can be changed easily. Some slates are electronic and display the time code of the particular shot (see Figure 3.9). Film slates have a clapper at the top. The clapper is raised and then snapped against the base. Film editors use the frame in which the slate closes to line the picture up with the sound of the clapper to synchronize picture and sound. This is unnecessary for video because video is usually shot single system.

The person holding the slate should try to position it so that the camera can use the same focus and focal length for the slate as for the beginning of the shot. (Near the actor's face is often the best place.) Sometimes this is not possible, and the camera operator will have to refocus after recording the slate. The slate holder should also read the information on the slate while holding it in front of the camera. That way, the tape will contain both an audio slate and a video slate, often a help to the editor.

Once the tape rolls and records the slate, the director's next command is "action." The actors should wait a second or two before beginning their movements and dialogue so that the "action" command will not be part of the shot.

While the shot is being recorded, the VCR operator should be watching the tape to make sure it is actually moving and recording. Many VCRs have a video meter that registers in a green area, indicating the tape is receiving a signal. The VCR operator should also watch for signals that the batteries are low or that the tape is coming to the end.

The boom operator should follow the action. If the mic must be moved because the actors move or because a different person begins to talk, it should not be panned too quickly because this will create noise. The person overseeing audio recording (this might be the mixer, the VCR operator, or the camera operator, depending on the equipment configuration) should also wear a headset to make sure the sound is recording properly. Audio can be double-checked on the volume unit (VU) meter, if one is available.

The camera operator should keep the camera shot properly framed and in focus and should execute any camera moves called for. If the moves involve changing the position of a dolly, a camera assistant will push the dolly (see Chapter 4).

The cinematographer should watch for lighting problems, and the script supervisor should look for potential continuity problems. The director should be constantly thinking about the shot in terms of its overall effectiveness and its relationship to the entire movie.

A second or two after the actors are finished, the director should say "cut." The VCR should continue to roll for about ten seconds so that the end of the shot contains strong sync information. Because of its importance in editing, the need for continuous material both before and after the shot cannot be overemphasized. Material will not edit if it does not have enough of a lead to get up to speed, and the edit may fall apart if it does not have strong sync at the end (see Chapter 11). The director decides whether to record the shot again, but any crew member should speak up if something went awry. If the camera operator knows the shot was out of focus, if the script supervisor noticed that a prop was misplaced, if the cinematographer saw a boom shadow, if the audio engineer heard a strange noise, they should say so. Of course, an actor totally blowing a line would be obvious to everyone.

If there is any doubt about the quality of the take, it can be played back on a monitor. In fact, someone involved with audio or video should play taped material back from time to time to make sure it is recording well. However, the director should not make a practice of viewing each shot—it's too time consuming.

If the shot is to have another take, whatever problem occurred should be fixed quickly. During this time the person holding the slate can change the take number, the person compiling the log can note the result of the take, and the script supervisor can make continuity notes and work on the editor's script. The director should restart the process as soon as possible—standby, roll tape, slate, action, and cut.

Once a particular shot such as the master shot is finished, the director moves on to the next shot, perhaps a close-up. The set must be relit, and cast and crew must reposition themselves and rehearse as needed. The director shoots as many different shots of a particular

scene as are necessary to provide the editor with options. The director and the sound mixer should be sure to remember at some point to record **room tone** and any other audio effects needed (see Chapter 9).

Once a particular scene is finished, the next scene starts. If the scene is in the same location, it can start rather quickly, although in all probability actors will need to change costumes and the crew will need to set new lighting. If the scene is in a new location, the crew will have to strike the set and move everything.

Striking

The word **strike** refers to the tearing down and cleaning up of everything that was set up and used for rehearsals and shooting. The electricians should turn off the lights, untape and coil the cords, and put all lights, stands, cords, and accessories in cases. Similarly, the camera operator, mixer, and/or grips should make sure cameras, lenses, microphones, and recorders are properly stored in their cases. All used batteries should be recharged overnight.

The VCR operator should rewind tapes and label each tape and the box.[12] Ideally, the labels include the producer's name, director's name, movie title, reel number, date recorded, type of time code, channel on which the audio was recorded, and camera and VCR used for the recording. This information will be of help to the editor and can also be used if there are any problems with the tape.

The set should be taken down, unless it is needed the next day. Props, wardrobe, hair pieces, and makeup should be stored for the night or packed away for transport to the next location. The people in charge of these items may want to reorganize them so that what they will need early the next morning will be readily available.

Before everyone leaves, the assistant director or whoever is in charge of call sheets should post the call sheets for the following day and several days thereafter. If the production is moving smoothly, these will not be very different from what everyone anticipated, but if the production has fallen behind schedule, major changes in who reports where and when may be necessary.

Figure 3.10

An example of a property checkout release.

PROPERTY CHECK OUT RELEASE

I hereby affirm that, on inspection of the property

located at _____ ,

where _____ days of shooting between the dates of _____

and _____ have taken place for the movie_____

_____ , I have found that the property has

been left in the state that it was originally in before the

shooting for the production began.

Signature_____

Printed Name_____

Title_____

Street Address_____

City and Zip Code_____

Phone Number_____

Date_____

When you leave a location, it should be in the same condition it was in before shooting started. The production manager should have the person in charge of the site sign a property checkout release form (see Figure 3.10) so that no bad feelings (or lawsuits) will arise later. The production manager should also fill out the daily production report so that it can be used for control and for payroll verification.

The director, if not too tired, may view the tapes shot during the day or begin planning the actor and camera blocking for the next day's shots. The cinematographer may start planning the lighting for the next scenes. Or the tasks may be undertaken early the next morning.

Notes

1. This is a paraphrase of a paraphrase that appeared in Steven Kane, "Videocy," *Emmy*, April 1989, p. 12.

2. For good advice for directors, see Alan A. Armer, "Part Two: Directing Fiction," *Directing Television and Film* (Belmont, CA: Wadsworth, 1990), pp. 92–240; Steven D. Katz, *Film Directing Shot by Shot, Visualizing from Concept to Screen* (Stoneham, MA: Focal Press, 1991); and Ron Richards, *Director's Method for Film and Television* (Stoneham, MA: Focal Press, 1992).

3. Information about actors can be found in Paul Newman, "The Players," in Roy Paul Madsen, *Working Cinema: Learning from the Masters* (Belmont, CA: Wadsworth, 1990), pp. 156–181, Richard A. Blum, *Working Actors* (Stoneham, MA: Focal Press, 1989); and Patrick Tucker, *How to Act for the Camera* (New York: Routledge Press, 1993).

4. The term *script supervisor* is a film term, and *script clerk* is a video term. Historically, most of the people who held these jobs were female, so the term *script girl* has also been used. In early TV, the script clerk's duties were different from the duties of the script supervisor of film. The script clerk was the woman who kept time during early TV

live shows, particularly dramas. She would back-time the show so that when a commercial break came, she could tell the director how many minutes were left until the program had to end. The director would then tell the actors how to adjust their lines and actions so that the program finished on time. For many years, the script supervisor and script clerk were the only women on most film and video crews. Although the functions of script supervisor are important, this is still a low-paying position.

5. *Production manager* is a film term, and *unit manager* is a video term. Now that the two media are merging, the term *unit production manager* is sometimes used.

6. Often the production manager does this in conjunction with the second assistant director. On many major union shoots the first assistant director works for the director, and the second assistant director works for the production manager. Of course, nowadays computer programs make it easier to produce the daily production report.

7. Four computer programs that can be used to create logs are *Log Producer* from Image Logic, 6807 Brennan Lane, Chevy Chase, MD 20815; *Script/ R* from The Adelaide Works, 445 Adelaide St. West, Toronto, Ontario M5V 1T1, Canada; *The Executive Producer* from Imagine Products, 1416 South Rangeline Rd., Suite 104, Carmel, IN 46032; and *Log Master* from Comprehensive Video Supply Corp., 148 Veterans Dr., Northvale, NJ 07647.

8. See Vilmos Zsigmond, "The Cinematographer," in Madsen, pp. 209–259.

9. Safety is important and should not be overlooked in the rush to shoot. The BBC has a policy of not letting anyone on the set until a safety check has been completed.

10. Sometimes the director and actors have been working on this during preproduction. For example, they may have been rehearsing in a big hall with the set boundaries taped on the floor. This allows them to determine blocking even before the sets are built. In some instances the writer may be with them. Some directors invite the writer for the first run-through so that any lines that do not read well can be corrected early.

11. James Caruso and Marvis Arthur, "Blue Lagoon's 8mm Secret," *Video*, October 1991, p. 33.

12. Sometimes tapes are stored tails out to minimize print-through and wear and tear caused by rewinding.

chapter four
Cameras and Lenses

Electronic moviemaking begins with the portable video camera and recorder. In some ways the process is similar to that for a film camera, and in other ways it is quite different. Both have lenses, viewfinders, and some means of recording what you see through the viewfinder. However, the method of creating the image—electronic versus photochemical—is different. In this chapter we highlight the portable video camera and recorder (or camcorder), camera mounting equipment, and lenses. We also look at the variety of film and video **formats** and, where appropriate, highlight some basic differences between capturing an image on video and capturing it on film.

Formats

Film formats have been standardized for many years, whereas new video formats are introduced regularly. Film formats are determined primarily by the actual width of the film in millimeters, but because it is possible to have two formats of the same width (Super 8 and regular 8mm, for example), film formats are also based on the differences in image area, perforations, and sound tracks. Video formats are based on such factors as tape size, the method used to record the video signal, the kind of processing that signal receives, and the speed at which the tape moves through the recorder.

Film Formats

The original motion picture format, invented by Thomas Edison and George Eastman in 1889, was 35mm, basically the same film format used today for most theatrical motion pictures. Perforations (**sprocket holes**) along the sides of the film, the area of the film available for the

image (the **frame**), and the sound tracks were quickly standardized.

In the 1920s Eastman Kodak introduced a new format, 16mm, intended to encourage amateur filmmaking. This format proved to be too costly for most amateurs, but it became the choice for many educational and training films.

Super 8 was introduced in 1965, preceded by 8mm. Both formats use film that is 8mm wide, but Super 8, by repositioning sprocket holes and making them smaller, allows for a larger image area.[1]

Formats larger than 35mm (primarily 70mm) have also been developed to improve the quality of theatrical films. Because 70mm is so expensive, it is usually reserved for big-budget epic productions that can truly take advantage of the more dynamic large-screen image.[2]

Obviously, the different formats require different cameras because they must be able to hold different sizes of film. Figure 4.1 shows examples of various cameras.

In film, the producer selects a format based on the cost and the ultimate place of exhibition. The larger the format, the better the image and the more expensive the production. Theatrical motion pictures use 70mm and 35mm. The less expensive 16mm format is used for productions that do not call for the large-screen image, particularly those by businesses, schools, the military, and other similar organizations. Because of the enormous cost associated with the theatrical film formats, student filmmakers usually work in 16mm and Super 8. Before the advent of small-format video, Super 8 was also the mainstay for recording family gatherings, baby's first steps, birthday parties, and vacation trips. (See Figure 4.2 for a comparison of different film formats.)

Video Formats

Video formats are much more numerous than film formats. The first video format, developed by Ampex in the 1950s, used tape that was 2 inches wide. The size and complexity of the videotape recorders ruled out their use in portable configurations.

Beginning in the 1970s manufacturers introduced a number of formats suitable for portable

a

b

Figure 4.1

Several motion picture cameras. (a) A Panavision 70mm camera; (b) an Arriflex 35mm camera; (c) a Bell & Howell 16mm camera; and (d) a Beaulieu Cinepro Super 8mm camera. (Photo a courtesy of Panavision; photo b courtesy of Arriflex Corporation; photo c courtesy of Alan Gordon Enterprises; photo d courtesy of Super 8 Sound)

c

d

operation. The first was **U-Matic,** which consisted of a camera and a separate videocassette recorder that used a ¾-inch tape. The camera and recorder were linked by a cable. This format almost immediately replaced 16mm motion picture equipment for television news production, and schools and businesses adopted it for training and production purposes.

A few years later two ½-inch formats intended primarily for the home consumer were introduced—Sony's **Betamax** and JVC's **VHS.** These were not compatible with the U-Matic because of the difference in tape size, but they also were not compatible with each other because the way the tape wrapped around the video recording heads and the speed at which the tape traveled were different. The main consumer use of these formats was (and still is) to play back entertainment programs rented from the video store or recorded off-air. However, a number of people bought cameras to go with their recorders in order to make home movies.

In the early 1980s several manufacturers introduced high-quality camcorder systems for professional television production; they combined the camera and videotape recorder in a

70mm

35mm

16mm

Super 8

Figure 4.2

A comparison of different film formats.

single highly portable unit. Two main formats dominated—Sony's **Betacam** and JVC's and Panasonic's **M-format.** Although they both used ½-inch tape, these formats were not compatible with each other or with the consumer-grade ½-inch formats. Consumer-grade recorders were **composite,** while the professional ones

were **component.** Composite systems record information about brightness (**luminance**) and information about color (**chrominance**) together. Component systems record luminance and chrominance information separately. The component systems are superior because recording the two types of information separately greatly reduces color smearing and improves picture quality. However, they are more expensive than the composite systems.[3]

Shortly after the camcorder configuration was introduced for the professional world, Sony and JVC also developed camcorders for their consumer formats. Betamax was not nearly as successful as the VHS format, which eventually dominated the consumer market. However, in the 1980s Sony introduced a new format, **Video-8.** This format used tape that was 8mm (about ¼-inch) wide and was the smallest, most portable format yet devised.

All major formats in existence in the 1980s—U-Matic, VHS, Betacam, M-format, and Video-8—improved their recording abilities (in large part by developing better tape stocks) and came out with new equipment—**U-Matic SP, Super-VHS** (also called **S-VHS**), **Betacam SP, M-II,** and **Hi-8.** In general, these newer formats are only partially compatible with the older formats from which they were derived. They usually can play the older formats, but material recorded on the newer formats cannot be played back on the older ones. For example, a tape recorded on a VHS recorder can be played back on an S-VHS recorder, but a tape recorded in S-VHS cannot be played back on a VHS recorder.

Another format, **Type C,** uses 1-inch tape. The equipment associated with it is rather bulky so it rarely is used in the field. But it is high quality and is often used in the editing and distribution phases of moviemaking. (Figure 4.3 shows a variety of equipment and formats.)

Format development today is concentrating on **digital** technology. All the formats mentioned previously are based on **analog** technology. Digital recording is far superior because it improves the picture quality and allows taped material to be copied without losing quality. Analog material suffers greatly when copies are made, as anyone who has seen a fourth-generation VHS tape can attest.

a

b

c

d

Figure 4.3

A sampling of equipment for different video formats. (a) a Sony 8mm Handycam; (b) a Sharp regular-VHS camcorder; (c) a Panasonic S-VHS Type C camcorder; (d) a Sony Betacam SP camcorder; (e) a Sony Digital Betacam SP camcorder. (Photo a courtesy of Sony Electronics, Inc. and Geltzer and Company, Inc.; photo b courtesy of Sharp and Dorf & Stanton Communications; photo c courtesy of Panasonic; photos d and e courtesy of Sony Electronics, Inc.)

e

1.33:1 Academy aperture

1.66:1 European standard widescreen

1.85:1 American standard widescreen

anamorphic 2:1 squeeze, 2.35:1 when projected

Figure 4.4
Some standard and wide-screen aspect ratios.

benefits of digital video recording technology in a format that further reduces the gap between professional and consumer-level equipment.

High-definition television (HDTV) is also likely to affect production processes. Many HDTV formats have been proposed over the years, and the Federal Communications Commission (FCC) is currently testing a format to be used in the United States. HDTV will provide the highest picture quality of any format because it will roughly double the number of lines of information seen on the TV screen. It will also improve color rendition and change other characteristics of the TV picture, such as the aspect ratio.[4]

Aspect Ratio

When a high-definition television format is eventually adopted, the basic shape of the video frame will change for the first time since television's inception. This shape is usually described by the term **aspect ratio,** the ratio of the width of the frame to its height. In film, the most popular early aspect ratio of three units of height to every four units of width was eventually adopted by the Academy of Motion Picture Arts and Sciences as the standard for theatrical films. This **Academy ratio,** also expressed by the ratio 1.33:1 (a square would have an aspect ratio of 1:1), remains the aspect ratio for standard 8mm, 16mm, and 35mm film. Although 1.33:1 was basically an arbitrary frame configuration, the fledgling television industry also adopted the mild rectangle when it standardized its frame shape, an aspect ratio that persists in television today.

Partly in an effort to lure television viewers back to movie theaters with a larger and more powerful film image, the motion picture industry in the 1950s developed several **widescreen** aspect ratios. One method was to mask off the top and bottom of the typical 35mm film frame, a procedure that created the commonly used widescreen aspect ratios of 1.85:1 in the United States and 1.66:1 in Europe. Another method involved the use of an **anamorphic lens** to squeeze the widescreen image optically into the film frame and then unsqueeze it onto the movie screen with an anamorphic lens on the projector.

A number of different digital formats have been developed (D1, D2, D5), and, as you might expect, they are not compatible with each other. Moviemakers are beginning to experiment with Sony's Digital Betacam format because it produces an image of such quality that tape-to-film transfers are virtually indistinguishable from footage shot originally on film. Both Sony and Panasonic have introduced consumer camcorders that employ a digital video (DV) format. With improved picture resolution and color fidelity, these camcorders provide all the

The anamorphic widescreen process created an extremely elongated rectangular frame with an aspect ratio of 2.35:1 for the popular Panavision process.[5] Figure 4.4 illustrates the 1.33:1, 1.66:1, 1.85:1, and 2.35:1 film aspect ratios.

Occasionally, widescreen films are shown on television (or released on videotape or disk) in the "letter box" format that masks off the top and bottom of the frame and displays the entire widescreen image within television's 1.33:1 aspect ratio. More commonly, this translation of aspect ratios involves some loss (or even reframing) of the original film image, a process frequently referred to as *panning and scanning*.[6] This will be less of a problem when HDTV arrives because all the proposed HDTV systems have an aspect ratio, approximately 1.66:1, that is close to the widescreen motion picture aspect ratio.

Choosing a Film or Tape Stock

Selecting a film or videotape stock begins with the format you choose for your production. A 35mm film camera requires 35mm film, and a ½-inch S-VHS VCR requires the right ½-inch videotape cassette. But the choice of a film stock has a far greater impact technologically and aesthetically than the choice of videotape. The film stock itself is the actual **imaging device** in a film camera, and the selection of a particular type of film profoundly affects the kind of image it produces.

Motion picture film is composed of a thin layer of light-sensitive silver halide grains suspended in gelatin, the emulsion. The layer of **emulsion** is supported by a flexible, transparent **base** of cellulose acetate. When the lens focuses light onto the emulsion, a photochemical reaction occurs. The areas of the photograph (each frame of the motion picture film is an individual photograph) that receive the most light will appear darkest when the film is developed (chemically processed and stabilized) in the laboratory. The result is a **negative** image that must be printed on another piece of film to produce a **positive** image with correct photographic tones (that is, black as black and white as white). Reversal film requires additional processing in the laboratory to convert the film (the original film run through the camera) into a positive image. After processing, reversal film can be viewed (or projected) without the need to make a print. Color film stock uses three layers (yellow, cyan, and magenta) of photosensitive dyes to produce all the colors in the visible spectrum.

Most people have bought film for a still camera and have some familiarity with the many choices available. You must decide whether to shoot in black and white or in color. You must also decide if you want to use the negative or reversal film system to create a positive image (like a slide) or a negative image (the kind used for most professional filmmaking) for making prints. If you want to shoot where there is not much light, you need to buy a **fast film stock** (one more sensitive to light) that has a high **exposure index** (**EI**) or **ASA**. Or you may want a **slow film stock** (with a lower EI) to produce a sharper, less grainy image. Film stock is also **color balanced** (designed to produce the correct colors in different types of light) for artificial light or for daylight. Finally, even similar film stocks from different manufacturers (like Kodak, AGFA, and Fuji) have different **tonalities**—the range of colors (or black and white) that they reproduce.[7]

In video, almost all these choices are predetermined by the recording format and the quality of the camera. Whether to shoot in black and white or in color is not determined by the selection of videotape because all videotape can record either color or black and white. The quality and sensitivity of the camera determines the ability to produce an image in low light as well as the overall sharpness and quality of the image. Given the same camera and VCR, the choice of one videotape over another has only a minimal effect on image quality and almost none on the cinematographer's artistic control of the image.

Videotape is composed of a polyester base coated along one side with a thin layer of metal oxide. If you have ever purchased a videotape for use at home, you have undoubtedly been exposed to different grades of videotape. Within a single format such as regular VHS a manufacturer will usually sell four or five different grades of tape with names such as *hi-fi, extra high gain, HQ,* or *high definition.*

The higher grade (and more expensive) videotapes usually (but not always) provide some slight gain in image quality and color rendition, a reduction in **dropouts** (loss of signal due to imperfections in the tape's surface), and some improvement in the videotape's audio recording capability. The cheapest tape may actually clog the recording heads on the VCR or even damage them.

The videotape used in component recording systems like the M-II or Betacam SP formats (or S-VHS or Hi-8 formats) has a finer metal particle layer than regular videotape. As a result, it can record a higher-quality picture. In many respects this difference is comparable to the differences between the chromium and normal audiocassettes used on home audiocassette decks or portable cassette players.[8]

All videotape used in portable video recorders or camcorders is packaged in cassettes. Although it is possible to vary the recording time of a cassette by changing the recording speed of the VCR (the familiar SP, LP, EP modes), the length of the tape within the cassette also governs the recording time possible at any of those speeds. In the popular VHS format videocassettes are priced according to the maximum time in minutes in the SP mode—T-120, T-60, and T-30.

A number of formats use **minicassettes,** which load shorter lengths of regular ¾-inch or ½-inch videotape into smaller cassette housings to increase portability. All ¾-inch portable VCRs use U-Matic minicassettes, which come in 5-, 10-, 15-, 18-, and 20-minute lengths. These smaller cassettes will play in a full-size studio VCR, but the full-size ¾-inch cassette will not fit into the portable machine. A similar minicassette has been developed for the VHS format—**VHS-C** (the C stands for compact). VHS-C tapes are made specifically for camcorders. They can be played in a home-size VHS deck only with the aid of a special adapter. The new consumer-level digital video (DV) format uses minicassettes that can record 30 or 60 minutes of digital video. Sony's version of the DV cassette includes a proprietary 4-kb memory chip that records exposure information, dates, and other indexes. DV cassettes can record up to 580 still frames, each lasting six seconds, on a single 60-minute cassette. With their massive storage capacity (11 gigabytes), DV cassettes are likely to be used in a variety of computer applications.[9]

Videotape can, of course, be recorded over and used many times. However, because videotapes show wear after being used only a few times, most professionals would never consider using "used" tape stock for an important shoot. Although this reuse capability is a definite advantage, especially in terms of cost, it is also possible to erase or record over something that you meant to save. Most cassettes have some temporary means of preventing an accidental rerecording. For ¾-inch tapes a red button protects against erasure or rerecording. If the button is removed from the bottom of the cassette housing, a recording cannot be made (nor can an erasure occur). Most consumer tapes have small tabs that can be moved to a different position or broken off from the cassette housing to ensure erasure/recording protection. If you change your mind later and want to record on a tape after you have broken off the recording tab, you can place a piece of masking tape over the hole.

The Camera

For our purposes any of the portable camera-recorder systems (U-Matic, Betacam, S-VHS, Video 8, and so on) provide the ideal tool for the beginning student moviemaker. We will emphasize the general principles of the video camera rather than any one format or type of gear. Undoubtedly, some of the points we make will not apply to the camera you have access to, and some of your camera's features will be missing from our discussion. You should always read the instruction manual for your particular camera to make certain you know its capabilities and idiosyncrasies.

Imaging Devices

Whether you are shooting with the finest broadcast-quality studio camera or working with a low-end camcorder from the local discount store, the main parts of the camera and the principles on which they are based are virtually the same. When the camera is pointed at a scene, the lens gathers the light reflected from that

photoconductive layer

electron beam

photosensitive surface

target

electron gun

Figure 4.5

The electron gun at the end of the pickup tube emits a beam of electrons that scans the image on the target.

scene and focuses it on an imaging device, either a solid-state element known as a **charge-coupled device (CCD)** or a camera **pickup tube.**

The compactness of CCD sensors (which greatly reduces the bulk and weight of the camera) and their low power consumption, ruggedness, and stability have made tube cameras virtually obsolete. The CCD sensor and camera pickup tube perform the same basic function—transforming the incoming light into electrical signals that can be recorded on videotape and/ or be seen in the camera's electronic viewfinder. They do this in very different ways, however.

A CCD sensor is a solid-state device (a chip) that contains an array of 200,000 or more *individual* light-sensitive picture elements (called **pixels**). When the image is focused on the sensor, each pixel builds up an electric charge containing color (chrominance) and brightness (luminance) information. This information is stored momentarily in a storage area (similar to the imaging area) in the chip until it is read out to create the video signal.

The more active pixels a CCD sensor contains, the higher the quality of the image it can produce. Given the direct relationship between number of pixels and image quality, the competition among camera manufacturers to produce ever higher pixel counts for their chips is ferocious. Even consumer-grade CCD cameras today tout sensors with more than 400,000 effective pixels.[10]

The other type of imaging device, the pickup tube, is a small glass vacuum tube (½-inch to 1¼-inch in diameter) with a photoconductive **target** at its front end (see Figure 4.5). The target contains more than 200,000 pixels laid out in a grid. As the light coming through the lens is focused on the target area, it changes the electric charge of each pixel according to the amount of light reaching it. An **electron gun** at the other end of the pickup tube begins **scanning** the target with a beam of electrons, reading each pixel from left to right as it moves from the top to the bottom. As it scans the image, the electron gun produces greater voltage levels in the bright areas of the photoconductive grid than in the dark areas.

In video, the scanning process creates the illusion of movement in a very different way than the process used in motion pictures. One sec-

ond of film is composed of 24 **frames,** actually 24 individual still pictures. When that film is projected, each frame is displayed on the screen for only a fraction of a second. While the projector is pulling the next frame into place, a shutter momentarily blocks the light and then swings out of the way to reveal the next frame.[11]

In the United States the video scanning process creates a series of 30 frames in one second. The video frame does not exist as a single, discrete frame like a motion picture frame. It is broken into 525 lines of information that are scanned one line at a time, line by line, as the electron beam moves across and down the image on the target area. To minimize brightness variations and reduce flicker, each video frame is broken into two **fields,** each composed of half the 525 lines in the frame. The first field contains the 262.5 odd-numbered lines (1, 3, 5, and so on), and the second field contains the 262.5 even-numbered lines (2, 4, 6, and so on).[12]

When the electron beam reaches the end of the first line (moving horizontally left to right), it goes into a blanking mode and then moves back across to the left edge to begin scanning the next line down. During this **horizontal blanking interval** the electron beam is momentarily shut off so that it cannot be seen as it moves back across the target to the next line. The process continues until the beam reaches the end of the last line in the odd-numbered field. The beam then goes into a **vertical blanking interval** while it moves back to the top of the even-numbered field to begin the downward scan again. The diagram in Figure 4.6 illustrates the basic scanning process.

All of this occurs at an incredible speed. In one second the electron beam scans 15,750 lines

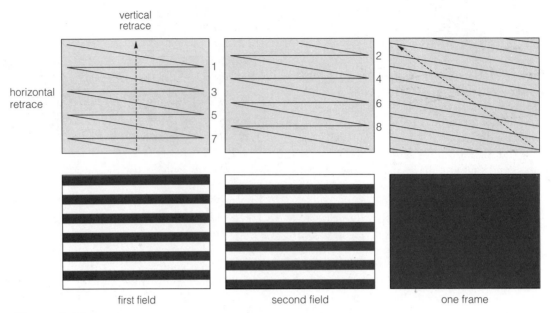

vertical retrace

horizontal retrace

first field   second field   one frame

Figure 4.6

The basic scanning pattern. First, the electron beam scans the odd field (lines 1, 3, 5, and so on), moving left to right across each line. At the end of a line the beam goes into a blanking mode and quickly retraces back to the left edge to begin scanning the next line. This continues until all the odd-numbered lines in the first field (half of the picture) are scanned. Then, the beam goes into another blanking mode while it moves back to the top of the picture to begin scanning the even-numbered lines that make up the other half of the picture. The scanning process for each field takes $\frac{1}{60}$ of a second. Combining the two fields, a pattern called interlaced scanning, produces the full video frame in $\frac{1}{30}$ of a second.

of 60 fields to create the 30 video frames. Combining two fields to make up one video frame, a process known as **interlaced scanning,** displays 60 half frames (60 fields) in one second.

A CCD sensor, of course, does not have an electron gun or an electron beam to scan the picture (one of the reasons a chip is so much smaller than a pickup tube). Instead, a CCD sensor uses an internal clock to read the image out of the storage area one line at a time in the same basic pattern and at the same scanning rate as a conventional pickup tube.[13]

A television set or monitor basically reverses the scanning process, using an electron gun at the back of the picture tube to focus an electron beam on the phosphorescent materials at the front of the picture tube. The image you see on your television set usually displays fewer than 525 lines because some lines are assigned to the vertical blanking interval.

In essence, then, the imaging device, be it tube or CCD, gathers the light information and converts it to electronic information in the form of a 525-line image. This electronic information is then sent out of the camera so that it can be

processed further (recorded, for example). Eventually, it is displayed in 525-line form on a monitor. Of course, not all systems use 525 lines. Europe and much of the rest of the world use a system that is based on 625 lines, and the proposed HDTV system promises more than 1,000 lines.

Color Video

In effect, the video signal created by a color camera superimposes the color information (chrominance) on the brightness information (luminance) that would be produced by a black-and-white camera. Color has two basic components: the **hue,** the specific tint of the color (for example, yellow, brown, red), and **saturation,** the intensity or purity of the color (for example, a highly saturated deep blue, a lightly saturated pale blue). The luminance information, which presents the full range of variations from the darkest to the lightest part of a scene, also has an effect on the **brightness** of a color, how dim or how bright a particular color appears to be. (See Color Plate 1.)

Figure 4.7

A prism block separates the light coming through the lens into its red, green, and blue components. Those three signals are then sent to the appropriate red, green, and blue pickup targets (either tubes or CCDs). Eventually, the three separate color signals are recombined by the encoder to produce the full-color image.

A three-chip or three-tube camera creates a color video signal by separating the light coming through the lens into its three primary colors of light, red, blue, and green—one for each of the three chips or tubes. (See Color Plate 2.) The light is divided into the primary colors (in proportion to the amount of each color in a scene) either by a **prism block** or by a special **dichroic mirror** system.

In a three-tube camera a device called the **encoder** recombines the separate red, green, and blue color signals together with the luminance information to produce a single composite signal (see Figure 4.7). As we mentioned earlier, this encoding process is what the component recording systems were designed to avoid. Keeping the chrominance and the luminance information separate throughout the entire video system, from camera to recorder, produces a higher-quality color signal.[14]

Evaluating Camera Performance

One of the most important ways of evaluating a camera's performance is assessing its ability to reproduce fine detail. Most camera manufacturers tout their particular camera's resolving power in terms of **horizontal resolution**—the maximum number of vertical lines per millimeter the camera's pickup tubes or CCDs can distinguish (together with the lens, optical system, and electronic circuitry). A camera with 600 lines of horizontal resolution will produce a sharper picture than one with 200 lines.[15]

A camera's **low-light sensitivity**—its ability to produce an acceptable image with minimal illumination—is another way to evaluate camera performance. You will recall from our earlier discussion that a filmmaker can select a faster (more light-sensitive) film stock for shooting in

low-light situations. In video, low-light sensitivity basically is built into the camera. Although the lens and the camera's electronic circuitry contribute to a camera's performance in low light, the light sensitivity of the CCD sensors or pickup tubes is the primary determinant. Camera manufacturers usually express a camera's low-light sensitivity by listing the minimum number of **footcandles** (such as 200 footcandles) the camera requires to produce an optimal image. Another measurement, **lux** (roughly 1/10 of a footcandle), is also used.

In general, three-chip or three-tube cameras outperform single-chip or single-tube cameras. They produce the most horizontal resolution, the best color rendition, and the highest **signal-to-noise ratio,** the ratio of background noise (visual distortion) generated by the camera's imaging system to the strength of the desirable video signal it produces.

Basic Camera Features

All cameras require electrical power to function. Portable cameras are battery (**DC**) powered, usually by a rechargeable nickel cadmium battery pack. Batteries usually insert into the camera, but they may also be carried in an external battery belt or shoulder pack. In a separate camera-recorder configuration, batteries in the VCR can sometimes be used to run the camera. Most cameras have some type of adapter (or power unit) that allows the camera to use **AC** current from the wall, and many consumer-grade cameras provide car battery adapters that plug into the cigarette lighter for power.

There often is a switch on the camera for selecting the type of power (AC or DC) a camera is to receive; another switch turns the power on or off. In some cameras the on/off switch has a **standby** position that allows the camera's circuitry to preheat or warm up without using full power.

Some rechargeable batteries can develop a "memory" problem if they are not handled properly. If a camera is used only for a brief time and then the battery is removed and placed in the recharger, it eventually will not be able to accept a full charge. This can be avoided if the battery is fully drained before being recharged.

The signal strength (brightness of the picture) of many portable cameras can be increased electronically by boosting the **gain.** Although this allows the camera to operate effectively at lower light levels, it creates more video noise (comparable to increasing the grain in a film image). Usually, a two- or three-position switch on the camera boosts the gain in large increments, such as +9 **decibels (dB)** or +18 dB.

Some consumer cameras are equipped with an **automatic gain control (AGC)** option that continuously adjusts the signal gain as the picture changes. In situations that call for a great deal of camera movement and different light levels, problems arise because the AGC will constantly try to compensate for varying levels of brightness and darkness. Being able to turn off the automatic gain control is a valuable asset.

Because they are designed for use by a single operator, portable cameras have a triggerlike switch on the handgrip for starting, stopping, or pausing the VCR. A camcorder has numerous control panels, each containing a series of buttons, switches, and knobs, usually grouped together according to whether they control functions in the camera or in the VCR.

Many consumer camcorders can insert the date and time on a recording, and some models can insert titles into a shot (some have a small keyboard). Another switch may record an index search pulse to help locate that position during playback. Also, digital technology has made it possible to generate a number of in-camera (and recorder) special effects, such as wipes, still frames, pictures in a picture, strobing, and fades in or out.

A power zoom lens is almost standard equipment in portable cameras and camcorders. A strap near the front of the camera or lens provides support for holding the camera by hand and should also place the hand close enough to the lens to allow for focusing or control of the power switch that governs the zooming operation. Such lenses normally have an **automatic iris** (auto iris), which continuously adjusts the iris opening to any lighting condition, and an **automatic focus** (auto focus) to keep the picture sharp and clear.[16]

Many newer cameras also contain an electronic shutter switch for different high-speed shutter settings. This is not, incidentally, the same as the shutter in a film camera. In a video camera, electronic shutters actually *reduce* exposure but sharpen the detail and help eliminate blurring in shots with fast action (such as a racing car). Another feature, **electronic image stabilization,** digitally magnifies part of the image and tracks the image if the camera moves. Although image quality diminishes somewhat, electronic image stabilization does make a camera movement appear steadier and less jerky.

Because the camera operator must be able to turn on or off many of these automatic functions, often while the camera is running, their layout and accessibility are important features. The electronic viewfinder, so standard on portable cameras and camcorders, is really an eyepiece-size television monitor that not only allows the camera operator to compose and focus the shot but also enables the operator to monitor a variety of camera and VCR functions. Most viewfinders are mounted on the side of the camera, can swivel to different viewing angles, and often contain some means of correcting vision for camera operators who want to shoot without their glasses. Most electronic viewfinders are black-and-white; a color viewfinder increases size, weight, and cost.

Although cameras vary, electronic **viewfinders** usually present some sort of visual display of information (a warning light or graphic) about such factors as the amount of power remaining in the battery, the status of the VCR (recording, paused, or running low on tape), the exposure (too much or too little light for proper exposure), which **filters** or **shutter speeds** have been selected, and the position or status of a range of camera controls (titling, special effects, standby, and so on).

Another set of controls on the camera is used to adjust the picture for proper color rendition. A filter wheel, or a switch on the less expensive cameras, permits selection of filters appropriate for various lighting conditions, such as sunlight or artificial light. (We deal with the issues of

a

lighting and filtering in much greater detail in Chapter 6.) A closely related function, **white balance,** enables the camera operator to make more subtle adjustments in the camera's ability to record white correctly, even in situations in which the lighting has a different hue—more red at sunset, more blue on an overcast day.

Increasingly, portable video cameras are incorporating a wide range of automated functions and controls such as automatic white balancing and automatic black balancing (setting the level of black in the picture). We have already mentioned a number of other automatic functions such as auto focus, auto iris, and auto gain control. Most of these automatic controls can be quite useful, particularly to a camera operator whose eye is glued to the viewfinder and whose attention may be focused on other elements of the production. In many instances, however, the auto-mania so rampant in consumer-grade equipment can mean a loss of creative control—an inability to make the camera do what you want it to do in certain conditions. The solution is simple enough—a switch that allows you to select a manual mode of operation.

b

c

Video Recording

A video recording system can be built permanently into the camera (a camcorder), it can be a VCR totally separate from the camera, or it can be a dockable recorder unit (see Figure 4.8). In the latter, the camera and recorder function

Figure 4.8

(a) A VHS camcorder with the recording system permanently built in; (b) a composite digital camera and a separate portable digital recorder; (c) a dockable camcorder. (Photos a and b courtesy of Panasonic; photo c courtesy of Sony Electronics, Inc. and Geltzer and Company, Inc.)

— control track

— video track

— time code address track
— audio channel track 2
— audio channel track 1

Figure 4.9
A videotape has a number of different tracks from top to bottom of the tape. On some recorders, the control track is at the top, and a time code address track and two audio channels are located at the bottom.

like a camcorder, but you can detach the VCR unit from the camera and use it in other configurations. The main differences among these different systems are convenience and connections. A totally separate recorder must be joined to the camera by means of cable and connectors. These are often the weak link in the recording system because they break or in other ways malfunction. Having a separate VCR is more cumbersome, but it allows one person to operate the camera while another monitors the audio and video signals, reducing the likelihood of error. A dockable VCR can be used with a variety of different cameras or detached from the camera for repair or use in an editing system.

Videotape recorders place a number of signals on videotape, including, of course, the basic picture signal. (See Figure 4.9 for a diagram of the various signals recorded on videotape.) A number of **heads** within the recorder take the scanning information fed from the camera and put it on the tape, one diagonal track at a time.

The recorder also places **control track** information on the tape. This consists of electronic timing impulses that keep the picture stable. The audio information also is placed on the tape. This process is discussed in Chapter 8.

Some recording systems can lay **SMPTE time code** on the tape. This is a numbering system that provides an address number for each frame of video. For example, 1:02:15:10 would mean the tape was at 1 hour, 2 minutes, 15 seconds, and 10 frames. For some video formats, the time code is laid on one of the audio channels. For others it is laid on a special section of the tape specially reserved for time code. Still other camcorders and recorders do not come equipped with the components for recording time code in the field, in part because this would

add to the cost. For this reason time code is often added to the tape in postproduction. See Chapter 11 for a further discussion of time code.

Whether they are separate, dockable, or permanently attached to the camera, recorders contain the same basic controls familiar to home audio and videotape recorder users—play, record, pause, fast forward, rewind, and stop. Even in a separate camera-recorder configuration, the cable connecting the two components usually allows the camera operator to control most VCR functions from the camera.

Most recorders also have some sort of metering system so that you can evaluate the quality of the signal you are recording. The most professional VCRs have three separate meters—one for video and one for each of two audio channels. Others have only one meter, but it can be switched so that it shows either video or audio. Sometimes this same meter indicates the amount of charge in the battery.

Most camcorders have **flying erase heads**, which means you can make clean edits between shots. This is sometimes referred to as *in-camera editing*. When you finish one shot, you can put the recorder in the pause mode while you set up the next shot. When you put the machine back into the record mode, it backspaces in order to get up to speed and then begins recording the next shot.

VCRs have a variety of inputs and outputs for video and audio. The basic video input is the signal from the camera. In a camcorder the signal goes directly from camera to recorder. The audio inputs are used primarily for microphones and are discussed in detail in Chapter 8.

Audio outputs are used to route audio signals to editing equipment or to headphones or speakers. Video outputs take the signal to a TV screen where it can be displayed.

Video Connectors

Whenever the video signal leaves one piece of equipment and goes to another, it travels through cables and connectors. This is true when the signal goes from the camera to a recorder or when it goes from the recorder to a monitor. Because it is all in one unit, a camcorder can operate without cables or connectors. The connectors you are most likely to encounter on a camera, VCR, or monitor are multipin, BNC, UHF, RCA, and RF connectors (see Figure 4.10). The **multipin connector** can carry video, audio, and remote control signals all in one cable. For example, a multipin cable might allow the camera operator to use a button on the camera to place the separate recorder in the record mode. Multipin connectors are not alike; usually a particular multipin can be used with only one specific type of camera and VCR. Multipins that connect a camera and VCR look quite different from those that connect a VCR and monitor.

BNC connectors carry video only. If a camera's video output is connected to a VCR with a BNC connector, the recorder cannot be operated remotely from the camera controls. BNC connectors also are frequently used to route signals between VCRs.

UHF connectors also carry video only. Although they are used less frequently than they once were, UHF connectors most commonly are used to carry the video signal from the VCR to a monitor or from one VCR to another.

RCA connectors can carry either video or audio, but not both at the same time, and **RF connectors** can carry both audio and video from a VCR to a regular TV set.[17]

multipin for a camera

multipin for a monitor

BNC

UHF

RCA

RF

Figure 4.10
Some basic video connectors. From top to bottom: a multipin connector for a camera, a multipin connector for a monitor, a BNC connector, a UHF connector, an RCA connector, and an RF connector.

Monitoring the Recording

Viewfinders, monitors, and TV sets all can show the picture recorded by a VCR, but they vary in design, construction, and accessibility. The viewfinder is part of the camera and can be used to play back the videotaped signal. This is easiest with a camcorder or with a system that has a multipin connector between the camera and the VCR. Using a camera viewfinder is a convenient way to make sure you have an acceptable recording. However, it can show you the picture only after the fact, and it can be viewed by only one person at a time.

Monitors look like home TV sets, but they cannot receive signals off the air. They receive a signal from a VCR through a multipin, BNC, RCA, or UHF connection. A cable run from video out (also called *line out*) of the VCR to video in (*line in*) on the monitor will enable the

monitor to display the picture. Some monitors have built-in speakers (although many do not), but connecting the video alone will not allow sound to be heard. For a monitor to play video and audio, either use a multipin connector or run a separate cable from audio out on the VCR to audio in on the monitor. Separate, small, battery-powered monitors can be helpful on a shoot because they enable you to evaluate your recording while the taping is in progress. They also allow a variety of crew members (not just the camera operator) to see what is being taped. This advantage may be outweighed by the slowdown in production that results when the producer, director, actors, and crew members are constantly viewing the tape.

a   b

Figure 4.11
(a) A Steadicam camera stabilization system. (Photo courtesy of Cinema Products Corporation and Lewis Communications); (b) a much smaller Steadicam JR™ is made for lightweight consumer camcorders. (Photo courtesy of Cinema Products Corporation)

Regular home **TV receivers** can be used to display what is shot on videocassette, provided the necessary components and connections are available in both the VCR and the receiver. Unlike monitors, TV receivers are designed to receive broadcast signals that are transmitted via **RF** (**radio frequency**); in other words, the signals have been **modulated** so that they will appear on a particular channel—2, 3, 4, 5, 6, and so forth. The video out signal from a VCR has not been processed in this way. It must first go through a modulator that places it on a channel—usually channel 3 or channel 4. Most 1/2-inch VCRs intended for home use have built-in modulators, and you can add RF units to many other systems. Home TV sets can be handy for viewing and assessing material shot for student movies.

Supporting the Camera

Many elaborate pieces of equipment have been designed to support cameras, including stands and clasps for holding a camera on an airplane wing and platforms that mount on the side of a speeding car. But the types of supporting devices most common in electronic filmmaking are the tripod and the human shoulder. Less common, mainly because of their cost and size, are the dolly and the crane.[18]

Hand-Held Cameras

Small lightweight cameras can be placed on the shoulder and hand held, even by people who are not especially strong. However, it is difficult to hold them steady for any long period, especially if you must walk or move in any other way. The result is often jerky pictures that are likely to cause motion sickness in anyone who watches them.

Many cameras can be equipped with a stabilized lens, which is a lens mounted in a housing in such a way that the lens moves counter to the camera's movement. Such housings improve picture stability, but they are expensive and cannot compensate for large movements.

More commonly, **shoulder mounts** are attached to the camera so that it rides comfortably on the shoulder. More elaborate **body braces**, such as a **Steadicam** (see Figure 4.11a), can also help the operator reduce unwanted camera movement. The Steadicam JR, a scaled-down version of the original Steadicam, was designed specifically for lightweight consumer camcorders (see Figure 4.11b).

Tripods

The **tripod** is a three-legged device for supporting a camera. The lengths of its legs are adjustable so that the tripod can be level even if the surface on which it is resting is not (see Figure 4.12a). Most legs will adjust so the camera can rise from 2 to 3 feet off the ground to slightly above eye level. If a camera needs to be lower, you can use a **high hat,** a board attached to very short legs.

Tripod legs have spikes or pads on the bottom so they can rest firmly on the ground or a floor. Sometimes wheels are attached to the legs to make the whole unit mobile.

Mounted on top of the three legs is a tripod **head,** a device with a handle that allows the camera to pivot smoothly (see Figure 4.12b). A screw on the head attaches it to the bottom of the camera. Some heads (usually inexpensive ones) are referred to as **friction heads** and use the resistance created by surfaces touching each other to provide smooth movement. More expensive **fluid heads** have adjustable hydraulic resistance that allows for easy, smooth camera movements. Both types have levers or screws that control the amount of freedom the camera has; heads can be locked down so they do not move at all, or they can provide varying degrees of movement.

Dollies

Professional **dollies** are wheeled carts that come in various sizes, from about the size of a wagon to the size of a small truck (see Figure 4.13). They are often motorized and have a pole in the middle on which the camera is mounted. Usually, one person drives or pulls the dolly while another operates the camera. They are excellent for moves that involve going forward and backward. Students are usually talented at concocting homemade dollies from wheelchairs, grocery carts, and the like.

Cranes

Cranes are large pieces of equipment, like the phone company's cherry pickers, that can move the camera from very low to very high above the set. Many cranes can also move forward, backward, to the side, and in arcs.

A crane often requires several people to move it from one position to the next. Cranes are very expensive and are not used frequently, so they are usually rented. Many manufacturers also

a   b

Figure 4.12
(a) A lightweight tripod and (b) a fluid head that allows smooth, fluid pans and tilts. (Photos courtesy of Miller Fluid Heads)

Figure 4.13
A camera dolly mounted on tracks. Taken off the tracks, this particular dolly could also be moved on its pneumatic wheels. (Photo courtesy of EPIX, Pty, LTD.)

make counterweighted **jib-arms** that can be used to swing the camera out over an area that would be inaccessible to a large crane holding the camera operator and camera. For additional flexibility, many camera jibs can be attached to

a

b

Figure 4.14
A camera mounted on a jib-arm (a) can provide up-and-down movements similar to those achieved with a larger crane (b). Note that the crane has space for mounting the camera and for the camera operator. (Photo a courtesy of EPIX, Pty, LTD.: photo b courtesy of Matthews Studio Equipment, Inc.)

Figure 4.15
A zoom lens with servo control mounted on the left. Note the lens hood, which keeps stray light rays from the lens surface. (Photo courtesy of Angenieux Corporation of America)

dollies or tracking bases. (Figure 4.14 shows a jib-arm and a crane.)

Moving the Camera

Mounting equipment also allows the camera to move. A number of terms describe these camera movements, whether they are accomplished by a crane, a dolly, a tripod, or a human body. A movement of only the camera from left to right is called a **pan.** Camera operators can pan left or right by moving the handle attached to the head. A **tilt** involves moving only the camera up or down and again involves using the tripod head's handle. Moving the camera and the supporting device left or right is called a **truck** (or **track**). For example, a tripod on wheels could be trucked left or right. The head would need to be locked down so that the camera did not move separately from the tripod. When everything moves in or out, the shot is called a **dolly,** a term that arose because the piece of equipment called the dolly is excellent to use for moving back and forth. An up-and-down movement of the camera and the supporting device is called a **crane** or **boom,** once again because the crane is the best mounting device to use to go from low to high.

These five movements—pan, tilt, truck, dolly, and crane—are the basic movements, although others, such as an **arc,** are used from time to time. Of course, you can make several movements; a camera can dolly in, pan left, and crane up all at the same time.[19]

Lenses

Lenses gather light reflected by a subject and concentrate it on the imaging device. A **lens hood** is often mounted on the front of the lens to keep stray light from hitting the lens surface and causing unwanted glare. A lens hood also may help protect the lens surface during transport.

Lenses consist of curved glass elements that turn the image upside down at the **optical center** of the lens and then focus it at a point where it begins its electronic or photochemical journey to being recorded. In a film camera, this focus point is the film itself; in a CCD video camera, it is the chip; in a tube camera, it is the target. Everything that is filmed or taped passes through the lens, so it is a very important part of moviemaking.

Focal Length

Most lenses on TV cameras and camcorders are **zoom lenses** (more properly called **variable focal length lenses**), capable of capturing close-ups, wide shots, and everything in between. Other lenses, called **fixed lenses** (or **prime lenses**), are capable of capturing only one distance. If you frame a close-up with a fixed lens, you cannot keep the camera in the same position and change to a wide shot unless you change to a different lens.

With a zoom lens you can make this change, either while you are taping or between shots. To do so you must move elements within the lens by turning a barrel on the lens. This barrel can be turned by hand but more often is turned remotely by a servo-controlled motor. (Figure 4.15 shows a zoom lens with servo control.) A switch on the camera allows the operator to activate and deactivate the zoom and control its speed. The motor allows for a smoother zoom than can be accomplished by hand.

All lenses, zoom or fixed, have measurements that designate their **focal length.** One fixed lens may be a 25mm lens, whereas another is 50mm. A variable focal length lens may have a range of 10mm to 100mm. The focal length is the distance from the optical center of the lens to the point in the camera where the image is focused. The longer the focal length, the more the shot is magnified. A 50mm lens will show greater detail, but less of a scene, than a 25mm lens. A zoom lens that is in the 100mm position will have a tighter shot than when it is in the 50mm position.

Zoom lenses often have a designation that specifies the ratio of the closest shot to the widest shot. For example, some lenses are 5:1, whereas others are 10:1. If the widest shot on a 5:1 lens is 20mm, the tightest shot will be 100mm. If the widest shot on a 10:1 lens is 20mm, the tightest shot will be 200mm. The bigger the ratio, the greater the zooming range—and the greater the cost of the lens.

Lenses or zoom lens positions that show shots that appear to be magnified are usually

a

b

c

Figure 4.16
From the same position a zoom lens can present (a) a wide angle of view, (b) a relatively normal angle of view, and (c) a telephoto view of the scene.

referred to as **telephoto;** those that show views roughly as the eye sees them are **normal;** those with a view wider than the human eye's are called **wide angle.** (These views are depicted in Figure 4.16.) The normal lens creates the most natural perspective. The telephoto not only makes things appear bigger, it also foreshortens them so that they appear to be closer to each other. If the objects are moving, they will appear to move more slowly than they actually are. The opposite is true of a wide-angle lens. It makes things appear smaller, farther apart from each other, and faster than normal if an object is approaching or receding from the camera position.

Figure 4.17
A cutaway of a zoom lens showing the many different elements within. (Photo courtesy of Canon USA Inc.)

Figure 4.18
A Canon LX-100 Hi-8 camcorder that can use many different Canon lenses. (Photo courtesy of Canon USA Inc.)

In effect, a zoom lens can be thought of as a lens having the characteristics of all the prime lenses that it can mimic within the extremes of its zoom range. It is so easy to go from wide angle to telephoto that operators sometimes do not weigh the advantages or disadvantages of a particular focal length setting. For example, an extreme telephoto shot can seem close to the subject and can fill the screen with detail but at the cost of foreshortened depth, difficulty in holding the camera steady, and a touchy focus because of the shallow depth of field. At the other extreme of the zoom range (wide angle)

the opposite may be true. For example, although there is depth, the amount of detail needed to understand what is happening may not be discernible.

Zoom lenses often have a **macro** setting that allows the lens to focus on an object very close to the front element of the lens. A button or some other control allows you to select the macro position for the lens in order to create a screen-filling close-up of a small object, such as a coin or fingernail.

Although zoom lenses are standard on most video cameras, they are not always the best lenses to use. They are more expensive, mainly because they have more elements than fixed lenses (see Figure 4.17). They need more light because light dissipates as it goes through these dozen or so elements. They cannot be manufactured to provide an optimum picture at all focal lengths. However, zoom lenses have the obvious advantage of changing magnification easily. They are also likely to deliver more consistent color than prime lenses. Color rendition changes slightly from one lens to another, so if a 25mm lens is removed from a camera and replaced with a 50mm lens, the color recorded may change slightly. Prime lenses, however, are generally faster than zoom lenses and may produce a somewhat sharper image.

Until recently, the question of whether to use prime lenses or zoom lenses was irrelevant for consumers with camcorders. The camera simply came equipped with a zoom lens that could not be removed or changed. However, a number of equipment manufacturers, including Canon, Hitachi, Matsushita, and Sony, have jointly developed a lens mounting system that does allow for interchangeable lenses that retain most automatic functions (auto focus, auto iris, zoom control, and so on). In addition, some of Canon's Hi-8 cameras feature a special adapter that allows the camera to accept a wide array of 35mm lenses from Canon still cameras[20] (see Figure 4.18).

Focus

A lens has a ring for controlling **focus**, with numbers on the ring that give distance in feet (and inches) and meters. When something is in focus, it looks sharp and clear; when it is out of f/22   f/5.6   f/1.2

Figure 4.19

The thin metal blades of the lens iris open or close the aperture to different f-stops. The smaller the iris opening, the larger the f-stop number (and the less light the lens will allow to enter the camera). Lens speed is based on how much light a particular lens will let in at its maximum aperture. Thus, a lens with a maximum aperture of f/1.2 is faster than a lens with a maximum aperture of f/2.

focus, it appears fuzzy and ill defined. When you look in the viewfinder while turning the focus knob, you usually can discern when the picture is in focus. However, a good practice is to look at the focus ring to make sure it reads a distance about the same as the actual distance to your subject. If you are 10 feet from a subject and your focus ring reads 3 feet, something is wrong with the optics. If focus is crucial, you can run a measuring tape from the camera imaging device to the subject and set the focusing ring to correspond to the measurement. For many years this has been a common practice in filmmaking.

The focusing mechanism for a fixed focal length lens is quite simple. It merely moves the lens elements closer to or farther away from the imaging device. When the object to be placed in focus is close to the camera, the elements should be far from the imaging device. If the shot is focusing on a distant object, the elements should be closer to the film, CCD, or tube.

To focus a zoom lens properly you should take advantage of the zoom by zooming in all the way (the most magnified or telephoto setting), focusing, then zooming out to frame the shot. This focusing technique allows you to zoom in or out during the shot without losing focus on the subject. This type of focusing sets what is referred to as the zoom lens **front focus** because it changes the glass elements at the front of the lens. Zoom lenses also have a back focus, which should be adjusted only by a qualified camera technician. If the lens is jarred, this back focus can come out of adjustment, causing a fuzzy picture.[21]

Aperture

In addition to the focus ring, lenses have a ring that determines how much light is let into the camera. This ring controls the size of the **aperture**—the opening in the lens that allows light to pass. The aperture has an adjustable **diaphragm** or **iris** that opens and closes to let in more or less light. The degree to which the aperture is open is measured in **f-stops,** which are numbers that usually appear on the aperture ring.

F-stops can be confusing, if for no other reason than they are depicted by rather strange numbers—1.4, 2, 2.8, 4, 5.6, 8, 11, 16, 22. The reason for these seemingly unrelated numbers involves a mathematical formula that calls for multiplying each preceding number by the square root of two. In this relationship each f-stop doubles or halves the amount of light of the f-stop next to it. This relationship adds to the confusion because the larger the f-stop number, the smaller the aperture. In other words, there is an *inverse relationship* between the two. An f-stop of 8 will let in half as much light as an f-stop of 5.6; an f-stop of 11 will let in twice as much light as an f-stop of 16. (Figure 4.19 shows various f-stops and their apertures.)

Some lenses may include a **t-stop** scale. T-stops are more accurate than f-stops and are more likely to be used in film than in video. All lenses lose a certain amount of light within the lens itself, depending on the quality of the lens and its coatings. T-stops denote the actual amount of light *transmitted* (thus the *t* in *t-stop*) through a particular lens.

Lenses are rated according to their lowest f-stop number—the greatest amount of light they can let in. An f/1.4 lens is considered a fairly **fast lens** because it can open up wide enough to let in a good deal of light. An f/4 lens would be a **slow lens** because it can let in much less light. One of the disadvantages of zoom lenses is that they are slower than fixed lenses because of the many elements they contain.

As with focus, many cameras have an automatic iris that adjusts to the amount of light hitting the image plane and sets the f-stop accordingly with a small motor that opens and closes the iris. Again, this is fine as long as you want average exposure. But if you want the

Figure 4.20
Depth of field and the one-third principle.

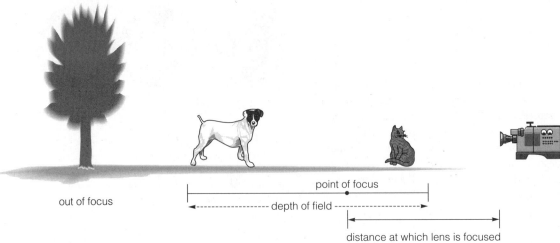

point of focus

out of focus

------------ depth of field ------------

distance at which lens is focused

scene to look dark, or if you have a scene with a bright background and a dark foreground, you may need to turn off the automatic iris.

Some situations require sacrificing overall exposure for the sake of correctly exposing the most important element in the frame. One way to make sure that your light reading is correct under these circumstances is to zoom in on that element and look at the automatic iris reading. Then zoom back out to your intended composition, and set the iris manually for the f-stop reading you had when you zoomed in. This is especially helpful if you have a person standing in front of a bright background. The automatic iris might expose for the bright background when what you want to be able to see is the person's features. If you have zoomed in and set the iris for the person's face, the face will be the element that is properly exposed.

Depth of Field

Depth of field is the distance (the range, really) through which objects will appear in sharp focus in front of and behind the point at which the camera is actually focused. The depth of field varies according to the aperture, the focal length of the lens, and the distance of the camera from the subject. The longer the focal length of the lens and the wider the aperture, the shallower the depth of field will be. Thus, wide-angle (or short focal length) lenses give a greater depth of field than telephoto (or long focal length) lenses. Generally, the closer the subject is to the camera the less the depth of field will be.

When two characters or objects are lined up at different distances from the camera, it some-

times may be necessary to split the focus to keep both subjects in clear, sharp view. This is not done by focusing on a point midway between the two; rather, it is done by focusing on a point one-third the distance behind the front subject. In other words, focus will be sharp for an area one-third in front and two-thirds behind the point of focus. (Figure 4.20 illustrates the depth of field and the one-third principle.)

Focal length affects depth of field because wide-angle lenses have a greater natural depth of field than telephoto lenses. They are designed to capture large, deep scenes.

The smaller the aperture (and the larger the f-stop number), the greater the depth of field. A lens set at f/22 will create a greater depth of field than one set at f/2.8. This characteristic can be used to highlight certain objects in the frame by having them, and only them, in focus. Most lens manufacturers and many publications such as the *American Cinematographer Manual* publish depth-of-field charts that give the depth-of-field characteristics for lenses of different focal lengths under various conditions.

Care of Equipment

All equipment and supplies mentioned in this chapter should be handled and stored carefully. They represent an investment on the part of an individual, a school, or a company. Careless handling shortens their life and causes unnecessary operating problems.

One good rule is *never force anything*. If a connector won't slide into its receptacle easily, you probably do not have it lined up correctly. If you force a knob on a tripod, you may strip the threads. If a lens ring is binding or feels excessively loose, you are going to make things worse by forcing it. Driving a lever, switch, or dial against the end of its movement range will damage the equipment.

You should also protect equipment while transporting and storing it. Whenever possible, store and carry cameras and their lenses in sturdy, well-padded cases that hold the equipment securely in place so that it will not bounce around. If possible, store and carry tripods in sturdy cases. Before putting a tripod in the case, be sure that all levers are locked, the legs are bound together, and the handle attached to the head is positioned so that it cannot be damaged. Similarly, monitors and recorders should have their own cases.

Even with cases to protect the equipment, everything should be moved as gently as possible. For cases that have wheels, use an elevator or handicapped ramp if available. If necessary, simply pick up the case and carry it a short distance.

Extreme heat or cold is not good for most equipment, and electronic gear must be protected from moisture. Keep lenses away from areas of high heat because the cement holding the elements in place may melt. Store tape and film in a cool place. Never leave film or tape in a parked car where the temperature can reach high levels.

Dirt is also an enemy of electronic components. Keep equipment and supplies off the ground, especially if the area has sand or loose dirt. Keep cameras, recorders, monitors, batteries, tape, film, and cables and connectors in cases, boxes, or bags when not in use.[22]

Lenses should be kept spotlessly clean. Although it is possible to clean a lens, doing so too often is not recommended. Anything touching a lens, even a cleaning cloth, can scratch it or wear down its antireflective coating. Fingerprints are especially bad for lenses. They produce a smear on the picture, and the oil from fingers can over time etch the lens. If the lens becomes dirty, remove dust gently with a camel hair brush. Next, place a drop of special lens cleaner on a special nonabrasive lens tissue and rub it lightly over the lens surface in a circular motion.

One of the surest signs of professionalism is the respect with which a person treats equipment.

Notes

1. Lenny Lipton, *The Super 8 Book* (New York: Simon & Schuster, 1975), pp. 9–12.
2. Film formats have never been quite as standard as this discussion suggests. The number of perforations per frame has varied from two to six, and at different times in film history ultra-large-screen film formats have been introduced with film widths of 62mm, 63mm, and 65mm. The Cinerama format, for example, initially required three cameras at a frame rate of 26 frames per second. In fact, much current experimentation with large-screen formats involves increasing the frame rate to a speed higher than the customary 24 frames per second (fps) standard. By increasing the filming and projection speed to 48 fps or 60 fps, much higher image quality can be achieved in terms of sharpness and clarity.
3. Robert Rivlin, "Composite-Component: Evolution or Revolution?" *E-ITV,* September 1987, pp. 16–24.
4. Some good general articles that cover the various formats are Michael Grotticelli, "Digital Betacam Makes the Film-to-Tape Transition," *Videography,* October 1995, pp. 66, 84–85; "Video Formats for the Past, Present, and Future," *Computer Video,* July/August 1995, pp. 24–32; Claudia Kienzle, "Camera Round-Up," *Film and Video,* October 1991, pp. 32–49; Frank Kelly, "Is the New DVC a Poor Man's Betacam," *Computer Video,* January-February 1996, p. 8; Frank Beacham, "Camcorders Take Another Giant Leap," *TV Technology,* November 1995, p. 1; Stewart Appelgath, "Big Shot: Sony's DCR-VX1000 Takes the Shot Heard 'Round the World," *Video,* November 1995, pp. 84–85; and David Brott, "Digital Frontier," *Videomaker,* November 1995, pp. 43–46.
5. There are actually far more aspect ratios in film. Between the two extremes, the 1.33:1 Academy ratio and the Cinerama 3:1 ratio, are nine sizes. For a good historical summary of different aspect ratios, see Lenny Lipton, *Independent Filmmaking* (New York: Simon & Schuster, 1983), pp. 182–183.
6. Bruce Elder, "Widescreen Fever: Letterboxed Films Find Passionate Following in the Laserdisc Age," *Video,* September 1991, pp. 53–54. See also "Widescreen Presentation," *LaserNews Spe-*

cial Report, 1991, pp. 1–4, for an excellent discussion of the problems associated with translating widescreen motion pictures to laser disk.

7. Film manufacturers continue to improve the speed and the resolution of their film stocks. See, for example, Tony Harcourt, "The Features and Benefits of T-Grain Emulsion," *In Camera,* Summer 1995, pp. 28–29; and "Selecting Your 16mm Film," in *Creating Better Video with 16mm Film* (Rochester, NY: Eastman Kodak Company, 1992).

8. For an excellent discussion of new videotape materials and coatings, see Ron Goldberg, "The Layered Look," *Video,* July 1992, pp. 34–36, 94–96. See also *1992 Buying Guide Issue* (Mount Vernon, NY: Consumer Reports, 1991), p. 27, and Lancelot Braithwaite, "VHS Tape Tests," *Video,* March 1993, pp. 38–43.

9. Cliff Roth, "DV Nation: The Digital Frontier Debuts with Camcorders from Panasonic and Sony," *Video,* November 1995, pp. 78–80.

10. See David Ranada, "In the Realm of the Sensors," *Video,* May 1993, pp. 50–53.

11. Early researchers credited this phenomenon to the so-called persistence of vision, the capacity of the human eye to retain each image (each projected frame) for a fraction of a second. Coupled with the Phi phenomenon, a response observed by Gestalt psychologist Max Wertheimer, the sense of motion on the screen is possible.

Scientists, however, are still debating precisely how this process actually works. The illusion of movement created by a series of projected still pictures is the result of complex physiological and psychological factors. If the film projection rate is too slow, 8 frames per second, for example, the image appears to flicker. When the speed is increased to 16 or more frames per second, the viewer no longer perceives the flickering.

12. Some exceptions to this should be noted. In color television the actual frame rates are 29.97 frames per second and 59.94 fields per second. See Chapter 11 for a discussion of non-drop-frame and drop-frame time code.

13. Improvements in CCD sensors continue at a rapid rate. One example is the frame transfer sensor developed by BTS, a system that uses a high-resolution frame transfer (FT) sensor and a shutter to eliminate smearing. In this system each separate image is transferred to storage before a new image takes its place. A shutter in the camera is timed to operate during this transfer, and it interrupts exposure during the frame shift. This allows each frame of the picture to be independent of the previous frames (just like a film camera) and virtually eliminates smearing. See Peter G. M. Centen,

"BTS: F-stops and the Angle of Perception," *TV Technology,* April 1992, p. 7.

14. First developed for the broadcast-quality Betacam and M-formats, something like this technology is now beginning to appear in consumer formats such as Super-VHS and Hi-8. These consumer systems, however, are not true component systems. They still modulate the color information onto a carrier for recording, unlike the Betacam and M-systems, which maintain chrominance/luminance separation throughout the entire process, thus avoiding partial encoding.

15. When you watch a broadcast television channel at home, you are probably seeing a signal (depending on the strength of the broadcast signal and how finely your receiver is tuned) with somewhere between 200 and 300 lines of horizontal resolution. The highest-quality cameras, recorders, and studio television monitors can produce an image with 600 to 800 lines of horizontal resolution. A regular VHS camcorder produces an image much closer to 200 lines of resolution. In comparison, a S-VHS or Hi-8 camera produces an image with more than 400 lines of horizontal resolution, though you can see the difference only if your television is capable of accepting the S-VHS or Hi-8 signal through a special connector.

16. Three main types of auto-focusing systems are used in camcorders today: range finding, phase detection, and blur reduction. For an excellent discussion of the pros and cons of the various systems, see David Ranada, "Inside Optics: How Camcorders See," *Video,* October 1990, pp. 38–43.

One of the newest offshoots in auto focusing, "fuzzy logic," was designed to avoid the "hunting" so typical of the earlier auto-focusing systems. When confronted with multiple subjects, many older auto-focusing systems go back and forth, in and out of focus. In contrast, a fuzzy logic system surveys many objects at different distances, chooses a compromise setting, and stops grinding back and forth. See, for example, "Fisher 8mm Fuzzy Logic Camcorder," *Video,* October 1990, p. 25.

It is worth testing any auto-focusing system before purchasing a camera. It is also important to be able to override or turn off the auto-focusing system when circumstances require it.

17. In order to do this, however, the signal must be modulated onto a regular TV channel. This requires a modulator unit, usually built into the VCR, that sends the signal to an unused channel (channel 3 or channel 4 in a typical consumer unit).

18. For articles on camera mounts see "The Pros and Cons of the Tripod," *TV Technology,* February 1993, p. 36; and Michael Wiese, "Zen and the Art of the Steadicam JR," *Videography,* December 1990, pp. 41–43.

19. A remote controlled, consumer-grade camera tracking system has been introduced by Parkervision (8493 Baymeadows Way, Jacksonville, FL 32256). This system allows the operator to execute camera movements entirely by wireless remote control with the camera mounted in special housing.

20. "Low Down on Lenses," *AV Video,* October 1995, pp. 62–70; and Ty Harrington, "Canon a la Carte," *Video,* June 1992, pp. 50–51.

21. This is tied to depth of focus, a concept that is often incorrectly confused with depth of field.

Depth of focus refers to the distance between the back of the lens and the target of the camera. If this distance is changed, the depth of focus is changed and the picture will not focus properly. The focus can be adjusted by setting the lens at infinity and zooming in on a distant object. Then adjust the distance between the lens and the target of the tube (the back focus) so that the image is sharp. When you zoom out, the image should stay sharp. If it doesn't, adjust the back focus in the zoomed-out position until the picture is sharp. Now zoom in. The picture should be sharp. Continue to do this until both the zoomed-in position and the zoomed-out position yield a focused picture.

22. Gordon McComb, "How to Triple Your Camcorder's Life," *Video,* December 1994, p. 26.

chapter five
Approaches to Image Making

After deciding what to shoot, the director's concern shifts to how to shoot it. The distinction here is between what is put in front of the camera and how the camera itself is used to record and manipulate the scene being shot. Film scholars have adopted the French theatrical term **mise-en-scène** to describe the director's control of the lighting, sets, locations, props, makeup, costumes, and blocking.[1] This concept is useful in defining more clearly the role of cinematography.

The director can make decisions about the mise-en-scène during preproduction or production (the last-minute blocking of the actors or adjustment of the lights) but before the camera comes into play. In effect, the mise-en-scène is what is visible through the viewfinder before shooting—the way the scene is staged for the camera. Once the director decides on the mise-en-scène, attention moves to how best to capture it with the camera. At this point the director and cinematographer must make a number of choices about composition.

Shot Determination

Interpreting the mise-en-scène involves determining how much of that scene to include within the shot. One of the special powers of the camera is its capacity to force the audience to see what the director wants the audience to see. This situation is quite different from real life or from a stage play, where the observer is freer to choose the point on which to concentrate. At a play, part of the audience may be watching the French maid; the rest may be watching the English butler. When a camera is used to interpret that scene, the viewer can virtually be forced to see a single area of the scene, such as the maid's eyes.

Of course, the director may also use elements of the mise-en-scène to direct the audience's at-tention, whether in a movie, at a stage play, or even in real life. The lighting, blocking, costumes, makeup, set design, and dialogue are elements that can direct the viewer's eye. But the camera directs the audience's attention in a more obvious and powerful manner.

The Basic Shots

Selecting what is to be seen in the frame is one way the camera can be used to direct attention. This capacity distinguishes a film from a play, where the frame is the entire proscenium arch. In the theater you buy the frame through which you are going to see the play when you pay for your seat. The cheaper the seats the longer your "shot" of the stage. Shots are constantly changing in a motion picture. You see a variety of **long shots (LS)**, **medium shots (MS)**, and **close-ups (CU)**. (Figure 5.1 illustrates these shots.)

Defining these terms is not always easy. A long shot may mean different things to different directors. It may even mean different things in film and television. A long shot in a three-camera television interview show may refer to a shot that includes guests and the host. In a film, a long shot might include a cowboy hero riding his horse through the wide open spaces of Monument Valley.

Generally, a close-up isolates the subject, such as an actor, from the surroundings. A medium shot provides not only a shot of the subject but also of some of the surroundings. A long shot emphasizes the surroundings and the subject's place in relationship to them. To some extent these terms are relative to each other. A shot might be called a long shot in one sequence of shots but a medium shot in another. Perhaps the simplest way to describe different shots is in terms of a spectrum, with an extreme long shot as the widest shot and an extreme close-up as the nearest shot. All other shots are spread somewhere between the two extremes.

Often the language we use to describe various shots is based on the human body. A long shot includes the entire body. A medium shot is from somewhat below the waist to the top of the head. A close-up is from the shoulders up.

Another common way to describe a composition is according to the number of people in the shot; for example, a two-shot has two people, and a three-shot has three people. Terms such as *head shot, head-and-shoulders shot,* and *full shot* are fairly self-descriptive, but none of these terms is exact. (Figure 5.2 shows some standard shots.) Given that there are many ways to describe a composition and that your medium shot may be somewhat different from what your friend means by a medium shot, the real translation often lies in the camera viewfinder. The director can look through the viewfinder and say, "That's what I want."

Subjective Shots

Another type of composition injects a subjective element into the composition. A shot in which the lens of the camera becomes, in effect, the eye of a character in the film is called a **point-of-view (POV) shot.** We are all familiar with a novel that is narrated by a character such as the hard-boiled detective. Narration from the viewpoint of a character within the story is more difficult in film and video. Nothing within the shot itself tells you that this is what James Bond sees. But a close-up of Bond's eyes (and a slight widening of the pupils) can be followed by a POV shot that approximates the height, angle, and direction of Bond's gaze.

Sustaining this for an entire film, however, greatly reduces a director's storytelling flexibility and can be almost silly. Robert Montgomery's film *The Lady in the Lake* (1946) tried, and not very successfully, to create a visual equivalent of first-person narration (like the hard-boiled detective novel on which it was based) by using POV shots for the entire picture. We see the detective's hands reaching into drawers or his pipe poking into the shot as if the camera were located precisely at eye level and the pipe were in our (his) mouth at the bottom of the frame. The detective in *The Lady in the Lake* is seen only occasionally, in a mirror or window reflection.

Most filmmaking uses POV shots far more sparingly. However, a director who does want to suggest a point of view can heighten the realism of this shot by using a slight movement of the camera to simulate an actor's head or eye movement. Another common subjective cue is placing a mask over the lens to simulate binoculars

a

b

c

Figure 5.1

(a) A long shot, (b) a medium shot, and (c) a close-up shot. (Photos courtesy of Video Producer: A Video Production Lab *by Herbert Zettl and Cooperative Media Group, published by Wadsworth Publishing Company)*

a

b

c

d

Figure 5.2

Other common shot descriptions: (a) a full shot; (b) a head-and-shoulders shot; (c) an extreme close-up, sometimes called a choker close-up; (d) a two-shot from Hill Street Blues. *(Photo d courtesy of MTM)*

or a keyhole that a character might be looking through.

The **over-the-shoulder (OS) shot** (see Figure 5.3) is also executed from a particular position. This shot literally looks over the shoulder of one character toward another character or object. An OS shot is a typical way of shooting two people talking. For example, a man might be seen from over a woman's shoulder. A reverse angle shot would then show the woman from over the shoulder of the man. Over-the-shoulder shots have a subjective element. We are seeing from approximately the same angle as the character whose shoulder we are looking across.

Lens Selection

Another aspect of composition concerns the choice of **lens** or the setting of the variable focal length zoom lens. This choice can determine how something appears in terms of physical and psychological distance. It can also direct attention by selecting what will and will not be in focus.

Focal Length Characteristics

The **normal lens,** so called because it shows things much as the viewer's eyes see them, might be the least manipulative and most realistic of the various lenses. It introduces the least distortion into the scene.

The **telephoto lens** (or **long lens**) tends to compress the perceived distances between the foreground and background within the shot. The television commercial in which the auto executives demonstrate their faith in the brakes of their company's luxury sedan is actually demonstrating their faith in the power of an extreme telephoto lens. This lens makes the car that is screeching to a halt near their legs seem much closer than it actually is.

In general, the long or telephoto lens may be the most obvious lens in the sense of calling attention to itself. It can draw the viewer into the scene, creating intimacy and involvement. An extreme telephoto lens can so distort perspective relationships that the result is an almost surreal, dreamlike quality. This lens can also give a voyeuristic feeling, almost as if the spectator is eavesdropping on the scene. *Mississippi Burning* was shot largely with a telephoto lens to give a closed-in feeling that evoked racial tension.

On the other hand, an extreme **wide-angle lens** (or **short lens**) calls attention to itself by distorting the image, albeit in the opposite way. It can create a feeling of size and scope by giving a wide horizontal field of view. This characteristic can be used to delineate relationships between characters in a film. Orson Welles's classic film *Citizen Kane* is noted for its extensive use of extreme wide-angle lenses to emphasize the physical distance and the psychological distance between its characters.

Figure 5.3
An over-the-shoulder shot. (Photo courtesy of Video Producer*)*

The object is to choose the focal length that fits the sense of the scene you are shooting. What kind of relationships do you want to emphasize through size, distance, and perspective? Do you want to distort or call attention to the way the *mise-en-scène* is being manipulated? (Figure 5.4 shows the same scene shot through a normal lens, a telephoto lens, and a wide-angle lens. The cars seem closer together with the telephoto lens.)

Depth of Field

By manipulating the **depth of field** the director has yet another way to direct the spectator's attention within the frame. A large depth of field allows the viewer's eyes to roam throughout every plane of action, all of which will be in focus. Some directors, like Orson Welles and Jean Renoir, are noted for using deep focus in their films. This technique can be more realistic because it approximates the way we see. It also allows the viewer to seek out an area of interest in a composition with many layers.

A shallow depth of field (or shallow focus) isolates a subject in one plane and throws all other planes out of focus. (Figure 5.5 shows examples of deep and shallow depths of field.) In the heyday of Hollywood studio production a shallow depth of field was often used to isolate the studio's major star from any visual distractions in the foreground or background. Using a shallow depth of field also makes it possible to shift the point of focus during the shot. This

a

b

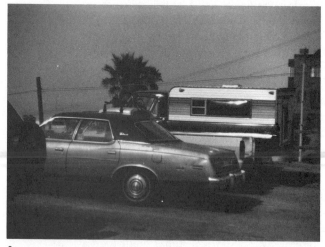

c

Figure 5.4

Photo a shows a parking lot shot with a normal lens. The distance between the cars in photo b, taken with a wide-angle lens, appears greater than it really is, whereas photo c, taken with a telephoto lens, makes the cars seem closer together than they actually are.

technique, as it is seen on the screen, is known as **rack focus.** It is the result of **pulling focus** (that is, changing focus) during the shot (see Figure 5.6). For example, a shot might begin with the star in sharp focus in the foreground, but as the focus is shifted, the star blurs out of focus while a character in the background comes into sharp relief.

Camera Angle

The angle of the shot can also affect composition. A camera can be placed above or below the scene, creating a **high-angle shot** or a **low-angle shot.** The standard (or conventional) meaning attached to these shots deals with the relative dominance of different viewing angles. A shot looking down usually diminishes or weakens the subject (or character), whereas a shot looking up tends to accentuate the power or dominance of the subject. In Orson Welles's *Touch of Evil* the corrupt and corpulent border police officer, played by Welles himself, is consistently shot from extreme low angles, making him grotesquely sinister and powerful at the same time.

These are examples of extreme angles, however. The normal camera angle in narrative motion pictures is chest high, not eye height, a practice that does not match the viewer's everyday visual experience (unless the viewer is very short). This angle does match the viewer's experience of watching motion pictures—a chest-high camera angle is the norm, the conventional angle for shooting "larger-than-life" film stars. Consequently, eye-height angles (as in shoulder-mounted camera work) look like high angles even though they are totally realistic in terms of our normal viewing experience. A **Steadicam** (see Chapter 4) allows stable, hand-held, mobile shooting at angles lower than eye height.

The framing of a shot may also be manipulated by the degree to which the framing is level with the horizon. A **canted shot,** or **tilted shot,** is so unusual and disorienting that it can be unsettling to the viewer. A POV shot that suggests someone is drunk or drugged frequently uses this composition, but it is wrong to suggest that a canted frame always means something is askew or out of kilter. The meaning of a canted frame,

a

b

Figure 5.5
(a) A shallow depth of field in "Married . . . with Children" (photo courtesy of Columbia Studios) and (b) a deep or large depth of field in Jean Renoir's classic film Rules of the Game *(photo from Janus Films).*

a

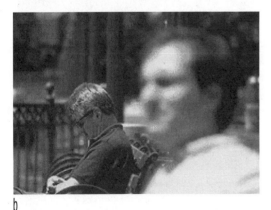
b

Figure 5.6
(a) The man in the foreground is in focus. Pulling focus (b) brings the man in the background into focus and throws the man in the foreground out of focus. (Photos courtesy of Video Producer*)*

or for that matter a high-angle or low-angle shot, is derived from the context of the film, not from some dictionary of camera aesthetics. (The photos in Figure 5.7 illustrate different camera angles.)

Composing Within the Static Frame

Some shots that the director composes are relatively static because the camera does not move very much. A number of conventions, or so-called rules, have evolved regarding the composition of a shot within a static frame. These involve such elements as balance, depth, relative strength of various planes of the shot, and the space on and off the screen.

Manipulating the Mise-en-Scène

Before the camera rolls, the way the event is staged for the camera has a profound effect on how the composition directs the viewer's eye. The director's storytelling technique is based on a subtle interplay of lighting, blocking, costumes, and setting and the way the camera emphasizes those elements.

In a culture that reads left to right, the left side of the frame is probably more powerful than the right. To counterbalance this tendency

a

b

c

d

Figure 5.7
Different camera angles: (a) a canted shot; (b) a shot with normal framing level to the horizon; (c) a two-shot from the conventional chest-high angle in Old Mother Witch; *(d) a high-angle shot; and (e) a low-angle shot from Jean Renoir's* Rules of the Game. *(Photo c courtesy of Phoenix Films, Mark Chodzko, and Carol Carrick, photos d and e from Janus Films)*

it may even be useful at times to place an object (or character) of greater size on the right side of the frame.

Usually, the element that has the greatest mass or that takes up most of the composition will draw the most attention. However, the placement of objects or characters within the scene is not the only way to attract the viewer's attention. The most brightly lit object (or person) in the composition also tends to dominate the frame. The colors of costumes, props, or the set itself can create a visual emphasis. In Robert Altman's *The Player* the appearance of Cher in a bright red dress at a formal social gathering, where everyone else is wearing black or white, absolutely guarantees that she will be noticed. During the liquidation of the Warsaw Ghetto in Steven Speilberg's *Schindler's List,* a young girl in a red coat is the only visible color in an otherwise black-and-white scene. The red coat is glimpsed again later in the film as the camera pans across a pile of discarded clothing, indicating that the girl is dead.

The different lines of interest established within the composition have a dramatic effect on how the viewer sees and interprets the image. Diagonal lines across the frame are often more

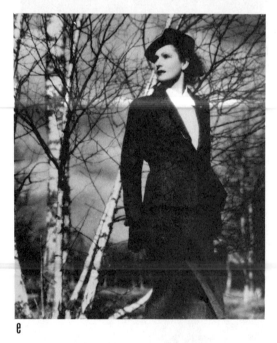

e

dynamic than horizontal lines. Shooting a group of choir boys in a circle rather than in a straight line may create a feeling of tranquillity. Shooting an actor framed by a window or archway says something far different visually than shooting the same actor in a flat, even composition.

The **blocking** of actors is one of the director's most basic tools for focusing the audience's attention. An actor closer to the camera is more dominating than one farther away. A performer facing the camera tends to grab the spectator's attention more than someone turned three-quarters, in profile, or away from the camera. A person in motion tends to attract the viewer's eye more than a person who is stationary. Similarly, an actor who is standing while the other actors are seated (or vice versa) receives greater emphasis. A performer alone, away from others in the composition, tends to attract more attention, as does an actor on whom all the other actors seem to be focusing their attention. Someone entering the scene usually is more dominating than someone leaving the scene.

Ultimately, the director's dramatic objective for a given scene determines the way the event is staged for the camera. What are you trying to emphasize? What do you want the audience to see? The answer to these questions lies somewhere between the manner in which the viewer's attention is directed by the mise-en-scène and the way in which the camera interprets the mise-en-scène.

Balance

Unbalanced compositions are considered more interesting than **balanced** compositions. When subjects within the frame are balanced so that the relative "weights" on the left and the right or on the top and the bottom are equal, the composition appears stable and solid but also tends to be flat and lacking in depth. Unbalanced compositions are more dynamic and visually active and often can be used to create a sense of instability or tension. One reason for this is that what is in the "heavy" (or weighted) half of the frame tends to draw the items in the "light" half of the frame toward it.

The real objective, of course, is not to create individual shots suitable for framing on the wall but to create a composition that is appropriate for the subject at hand. Sometimes a perfectly stable and relatively flat composition is exactly right. For example, George Cukor used many balanced frames in his film *Adam's Rib* to convey equality between Spencer Tracy and Katharine Hepburn (see Figure 5.8). There is nothing in-

Figure 5.8

A balanced and relatively flat composition from Adam's Rib. *(© 1949 Turner Entertainment Co. All rights reserved)*

herently correct or incorrect about a balanced or unbalanced composition. What really matters is how the composition contributes to the overall production.

Rule of Thirds

Closely related to the concept of balanced-unbalanced compositions is the **rule of thirds**, which states that you should try to avoid breaking the frame in half (top and bottom or left and right) because such compositions tend to be overly balanced and flat. Breaking the frame into thirds tends to create less symmetrical and more active compositions. Because the lines of interest are more on the diagonal, the viewer's eyes may be drawn more powerfully across the frame, and a sense of depth may be enhanced by the more angular, less even composition (see Figure 5.9). Of course, the director can use the shape of objects within the frame, the lines of interest they create, and even their color to direct the viewer's eyes within the composition.

Creating Depth

A director can accentuate the sense of depth in a static shot in a number of ways. For example, giving a frame a definite foreground, middle ground, and background provides a sense of depth. A shot of a person (foreground) placed in front of a wall (background) does not appear

Figure 5.9

A shot from "Married . . . with Children" provides a good demonstration of the rule of thirds. A strong diagonal line of interest flows from the kneeling shoe salesman in the lower left third to the woman trying on shoes up to the reaction by coworker Al Bundy in the upper right third. This picture also demonstrates how the sense of depth can be enhanced by having objects in different planes throughout the composition. (Photo courtesy of Columbia Studios)

to have much depth, but if a middle ground figure such as a bush, or even a shadow, is added between the person and the wall, the frame will assume more depth. Overlapping foreground objects with middle ground or background objects enhances the sense of depth even more. Variations in size of objects within the frame or in their position within the picture plane can also serve as depth cues, as can color and brightness.

Unbalanced compositions and strong diagonal lines in the composition tend to increase the depth cues and draw the viewer's eyes back into the frame. A director must take care, however, to keep background objects, such as potted plants and telephone poles, from appearing to grow out of a person's head.

Composition is too complex and too subjective for a simple rule book. There is nothing inherently right or wrong about a composition that is flat as opposed to one that emphasizes depth.

On-Screen/Off-Screen Space

Another important element of composition involves the director's use of space outside the frame of the film or television image. The frame limits what we can see of a scene, but a director can choose to open up the frame by having ac-

tors leave and reenter the frame or by framing shots that make us more aware of the space outside the frame. We may see only the front half of the dog in the frame, but we are at least subliminally aware that the rest of the dog exists just outside the frame. Conversely, during the heyday of the Hollywood studio system the frame was generally more closed. Actors were usually placed in the center of the frame and seldom left it.

The **off-screen space** in film or video is more "real" than in a stage play. When actors go offstage (out of the frame imposed by the proscenium arch), we do not expect to follow them. In film or television, the frame is more like the frame around a window. Viewers have the sense that if the camera moved just slightly forward and more to the right they could see through the window and continue to watch the characters who just went out of frame. By having a character simply look off screen, the director to some extent can open up the frame and heighten the use of that off-screen space.[2]

The Edge of the Frame

Regardless of a director's attitude toward on-screen or off-screen space, the frame does pose limits. We generally expect the edges of the frame to remain relatively steady. A shaky camera creates a disconcertingly unsteady frame. Thus, the camera is usually mounted on a tripod to minimize awkward and unwanted camera movement.

The sides of the frame create another kind of limitation, particularly in shots in which a person is the subject. A viewer usually perceives that something is wrong if the framing of a person does not leave enough (or leaves too much) **headroom** between the top of the frame and the top of the person's head. **Noseroom,** sometimes called **look space,** refers to the space to the sides of the frame and the direction a person is looking within the frame. If the person is looking to the left, placing him or her on the right side of the frame leaves noseroom to the left and focuses attention in the direction the person is looking. If a person looking left is placed on the left side of the frame (with his or her nose virtually touching the left side of the frame), attention focuses on the empty space behind.

a

b

c

d

e

f

Figure 5.10

Photo a shows a composition with too much headroom, while photo b shows a more typical or conventional amount of headroom. Photo c shows inadequate noseroom that makes a character appear to be bumping up against the edge of the frame. Photo d shows a composition with better look space to the right side of the frame. Photo e does not give the man on the bicycle enough leadroom. Photo f is better. (Photos a, b, e, and f courtesy of Video Producer)

These same general principles apply when a person is moving in the frame and the camera is following the action. The convention is to provide **leadroom** in the direction the person is moving. In a chase sequence, however, allowing the people being pursued to bump up against (or move closer to) the side of the frame in the direction they are moving may help create the sense that they are hemmed in and about to be overtaken. The photos in Figure 5.10 illustrate proper and improper use of headroom, noseroom, and leadroom.

The Moving Frame

Most of the concepts we have talked about in this chapter thus far would apply equally well to still photography or painting. The mobility of the camera itself, however, is one of the distinguishing characteristics of film and video. When the camera moves, the framing of the scene moves with it. Within a single shot the framing changes as we move closer to, around, above, or away from the subject. A composition that was unbalanced one second may be balanced the next, or a shot that was high-angle can become straight-on. A medium shot can become a close-up, or the foreground can become the background. A camera moving in toward a character gives that character more impact or emphasis. Moving the camera away tends to diminish or deemphasize the character the farther away the camera moves.

Camera Movements

The major camera movements—pan, truck, tilt, crane, and dolly (see Chapter 4)—can be used not only to follow moving people or objects but also to provide different psychological feelings. In general, when just the camera moves, the feeling projected is one of an onlooker. When the camera and its mounting support—crane, tripod, human shoulder—move, the feeling projected is one of a participant.

Take, for example, the difference between a **pan** and a **truck.** Both are side-to-side movements, but for the pan only the camera moves left to right, a movement that produces an effect similar to someone moving his or her head from side to side as someone would who was observing the scene. A truck, on the other hand, moves the camera and tripod and produces a feeling of someone walking or running alongside whatever is being photographed, a much more involving type of shot. The movement of the background is also very different with a pan and a truck. For the pan, the background moves at an angle; for the truck, it stays parallel. Similar differences in feeling and background occur with a **tilt,** which involves swiveling the camera up or down, and a **crane,** which moves the entire camera and supporting mechanism up or down.

Zooming

In a **zoom** the elements of the lens move, magnifying or reducing objects in a way that the human eye cannot. With a dolly, the camera and the camera support move together into and through the space in the scene, creating a greater sense of what that particular space is like. A zoom in tends to flatten things out and bring everything in the composition closer. With a dolly in, things on screen appear to move out of frame as the movement occurs, forcing the viewer to experience the space at a more visceral level.

Student cinematographers have a tendency to rely too much on the zoom, using it as an excuse not to put the camera in the proper place for the appropriate field of view and depth of field for the lens setting. Rather than placing the camera closer to the scene (or farther away), the novice often relies on the zoom to set up and compose the shot.

Students also have a tendency to use a zoom as a substitute for a dolly. In theatrical feature films zooms are fairly rare. When a zoom is used it is often in a situation in which the artificiality of the zoom lends some particular meaning to the shot. It may also be used in a situation in which a dolly is impossible or too expensive (as across a deep open space like the ocean). Otherwise, professionals rarely use the zoom.

One of the surest signs of a novice camera person is excessive zooming. Constant zooming during shots can create a feeling of uncertainty (if not vertigo); it conveys a subliminal message that the director (or camera person) is trying to find the shot, even while the camera is running. Like any shot, a zoom should have a purpose.

Reframing

The almost infinite number of camera movements presents the director with a huge variety of strategic choices. Camera movement (and the moving frame) constantly shifts on-screen and off-screen space, opening up the frame by providing new and changing information about the space through which the camera is moving. One of the most common camera movements is re-framing, the slight adjustments made to shift the framing of the shot as characters change positions within the frame. Reframing is common in Hollywood movies: three-shots that become two-shots and subtle shifts of the frame to compensate for the different heights of various characters in the film.

Directors use the subjective feeling created by most camera movements to provide an additional cue that a shot is coming from a particular character's point of view. Hand-held camera movements, as we noted earlier, can also suggest a POV.

A number of action-oriented TV shows, such as *NYPD Blue,* use reframing to a much greater degree than conventional films. Often directors of these shows work their way into a scene through a series of long shots that move about as though someone were turning his or her head quickly to take in the whole area. This is sometimes referred to as a **rock 'n' roll** into a scene. They also use shaky movement that gives the appearance of hand-held shots although the cameras usually are actually mounted on tripods. Some Hollywood practitioners refer to this unstable movement as **Richter,** after the Richter scale that measures earthquakes. The more Richter the director calls for the shakier the camera movement is supposed to be.

Time

Any camera movement also involves a time element. Moving the camera takes time, and a director who chooses to use elaborate camera moves generally tends to emphasize the mise-en-scène (as opposed to editing) to tell the story. Moving back from a close-up to a two-shot usually takes longer than cutting directly from a close-up to a two-shot.

Camera movements can be slow or fast or any speed in between. Many directors have used the rhythmic quality of camera movement as a powerful, expressive tool. Abrupt, quick movements create a different feeling than long, majestic ones. Even a brief look at music videos on MTV provides many examples to illustrate the importance of time in camera movement.

Camera movements are most frequently based on the movement of the characters within the frame. But a director may also use camera movement to create a sense of expectation or suspense unrelated to the characters. A camera movement can also change our focus to some object or some part of the mise-en-scène that the director wants to emphasize.

In actual practice composing a shot is probably more intuitive than analytical. Through the composition of the image within the frame the director can choose to highlight, modify, shade, reinforce, or even undercut almost any element in the scene. A director making a narrative movie is undoubtedly working with a script, and whether the composition of a shot is good or bad depends more on what the director is trying to accomplish with a shot than on some abstract principle of pictorial composition. In some nonfiction productions, particularly documentary work, it may be perfectly acceptable, even normal, to refocus and reframe in the middle of an unsteady, hand-held shot. The same camera work would usually be considered out of place in a conventional theatrical film, however.

Color and Tonality

Manipulating the filmed image through the choice of film stock or in developing and printing is strikingly different from capturing an image on videotape. A black-and-white **slow film stock** (one less sensitive to light) records a richer range of grays and a sharper image than a **fast film stock** (one more sensitive to light). Faster film stocks also tend to yield grainier images with more contrast, an effect that may be enhanced in the processing and printing of the film. Slow and fast color film stocks have similar differences. In video, the color and tonal qualities do not depend on the choice of the stock.

Film Color

Different color film stocks (and even different stocks from different manufacturers) offer perceptibly different tonal qualities (one stock may emphasize the reds and yellows, another the blues and greens). And the lab can further manipulate all these differences when the film is processed and printed.

Color film is somewhat more expensive to shoot and process than black-and-white, which may be an important factor for student filmmakers. Furthermore, altering the image during processing or printing entails additional expense. But what filmmakers lose at the bank may be offset to some extent by the many ways they can manipulate the visual quality of the image.

Video Color

There is no such thing as color videotape or black-and-white videotape. In video, the same tape can be used to record both. In most cases it is easier to obtain black-and-white in postproduction than in production because most video cameras do not allow the user to shoot in black-and-white. During its early history the objective in black-and-white (and later color) video was for all pictures to have a similar tonality. Equipment was complicated and the engineers who operated it concentrated on obtaining consistent quality rather than artistic interpretation. As equipment has improved, directors and cinematographers have begun to experiment with the color and tonal qualities of video.

Black-and-White or Color

Despite the technical differences (and differing traditions) of the two media, most of the creative choices confronting the director and the camera operator remain the same. Color is the norm for commercial production in film and video, so the absence of color calls attention to itself. Television advertisers have clearly begun to recognize the attention-getting value of a black-and-white commercial. Some commercials extend this idea even further by colorizing the product in postproduction (the pink cherry cola can or ravishing new red hair rinse) to highlight the product in an otherwise black-and-white environment.

More commonly, black-and-white is used to evoke the past. Both film and television began as black-and-white media, with color becoming the standard as the technology evolved. An award-winning episode of the popular television series *Moonlighting* was shot in black-and-white to enhance its parody of the classic black-and-white film *Casablanca*. Woody Allen's comic "documentary" *Zelig* uses black-and-white in much the same way, suggesting not only the past but old movie newsreels as well. In fact, one of the clichés of student moviemaking is the use of black-and-white to cue flashbacks in a color film.

Director Martin Scorcese seemingly inverts this cliché in his black-and-white film *Raging Bull*. The only color material in this film consists of flashbacks to the La Motta family's faded color home movies. As noted earlier, Steven Speilberg's *Schindler's List* is shot in black-and-white, although the film is framed by color sequences at the beginning and end, and it contains two sequences with the red coat painted into what are otherwise black-and-white shots.

Black-and-white may be more appropriate than color for certain subjects. Movies meant to be somber or earthy may convey this mood better if shot in black-and-white. Woody Allen is one modern filmmaker who has shown an interest in using black-and-white for films, including *Stardust Memories* and *Manhattan*. With the evolution of the music video and MTV new interest is emerging in the many ways black-and-white (or black-and-white in combination with color) can be used to enhance the mood or meaning of a particular piece of music. Oliver Stone's *Natural Born Killers* switches between black-and-white and color within the same scene, mimicking the intercutting of color and black-and-white in many music videos.

Color Considerations

Much has been written about the aesthetics of color.[3] But even beyond the theorizing of the artists and scholars about the power of color to evoke specific emotions, most of us accept a number of cultural conventions about color. Whether we are buying fabric at the fabric store or talking to the interior decorator or housepainter, we have a tendency to describe certain colors (reds and yellows) as emotionally warm and other colors (blues or greens) as emotionally cool. One theory holds that warm colors make items appear large, close, heavy, and enduring, whereas cool colors make items appear small, far, light, and temporary.[4]

Certain colors seem to go together, and others seem to clash. Mixing colors opposite each other on the **color circle,** such as green and red, creates color contrast. Working with colors on the same side of the color circle creates color harmony. (See Color Plate 3.) Advertisers go to great lengths to determine what color of packaging encourages us to buy their products.[5]

In moviemaking many decisions about color are made during preproduction. The director, in conjunction with the art director, decides which colors are appropriate for the sets, costumes, props, and even makeup. Color can emphasize or deemphasize any element of the mise-en-scène. The camera can also be used to alter the emotional content of the shot with subtle shifts in color tonality. Think of the warm and homey glow of the typical hamburger chain's television commercials, or the way beer commercials tend to be shot in the orangish light of late afternoon (after work when the world is beautiful). In Robert Altman's western *McCabe and Mrs. Miller* the Golden West comes to life visually on screen. A dreamlike golden tone pervades most of this film, a technique that further heightens the contrast with the cold blue death of McCabe in a snowstorm at the end. Warren Beatty's film *Dick Tracy* uses vibrant primary colors to emphasize the story's comic book origins.

In filmmaking these effects can be produced to some degree in the laboratory as the film is being processed or printed. They can also be enhanced by placing a filter on the lens to warm (orange or reddish) or cool (blue or green) the image. Other types of filters can alter the contrast range of a shot or diffuse and soften the subject being photographed. You can use these same filters with a video camera, and a growing tendency in video seems to be to treat the image in a more photographic manner. See Chapter 6 for a discussion of filters.[6]

The same scene or subject can read in very different ways, depending on shot composition, framing, camera movement, and manipulation of the color and tonality of the image. The power to interpret the mise-en-scène with the camera is basic to the art of moviemaking. Choosing and controlling the type and quality of the shot is one of the most important decisions confronting the moviemaker, student and professional alike.

Shooting to Edit

The camera can move from a medium shot to a close-up (or the actor can move toward the camera and change a medium shot to a close-up), but this change of view is normally created through editing. Material shot during production will almost certainly be edited during postproduction. The eventual editing of the shot has a profound effect on the composition, framing, and movement created by the camera. (We discuss the aesthetics of editing in Chapter 12.)

Shot Selection

A **shot** begins the moment the camera begins recording the subject and ends when it stops. It can be long or short, but eventually it will be joined with other shots during editing. In narrative moviemaking the basic building block in the construction of the story is the **scene,** a unified action occurring in a single place and time. A scene is usually composed of a series of shots, though an entire scene can be one continuous shot.

To provide complete coverage of the scene the director usually shoots more shots than will actually be used in the final edited version. At the simplest level the objective is to provide a variety of shots of the physical action and dialogue in the scene. Imagine a simple one-minute scene in which a man and a woman eat breakfast while talking at the kitchen table. To ensure adequate coverage of this scene and to make certain that the needed shots will be available during editing, many directors begin by shooting a **master scene shot,** a fairly long shot showing both characters at the table as they play out the scene in its entirety. If used in the edited version of the motion picture, this one master scene shot would present all the dialogue and action within a single shot—a one-shot scene.

A director using the master scene shooting method would then begin to provide coverage of the scene with shots from a variety of angles and perspectives: close-ups of each actor delivering lines, two-shots, reaction shots of one character listening to the other talk, and **cut-ins** to some essential detail within the scene (for example, a piece of burned toast). Perhaps the last element in providing complete coverage of a scene is to shoot **cutaways,** shots of related details that are not actually part of the scene (such as the kitchen clock on a wall off-screen).

In the editing room these different shots will be cut together to build up the scene—beginning, perhaps, with a master shot of both actors, then cutting to a close-up of the clock, a two-shot of the woman talking, and a CU of the man listening. It is important that the director select shots that can be edited according to the action, dialogue, and dramatic needs of that particular scene. Directors always select shots with an eye to how they might be edited later.

Shot Duration

The director must also decide how long to shoot each shot. The dialogue or the movement of the actor within the scene often dictates the length or duration of a shot. Moving the camera (because it takes place in time) can also determine shot duration. In addition to the composition, framing, and use of camera movement, the duration of the shot deeply affects how we see and understand it. The viewer can absorb more during a shot of long duration than during one of short duration.

On the purely technical level providing extra time at the beginning and end of a shot for identification and editing purposes is important. In film and video the first few feet are needed to **slate,** or identify, the shot. In film-making the first few frames of the shot often contain overexposed frames (or *flashframes*), which are created while the camera is getting up to speed. Having a little more *head* or *tail* on each shot can prove invaluable in the editing room. Providing extra material for a given duration (five or ten seconds) can be just as vital for electronic editing, which requires preroll material.

The Long Shot, Medium Shot, Close-Up Pattern

The most conventional way to shoot a scene is to begin with an **establishing shot,** a shot that sets the scene and establishes the location. This often is a long shot (the apartment building), but it could be something like a sign (Mastroianni's Cafe) that tells us where the scene is taking place. Next, we move into the scene from long shots to medium shots and finally to close-ups. If the angle of view does not change sufficiently between the LS, MS, and CU, the shots will appear to jump when they are edited together. The conventional way to avoid this problem is to vary the angle of view at least 30 degrees from the previous shot (the so-called **30-degree rule**). Some critics have argued that the LS–MS–CU pattern is the most psychologically correct way to construct a scene because it is similar to the way our minds work.[7] When we walk into a dance in a large ballroom (establishing shot), we tend to survey the entire room (the long shot) until we spot a group of friends (the medium shot) and move over and begin talking to them (the close-up). The establishing shot, long shot, medium shot, close-up pattern draws us into the scene. We gather more and more information as the shots move closer and closer.

This pattern can also be reversed. Beginning with a close-up can create questions. Who is this character talking to? Where are we? Moving from close-up to the medium shot and long shot can answer these questions as each shot provides additional information about the scene. Again, there is nothing inherently right or wrong about any pattern, but unless the director selects the shots during the shooting phase of production (shooting to edit), they will not be available when the editing begins.

Shooting for Continuity

Technically, a single shot maintains **continuity,** a sense that the space we see in the shot and the time in the shot are continuous and uninterrupted. In conventional moviemaking continuity most often becomes an issue in the scene. Usually, scenes take place in a single location and in a continuous segment of time. This ar-

Top view

Camera view 1

Camera view 2

Figure 5.11
Anywhere within the 180-degree arc established from camera view 1, the two football players (A and B) will maintain the same spatial relationship—A on the left and B on the right. Crossing the axis, however (as in camera view 2), will reverse, or flip, A and B to the opposite sides of the screen.

rangement would not be a problem if the scene was shot with a single run of the camera. But because most scenes are composed of a variety of shots taken at different times and from different angles, continuity is often difficult to maintain during editing.

On the set of a typical Hollywood film continuity is almost an obsession. Crew members such as the **script supervisor** are constantly checking for continuity errors. Some of the most common gaffes involve costumes or props: the tie that changes color from one shot to the next or the cigarette that is a stub in the first shot but full-length in the next. Even something as simple as changing light values (when shots taken at different times of the day are edited together in what is supposed to be a continuous sequence of time) can violate continuity. This kind of error involves the mise-en-scène, but unless a director is consciously shooting to maintain continuity, the placement of the camera can also create problems.

Perhaps the most common technique for shooting to maintain continuity involves the **axis of action,** or the so-called **180-degree rule.** In any shot, whether it contains two people talking or a single person walking down the sidewalk, the principal axis of the action is identifiable. It is the imaginary line between the two people talking or the **screen direction** established by the walking character or moving object. If the camera is placed on one side of this imaginary line (anywhere within the 180-degree

arc on the same side of the line), spatial continuity will be maintained (see Figure 5.11). A shot that crosses the axis would, when edited, flip-flop character A and character B to opposite sides of the screen.

Similarly, crossing the axis of a walking character or moving car would make the person or car appear to reverse screen direction on the cut. As long as the camera is placed on the same side of the action line (again, within the 180 degrees), the character will seem to be moving in the same direction across the screen. A shot taken right on the axis (a neutral position in regard to the line) can be used as a transition between shots that would otherwise appear to cross the axis or reverse screen direction.[8] The photos in Figure 5.12 illustrate screen direction for a moving object.

Maintaining a constant screen direction also extends to the line of action established by a character looking off-screen. Imagine, again, two characters talking. We see character A in a close-up talking to character B, who is off-screen. In the next shot we see a close-up of character B responding to character A, who now is the one off-screen. Unless there is an **eyeline match** between the two shots, character A and character B will not appear to be talking to each other and might even appear to be distracted by something else off-screen (see Figure 5.13).

A radical change in the speed of a character or object (a car, for example) from one shot to the next also can violate continuity. The first few

Figure 5.12

Once a screen direction is established for a moving object, that direction needs to be clearly maintained. Photo a shows a vehicle moving right to left. A cut to a shot of the vehicle from the other side of the axis (photo b) would make it appear that the vehicle has reversed its direction of travel just at the moment the cut occurs. Once the right/left screen direction has been established as in photo a, it is normally maintained in subsequent shots, as in photo c.

Figure 5.13

Once the eyelines have been established in one shot (a), the eyes must maintain those directional lines in subsequent shots in order to match. The woman in photo b (correct eyeline match) appears to be looking in the correct direction for the man established in photo a. If the woman is supposed to be listening to the man, the eyeline match is wrong in photo c because she is looking away from him (and his eyes). The implication of cutting from shot a to shot c is that she is not really listening to him or that she has been distracted by something off-screen in the other direction.

steps people take when they are getting up to walking speed (almost always near the beginning of the shot) are appreciably slower than when they are already at full walking speed. If you cut together two shots of people walking down the street, you want their relative speed (and gait) to match up as you edit from one shot to another. A **match cut**—a cut that maintains a continuous sense of space and time from one shot to the next—can be extremely difficult to make unless the director has shot the material with an eye to editing.

The time-tested method of ensuring footage that can be match cut is to **overlap action** during shooting. Imagine two shots that are going to be match cut. A character (from an angle in the hall) comes up to a door and opens it. The next shot shows the character entering the doorway and coming into the room from an angle inside the room. To overlap the action during shooting the director should shoot the entire action (walking up to the door, opening it, and walking into the room) in both shots. By overlapping the action in this manner the director provides the editor with an almost infinite number of cutting places for matching the two shots.

Of course, continuity entails much more than the placement of the camera. It also depends on how the director stages the mise-en-scène for the camera and the way in which the editor puts the material together in postproduction. (We deal with the conventions of the continuity system in much greater detail in Chapter 12.)

Notes

1. See, for example, David Bordwell and Kristin Thompson, *Film Art: An Introduction* (New York: McGraw-Hill, 1993), pp. 145–184; and James Monaco, *How to Read a Film: The Art, Technology, Language, History and Theory of Film and Media* (New York: Oxford University Press, 1981), p. 148.
2. Noel Burch, *Theory of Film Practice,* trans. by Helen R. Lane (New York: Praeger, 1973), pp. 17–31.
3. Monaco, pp. 96–98; R. T. Ryan, *A History of Motion Picture Color Technology* (New York: Focal Press, 1977); Raymond Durgnat, "Colours and Contrasts," *Films and Filming,* November 1968, pp. 58–62; and Vincent LoBrutto, "Three Moods Prevail in *Dead Presidents,*" September 1995, pp. 59–66.
4. Herbert Zettl, *Sight-Sound-Motion: Applied Media Aesthetics* (Belmont, CA: Wadsworth, 1990), pp. 66–68.
5. Roy Paul Nelson, *The Design of Advertising: An Exploration of Current Practices and Techniques* (Dubuque, IA: William C. Brown, 1967), pp. 133–139.
6. In particular see Harry Mathias and Richard Patterson, *Electronic Cinematography: Achieving Photographic Control over the Video Image* (Belmont, CA: Wadsworth, 1985).
7. André Bazin, *What Is Cinema?* trans. by Hugh Gray (Berkeley: University of California Press, 1971), pp. 23–40.
8. Frank Beacham, "The Art of Crossing the Line," *TV Technology,* October 1991, pp. 30–31.

chapter six
Lights and Filters

Light is the key to recording an image on film or videotape. Whether the light record is created photochemically or electromagnetically, the cinematographer's first concern is to determine if there is enough light to record the image. The cinematographer's attention next shifts to how the light can best be shaped to fit the dramatic needs of the shot. Thus, creative control of the image involves not only the means to measure the light accurately but also the means to control it. This chapter deals with the tools needed to accomplish those tasks.

Measuring the Light

To obtain the correct exposure the amount of light reaching the film emulsion or electronic imaging device must be carefully governed. Too much light will result in an overexposed image; too little light will result in an underexposed image. The adjustable diaphragm in the lens is used to obtain the correct exposure setting. To calculate that setting an instrument called a **light meter** is used to measure the amount of light falling on or reflected by the subject.

A needle on a scale or dial usually presents this information, but many modern light meters produce a digital readout of the light reading. Cameras with built-in metering systems may display this information in the viewfinder. There are several basic types of light meters including incident and reflected meters.

Incident Meters

An **incident light meter** measures the amount of light falling on a particular person or area of a set. Commonly used incident meters, such as the Spectra, have a plastic hemisphere (which looks like half a Ping-Pong ball) over the light-sensitive cell on the meter (see Figure 6.1a). To use an incident meter, hold it next to the subject with the light-collector bulb pointed at the camera position. The intensity of the light reaching the hemisphere creates a light reading that can be measured. Usually, the top half of an incident meter swivels so that the person taking the light reading can read the scale without casting a shadow over the light-sensitive photocell.

An incident meter is generally considered the standard meter for professional cinematography. It is accurate, easy to use, and highly reliable. Because it measures the light hitting a *specific* area, it is not fooled by background light (or darkness). Therefore, it gives an objective light measurement from scene to scene. An incident meter is especially helpful when setting lights to a particular intensity for more than one camera setup.

Reflected Light Meters

A **reflected light meter** measures the amount of light reflected by the subject, providing an overall light reading for the entire scene (see Figure 6.1b). A reflected meter operates differently than an incident meter. You hold it next to the camera and point it at the subject or scene. Reflected light meters typically gather light from a relatively wide angle of view (or *acceptance*), creating a light measurement that is the average of the range of **brightness** levels within the scene. You can adapt many professional-quality incident meters for use as reflected meters.

A **spot meter** (see Figure 6.2) is a reflected light meter with a narrow angle of acceptance, often as little as one degree. Instead of averaging brightness across the entire scene, it provides a reading of a small, individual spot within the composition. A spot meter usually is shaped like a small camera. It has a pistol grip, eyepiece, and viewfinder to enable the operator to target the exact spot (usually designated by a small circle in the viewfinder) being measured. This is particularly useful when you are comparing brightness levels of different parts of the scene. Although they are reflected meters, spot meters can provide the same information as incident meters because they read light for small areas. In this way they combine the best features of incident meters and reflected meters.

a

Figure 6.2
A Minolta spot meter. (Photo courtesy of the Minolta Corporation)

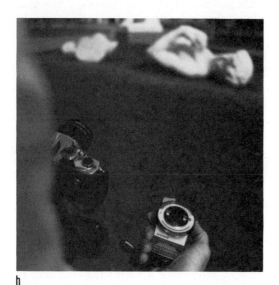
b

Figure 6.1
Photo a shows a Spectra incident meter with an ASA slide. The meters come with a packet of slides keyed to different ASAs. An incident meter is held next to the subject and pointed back toward the camera. Be careful not to skew the reading by blocking part of the light with your body. Photo b shows a reflected light meter held next to the camera and pointed toward the scene.

Automatic Metering Systems

The automatic exposure system built into most modern cameras is really just another type of reflected light meter. It measures the light com-

ing through the lens (usually a zoom lens) and automatically adjusts the iris to the proper setting. Because it is behind the lens, it will compensate for any light lost to filters or to the many elements within the lens itself. Some cameras use a zebra stripe pattern visible within the viewfinder to show areas at the upper limit of the camera's exposure range.[1] Others blink the words *low light* in the viewfinder when there is not enough light for an acceptable image.

Automatic exposure systems are extremely easy to use, which is one reason they are virtually standard on consumer-level cameras. They can be invaluable in situations in which the light cannot really be regulated or when shooting entails rapid, uncontrollable shifts in exposure levels, as in sports or documentaries.

Getting Correct Exposure

Light meters are simply tools. They cannot think nor can they know what you are trying to expose for within a shot. The brightness levels in a particular shot might range from f/2.8 to f/22 (or beyond), and this can pose problems for any type of light meter. In-camera meters, as noted previously, try to solve this problem either by averaging the light readings from the entire scene or by metering a smaller area in the center of the frame, which is called **center-weighted**

Figure 6.3
*A lighting situation such as this easily fools an automatic iris. The iris will close
too much because of the large amount of light in the scene's background. A center-
weighted light meter offers some correction. Other cameras have backlight compensation systems that increase exposure to make up, at least in part, for strong backlight.*

metering. It is also possible to use a hand-held
meter to take readings of different areas within
the frame and work out the average mathemati-
cally. What is important is interpreting the light
readings to suit your purpose.

Problems with Automatic Metering Systems

Certain lighting situations can easily fool reflected light meters, whether they are hand-held
or built into an automatic metering system in
the camera. Strong backlighting causes the most
common problem. A shot of the face of a person
who is standing in shade that is in front of a
bright, sunny background can result in a reading that greatly underexposes the face. The
meter averages the light for the entire scene, not
just the face, and produces a reading that over-
values the bright background. (See Figure 6.3
for an example of underexposure because of
backlighting.) The opposite could occur in a
shot of the face of a subject standing in bright
light against a large dark background.[2]

Using a spot meter or an incident meter is
one way to get a correct reading of the area of
the frame you are trying to expose. A zoom lens
with an in-camera metering system can also be
used as a kind of spot meter. By zooming in and
filling the frame with the person's face, you can
obtain the correct exposure setting. Then you

must manually override the automatic exposure
system (if that is possible with your camera) or
change the lighting setup (if that is possible). If
neither of those options is viable, it is probably
time to consider shooting the shot in a different
way.

Some cameras have a backlight control button that opens up the iris one f-stop (or more or
less) to compensate for strong backlighting.
Other cameras have an exposure lock that enables you to lock in a particular f-stop setting,
thus overriding the automatic iris system. Another technique for obtaining correct exposure
is to **bracket** your shots. Provided you can manually adjust the iris, you simply shoot the scene
with several different f-stop settings.

Because different types of light meters have
different strengths and weaknesses, it is probably wise to supplement an in-camera reflected
meter with a hand-held incident meter. When
working outdoors, many cinematographers prefer a reflected light meter. They usually choose
an incident meter when working indoors, where
the lighting can be totally controlled. You might
also consider bringing along your still camera.
You are probably quite familiar with its built-in
metering system and can use it to back up your
light readings on the set, as well as to provide
stills of your production.

Footcandles, F-Stops, and EI

Most light meters are calibrated to produce
readings in either footcandles or f-stops or in
both. A **footcandle** is an international unit of
illumination. It represents the amount of light
falling on a sphere 1 foot from a light source of
1 candlepower. In effect, a footcandle reading
on a light meter is a measurement of light intensity. If the light meter provides an **f-stop** reading, it must have some means of translating the
light intensity in the scene to a lens f-stop that
is accurate for the particular camera being used.

When metering for film, this usually means
that it is necessary to set the **ASA**, or **exposure
index (EI)**, of the particular film stock being
used. A film stock with an EI of 400, for example, is twice as sensitive to light as a film stock
with an EI of 200. Thus, the proper f-stop depends not only on the amount of light available
but also on how sensitive a particular film stock

is to light. With exactly the same light (that is, the same footcandle reading) an ASA of 100 might require an f-stop of f/8, whereas an ASA of 200 would require f/11. Each f-stop change (from f/2.8 to f/4, f/5.6, f/8, and so on) cuts the light that reaches the film in half.

The EI is set either by slipping a slide in front of the photosensitive cell or by turning a dial similar to the type used to set the film speed on a still camera.

Calculating the exposure index for a video camera is more complicated. The light sensitivity of a video camera cannot be boosted by changing the imaging device (as in buying a roll of faster film). Its responsiveness to light is, in effect, built in to that particular imaging system, whether pickup tubes or CCD sensors. Of course, many video cameras can boost the image signal electronically (a 6-dB increase in gain approximately doubles the exposure index). At the normal setting, however, most video cameras have an exposure index that is in the range of 100. With the proper video test equipment, determining the effective EI rating for any video camera is not difficult.[3]

Contrast Range

Contrast refers to the varying levels of brightness and darkness within a particular scene. A high-contrast scene would have extremely bright and dark areas with almost no gradations in between. In comparison, a low-contrast scene would be relatively flat, with the brightest and darkest areas of the scene at roughly the same luminance level. Normal contrast would exhibit a rich, full range of brightness levels between the darkest and brightest parts of the scene.[4]

By taking a light reading of the brightest and darkest areas of the scene, it is possible to calculate the contrast range, the ratio of the brightest value to the darkest value. For example, if the brightest area in the scene is eight times brighter than the darkest area of the scene, the contrast ratio for that scene would be expressed as 8:1 (a range of light three f-stops wide). A 16:1 contrast ratio would produce a range of light roughly four f-stops wide. Calculating the contrast ratio is relatively simple with a spot meter, but any reflected light meter can be used for this purpose by moving in closer and measuring the amount of light reflected by different objects across the scene.[5]

All film stocks and electronic imaging devices are limited in the range of brightness they can accurately reproduce. That range or latitude is designed into a particular film stock or video imaging system, although the contrast ratio in film is frequently altered during the developing process. Negative film stock has a greater latitude than reversal, and film generally has a greater latitude than electronic imaging systems. A shot exceeding the latitude of a particular imaging device will create areas of brightness or darkness in which all distinguishing details are lost. Thus, measuring the range of brightness within a scene is important not only for obtaining correct exposure but also for creatively manipulating the lighting for a scene.

Color negative film stock has a contrast ratio of approximately 128:1. This means it can record more discernible brightness levels (or shades of gray) than a typical video camera. In other words, a scene shot on film will produce a greater range of brightness levels than that same scene shot with the same lighting with a video camera. Details that would be discernible in the shadow area of the film version may not even be visible in the video version of the same scene. This reduced contrast range is one of the primary differences between film and video.[6]

Thinking of a video camera as just another kind of film stock may be helpful. The typical professional-level camera has an EI of about 100. Its contrast range exceeds reversal film stock but is an f-stop or so less than the contrast ratio for negative film. Many of the newer top-of-the-line chip cameras have an EI closer to 200, and they often contain circuitry that compresses the highlights and produces a contrast ratio equal to most film stocks.

Using a Monitor to Evaluate Exposure

One of the great advantages in shooting video is the ability to play back the recorded image and sound immediately after it has been recorded. This can be accomplished by rewinding the videotape in the camcorder (or VCR) and playing

Figure 6.4

A highly portable combination color monitor and waveform monitor. (Photo courtesy of Leader Instruments Corporation)

black level setup
(7.5 IRE)

Figure 6.5

The display on the waveform monitor allows the picture to be represented on a luminance scale. The bright areas in the picture register near the top (near 100 IRE). The monitor displays the darkest areas at the bottom, where the black level (7.5 IRE) is normally set. This is often called the pedestal level. If image brightness exceeds 100 IRE or falls below 7.5 IRE on the waveform monitor, the image will be distorted.

it through the camera viewfinder or through a portable television receiver, monitor, or combination monitor/receiver. This provides the director and cinematographer with immediate feedback about the overall look of the shot as well as the performance of the actors. In fact, this capability is available with many professional motion picture cameras that can be adapted to record an image on film and videotape simultaneously. This is usually referred to as **video assist.**

Most camera viewfinders display only a small black-and-white image, which reduces their usefulness in evaluating image quality. A portable color television monitor that can operate on batteries (in addition to AC power) is a better tool for judging a recording. Some portable VCRs or camcorders, particularly at the consumer level, have an RF output, which means you can use a regular television receiver for monitoring.

Despite the obvious benefits of instant picture review, a monitor can sometimes cause problems when used for image evaluation. It is seldom a satisfactory substitute for a light meter because the actual quality of the image being viewed depends on how accurately the portable monitor is calibrated. With portable gear that is constantly knocked around in transit or television receivers that are adapted for use in the field, image reproduction is seldom trustworthy. A light meter provides a comparable measurement of light values from one lighting setup to the next. Trying to use a monitor for this purpose is haphazard at best. Without the numeri-

cal values provided by a light meter, trying to match lighting setups can be total guesswork.

Using a Waveform Monitor to Evaluate Exposure

A **waveform monitor** is a far more accurate way of measuring and evaluating lighting. This piece of equipment is standard in any television studio, and it is also available in portable versions for use in the field. These portable units (see Figure 6.4) can operate on either DC (batteries) or regular AC power.

When a video signal from a camera is looped through a waveform monitor, the monitor's screen presents a graphic representation (see Figure 6.5) of the signal (the waveform). That signal is superimposed on a scale divided into 140 IRE units (IRE refers to the Institute of Radio Engineers). The picture information falls in the area between zero IRE units (the darkest area of the scene) and 100 IRE units (the peak white area of the scene). The blackest areas of the scene are actually set slightly above zero, at 7.5 units. The negative area at the bottom of the scale (between zero and −40 IRE units) displays

a

b

Figure 6.6

*The two fields on the waveform monitor show the waveform (photo a) of the 1-inch
metal videotape reel in photo b. Notice how the dark black cutouts in the videotape reel
are mirrored in the two rectangular areas just above the 7.5 IRE line on the waveform
monitor. The hole in the center of the videotape reel is less distinct on the waveform
monitor because it is reflecting some light. It is not as black as the rectangular cutouts
beside it. (Photo b courtesy of Maxell Corporation of America)*

information about the blanking and synchronizing pulses (see Figures 6.6a and 6.6b).[7]

The waveform monitor provides more information about the brightness and contrast range of a scene than any light meter. The area between 7.5 and 100 IRE units provides information that you can use to adjust the camera's imaging system (20 IRE units equal approximately one f-stop, hence a latitude of approximately five f-stops). Any area of the scene exceeding 100 IRE will be overexposed, and any area of the scene below 7.5 will be too dark to render visible detail. Obviously, this information can be used to set up and adjust lights. The waveform monitor displays the exposure levels for every point in the scene, like a full-frame spot meter. It also shows precisely which areas of the scene are above or below the contrast range the camera is capable of reproducing.

Some of the more professional video cameras display a crude waveform in the viewfinder, but this does not present the same kind of detailed information as a waveform monitor. Few schools have portable waveform monitors set aside for student use. The waveform monitor is usually mounted in the studio and used primarily by the college's video engineer. But as sophisticated location lighting becomes more commonplace in video, students will need increased access to portable waveform monitors and the training to use them properly.

The Color of Light

Thus far we have been concerned primarily with different ways to monitor and measure light intensity. The color of light in the scene is also an important concern for the cinematographer. Different light sources produce different colors. Being able to measure and compensate for those color variations is as much a part of quality image making as controlling exposure.

The Electromagnetic Spectrum

Our eyes can see only a small portion of radiated energy in the **electromagnetic spectrum.** Electromagnetic energy is measured according to **wavelengths** and ranges from the microscopically small wavelengths of cosmic rays to electrical power waves several miles long. Visible light is only a tiny portion of that spectrum, ranging from the shorter violets to the longer blue, green, yellow, and red wavelengths. The wavelengths just below and above the visible spectrum, X rays and infrared, cannot be seen by the eye but can be recorded on special film. (See Color Plate 4.)

Our eyes see different wavelengths as different colors. White light is composed of all the visible wavelengths. When white light falls on an object like a red flower, it reflects the red wavelengths and absorbs the other wavelengths (primarily the greens and blues). If the color of the light illuminating that flower is changed, our perception of that flower's color will also change. The way we perceive colors is based on both the particular wavelengths (colors) of light illuminating an object and the wavelengths of light that the object absorbs. This fact has important implications for cinematography. It means that a filter can be used to modify the light by absorbing certain colors and letting other colors pass through.

Figure 6.7

A color temperature meter with digital readout. (Photo courtesy of the Minolta Corporation)

The Kelvin Scale

What we perceive as the white light of the sun is actually made up of roughly equal parts of red, green, and blue light. The color of sunlight is constantly changing, according to the time of day or the way that light is reflected through clouds or smog in the air. As the sun sets toward the horizon, the longer red wavelengths and denser atmosphere create a redder color. If the noonday sun is reflected through a cover of clouds, the light may seem almost blue.

A **color temperature** scale was developed to provide a precise and accurate measurement of different colors of light. This scale is expressed in degrees **Kelvin** (K). As a theoretical black body source is heated, it will give off light. Imagine a chunk of iron heated over a powerful flame. As the metal begins to heat, it will start glowing red. As it gets even hotter, it will turn orange and then white and finally blue-white. These changes can be measured on the Kelvin scale. The sun at noon, for example, has a color temperature of about 5,500 degrees Kelvin, whereas the color temperature at sunrise could be as low as 1,800 degrees Kelvin. This can be a little confusing because we tend to think of red

light as hot and blue light as cold. But in terms of color temperature, the lower the color temperature the redder the light and the higher the color temperature the bluer the light. (See Color Plate 5.)

A special type of light meter, called a *color temperature meter,* registers the specific color of light in degrees Kelvin. It also specifies the type of filters that should be used to obtain a particular color temperature (see Figure 6.7).

Tungsten and Daylight-Balanced Light

Our eyes (and brains) have the ability to compensate for large changes in the color of light and still see seemingly accurate, believable color. Film and video cameras cannot do this, however. Color film stocks and electronic imaging devices can only produce correct colors within a relatively limited range on the Kelvin scale. This is accomplished in film and video in a somewhat different manner, but the basic principles are the same.

Color Plates

Color Plate 1

The actual properties of the color video image are based on the hue (the specific color), of strength or purity of the color (its saturation), and the brightness information (luminance), which indicates the amount of light being reflected or given off. In the development of NTSC color video, the chrominance information (hue and saturation) was designed so that if could be added onto an existing black and white signal (the luminance information). This maintained compatibility with existing black and white television receivers that could simply ignore the color information of a program broadcast in color.

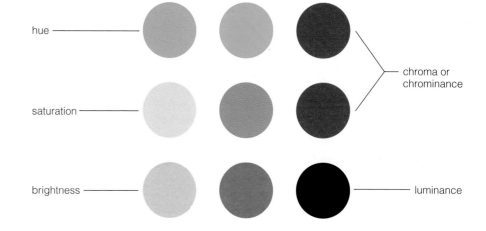

hue

saturation

brightness

chroma or chrominance

luminance

Color Plate 2

Additive color mixing. In video all colors can be produced by mixing together various quantities of the three primary colors (red, green, blue). Where the primary colors overlap, they produce the secondary colors cyan, yellow, and magenta. Magenta, for example, results from mixing red and blue. An equal mixture of the three primary colors produces white.

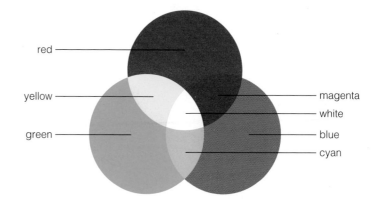

red

yellow

green

magenta

white

blue

cyan

Color Plate 3

This color circle shows the colors of the visible spectrum as they gradually merge into each other. The primary colors (red, green, blue) are on the opposite side of the color circle from their complementary colors (cyan, magenta, yellow).

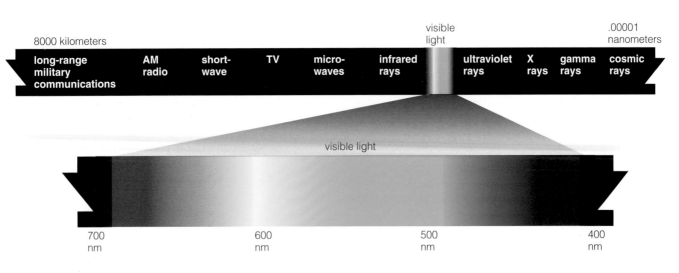

Color Plate 4

Electromagnetic spectrum wavelengths. The human eye can see only a small part of the visible spectrum, ranging from the short violet wavelengths to the longer orange and red wavelengths.

Color Plate 6

Color conversion filters. The commonly used orange 85 filter (left) is used to convert 5500-degree-Kelvin daylight to 3200 degrees Kelvin for use with a tungsten-balanced film stock or electronic imaging device. The blue 80A filter (right) is used for shooting daylight-balanced film (5500 degrees Kelvin) under lights that are balanced at 3200 degrees Kelvin.

reflected sunlight	9000°K
hazy sky	8000°K
overcast sky	7000°K
bright sunlight	6000°K
sunlight at noon	
	5000°K
light in the morning and late afternoon	4000°K
quartz light	
household light bulb	3000°K
sunrise and sunset	2000°K
candle flame	1000°K

Color Plate 5

The color temperature of some common light sources.

a

b

Color Plate 7

(a) Shooting in sunlight (5500 degrees Kelvin) with film or with an electronic imaging device balanced for 3200 degrees Kelvin produces a bluish image.
(b) With the orange 85 color conversion filter in place, the daylight is converted to a color temperature that more correctly matches the imaging system.

Color Plate 8

Cinematographer Vittorio Storaro utilizes "golden time" throughout Francis Ford Coppola's Tucker: The Man and His Dream. *In this scene the rich, warm lighting underscores a happy family moment in the Tucker front yard. (™ and © Lucasfilm Ltd. [LFL] 1988. All Rights Reserved. Courtesy of Lucasfilm Ltd.)*

Color Plate 9

Night-for-night lighting in Tucker. *Turning all the lights on in the Tucker car assembly plant provides not only backlighting for the actors but also motivation for the unseen light source illuminating them form the upper right-hand side of the frame. (™ and © Lucasfilm Ltd. [LFL] 1988. All Rights Reserved. Courtesy of Lucasfilm Ltd.)*

Color Plate 10

As more and more production and post-production employs digital technologies, computer programs play an increasing role. For example, this multi-screen display from Cakewalk *shows different windows for music, timing, track building, and editing. (Photo courtesy of Cakewalk Music Software)*

In film, you can compensate for color changes by purchasing a film stock that is **color balanced** for use in either daylight (5,500 degrees Kelvin) or tungsten light (3,200 degrees Kelvin). When used with lights rated at 3,200 degrees Kelvin, tungsten-balanced film will produce correct colors. If that same stock is used outdoors, color rendition will be skewed by the much bluer 5,500-degree-Kelvin color temperature of the sunlight. Using tungsten-balanced film stock outdoors requires a **color conversion filter** such as a Wratten 85 or 85B filter. These orange filters effectively convert the more bluish sunlight outdoors to the color balance of the tungsten film. Conversely, a daylight-balanced film stock can be used outdoors without a filter. But using that same daylight-balanced stock in the more reddish tungsten light requires a blue filter, such as a Wratten 80 or 80A, to obtain the correct color balance. (See Color Plates 6 and 7.)

Video does not have daylight-balanced pickup tubes or CCD sensors. Video imaging systems are always balanced for tungsten light. Using a video camera outdoors in daylight requires the same type of orange 85 filter used in film, but because it is built into the camera it is not easy to see. Many video cameras have a built-in **filter wheel** that enables the operator to dial in the correct filter for a variety of lighting sources. Such cameras typically have a setting for tungsten lights at 3,200 degrees (actually no filter), a setting for daylight (5,500 degrees), and perhaps an intermediate setting at 4,500 degrees. Some cameras may have only two settings, one for daylight and one for artificial light. These are often represented by graphics of the sun and a lightbulb. Other less expensive cameras may have no filter settings. They have an automatic color correction circuit that makes all color adjustments, and they may not have a manual override.

Small-Scale Color Corrections

The human eye can detect changes in color temperature as small as 100 degrees Kelvin. For this reason, you often must correct for slight variations in color that are much smaller than the broad changes made by color conversion filters such as the orange Wratten 85 filter. Another category of filters, called **light-balancing filters** or **color-compensating filters,** has been de-

signed for this purpose. They are used on the film camera to compensate for subtle shifts in color temperature.

Generally, these filters are paler in color than the heavier color conversion filters used to correct between sunlight and artificial light. Their colors tend to fall at either the blue end or the red end of the color spectrum. Cinematographers often use them to warm up (a yellow to red filter) or cool down (a blue to purple filter) a particular light source.

In video, obtaining this kind of small-scale color correction is much easier. In fact, it is precisely the type of color correction produced by **white balancing.** Once you set large-scale color correction with the filter wheel, white balancing fine-tunes the color, adjusting the camera precisely to the color temperature of any light source.

You do this by pointing the camera at a white surface such as a piece of white paper or a white T-shirt. Zoom the lens in to fill the frame with the white surface, and then press the white-balance button on the camera. A microprocessor in the camera automatically adjusts the imaging device to produce an accurate white in that light. In effect, the automatic white circuit knows what white is (almost equal amounts of red, blue, and green), and white balancing simply adjusts the system to reproduce white at the specific color temperature of the light in a scene. This setting for white will remain in memory until you press the white-balance button again, which you should do with any change of lighting. You could rebalance as often as every shot outdoors, where the color temperature may be constantly shifting because of the movement of the clouds or sun. Some video cameras have an automatic white-balance circuit that operates continuously unless the operator specifically sets an override mode.

You can also use the white-balancing circuit to produce the kind of warming and cooling effects created by light-balancing filters. By white balancing the camera on a colored card rather than a white one, you tint the entire scene. When you do this, you are in effect lying to the white-balancing circuit of your camera. Pressing the white-balance button automatically equalizes the amount of red, green, and blue (the definition of pure white) and produces all the other colors in their natural relationship to white. White balancing on a light blue card, for example, produces a color tint toward the opposite end of the color spectrum (that is, a warmer orange), whereas balancing on an orangish card produces a cooler, more bluish tint. You may need to experiment a little to get the effect you want, but you can check the results immediately with an accurate color monitor.

To obtain comparable control of small color variations in film requires a color temperature meter and a case full of finely graded light-balancing filters. And the color correction still would not be as accurate as the white-balancing process in video cameras.

The Vectorscope

In video, a **vectorscope** is used to monitor the color information in the video signal. It is used primarily to match the color between cameras in multicamera productions and to analyze and adjust color during postproduction (see Chapter 11).

The screen of a vectorscope presents a graphic display of the color information in the video signal. It shows the **hue** (the specific tint, such as blue, yellow, or orange) and the **saturation** of that hue (the degree to which the color is mixed with white light). A royal blue, for example, contains less white light than a baby blue. In other words, the royal blue is more saturated (less diluted) than the baby blue. Portable vectorscopes (see Figure 6.8) are used in the field to analyze the color characteristics of various scenes, but a vectorscope is generally less valuable than a waveform monitor as a location production tool.[8]

Filters for Film and Video

In addition to the filters used to correct color balance and color temperature, there are many other filters that change the image in a variety of ways. Among the most common are **neutral density filters.** They reduce the intensity of the light reaching the imaging system without altering the color of the light in any way. They are designed primarily to bring the light down to a level that the camera can handle. For this reason they are most commonly used for shooting in very bright light. Neutral density filters are cali-

Figure 6.8
An extremely small battery-powered vectorscope. (Photo courtesy of Leader Instruments Corporation)

brated according to their density, the amount of light they block. An ND-3 filter, for example, reduces the amount of light transmitted through it by one f-stop, an ND-6 by two f-stops.

A **graduated neutral density filter** is a special type of neutral density filter that darkens only part of the frame, usually the top. This is helpful on bright sunny days when the sky is too bright to allow correct exposure of the foreground. If you expose for the foreground (probably the most important area of the shot), you will overexpose the sky, hence the graduated neutral density filter. Such filters have a clear area that gradually becomes a neutral density gray. You align the neutral density half of the filter with the sky at the horizon, which allows proper exposure of the sky and clouds without affecting exposure (in the clear part of the filter) at ground level in the foreground.

Neutral density filters reduce all wavelengths of light equally, so they do not change the color temperature of the light transmitted through them. This neutrality means they can be combined with many other types of filters. An 85ND-6 filter combines the orange 85 color correction filter with a neutral density filter that reduces the light transmission by two f-stops. The filter wheels on many video cameras contain this type of combined neutral density–color conversion filter. Cameras that have a setting for clouds and bright sunlight usually have a plain 85 filter for the former and a combined 85–neutral density filter for the latter.

Several types of filters eliminate haze. A **haze filter** is particularly useful for eliminating the bluish cast often seen on overcast days. The **ultraviolet (UV) filter** performs a similar function by blocking out ultraviolet rays. Outdoors, many photographers simply leave a UV filter on their camera at all times. It is clear and has no effect on regular light frequencies. In black-and-white photography a pale yellow **sky filter** usually corrects the overexposure and loss of detail caused by haze.

Polarizing filters may also help eliminate haze and darken a blue sky, but their primary use is to minimize reflections from water or glass. The amount of polarization depends on the angle of light between the camera lens and the surface of the glass or water. Shooting at about a 30-degree angle to the reflective surface and then rotating the filter for maximum absorption of glare usually yields the best results.

Diffusion filters have a rippled surface or an extremely fine, netlike pattern that scatters (diffuses) the light and creates a softer, less detailed image. In the heyday of the Hollywood studio system cinematographers would often put a fine silk mesh over the lens to photograph the movie's female star. This reduced wrinkles and other blemishes and produced the same effect created by diffusion filters—a softer, more dreamlike, and romantic image. The amount of diffusion a filter provides depends on its grade (how dense it is) as well as the lighting, contrast, and size of the subject in the shot. In general, long shots require less diffusion than close-ups.

Star filters are a special kind of diffusion filter. A grid of parallel lines etched into the filter surface turns any bright point of light in the scene into a bright star pattern.

Fog filters break up the light like diffusion filters but scatter that light from the bright picture areas into the shadow areas. The result is a light fog effect that tends to lower contrast and soften the shot, creating a mysterious, foreboding feeling. **Double-fog filters** also produce a fog effect but without reducing sharpness.

Not surprisingly, **low-contrast filters** reduce contrast and color saturation. They are among the most useful filters for exterior shooting and are frequently credited with creating a film look in video. On a bright sunny day the direct sun casts extremely hard shadows. It also produces a much greater range of brightness levels in the scene. As a result, the camera cannot properly expose the shadows and the highlights. This is where a low-contrast filter is most useful. It uses light from the highlights within the scene, scat-

tering the light to brighten up the shadow areas, usually without reducing sharpness. This can be invaluable in any high-contrast lighting situation and can be particularly helpful in video.

Soft-contrast filters also reduce contrast but preserve a darker shadow area than low-contrast filters. They diminish the highlights without lightening the shadow area. The bottom line for both low-contrast and soft-contrast filters is reducing the contrast range. Whether you do this by brightening the underexposed areas of the shot or darkening the overexposed areas is less important than reducing the contrast range to a level the imaging system can handle.[9]

Using Filters

Filters are normally made out of either gelatin or glass. **Gelatin filters** are the least expensive and come in small sheets that you can cut to the proper size for the lens or filter holder. You can also place large sheets (or rolls) of gelatin filter over windows or fit them into holders on the front of lighting instruments to change the color temperature in mixed lighting situations.[10]

Glass filters may have a gel cemented between two sheets of optical glass, or they may have dyes laminated between two sheets of optical glass. The least expensive glass filters have dyes added directly to the glass during manufacturing.

Mounting Filters

Glass filters normally mount in front of the lens and must be of the proper size and type for a particular piece of equipment. Some glass filters screw directly into threads on the front of the lens and must be sized exactly to the diameter of that particular lens. Others mount on the lens with a special adapter ring and are held in place by a lens hood or matched retaining ring. You can also mount glass filters in a **matte box**, sometimes called a *filter box*. It is an adjustable bellows that attaches to the front of the camera body and extends beyond the lens. Squares of filter glass simply drop into the matte box, an arrangement that offers several advantages. Filters used in a filter box are cheaper because they do not have to be mounted (and threaded) on a specific lens. A matte box makes it easy to stack multiple filters, to drop in a cutout for such effects as binoculars or a keyhole, or to use the same filters with different cameras (because the filter does not have to screw into a particular lens size).

You can mount gelatin filters in a variety of ways. With a matte box you cut the filter to the proper size, place it in a holder, and mount it at the rear of the matte box. It is also possible to attach gelatin filters to the front of the lens with an adapter and retaining ring. Some film cameras, such as the Bolex or CP-16, have a filter slot behind the lens. A gelatin filter is cut to fit into a small metal holder and then inserted in the filter slot behind the lens. In some of the better video cameras a new filter can be added to the filter wheel.

Compensating for Filters

As we have already seen, filters work by absorbing certain wavelengths of light and transmitting others. This means that obtaining proper exposure usually requires some iris adjustment. A camera with a built-in light-metering system automatically compensates for the amount of light absorbed by a filter. When working with a separate meter, however, you must change the exposure according to the amount of light the filter prevents from reaching the imaging system. The degree of exposure compensation required for different grades of filters is usually expressed as a filter factor, a number based on the amount of light transmitted through the filter.[11]

The filter manufacturer normally supplies exposure compensation tables and an explanation of the filter grading system. In film production, recalculating the EI, taking into account how much exposure is affected by the filter, may be easier. Kodak does this on the film box for its motion picture film stocks. For example, Kodak's Video News Film (7240) has an EI rating of 125 without a filter but an EI of 80 when it is shot with the orange 85 filter required for daylight shooting.

Care of Filters

Because filters sit directly in the light path (either in front of the lens or behind it), they should be treated with the same care as a lens.

Gelatin filters are so soft and easily damaged that they should be handled only by their edges and cleaned with a camel hair brush. Fortunately, gelatin filters are inexpensive and if damaged should simply be replaced.

Fingerprints can scratch or smudge glass filters. Carry them in a protective case and keep them immaculately clean. Once damaged, they cannot be repaired. It makes no sense to shoot with a high-quality camera and lens and then degrade the image they create by using a damaged filter.

A plain, clear glass filter is one of the least expensive ways to protect the costly lens on your camera. Mounted in front of the lens, it will shield the irreplaceable lens surface from scratches, water, and dirt. If it is damaged, you simply throw the $10 glass filter away, something you would not do with an expensive zoom lens. Many professional cinematographers use relatively inexpensive daylight or UV filters in the same manner.

Artificial Lighting

The lights used in film or television production come in a seemingly infinite variety of sizes and shapes. They are categorized by the intensity and quality of light they produce and by other characteristics, such as the way they are mounted or how they control the light they emit.

Types of Lamps

Incandescent lights, similar in construction to a typical household lightbulb, are common sources of artificial illumination. They contain a metal tungsten filament sealed to form a vacuum in a glass bulb or lamp. When electric current passes through the metal filament, the filament heats up and produces light. The more resistance the filament has, the brighter (and hotter) the light glows and the more power it consumes. This difference is expressed in **watts,** a measurement of the amount of electric current a particular bulb draws. Thus, a 500-watt incandescent bulb produces more illumination and requires more power than a 100-watt bulb.

The incandescent tungsten lightbulbs used for television and film lighting come in a wide

Figure 6.9
Many photoflood bulbs have a built-in reflector.

Figure 6.10
A quartz-halogen bulb in a highly portable lamp housing. (Photo courtesy of Mole-Richardson, Hollywood, U.S.A.)

range of wattages.[12] They insert in a lighting instrument with either a flanged base that is pushed down and locked into place or with thin pins that plug directly into the lamp socket. Another common type of tungsten-filament incandescent lamp, called a **photoflood** (see Figure 6.9), has a standard screw base so it can be used with a normal household lighting fixture. The photoflood lamp is one of the least expensive lamps.

The principal drawback of regular tungsten incandescent bulbs is that their color temperature and light output drop as the bulb is used. As the tungsten filament evaporates, it deposits a tungsten coating on the inside of the glass lamp. This can occur after only a few hours of use, and although it may not be immediately visible to the naked eye, the color temperature can easily drop below the standard 3,200-degree Kelvin rating.

Because of this problem most modern professional lighting equipment has converted to **tungsten-halogen lamps**, also called **quartz-halogen** or **quartz lamps** (see Figure 6.10). These lamps also are incandescent lamps, but the bulb itself is made of quartz glass (to withstand the heat), and it is filled with a halogen gas. This creates a sort of restoration cycle. The halogen gas helps to deposit the evaporating tungsten back on the filament as the lamp burns.

The result is a lamp that maintains its color temperature and light output far longer than regular tungsten-filament incandescent lamps. Quartz lights are also smaller and more portable than regular incandescent lamps.

Be especially careful to avoid touching the surface of a tungsten-halogen bulb. Oil from the fingers, or any foreign material for that matter, will weaken the quartz envelope and cause it to burn out much more quickly. The bulb might even explode when it gets hot. When changing a quartz bulb, you must use a glove or a piece of cloth or paper to protect it.

Situations that call for daylight-balanced lighting of about 5,500 degrees Kelvin often use special **HMI lights** (HMI is the abbreviation for *hydrogen medium-arc-length iodide*). (Figure 6.11 shows an HMI light.) This type of discharge light represents an improvement over the bulky carbon arc lights once used for this purpose. HMI lights are lighter and extremely efficient. They generate more illumination and produce less heat than an incandescent or tungsten-halogen lamp of the same wattage. HMI lights have a restoration cycle similar to that of a quartz light and maintain their color temperature and light output for long periods. They are frequently used as a supplemental light outdoors or to illuminate large areas. They are expensive, however, and require a large and bulky ballast unit

Figure 6.11

An HMI light, shown with its ballast, produces daylight-balanced light with less heat and lower power requirements than incandescent lights. (Photo courtesy of LTM Corporation of America)

(high-voltage power supply) to produce consistent lighting.

In some lighting situations converting regular 3,200-degree-Kelvin tungsten-balanced lamps to the color temperature of daylight may be necessary. This is done by using blue **dichroic filters** that attach to the front of the light housing. Because these filters reduce the light output of the lamp by 30 to 40 percent, additional lighting instruments may be necessary to obtain the same amount of illumination.

In the last few years a new type of light source that uses special "full spectrum" fluorescent bulbs has been developed. Traditionally, fluorescent lights—the kind so common in schools and office buildings—have proved a difficult and unpredictable light source for shooting film or video. Their color rendering in the reds is usually poor. This new type of three-band lighting, however, uses improved fluorescent/phosphorescent bulbs that produce a sustained and stable light source in the red, green, and blue (RGB) portions of the visible spectrum. This kind of lighting uses much less energy than typical tungsten lighting and generates far less heat.[13]

Basic Lighting Instruments

Lighting instruments also are typically classified by the quality of the light they produce and how the light can be shaped and controlled by the lighting instrument itself. *Hard* and *soft* are the most common terms for describing light quality. A **hard light** has a narrow angle of illumination and produces sharp, clearly defined shadows, whereas a **soft light** scatters the light to create a much wider angle of gentle, diffused illumination.

Most lamps sit in some type of reflective housing that helps to control and direct the beam of the light. A **parabolic reflector** tends to produce a more concentrated beam of hard light. In contrast, a **softlight reflector** blocks the light directly in front of the lamp and bounces the light back into and off the reflector's surface. The result is soft, diffused light with the degree of softness determined in part by whether the reflector's surface is highly polished or matted.

Lighting equipment manufacturers and rental houses frequently categorize different types of lights according to their primary function. From this perspective lighting instruments are often classified as **key lights, fill lights,** or **scenery** (or **background**) **lights**. Key lights provide the main source of illumination in a typical lighting setup, so they tend to be powerful lights with a beam width that can be focused. Key lights come in a variety of closed-face (usually with a lens) and open-face designs. Fill lights supplement key lights, reducing the shadows and contrast range in relation to the key light. Fill lights usually produce a softer, more diffused light. They are often open faced and are usually more limited in their ability to vary the angle of illumination. Many, in fact, have fixed focus. Scenery lights add depth and control contrast between the subject and the background or set. They are often a form of soft light and provide flat, even lighting over a wide area.

Describing lights by their function has definite limitations. A lighting instrument can serve many purposes. A light sold as a key light can easily be used as a fill light. The real issue is not what the light is called but whether the light does what you want it to do in a particular situation. Nevertheless, some understanding of the basic strengths and weaknesses of different types of lighting instruments is important.

a

b

Figure 6.12
(a) A spotlight in the spot position with the bulb moved toward the back of the lamp housing, and (b) a spotlight in the full flood position with the bulb moved toward the front lens.

Figure 6.13
A Fresnel spotlight with barndoors attached. (Photo courtesy of Strand Lighting)

Figure 6.14
An open-face quartz spotlight with barndoors. (Photo courtesy of Sachtler Corporation of America)

Lights are also classified as to whether they are **spotlights** or **floodlights.** The former usually illuminate small, concentrated areas while the latter cast a diffused and even beam of light over a fairly large area. However, many spotlights are variable and can cover either a small or large area. The **Fresnel spotlight** is one of the most widely used lights in professional film and television production. You can vary its beam width by adjusting a control knob or lever on the back of the light that moves the bulb-reflector unit toward or away from the Fresnel lens. In some cases moving the lens itself produces this effect. At the **spot** position the lamp is farthest from the lens. This converges the light rays and produces a narrower, more concentrated beam. At the other end of the adjustment range, the **flood** position, the lamp moves closer to the lens (see Figure 6.12). Flooding creates a wider and somewhat more diffused beam of light that illuminates a broader area.

Common uses of Fresnels are as key lights or to light essential areas of the set, but their controllable beam width means they can be adapted for almost any application (see Figure 6.13). They come in many wattages and with various types of lamps—regular tungsten incandescent, tungsten-halogen, or HMI.

Some variable beam spotlights do not have lenses. For the lightweight and highly portable quartz spotlights used for location lighting, an open-face design is commonplace (see Figure 6.14). Although providing less beam control than a Fresnel, this type of instrument does allow the beam width to be varied from spot to flood.

Another type of spotlight has the reflector unit and focusing lens built right into the bulb. The beam width of such **internal reflector spotlights** is fixed, but different bulbs can be purchased with a greater or lesser degree of spotting. This same basic internal reflector lamp design is used in **PAR lights** (PAR stands for *parabolic*

Figure 6.15
A nine-lamp MicroBrute PAR light is small enough to be transported easily. (Photo courtesy of Great American Market)

Figure 6.16
A scoop. (Photo courtesy of Strand Lighting)

Figure 6.17
A quartz lamp broad on a lightweight stand. (Photo courtesy of Mole-Richardson, Hollywood, U.S.A.)

aluminized reflector). PAR lights are available in clusters of six to twelve bulbs with varying beam widths and a color temperature of either 3,200 degrees Kelvin or 5,500 degrees Kelvin. (Figure 6.15 shows a PAR light bank.) Filmmakers use them to light large areas or to provide daylight-balanced fill light outdoors.

Lens-less, open-face lighting instruments come in many other varieties. Most of these lights are some form of floodlight. One of the oldest types, a **scoop**, contains a single bulb in a bowl-shaped metal reflector (see Figure 6.16). Scoops range in diameter from 10 to 18 inches, and the beam width of some scoops is somewhat adjustable.

Broads are rectangular floodlights that typically use quartz lamps in an open-face housing (see Figure 6.17). They produce a broad beam of relatively diffused light and are often used for fill lighting.

Softlights (see Figure 6.18) create a more diffused and even light than broads. The light they provide is virtually shadowless because the bulbs are either recessed at the bottom of the instruments, usually in the larger softlights, or hidden behind a shield at the front of the housing in the smaller, more portable units. The light from the lamp never reaches the subject directly. Instead, it bounces off the reflective surface at the back of the instrument, producing an extremely soft light that is often used for fill or contrast reduction.

Many lighting equipment manufacturers sell portable lighting kits for location use. Such kits

Figure 6.18
A softlight with the lamps recessed along the bottom. (Photo courtesy of Strand Lighting)

a

Figure 6.19
A portable location lighting kit with case, stands, flags, umbrellas, and various lighting instruments. (Photo courtesy of Lowell-Light Manufacturing, Inc.)

b

Figure 6.20
A small portable battery-powered sun gun (photo a) is most often used in a news/interview setting. A camera light (photo b) mounts on a shoe on the top of the camera. (Photo a courtesy of Sachtler Corporation of America; photo b courtesy of Sima Products Corporation)

usually contain three or four small lighting instruments with stands, extension cords, and other accessories in a carrying case (see Figure 6.19). Location kits typically use quartz lamps ranging from 500 to 1,000 watts, and most portable instruments are open faced (broads or softlights). Small Fresnel spotlights are also available.

The smallest and most portable lighting instruments, called **camera lights** or **sun guns** (see Figure 6.20), are used primarily for electronic news gathering or documentary work and only then in situations in which the flat, straight-on

Figure 6.21

(a) A lightweight telescoping light stand, and (b) a somewhat heavier light stand. (Photos courtesy of Mole-Richardson, Hollywood, U.S.A.)

Figure 6.22

A softlight mounted on a boom arm. (Photo courtesy of Lowell-Light Manufacturing, Inc.)

lighting they provide is absolutely necessary. This type of light is usually battery powered and can be mounted directly atop the camera or held with a pistol grip. For maximum efficiency battery-powered lights typically use low-wattage tungsten-halogen lamps. Battery-powered lights begin to lose color temperature as the battery drains.

Mounting Equipment

In the studio lights usually hang from a grid of pipes on the ceiling. Elsewhere, the most common mounting device is a **light stand.** Stands are made of metal, have tripod bases, and vary in size from the light alloy stands found in portable lighting kits to heavy-duty C-stands equipped with casters. They can be telescoped to a height of 6 to 8 feet (see Figure 6.21).

Telescoping **boom arms** (see Figure 6.22) and **extendable lighting poles** often hold lighter, more portable instruments. Another common mounting device is the **trombone,** which hooks over and behind the set wall with the light supported by a pin at the bottom. **Wall plates** or **base plates** are sometimes used to attach lights to flat surfaces.

Alligator clamps (also called **gaffer grips**) are spring-loaded clamps that can be used to secure a lightweight instrument almost anywhere. They are frequently found in portable lighting kits, as are **universal clamps,** small metal clamps

that attach to a porcelain socket for holding photofloods. One of the most widely used light-securing devices, a **C-clamp,** attaches lighting instruments to a lighting grid or lighting pole. The screw in the C-clamp locks the clamp securely to the support. Figure 6.23 shows a variety of clamps and mounts.

Controlling the Light

If lighting is going to be used expressively, it must do more than simply provide enough illumination to ensure proper exposure. It must in some way be controlled so that it falls in the proper places, assumes the desired shapes, and creates the proper intensity of illumination. A number of lighting aids have been developed to control and direct the light.

Barndoors, for example, block off the beam of light, preventing unwanted shadows and keeping direct light out of the camera lens. They are thin metal sheets on a frame that attaches to the front of the lamp housing. They are available for most lighting instruments in either a two-leaf or four-leaf design (see Figures 6.13 and 6.14). **Snoots** serve a similar purpose. They are metal funnels of different diameters that attach to the front of the light and restrict the beam to a circle pattern.

Other light-directing accessories, such as **flags, dots,** and **fingers,** are made with heat-resistant opaque cloth or thin metal sheets. Film-

Figure 6.23

A variety of clamps and mounts. (Photo courtesy of Lowell-Light Manufacturing, Inc.)

Figure 6.24

A portable light with flags attached to flexible shafts. (Photo courtesy of Lowell-Light Manufacturing, Inc.)

Figure 6.25

A reflector with a handy carrying case. (Photo courtesy of Lowell-Light Manufacturing, Inc.)

Figure 6.26

A lightweight umbrella reflector. (Photo courtesy of Lowell-Light Manufacturing, Inc.)

makers put them on stands and place them between the light and the subject to create shadow areas or to keep light from reaching certain surfaces (see Figure 6.24).

One of the most valuable light-directing accessories is a **reflector** (see Figure 6.25). It bounces light (for fill) back into the scene from a bright light source like the sun or a powerful key light. Reflectors are mounted on stands or

held by grips during production. Any movement of a reflector, however, whether caused by a person holding it or the wind, will create a moving light pattern and may make the light unusable.

Some portable lighting kits use an **umbrella reflector** (see Figure 6.26) to create an extremely soft light source. The umbrella attaches to the light stand, and the light is turned into it. The

a

b

Figure 6.27

Photo a shows an accessory holder for different filters; photo b shows a lightweight frame for holding various gels. (Photo a courtesy of Mole-Richardson, Hollywood, U.S.A.; photo b courtesy of Lowell-Light Manufacturing, Inc.)

beam bounces off the umbrella's reflective interior surface, producing a highly diffused pool of light.

A piece of white cardboard, a sheet of white Styrofoam, a space blanket, or even crumpled aluminum foil taped with **gaffer tape** to a cardboard backing can provide a homemade reflector. Professional reflectors typically have a different surface on each side of a sturdy base: a hard, highly reflective side that redirects the light without scattering it and a more matted side that redirects and softens the light bounced from it.

Placing a light-diffusing material in front of the light source changes the quality of the light a lamp emits. Common light-diffusing materials such as fiberglass, silk, frosted glass, Dacron, and heat-resistant plastics can alter light quality

according to the diffusion characteristics of the material employed.

Diffusion materials can be mounted in a filter holder or filter slot in many lighting instruments (see Figure 6.27). They can also be placed on a stand between the subject and the light source. Because they are used with intensely hot lights, the stronger, more heat-resistant materials are preferred. Large diffusers can be suspended on frames over the entire set for location shooting.

A **scrim** is an accessory for reducing light intensity without changing the color balance of the light transmitted through it. Scrims are made of translucent black fabric or stainless steel mesh similar to a common household window screen. They mount in a holder on the lamp, or they can be placed on a stand between the light and the subject. Outdoors, large scrims such as a **butterfly scrim** (Figure 6.28a) suspended on a large frame reduce the intensity of sunlight in an area as large as 20 square feet. Scrims are available in varying thicknesses. Single scrims (Figure 6.28b) cut the light by one half-stop, and double scrims (Figure 6.28c) cut the light by a full stop. Half-scrims cover only half of the instrument's opening.

Dimmer boards control the intensity of the light, but they are somewhat bulky and therefore are rarely used for remotes. Dimmers use varying resistance to change the amount of voltage reaching the lamp. However, reducing the voltage changes the color temperature, so dimmers can adversely affect color rendition.

Neutral density gelatins also reduce light. Neutral density filters for cameras are more common than neutral density gelatins, but these gelatins are sometimes hung over windows to reduce the relative intensity of sunlight in interior scenes.

One of the most obvious ways to change light intensity requires no special equipment or supplies. It involves simply moving the light closer to or farther away from the subject being illuminated. As the light is positioned farther away, the intensity of the light decreases. The falloff is not proportional to the distance, however. According to the **inverse square rule**, the intensity of the light decreases by the *square* of the distance from the subject. In other words, moving a simple light source (such as a candle)

40 ft   20 ft   10 ft

16 footcandles

4 footcandles

1 footcandle

Figure 6.28

A butterfly scrim (photo a) can diffuse light over a much larger area than a single or a double scrim. Made from stainless steel, a single scrim (b) and a double scrim (c) fit into a variety of accessory holders. (Photo a courtesy of Matthews Studio Equipment, Inc.; photos b and c courtesy of Mole-Richardson, Hollywood, U.S.A.)

Figure 6.29

The inverse square rule. The intensity of the light varies according to the square of the distance from a simple light source.

from 10 feet to 20 feet from the subject will reduce light intensity on the subject by roughly *four times*. (Figure 6.29 illustrates the inverse square rule.) Most lighting instruments, of course, have some means of directing or focusing the light rays, which alters this formula. In actual practice this axiom simply means that close-ups of actors require less light than medium or long shots, for which the lights must be placed farther away to remain out of the frame.

Electric Power Requirements

Artificial lights require electricity to function. The three basic sources used to power lighting equipment in film and television production are

batteries, gas-powered generators, and household current. Battery-powered lights have limited uses. They provide a small amount of illumination and can operate for only a short time before the batteries must be recharged. In contrast, generators can provide large amounts of electricity. They are used primarily by professional production companies that need to illuminate large areas (and power many lighting instruments) with a power source that can be transported to virtually any location. For the majority of productions, however, the most common power source is the current supplied to a house or building by the utility company.

Portable lighting instruments are usually designed to operate with the 120-**volt** current available from wall outlets in almost every building or home. Lamps of different sizes draw greater or lesser amounts of power. Exceeding the power limits that a household electrical system can provide will cause an overload, resulting in tripped breakers, blown fuses, and sometimes burned connectors or cables.

Power circuits in most buildings or houses have breakers that handle either 15 or 20 **amps** per electrical circuit. If the lights plugged into a circuit exceed that limit, the circuit breaker will cut off the current. To determine the amperage rating for a circuit you must find the breaker box or boxes and read the breaker limit, either the 15 amps usually found only in older buildings or the more common 20 amps listed on the breaker switch handle. All electrical outlets and lighting fixtures at the location are routed through these breakers, and each power circuit has its own breaker switch. If you blow a circuit, the switch will flip to the middle, neither off nor on. You will need to unplug the lights that blew it and reset the circuit breaker by flipping the switch off, then on. The circuit is working if the breaker stays in the on position.

Obviously, it is vital to know which wall outlets are controlled by each breaker switch so you don't overheat a circuit. If that information is not written in the breaker box, you will need to compile your own map of the circuits. To do this, plug a light into each wall outlet in a particular room and switch the breakers off and on to determine which outlets are on which circuit. An inexpensive night-light is ideal for this purpose. A single circuit may have wall outlets in several rooms, such as a hallway, bedroom, and bathroom.

Once you have mapped a circuit, you will need to do some simple mathematics because circuit breakers (and most generators and batteries) are rated in amps, but appliances and bulbs are labeled in **watts**. Fortunately, a relatively simple formula converts watts and amps: *amps times volts equals watts*. The power voltage in the United States is about 120 volts. But to make the calculation even easier to do in your head, do the calculations using 100 volts instead of 120. This provides a margin of safety to keep from blowing circuits and also makes the multiplication simpler because you can multiply the number of amps given on the breaker box by 100. This tells you how many watts you can

safely plug into the circuit. For example, if the circuit can carry 20 amps, you can plug in 2,000 watts' worth of lights (2,000 watts = 100 volts × 20 amps).

This would mean you could plug in four 500-watt lamps, two 1,000-watt lamps, or any other combination of lamps adding up to 2,000 watts. Of course, you can use this much only if nothing else is plugged into the circuit. If a refrigerator or other power-consuming equipment is operating, you must deduct the number of watts each uses.

If the circuit in a room you are lighting cannot provide enough power for all your lighting instruments, you will have to route power to your lights from a different circuit. Extension cables used for this purpose should be of a heavy enough gauge to handle the wattage they are expected to carry. Common household extension cords are too lightweight and can be dangerous. Long extension cable runs can also reduce the voltage supplied to the lamps and may affect color rendition. A 1-volt drop in power supplied to an incandescent lamp lowers the color temperature by 10 degrees Kelvin.

As noted earlier, renting a generator is the common solution to limited location power. Generators are not cheap, but some rental houses provide student discounts, and in many cases a rented generator may be the only way to assure reliable power. Another option might be to negotiate with a neighbor to buy power from them. Finally, another option available from most lighting rental houses is a range plug. This plug is different from the standard two- or three-pronged Edison plugs. It plugs into the 240-volt outlet used for electric stoves and clothes dryers and breaks it down into two 120-volt legs. The lighting manufacturer, Mole-Richardson, calls this conversion plug a "range to Edison box," but there is really no standard term for this device. In a house with limited circuits it can be invaluable.

Professional film and television crews typically hire a licensed electrician to help deal with electrical problems. An electrician can bypass the breaker box and route the power into a separate distribution box that has its own breakers. This enables power cables to be run directly to the distribution box and be routed where they are needed without the constant risk of tripping circuit breakers or blowing fuses. Bypassing the circuit breaker box, however, should be done only by a qualified electrician.

Lighting Safety

Setting up and operating lighting equipment, especially on location, requires planning and care. Lights must be securely mounted, and barndoors or filter holders should be locked in place or taped to any supporting structure for additional stability. Electrical cords and extension cables should be taped down with gaffer tape or paper tape or be covered with rubber matting to keep people from tripping and pulling the lights down (see Figure 6.30). Power cables coming from the light should be secured to one of the legs of the light stand.

A fully extended tripod-base light stand is inherently unstable, and you should secure the legs with sandbags to keep them from tipping over (see Figure 6.31). Some heavy-duty light stands have antisway bars to increase their stability or come with rings at the base for securing power cords. Pointing one leg of the light stand in the direction the lighting instrument is facing helps to distribute the weight more evenly and improve the stand's steadiness.

Because lighting instruments get extremely hot, never place them near flammable materials such as curtains or upholstered furniture. An overloaded circuit or inadequate extension cable can also cause a fire. The placement of gels, filters, or diffusing materials on the lighting instrument also requires careful attention. It is imperative to attach these light-shaping materials in such a way that the heat can escape from the bulb and surrounding area. Even if a light has only been on for a short period, it is usually too hot to touch. If it is not possible to let the light cool down, use insulated electrician's gloves to adjust barndoors or to change scrims or filters. Turn lights off as soon as production is completed so they have time to cool before being packed away. Be careful when removing tape from floors or walls; it is easy to damage wallpaper or painted surfaces as the tape is peeled away.

Figure 6.30
Taping down extension cords can prevent injuries and reduce the chances of lights being pulled over.

Figure 6.31
A sandbag can be used to secure top-heavy light stands. (Photo courtesy of Matthews Studio Equipment, Inc.)

Most of these safety precautions are just common sense. In the heat of production, however, with time running short and pressure building, cutting corners is a real temptation. That is when accidents occur. To protect the crew and cast from injury you must always handle electrical power and lighting instruments in a careful, systematic, and professional manner.

In addition to well-maintained lighting instruments and the proper filtration materials and securing devices, a number of items should be part of your location lighting kit. These include a fire extinguisher, insulated gloves for each crew member handling lights, burn ointment, rubber matting, gaffer tape, and spare bulbs. If your location has an old breaker box with fuses, you had better bring some spares. You will probably need them. Finally, the quality and safety of location lighting are directly related to the amount of advance planning. Scouting a location for power requirements *before* the shoot tells you what to bring.

Notes

1. Several camera models use the zebra pattern. Its stripes are visible in the viewfinder over the areas of the picture that are near the 100 IRE unit level, the uppermost limit of brightness. It is adjustable in cameras such as the Betacam. The zebra stripes could be set to a level, for example, of 65 to 70 IRE, the approximate level for Caucasian skin tone and a level that is not so close to the camera's clip levels.

2. Overexposure in video can be especially troublesome. For an excellent discussion of this issue, see Harry Mathias and Richard Patterson, *Electronic Cinematography: Achieving Photographic Control over the Video Image* (Belmont, CA: Wadsworth, 1985), pp. 99–109, 164–173, 180. They recommend exposing for extreme highlights and then moving down to the required fill levels.

3. Ibid., pp. 171–172. Mathias and Patterson describe a simple procedure for establishing an ASA rating for any video camera. This requires a chip chart and waveform monitor in addition to the light meter and camera you will be using. After lighting the chip chart evenly, open the camera's iris to the point at which the white chip on the chart is at 100 IRE units on the waveform monitor. After checking to see which f-stop that requires on the camera, change the ASA slide or dial on the light meter until you reach the same f-stop reading as the one on the camera. You then can use that ASA slide or setting as the ASA for your camera.

4. For an interesting discussion of the way camcorders "see," read James Caruso and Mavis Arthur, "Learning the Light Stuff," *Video*, July 1989, pp. 43–46.

5. Remember that the range of f-stops is a result not only of the variance of light falling on the scene but also of the varying reflections of different surfaces within the scene. A single light source can result in different ranges, depending on the nature of the subject. For example:

Contrast Ratio	Range in F-Stops
1:1	0
2:1	1
4:1	2
8:1	3
16:1	4

6. Make the effort sometime to really compare the theatrical exhibition of a film that truly exploits the ability of color negative film stock to capture detail in the shadow areas of the scene (*Unforgiven, Godfather III, Barton Fink, The Crying Game*) with the look of that film when it becomes available on videotape.

7. For excellent explanations of the waveform monitor, see also Chapter 5 in Mathias and Patterson; Eileen Tuuri, "Scoping Out Your Video," *Videography*, November 1991, pp. 29–34; and Peter Utz, "Bars and Stripes Forever," *AV Video*, November 1995, pp. 77–87.

8. Again, see Tuuri, Utz, or Chapter 5 in Mathias and Patterson for a full discussion of the vectorscope. Rosco Laboratories, one of the biggest manufacturers of filters for film and television, has developed complete vectorscope readings for every Roscolux filter, including phase angles, chroma amplitudes, and waveform monitor luminance values. Thus, various colors will plot at different places on the vectorscope, according to their phase angle and chroma amplitude. Information about this may be obtained from Rosco Laboratories, 36 Bush Ave., Port Chester, NY 10573; (914) 937-1300.

9. For a good discussion of filters, see Peter Utz, "The Filter Factor," *AV Video*, October 1995, pp. 55–60; and Ira Tiffen, "Filters in Focus," *In Motion*, October 1991, pp. 34–35. In addition, Tiffen Manufacturing Corp., one of the biggest filter manufacturers, has produced a videotape entitled *Which Filter Should I Use?* that demonstrates a variety of specialty filters. For information about the tape, write to Tiffen Manufacturing, 90 Oser Ave., Hauppauge, NY 11788; (800) 645-2522.

10. Most lens manufacturers make filters, but there are many other sources as well. Some of the more consumer-oriented companies are Ambico, 50 Maple St., Norwood, NJ 07648, (201) 767-4100; Cokin/Minolta Corp., 101 Williams Dr., Ramsey, NJ 07446, (201) 825-4000; Schneider, 400 Crossways Park Dr., Woodbury, NY 11797, (516) 496-8500; Harrison and Harrison, 677 N. Plano St., Porterville, CA 93257, (209) 782-0121.

Some of the bigger manufacturers more oriented to professional-grade filters are Tiffen Manufacturing Corp. (which also makes a variety of consumer filters), 90 Oser Ave., Hauppauge, NY 11788, (800) 645-2522; Rosco, 1135 N. Highland Ave., Hollywood, CA 90038, (213) 462-2233; Belden Communications (the U.S. distributor of Lee Filters), 534 West 25th St., New York, NY 10001, (212) 691-1910; and Great American Market, 826 N. Cole Ave., Hollywood, CA 90038, (213) 461-0200.

11. The filter factor is the *inverse* of the fraction of the light transmitted (for example, 1/4 is two f-stops). You can divide filter factors into ASA and make all subsequent exposure calculations based on the new or recalculated ASA. With a filter factor of 4, for example, the ASA might be 320 without the filter but 80 (320/4) with the filter.

12. Such lights can also be purchased with a color temperature of either 3,200 degrees Kelvin or 3,400 degrees Kelvin, primarily because some color film stocks, such as Type A, are color balanced for the slightly higher 3,400-degree-Kelvin color temperature.

13. See "Videessence Receives Lighting Patent," *Videography*, August 1991, p. 63. For a full technical discussion of this type of lighting, see Paul D. Costa, *VIDESSENCE: Sustained RGB Light and Camera Theory* (Burlingame, CA: Videessence Press, 1992). Videessence details its television studio lighting installations in a pamphlet entitled *Videessence: Television Lighting*. The address for Videessence is P.O. Box 1188, Burlingame, CA 94011.

chapter seven
Lighting Approaches

The opening section of Carrol Ballard's *The Black Stallion* (1979) tells the story of a young boy shipwrecked on a deserted island with a beautiful untamed black stallion as his sole companion. The first fifty minutes of the film, from the shipwreck to the rescue of the boy and horse from the island, contain no more than five to six minutes of dialogue. Instead of words, *The Black Stallion* tells its story primarily through an incredible series of images photographed by Caleb Deschanel, director of cinematography. One breathtaking shot follows another: shimmering seas, moonlit cliffs, glowing sunsets, and dark, foreboding rain clouds. The first fifty minutes of *The Black Stallion* are a virtual textbook in image making, an advertisement for Kodak.

For great cinematographers like Caleb Deschanel, Conrad Hall, Vilmos Zsigmond, and Gordon Willis, lighting is more than simply obtaining adequate exposure. It is a way to direct the viewer's eye in the frame, to establish the character, the mood, and the dramatic quality of the image. Lighting can establish the time of day, bring out or mute certain colors, or create a feeling of safety or danger. Light can be used to emphasize or deemphasize depth. Layered in planes from the front to the rear of the frame, light can also help define the space in three dimensions.

Lighting Styles

The lighting in most modern dramatic motion pictures tends to be more or less realistic; it looks like the natural light we experience in everyday life (see Figure 7.1a). The key to this style of lighting is that the light must *appear* to be coming from some real light source in the movie, such as a streetlight, a ceiling fixture, a table lamp, or the sun. This kind of lighting is often called **source lighting** because it mimics or augments the direction of the light and the light source in the scene.

The opposite lighting approach, one that could be called *expressionistic* (or *stylized*), is more concerned with creating a particular mood or feeling in the shot than in seeming realistic (see Figure 7.1b). Such distinctions are not always clear-cut. To produce an image requires light, even in places where light is unlikely. It may be totally unrealistic to have a spotlight illuminating the slimy monster in a dark sewer, but realistic lighting is not the primary objective in such movies. Even motion pictures that make every effort to employ realistic lighting can slip into movie lighting conventions that totally defy our experience with light in real life: the pitch-black alley behind the bar that is *always* lit by a convenient full moon or the light streaming from beneath the dashboard in the front seat of the otherwise dark automobile.

There are many different approaches to lighting. Numerous books and magazines discuss the aesthetics of lighting,[1] but ultimately the style of lighting employed tends to defy any simple formula or rule book. A lighting setup must take into account not only the technical limitations of the camera, lens, and recording medium but also the dramatic needs of the scene being shot.

Basic Three-Point Lighting

Every imaging system (whether electronic or photochemical) requires a sufficient amount of light, called the **baselight level,** to ensure proper exposure. Base illumination typically is diffused, overall lighting coming from no discernible direction. The minimum baselight level for most video cameras is in the range of 100 footcandles, but this level does little to emphasize the subject or define the space. It simply means that the camera has enough light to operate.

Three-point lighting is perhaps the most traditional approach to lighting. It creates a balanced, sculpted image, one that emphasizes three-dimensionality in the otherwise flat, two-dimensional film or video frame. In the studio, of course, it is possible to control the light totally, but the same basic principles apply to location lighting.

a

b

Figure 7.1

In an episode of the TV series Werewolf, *actor Chuck Connors is seen (a) in a lighting setup that is basically realistic and (b) in a lighting setup that is more expressionistic. (Photos courtesy of Columbia Studios)*

a

b

Figure 7.2

(a) The basic angles for the key and fill lights in relation to the camera subject and (b) the vertical angle above the camera subject for the key and back lights.

The primary light source in three-point lighting is called the **key light.** The key light simulates the main source of illumination for a scene—the sun (or streetlight) outdoors, a lamp or lighting fixture indoors. It typically is placed 30 to 45 degrees from the camera-to-subject axis and is elevated at an angle of 30 to 45 degrees above the camera-to-subject axis (see Figure 7.2). The key light is often a focusable lighting instrument like a Fresnel and is adjusted somewhere in the middle of the flood-to-spotlight range. It creates some shadows, giving shape to the subject. As the dominant lighting source, it is the light most

responsible for setting the basic f-stop used to shoot the scene.

The **fill light** is placed on the opposite side of the camera from the key light, from near the camera to as much as 45 degrees away, and usually at camera height. It fills in, at least to some degree, the shadows created by the key light. For that reason it is never more intense than the key light and almost always employs a softer, more diffused light source. Too much fill light can create a flat, low-contrast image.

The third basic light in a three-point lighting setup is called the **back light.** It is placed above

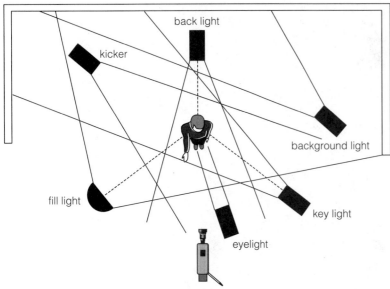

Figure 7.3

A complete lighting setup with key light, fill light, back light, kicker light, background light, and eyelight in their typical positions.

and behind the subject at enough of an angle to keep the light from coming directly into the camera lens. The back light helps to outline the subject (particularly in the head and shoulder area because the light is coming from above and behind) and separate it from the background.

Additional lights, sometimes referred to as **separation lights,** often amplify or enhance the modeling provided by traditional three-point lighting (see Figure 7.3). An **eyelight** is a small, focusable light placed near the camera (at eye level) to add a sparkle to a person's eyes. A **background light** illuminates the background, not the back of the subject like a back light. It helps to separate the performers from the background or set. A **kicker light** is similar to a back light in function. It is usually placed low, behind the subject, often directly opposite the key light. It too helps to separate, or "kick," the subject out from the background. The intensity needed for a back light or kicker light can vary greatly. A brunette requires more light, a blonde less, and a bald person even less. A properly lit scene may not even require separation lighting, and some lighting directors avoid kickers and back lights in order to achieve greater realism.

Film Versus Video Lighting

Television lighting originated in the studio. Early video cameras required a high baselight level just to produce an image. Thus, the typical multicamera studio production tended to pour

a great deal of light over the entire action area, producing the relatively flat, even lighting still seen in many game shows and situation comedies. In contrast, the much greater sensitivity of film stock made it far easier for filmmakers to shoot on location with lower light levels and more natural (or realistic) lighting techniques. **Film-style lighting** grew out of the single-camera shooting method for film: the lighting setup is changed as the camera position is changed for virtually every new shot. This is a slow and tedious process, of course, but what film-style lighting loses in time it makes up for in control.

As technological improvements in video equipment have begun to narrow the differences between film and video, applying film-style lighting techniques to video production has become increasingly possible. Differences in lighting for film and video remain, of course, but the same basic lighting principles apply to both media. Continuing advancements in electronic imaging will reduce these differences even more.

The most important difference between lighting for film and lighting for video, as noted in Chapter 6, stems from film's greater **latitude** or **contrast range.** Color negative film stock can accurately reproduce a range of brightness levels (from the darkest to brightest points in the scene) of more than seven f-stops. Video cameras can record a more limited range of approximately five f-stops. A shot exceeding the contrast range of the imaging system loses visible details in the dark or bright areas that are below or above the camera's range.

Altering the electronic imaging system so that it records more detail in the light or dark areas is possible but does not change the contrast range. If the imaging system is adjusted toward the bright end of the range, it will lose detail in the shadow areas. If it is shifted toward the dark area, it will lose information at the bright end of the scale. Film's greater contrast range gives it an advantage over video. This may partially explain why so much material produced solely for television (as opposed to theatrical distribution) is still shot on film. Even when a production is shot on film and copied (and postproduced) to videotape for display on television, the film tends to act like a filter, compressing the contrast range and making the transition into bright or dark areas less abrupt than if the same material had been shot on video originally. Furthermore, the film image is less affected by strong highlights because each successive film frame presents an entirely new recording area, unaffected by the previous frame. In a video camera, the target area—the video tubes or CCD chips—does not change. Each video frame is scanned from the same unchanging target. Thus, an overly bright highlight can be retained long enough in the electronic imaging system to bleed over and affect a number of successive frames.[2]

These differences do not mean that video must be lit in an entirely different way from film. They do mean that video lighting must take into account the more limited contrast range of five f-stops. The more expensive professional cameras have electronic compression circuits that help to reduce these problems, and a new generation of imaging sensors is beginning to eliminate some of the highlight retention problems,[3] but in most cases video lighting involves some type of contrast reduction in order to stay within the five f-stop range. Incidentally, less sophisticated cameras are likely to have a smaller usable contrast range.

In film, one of the most common methods of reducing contrast is a procedure called **flashing.** This involves exposing the motion picture film to a low but precisely controlled level of light *before* it is exposed in the camera (that is, *preflashing*) or *after* it has been shot (that is, *postflashing*). Whether it is done before or after shooting, flashing must be done *before* the film is developed. Flashing reduces contrast and increases visible detail in the shadow areas. It can also be used to mute colors or to create a softer image without losing image sharpness or resolution.

A video camera can achieve much the same effect. Although the tradition in video has been to set a camera up strictly according to factory specifications, a qualified video engineer can readjust the imaging system to produce changes in color balance, tinting, and contrast shifting, similar to the way film stock can be manipulated in the laboratory. This requires, of course, a highly sophisticated understanding of video cameras, electronic signal processing, and video testing equipment. As the differences between film and video continue to blur, such creative manip-

ulation of the electronic image will undoubtedly increase in production and postproduction.

In general, video cameras do not accurately reproduce detail in the shadow areas. Furthermore, large dark areas in a video frame can show a great deal of **noise.** The answer to this problem may be to use fill lighting to bring up the light level in those dark areas. Conversely, extreme highlights can result in a blooming or burning effect.

It is important to keep the light in the scene within the brightness range of five f-stops and, if possible, to make sure that the entire range is filled by including both a **black reference** (some black object within the shot) and a **white reference** (such as a white handkerchief). Video cameras have difficulty when the lighting for a scene is low contrast—at relatively the same brightness level at either end (dark or bright) of the contrast range. Using a white and a black reference helps to fill in or extend the video signal over the full range the camera is capable of reproducing. In a scene that is darkly lit overall, a white reference helps to restore the full contrast range. This can be provided by a practical light within the scene, such as a table lamp, or by any strong back light or side light that can create enough highlights to provide a white reference. In a scene in which the overall lighting is bright with no shadow areas, a black reference helps to produce the full video range.[4]

In most cases you should avoid strong backlighting and extreme highlights in video. Electronic imaging systems respond poorly to overexposure. As long as the image is exposed for the highlights and the difference between the brightest point in the frame and the subject (usually a face) for which you are exposing is no more than 1.5 to 1.75 stops, a video camera can probably handle a backlit scene.

It is easy to see why a portable **waveform monitor** can be such a valuable tool for video lighting. It displays the brightness levels across the entire scene and provides an extremely accurate guide for setting up or adjusting the lighting for the brightness range the electronic imaging system is capable of recording.

Producing the same lighting effect can be more time consuming in video than in film. With its more limited latitude, video usually requires extra fill light to reduce contrast. Filling in the entire video range with small, carefully measured increments of light can make video lighting a painstakingly slow process.[5] This is offset to some extent by the ability to instantly review lighting results on a monitor. And, as is the case in most student productions, as long as you are not paying the crew for the extra time it takes to light, the low cost of videotape encourages experimentation—shooting until you get exactly the lighting effect you desire.

Preparing to Light

Lighting, like any other element of the production, requires advance planning. The lighting director needs to understand the exact nature of the scene being shot. What kind of mood is the director trying to create? What kind of lighting instruments does that require? Are any special lighting accessories needed? At what time of day is the scene supposed to be taking place (and will the scene actually be shot at that time)?

If you are not going to be shooting in a studio, careful and systematic location scouting is imperative. You will need to survey each location to determine how much light it will require and how lights can be mounted at each location. How many crew members will you need to set up the lights or handle the reflectors? Seeing the site at the time of day you are actually planning to shoot is important. The position of the sun (and the prevailing lighting conditions) changes dramatically from early morning to late afternoon. Will it be possible to use reflectors? It is a good idea to take a camcorder along to log each location.

Once you have some idea of how many lights you are going to need and how they will be mounted, you should survey the location for electricity. How much power will you need and how much is actually available there? This is the time to find the breaker box and map out the power circuits. How many wall outlets do you have and where are they located? If you need to run power from additional circuits, how long do your extension cables need to be? Do you have a contact person so you can gain access to the breaker box? Do you need to hire a qualified electrician? If the power at the location is inadequate, you will need to rent a generator or per-

haps negotiate with people nearby to buy power from them.

You also need to consider how you will transport your lighting equipment. Lights and lighting accessories are large and bulky. They are also fragile. What kind of vehicle do you need to transport the equipment? What kind of access do you have for the vehicle when you reach the location? Ultimately, you will need to develop a checklist so that you don't forget anything. Here are some of the major items:

1. Lighting instruments and spare lamps (number, type, and size)
2. Mounting equipment (number, type, and size)
3. Lighting accessories (barndoors, flags, filters, diffusers, reflectors)
4. Power cables and mats, sandbags, and gaffer tape
5. Generator (if needed)
6. Safety equipment (fire extinguisher, gloves, and such)
7. Transportation
8. A weather report

Outdoor Lighting

Shooting outdoors usually means that you will have enough light to meet the baselight requirements of almost any film stock or electronic imaging system. The sun itself can be a powerful key light, not only defining the time of day (based on the color temperature and angle of the shadows) but also dictating the direction of the light in the scene. Shooting with the light (in the direction the light rays are falling) is the simplest and most common technique for outdoor shooting. Keeping the sun at your back usually eliminates the problems associated with lens flare and backlighting. The photos in Figure 7.4 illustrate shooting with the light and against it.

Light in the early morning or late afternoon casts longer, more clearly defined shadows, creating a greater sense of relief or modeling and a more dramatic image. A shot of a high mountain lake looks quite different in the flat light of midday than early or late in the day. The time of day also affects the color tones in the image. The late afternoon sun casts a particularly warm

a

b

Figure 7.4
(a) Shooting against (into) the light can create many problems with exposure, flare, and unwanted reflections. Shooting with the light (b) usually eliminates these problems and is almost always easier.

golden light. Many cinematographers prize the look of this "golden time" and set up their shooting schedule to take full advantage of the atmosphere it establishes for a scene. (See Color Plate 8.) For similar reasons they have used the dramatic red glow of a sunset as the backdrop for scenes in countless motion pictures.

The quality of the outdoor light we actually experience ranges from very harsh and direct to soft and diffused. In fact, natural light is usually a mixture of different light qualities. The sun can be both a source of hard direct light and a source of fill as the sun's light is reflected from clouds, buildings, and the ground to form a softer, more diffused general skylight. In most cases, however, reflected skylight does not provide enough fill for outdoor shooting. Without adequate fill light a sunlit image can easily exceed the latitude or contrast range of a camera's imaging system. As a result, outdoor lighting usually involves some kind of contrast reduction, a way to reduce the enormous range between bright sunlight and the dark shadows of the shade.

Contrast Reduction

Throwing additional fill light into the scene, as we have already discussed, is one way to reduce contrast outdoors. This is why professional film and television companies so commonly use artificial lighting outdoors, even on a bright sunny day.

Figure 7.5
Using reflectors is an efficient way to provide fill lighting in many outdoor situations.

This situation necessitates the use of daylight-balanced light sources such as **HMI lights**, or tungsten-balanced lights converted (with a **dichroic filter**) to daylight color temperature.

An even easier and cheaper method of providing daylight-balanced fill light is using **reflectors** (see Figure 7.5). Reflectors can bounce direct sunlight back into the scene for fill lighting. If the sun is the primary light source in a scene, the reflector will have to be placed in the standard fill light position (on the opposite side of the camera from the "key" light) in order to reflect the sunlight into the scene. Reflectors are usually mounted on stands (or hand-held) above eye level to simulate skylight. If they are too low, or if they create a too clearly defined light pattern, the reflected light they cast can look artificial and unnatural.

Another way to reduce contrast is to suspend a large **scrim** or light-diffusing medium over the entire set area. This can virtually eliminate shadows, creating the kind of soft, dreamy, highly diffused lighting commonly seen in many television commercials. Virtually the same thing can be accomplished by simply shooting the shot in a shaded area or shooting on an overcast day.

Sometimes you can put a filter on the camera to control outdoor lighting conditions. A **neutral density filter** reduces the overall light level in an excessively bright outdoor scene. This can be helpful when you want to reduce the **depth of field** by forcing the camera to shoot at a wider **f-stop** (see Chapter 4). **Haze filters** and **UV filters** reduce the bluish cast on overcast or hazy days. **Polarizing filters** minimize unwanted reflections from water or glass. **Fog filters** can create a fog effect, and **low-contrast** or **soft-contrast filters** reduce the contrast range. Filters generally cause some loss in image quality, but in many situations they may be the only workable way to deal with existing lighting conditions.[6]

Maintaining Continuity in Changing Light

When the sun is the primary light source, there is always the potential for lighting-induced continuity errors. Movies are usually shot out of sequence, and long delays between camera setups are commonplace. Shots that supposedly occur sequentially in time may have been shot at different times during production, even days or weeks apart. If those shots are to flow together seamlessly in the final motion picture, the lighting within the scene must be consistent from shot to shot.

This means that the light quality must be the same for each shot in the scene. If the first shot takes place in direct sunlight, it will look strange if the light in the next shot is suddenly the more diffused light caused by a passing cloud. Similarly, the direction of the light must be consistent. The angle of the sun creates appreciably different shadows at different times of day. A shot taken at noon when the sun is almost directly overhead contains few shadows. If that shot is followed immediately by a shot that clearly displays the long shadows of late afternoon, the continuity violation is obvious.

Even the natural changes in the sun's **color temperature** throughout the day can be the source of continuity errors. The color temperature of sunlight at 4 P.M. is visibly different from the color temperature at 6 P.M. The automatic **white-balancing** circuit in a video camera, or **color-compensating filters** on a film camera, can correct for these small shifts in color temperature. However, you cannot eliminate gross changes in the shadows or in the overall quality of the light.

The only way to avoid such lighting-induced continuity problems is to organize your shooting schedule carefully when working in natural light. Trying to shoot a long complicated scene late in the day when the light is changing rapidly will almost certainly lead to problems. Group similarly lit scenes together in your shooting schedule, and try to avoid shooting different sections of the same scene at different times of day. Shooting part of a scene before lunch and then finishing the rest of the scene after a long break can easily create incompatible lighting conditions.

Shooting at Night

Night scenes abound in feature films. Shooting at night, what filmmakers call **night-for-night**, produces the most convincing results. One of the biggest battles in night lighting is finding a convincing (well-motivated) source—a store window, streetlight, or bright moon—that could provide a believable source for the illumination of the scene. Artificial lights are then used to simulate the light that would be coming from that source. (See Color Plate 9.) Night lighting is easier if the actors avoid wearing dark clothing that makes them blend into the background. When shooting at night, cinematographers sometimes water down the street to increase reflections and pick up new highlights.

Dusk-for-night shooting is just what it sounds like—shooting at dusk. The sky at twilight provides a natural blue fill. Artificial lights provide the key. The biggest problem with dusk-for-night shooting is that twilight is so short. The rapidly changing lighting conditions require constant monitoring and readjustment of lights.

Another method, called **day-for-night**, is a well-known film technique for shooting "supposed" night scenes during the day. This involves increasing the contrast and darkening the sky usually by using a deep blue filter for color filming. Or some cinematographers use film that is balanced for artificial (3,200 degree) light and shoot without an 85 orange filter, thus enabling the film to "see" the daylight as blue. The scene is then underexposed by 1.5 to 2.5 f-stops. The film laboratory can also enhance the day-for-night effect during printing. With the proper tinting and some trial and error many of these night effects may be possible in video as well.

Shooting night-for-night on video generally is more difficult than shooting on film because of video's limited contrast range. What makes a shot read as night is having large dark areas in the background and a fairly large contrast between the light and dark areas. Video cameras have difficulty recording this, although even consumer-level cameras have continued to improve in this area. The best solution may be a subtle boosting of the fill light in the shadow areas, enough to reduce the contrast range but not enough to eliminate the sense of darkness in the background areas. A scene shot in color can also be made to look more like night if a light blue gel is used on the lighting instrument. This is because moonlight is conventionally enhanced by a bluish cast.

Adapting to Weather Conditions

When shooting outdoors, natural weather conditions can change the quality of the light dramatically. A funeral scene shot on a dark overcast day reads differently than the same scene shot in bright cheery sunlight. The highly diffused light of an overcast day often improves a color image. The low-contrast lighting can mute certain colors, making them more subtle and pastel. Shooting just after a rain has stopped can pick up a myriad of reflections and moving water patterns. Snow, fog, and mist each create a distinct mood-provoking atmosphere (see Figure 7.6). Even extremes in temperature can alter the quality of the light. On a cold day the steam curls from virtually every heat source. In the desert the hot air rising from a highway can imbue a shot with a sense of unbearable heat as the light is distorted through the shimmering haze.

Obviously, you cannot control the weather or the temperature, but you can use naturally

a

b

c

Figure 7.6

The same scene from virtually the same angle reads in very different ways on a bright sunny day (a) and in fog (b). Director Carl Dreyer exploits the diffused light of a fog-shrouded forest (c) in Day of Wrath *(1943).*

occurring conditions when the opportunity arises. Professional filmmakers, of course, can "make" weather to some extent with fog and rain machines. Wetting down the streets to create water reflections and glitzy highlights is a time-honored movie tradition. But even without such resources the lighting in different weather conditions can provide the perfect atmosphere for a special scene. With a weather report, a little patience, and some luck, there is nothing to stop you from using natural weather conditions to your advantage.

Indoor Lighting

Interior lighting demands a certain amount of flexibility, a willingness to make things work even in difficult conditions, especially on location. In a studio equipped with an overhead grid, a full complement of lighting instruments, and other accessory equipment, lighting is much easier to set up and control. A friend's living room, a neighborhood restaurant, or a lecture hall at school may be the perfect setting for your movie but a nightmare to light in terms of mounting the lighting instruments or obtaining adequate power. Good location scouting can alleviate some of these problems, but successful indoor lighting still requires an ability to adapt to each new situation.[7]

Shooting in Available Light and Low Light

In some cases it may be possible to shoot indoors relying totally on available light, such as the light provided by an overhead fixture or sunlight coming through a window. In both film and video, shooting in available light is a more viable option than ever before. Each new generation of lenses seems to be faster, and new film stocks and electronic imaging systems require less light to record an image. Still, even with these improvements shooting in available light may not produce a satisfactory image. It may be difficult, if not impossible, to control adequately the intensity of available light, its color temperature, or its direction. Thus, shooting with available light almost always involves trade-offs and compromises. And available light almost always means low light levels in interior locations.

In general, low-light shooting is somewhat easier in film than in video. Some film cameras have **variable shutters** that can be adjusted to allow more (or less) light to reach the film. Incidentally, these are not the same as the variable shutters that are on many video cameras. The electronic high-speed shutters on video cameras *increase* the shutter speed, making it possible to record extremely fast action without the blurring that would occur at the camera's normal shutter speed. This is the reverse of allowing more light to reach the film with a variable shutter. In effect, raising the shutter speed on such video cameras will make it more difficult to shoot in low-light situations.

If the available light is inadequate for a particular film stock and lens combination, the most common solution is to switch to a faster, more light-sensitive film stock. Professional filmmakers, in fact, often use two types of film when shooting a movie: a slower, more fine-grained stock for outdoor shooting (where light levels are seldom a problem), and a faster tungsten-balanced stock for shooting interiors or low-light situations. Film manufacturers have continued to improve film speed, producing stocks that not only are more light sensitive but are finer grained as well.[8]

In a situation in which the light levels are still too low for the film stock, the film can be shot *as if* it actually had a higher EI. This requires a special laboratory procedure called **pushed processing**, or **forced development**. Pushed processing entails increasing the developing time (or temperature of the developing chemicals) as the film is processed. It can raise the effective EI of film stock by as much as one or two f-stops. There is a trade-off, however. Pushed processing tends to increase grain and contrast in the image. Negative film can be pushed more than reversal film, but pushed processing usually results in reduced image quality. Much the same thing occurs when you boost the **gain** of the video signal electronically.

Bounce Lighting

One of the most common problems in location lighting is hiding lights (particularly the back light) from the camera's view. The low ceilings in most locations make it impossible to suspend the lights above the scene, the usual procedure in a studio with an overhead lighting grid. One way to provide back light or additional fill in a cramped interior location is to bounce light into the scene. **Bounce light** is light reflected into the scene from the ceiling or wall. Aim a lighting instrument at the ceiling and adjust it to the proper angle so that the reflected light falls where you want it (see Figure 7.7). This tends to create a diffused, even kind of lighting and can be a valuable way to establish an overall base-light level for an interior location.

Obviously, bounce lighting will not work if the ceiling is too high or too dark to reflect the light. It works best if the ceiling is a white or light-colored material such as the acoustic ceilings found in many homes. If the ceiling is dark, some white material such as a bedsheet can be attached to it and the light can be bounced from that. Bounced light will pick up the color of the surface from which it is reflected. This kind of subtle color shifting is difficult to compensate for in film, but white balancing in that light should adjust the color balance correctly for a video camera.

If bouncing light is not workable in a particular location, one solution might be to amplify the light in the **practical lights** on the set, the table lamps or lighting fixtures that already appear in the scene. This entails replacing the bulbs in those lamps or lighting fixtures with 3,200-degree Kelvin bulbs. You sometimes can achieve a similar effect by placing a very small lighting instrument, such as a Nooklite (see Figure 7.8), in a corner of the set where it can be blocked from view by a piece of furniture.

Mixed Lighting

When the lighting for a scene contains both daylight and artificial light, maintaining the proper color balance is extremely difficult. **Mixed lighting** is common when shooting location interiors. Imagine a scene with a person sitting in an easy chair in a living room (see Figure 7.9). Some light in this scene is streaming through a large window behind the person. The sunlight has a color temperature of 5,500 degrees Kelvin or even higher,[9] but the key and fill lights illuminating the character's face are provided by tungsten-balanced lights rated at 3,200 degrees Kelvin. Trying to

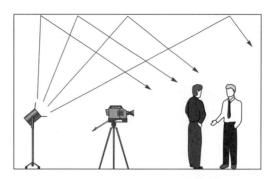

Figure 7.7

As long as the ceiling and walls are light (preferably white), light can be bounced back into the scene to produce relatively soft, even illumination.

Figure 7.8

A tiny Nooklite can be hidden easily behind objects within the set. This kind of instrument can be invaluable for lighting hard-to-reach areas. (Photo courtesy of Great American Market)

Figure 7.9

A typical mixed-lighting situation. The sunlight's color temperature (5,500 degrees Kelvin) is different from the tungsten-balanced (3,200 degrees Kelvin) instruments providing the main light for the man's face.

color balance for such mixed-lighting conditions can cause problems for any cinematographer.

If you shoot this scene on daylight-balanced film stock, the person's face will be red. With tungsten-balanced film stock the face would be correct, but the sunlit background would be very blue. There are several ways to solve this problem. One is to place sheets of orange Wratten 85 **color conversion filter** (the same filter used to shoot tungsten-balanced film in daylight) over the window. Another is to match the color temperature of daylight by using daylight-balanced 5,500-degree lighting instruments, such as HMIs. A third method is to convert

Figure 7.10

Three solutions for a typical mixed-lighting situation. Gel the windows with orange 85 filter gels (a). This will match the more bluish sunlight to the much redder 3,200-degree Kelvin light indoors. By using a daylight-balanced (5,500-degree) HMI light indoors (b), the color temperature will match the sunlight streaming through the window. A 3,200-degree Kelvin light could also be converted to a temperature of 5,500 degrees Kelvin with a dichroic blue filter placed on the lamp (c). The disadvantage of this approach is that the dichroic filter greatly reduces the amount of light from the 3,200-degree instrument.

tungsten lights to 5,500 degrees by placing dichroic blue filters over them. Any of these methods will make all the light roughly the same color temperature. (Figure 7.10 illustrates these solutions for mixed-lighting situations.)

The mixed lighting in this scene creates the same problems for a video camera, and the solutions are basically the same: using orange filter sheets to convert the daylight to tungsten-balanced light, using daylight-balanced lighting instruments to match the color temperature of the daylight, or covering tungsten lamps with dichroic blue filters. These last two approaches require an orange 85 filter on the camera. Either way, you will need to white balance the camera once the lighting has been established.

In some cases the simplest solution for mixed lighting may be to block out one of the sources. Closing a heavy curtain over the window might eliminate (or reduce) the sunlight enough to allow the tungsten lights to dominate the lighting of the scene. Depending on what is being shot, it may be acceptable to let the light coming through a window in the background go blue.

Certainly this seems to be more common than it once was in film and video.

In general, subtle shifts in color temperature are much easier to correct in video than in film. The white-balancing circuit in a video camera can instantly and accurately fine-tune the color temperature in most lighting situations. This same kind of color correction in film requires a color temperature meter and a case of finely graded light-balancing filters. Even then it can be difficult to obtain faithful color reproduction.

Fluorescent Lighting

Fluorescent lighting is commonplace in offices, schools, and commercial buildings, but it may cause color-balancing problems.[10] White light contains roughly equal amounts of all colors in the visible spectrum. Tungsten-balanced lights contain all colors, too, but with a higher percentage of red and a lower percentage of blue. Fluorescent lights, however, break up the spectrum, usually emitting only a few wavelengths, primarily the greens and blues. Similar problems occur with other "noncontinuous" light sources such as the mercury vapor or sodium lamps commonly used in streetlights or in large commercial applications.

In most cases, white balancing a video camera under fluorescent lights will produce satisfactory results, particularly if the fluorescent bulbs are of the popular daylight or warm-white varieties. This may not totally correct the color balance, however. There are many different types of fluorescent bulbs, each with slightly different color characteristics. The easiest solution might be to turn off the fluorescent lights and light the scene entirely with tungsten lighting instruments.[11]

Shooting in fluorescent light is uncertain in film as well. The broken color spectrum presented by fluorescent lights will fool some color temperature meters. Most cinematographers use tungsten-balanced film to shoot under fluorescent lights, but depending on the bulb type, daylight film might be more appropriate. If the fluorescent lights cannot be turned off, special fluorescent filters made by several manufacturers will provide at least some degree of color correction. As long as the color is not too far off, the film laboratory can usually color-correct enough

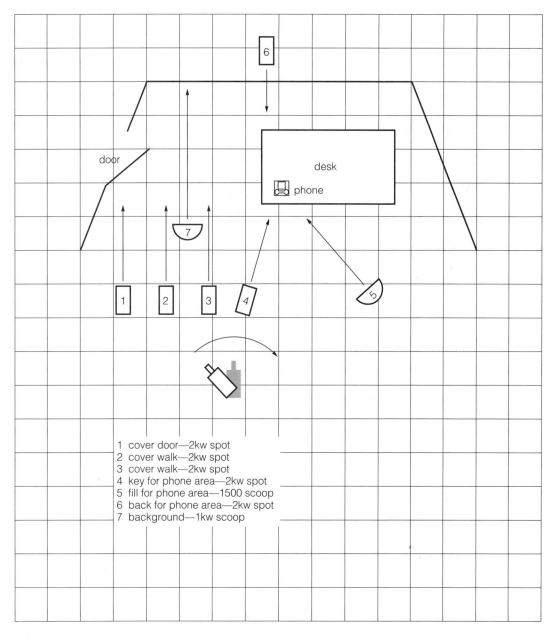

1 cover door—2kw spot
2 cover walk—2kw spot
3 cover walk—2kw spot
4 key for phone area—2kw spot
5 fill for phone area—1500 scoop
6 back for phone area—2kw spot
7 background—1kw scoop

Figure 7.11
A lighting plot with a key explaining the type, power, and function of each instrument. In this example, the lights are hung from a grid.

to produce proper skin tones. Perhaps the only way to be sure of your results is to experiment, to shoot a test roll with the film stock and filters you think will yield the best image in that specific type of fluorescent light.

Lighting for Movement

Lighting a scene in which a character (or the camera) moves is much more difficult than lighting a single fixed area. Most directors draw up a blocking diagram for shots that contain complicated movement. The cinematographer needs to look at the blocking diagram or at least

consult with the director to see precisely where the movement occurs and to see if any particular areas within that movement require special emphasis. For example, a woman walking from the door to a desk needs to be lit as she walks but may need more balanced, three-point lighting when she picks up a phone from the desk at the end of the movement.

Drawing up a **lighting plot** on graph paper is a good way to begin planning. A lighting plot is a diagram of the set that also shows the camera position, the location of lights, their size and type, and the direction they will be pointing (see Figure 7.11). Using one means the lights can be set up and placed in position even before the

Figure 7.12
A half-scrim is invaluable when the subject must move closer to the lighting instrument (with a subsequent increase in illumination as the subject moves nearer the light). By reducing the light emitted from the bottom half of the instrumet with a half-scrim, the light intensity can be balanced more evenly between the two positions.

actors arrive on the set. The lights cannot be focused or finely adjusted, however, until the director actually blocks out the scene with the actors. Their positions are marked on the floor with chalk or tape before the final stages of the lighting can begin. This is one reason why stand-ins are used in movie production. Lighting a spot where the actor will stand is not the same thing as lighting a 6-foot actor or his stand-in.

Perhaps the easiest method of lighting for movement is simply illuminating the entire area with soft, diffused lighting. This avoids some of the problems associated with uneven lighting in a large area: actors walking in and out of hot spots or disappearing into darkness between pools of light. Using diffusers or bounce lighting over the entire shot area can provide an even, overall baselight level.

For a shot in which a character moves toward or away from a light, you can place a half-scrim on the lighting instrument to even out the lighting. The half-scrim should mask the bottom of the light with the open (unscrimmed) half at the top (see Figure 7.12). If the light is angled correctly, the half-scrim will reduce light intensity near the light but will allow full illumination farther away, evenly balancing the light intensity between the two positions. This allows the character to walk closer to the light without the illumination becoming excessive.

Another common technique for lighting movement is to use standard three-point lighting for the areas that require it and to add fill lighting in the gaps between those areas. In this situation an **incident light meter** is especially helpful for checking light levels across the entire scene area, particularly in the gaps between lighting triangles. A similar technique involves *overlapping* the areas of key, fill, and back lights. This way, the same light performs different functions in different parts of the set. The key light can be the primary light source when the

actors are in one area, but when they move over into another area, that light might provide fill.

In any lighting setup special care must be taken to avoid unwanted shadows. Multiple shadows or the shadow of the sound boom draws the viewer's attention to the lights. These problems intensify if the shot contains movement. The shadow of a moving sound boom (as it follows the actors) is too obvious to ignore.

You can reduce or eliminate such shadows in several ways. Shadows tend to be much more conspicuous against a light-colored background than against a dark background or dark floor. Adjusting the lights to a different angle can eliminate shadows or at least shift them out of frame so they are not visible in the shot. Placing the actors farther from the wall will also make their shadows less visible. Sometimes a **flag** or **barndoor** can block the light that is causing a boom shadow. If that is not possible, moving the boom to a different position or miking the sound without a boom might work. Finally, altering the quality of the light in the scene may be the easiest way to reduce shadows. If the lighting is hard, the shadows are more intense. Simply diffusing the light to produce a directionless, overall illumination will diminish or eliminate most shadows.

The director's rehearsals with the actors provide a final opportunity to recheck the lighting to see whether movement in the shot introduces shadows that were overlooked as the lighting setup was being completed. The time to catch hot spots, dark areas, or moving shadows is before shooting begins.

Variations in Lighting

The mood created by lighting is established to a great degree by the **lighting ratio**—the ratio of the key light plus the fill light to the fill light alone. If, for example, the key light and the fill light together have an intensity of 300 **footcandles,** and the fill light alone equals 100 footcandles, the lighting ratio is 3 to 1 (3:1). You add fill light to the key light because the fill light actually provides some illumination to the key side of the subject.

Do not confuse the lighting ratio with the contrast ratio or brightness range. Those terms refer to the range between the brightest point and the darkest point in the frame. The lighting ratio is concerned only with the *ratio* of the key and fill to the fill alone. This ratio is often expressed as the f-stop difference between the key and fill. A 2:1 lighting ratio has one f-stop difference between key and fill and the fill alone; a 4:1 ratio has a two f-stop difference; an 8:1 ratio has a three f-stop difference.

The commonly recommended lighting ratio for color film is 3:1, though film will still show some shadow detail with a lighting ratio as high as 8:1 or 10:1. In video the traditional advice is to maintain a lighting ratio of 2:1 or 3:1. However, with the continuing improvement in video cameras, producing a quality image with lighting ratios as high as 6:1 or 8:1 is possible.[12]

The lighting ratio between the key light and the other lights on the set, such as the back light, the kicker light, or the background light, is far more subjective. It depends in part on how much light the subject or background will reflect and on the particular mood you are trying to create.

Lighting is often described as *high key* or *low key*. These terms can be extremely confusing. **High-key lighting** is generally bright, even illumination. The key-to-fill ratio is low, resulting in a low-contrast image. It might be easier to understand high-key lighting if we used the term high-fill, because the fill light intensity is actually high in relationship to the key. Conversely, **low-key lighting** uses a low amount of fill light in relationship to the key. That is, the ratio of key to fill is high in low-key lighting, as much as 8:1 or higher.[13]

Historically, the tendency has been to use high-key lighting for lighter subjects, such as comedies, musicals, and romances. High-key lighting is bright, happy, and relatively flat. Low-key lighting is much darker, more brooding, and harsh. Dramas (some might say melodramas), horror films, and thrillers—the kinds of movies in which something, good or evil, is always emerging from the shadows— traditionally use low-key lighting. (Figure 7.13 illustrates high-key and low-key lighting.)

Other factors help to determine the emotional impact of the lighting. The direction of the light (front, side, or back), the angle of the light (above, below, or eye level), and the quality

a

b

Figure 7.13
The same scene with low-key lighting (a) and with much brighter high-key lighting (b). (Photos courtesy of Claudia Sternberg)

of the light (hard or soft) can affect the image as profoundly as the lighting ratio.

For example, lighting from the front tends to reduce shadows and flatten the image. If frontal lighting is soft and diffused, it will also smooth out the texture of the surface it illuminates. Lighting from the side creates sharper shadows, particularly with a hard light source. Side lighting throws the subject into relief and can highlight texture with small shadows. Backlighting can be used to emphasize depth. Shooting directly into the light silhouettes the subject, accentuating its outline while minimizing specific

Figure 7.14

(Photo a) In a scene from "Werewolf," actor John J. York prepares to cauterize a wound. The lighting in this scene is basically low key—the ratio of key light (screen right) to fill light is fairly high. Remember, however, that the placement of the key light and the ratio of key to fill are what determine whether the lighting is high key or low key, not the overall intensity of illumination in the scene. A light next to the camera (with an almost equal amount of fill lighting) hides the shadows and produces a high-key scene. If the key light is placed more to the side, shadows increase and the lighting becomes more low key. (Photo b) In Carl Dreyer's Day of Wrath *the lighting consistently casts shadows across the face of the young woman, Anne, who is accused of witchcraft. The brooding low-key lighting in this film underscores its deep sense of mystery and ambiguity. (Photo c) In another scene from* Day of Wrath, *the light appears to be coming from a candle in the lower left-hand corner of the frame. There is too much light, of course, for a single candle, but the angle of the lighting within the scene roughly matches the angle of illumination from the flickering candle. Note the deep shadows on the right side of her face and in the background and the relatively high ratio of key light to fill light. (Photo d) A generally high-key scene from the television show "21 Jump Street," and (photo e) a typically low-key shot from Ingmar Bergman's* The Seventh Seal. *(Photo a courtesy of Columbia Pictures; photo d courtesy of Stephen J. Cannell Productions; photo e from Janus Films)*

a

b

c

d

e

details. This can make the image more abstract. Lights angled sharply from above or below create more distinct, dramatic shadows than lights closer to eye level. The shape, the color, and the sense of depth can change dramatically, ac-

cording to whether the illumination is hard and direct or soft and diffused. The number of variables in lighting makes the combinations almost infinite. The photos in Figure 7.14 show various lighting strategies.

Technological advancements make possible at least one generalization about lighting: The tendency today is to use fewer lights. Faster lenses and more sensitive imaging systems in both film and video make it possible to use less lighting, to place lights farther away, and to have more shadow areas within the shot. This not only makes the set or location more comfortable for the actors but also makes changing lighting setups much faster.

One of the best things about the video revolution is the widespread availability of VCRs and video rental stores. The opportunity to rent and watch a wide variety of films means you can study lighting as never before. Lighting defines the tone and style as much as any element in a movie. In the hands of talented directors, production designers, and cinematographers, the approaches to lighting are almost infinite.

Notes

1. See, for example, almost any issue of *American Cinematographer* or *Lighting Dimensions*. Some books that deal with lighting include Brian Fitt and Joe Thornley, *The Control of Light* (Stoneham, MA: Focal Press, 1993); Ross Lowell, *Matters of Light and Depth* (Philadelphia: Broad Street Books, 1992); Gerald Millerson, *Technique of Lighting for Television and Film* (Stoneham, MA: Focal Press, 1991); Blain Brown, *Motion Picture and Video Lighting* (Stoneham, MA: Focal Press, 1995); and Dave Viera, *Lighting for Film and Electronic Cinematography* (Belmont, CA: Wadsworth, 1993).

2. Anton Wilson, *Cinema Workshop,* (Hollywood: American Society of Cinematographers, 1983), pp. 243–245.

3. The camera manufacturer BTS, for example, has introduced a Frame Transfer CCD with a shutter that virtually eliminates smearing. Each image is transferred to storage before a new image takes its place. The shutter is synchronized to operate during this transfer, interrupting exposure during the frame shift much as a film camera's shutter blocks the light while a new frame is being pulled into place. Thus, each frame of the picture is independent of previous frames and highlights. An off-shoot of this kind of chip is called a frame interline transfer sensor (FIT), a merging of frame transfer and interline transfer sensors. Sony uses its new sensor, the Hyper HAD CCD imager (also FIT), in its top-of-the-line cameras, such as the Betacam SP camcorder.

4. Wilson, p. 247.

5. Harry Mathias and Richard Patterson, *Electronic Cinematography: Achieving Photographic Control over the Video Image* (Belmont, CA: Wadsworth, 1985), pp. 6–12.

6. John Premack, "Taking the Sun at Face Value," *TV Technology,* October 1995, pp. 39–45.

7. James Caruso and Mavis Arthur, "Interior Lighting Techniques," *Video Pro,* March 1995, pp. 34–37.

8. See, for example, Kodak's line of EXR films. Kodak's EXR 5296 is a tungsten-balanced 35mm color negative film that uses the "T-grain" emulsion technology to produce an extremely sharp, fine-grained stock while also improving the film speed to 500 ASA.

9. Depending on atmospheric conditions and the time of day, the color temperature of blue skylight can range from 7,000 to 30,000 degrees on the Kelvin scale.

10. This section refers to normal fluorescent lights, not the wide-band or three-band fluorescent lights that are beginning to come into use. See Chapter 6 for a discussion of some of these instruments.

11. When using all tungsten lighting is not possible, some of the high-output flicker-free fluorescent lighting instruments for fill or side lighting may be necessary. These special tubes are usually mounted in four-, six-, or eight-tube reflectors and are available in a variety of color temperatures. Two examples of this type of instrument are the Sunray from the Leonetti Co. (5609 Sunset Blvd., Hollywood, CA 90028) and the LightArray System from the Lowell-Light Manufacturing Co. (140 58th St., Brooklyn, New York 11220).

12. Mathias and Patterson, pp. 178–179.

13. Sonny Sonnenfeld, "The Basics of TV Studio Lighting," *Videography,* August 1991, pp. 57–59.

chapter eight
Microphones and Recorders

Sound is an essential element of movies and should be given much thought and care. If you need proof, watch your TV set with the sound off for a while and see how well you understand what is happening. Then turn the sound up, cover your eyes, and listen without seeing the picture. You probably will be able to understand what is happening much better without the picture than without the sound.

Nevertheless, student (and professional) moviemakers often become so absorbed in setting up proper picture composition that they forget to leave time for proper microphone positioning. They hastily place a microphone in front of the talent and then fret over the poor sound quality during postproduction—when it is too late.

Much of what is needed for good sound is the same for film and video. Recording equipment differs, but microphones, cables, and connectors are identical. Most significant, the basic principles of sound are the same for virtually all media.

The Nature of Sound

Sound has a number of characteristics that are important to understand in order to select the right audio equipment and record properly. These include pitch, loudness, timbre, duration, and velocity.[1]

Pitch and Frequency

Sound waves travel in well-defined cycles. The number of times per second that the wave travels from the beginning of one cycle to the beginning of the next is its **frequency,** which is measured in **hertz (Hz).** For example, a sound wave that goes from the beginning of one cycle to the beginning of the next at 200 times per second is said to have a frequency of 200 Hz. (Figure 8.1 shows high and low frequencies.)

The sound made by the differing frequencies is the **pitch.** Bass sounds have lower frequencies and lower pitch than treble sounds. For example, a bass violin has a frequency of about 100 Hz, whereas a triangle has a frequency of about 13,000 Hz. Men's voices have a lower frequency (hence lower pitch) than women's voices. People with exceptionally good hearing can hear about 20 Hz to 20,000 Hz.

Each microphone and tape recorder has its own **frequency response**—the range of frequencies that it will pick up. The frequency response needed depends on the type of sound being recorded. For example, the range of frequencies used by the human voice is from about 200 Hz for a deep male bass to 3,000 Hz for a high female voice. For recording speech, a mic and recorder with a somewhat limited frequency response will probably be adequate. On the other hand, for recording music, you would want a wider frequency response, perhaps as broad as 20 Hz to 20,000 Hz.

Microphones and recorders may not pick up all frequencies equally well. As a result, equipment manufacturers usually represent the ability to pick up various frequencies with a graph called a **frequency curve** (see Figure 8.2). Some mics and recorders do not pick up the very high and very low frequencies as well as they pick up midrange frequencies; therefore, the frequency curve will be higher in the middle. Sometimes this is because the equipment is inexpensive and not well constructed, but other times this is entirely intentional. For example, some mics have a **speech bump;** they *intentionally* pick up human speech frequencies better than they pick up other frequencies. Other mics have a switch with two positions, one for speech and one for music. When the mic is in the speech position, it records a narrower band of frequencies than when it is in the music position. Microphones and recorders that pick up all frequencies equally well are said to be flat because they have a flat curve.

You can manipulate frequency characteristics in other ways. For example, some mics boost the bass frequencies as a person moves closer to the mic. This is called **proximity effect** and is usually undesirable because it gives the voice a fuzzy sound. However, it can make some male voices sound more mellow.

There is no universally correct frequency response or frequency curve. The choice depends on the use intended. Sometimes a very limited frequency response, perhaps 1,000 Hz to 2,000 Hz, is desirable to create a tinny sound similar to an answering machine.

Obviously, all the equipment within a complete recording system should have a similar frequency response. A symphony orchestra recorded with high-quality wide-frequency response mics should not be fed into a $50 cassette tape recorder with narrow frequency response.

Loudness and Amplitude

In addition to having a frequency, a sound wave has a height or **amplitude.** Amplitude is related to loudness. As the amplitude increases, the sound will appear to become louder. Loudness is measured in **decibels (dB).** A whisper is about 20 dB, conversation is about 55 dB, and a rock concert can get well above 100 dB. The **threshold of pain** starts at about 120 dB.

The range of quietness to loudness is called **dynamic range.** Different pieces of equipment have different dynamic ranges. If something is recorded louder than the system can handle, the result is **distortion.** For example, if a system has a 60-dB range and you plan to record at 20 to 100 dBs, some of the sound will not record well. The loud notes will become a muddy jumble, and the frequencies will not come out of the equipment with the same clarity with which they went in. For recording speech, mics and recorders with a limited dynamic range will be quite adequate. But for recording a rock band or symphonic music, every piece of equipment in the system should have a large dynamic range in the neighborhood of 90 dB, or the recording will be distorted.

Another element related to loudness is the **signal-to-noise ratio (S/N).** Most electronic equipment has inherent **noise** built into it; it comes from the various electronic components, such as those used for amplification. One of the specifications provided for equipment is its signal-to-noise ratio, usually something like 55:1. This means that for every 55 dB of signal re-

Low Frequency

High Frequency

Figure 8.1
A low-frequency sound has fewer cycles per second than a high-frequency sound.

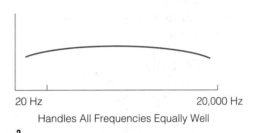
20 Hz — 20,000 Hz
Handles All Frequencies Equally Well
a

20 Hz — 20,000 Hz
Handles Mid-Frequencies Best
b

20 Hz   200 Hz   3000 Hz   20,000 Hz
Speech Bump
c

Figure 8.2
These drawings show three common frequency curves for microphones and other electronic equipment. The curve in drawing a is often referred to as a flat curve because the equipment it represents reproduces all frequencies with about the same accuracy. The curve in drawing b represents equipment that produces middle frequencies better than it produces high or low frequencies. Drawing c represents a mic that best reproduces frequencies in the human speech range.

corded 1 dB of noise is present. A ratio of 55:1 is considered good, whereas one as low as 20:1 is considered poor. Generally, the more expensive equipment has the higher signal-to-noise ratio.

Timbre

Timbre deals with such characteristics as mellowness, fullness, sharpness, and resonance. It is what distinguishes a violin from a clarinet when both are playing the same pitch at the same loudness. It is also what distinguishes each person's voice.

Harmonics and **overtones** contribute to the production of timbre. A sound has one particular pitch, called a **fundamental**, but it has other pitches that are exact multiples of the fundamental frequency (harmonics) and pitches that may or may not be exact multiples of the frequency (overtones). The way the fundamental combines with its harmonics and overtones is part of what creates timbre.

The room in which something is recorded can also affect timbre. All other things being equal, a voice will sound more hollow in a large room than in a small room.

Timbre can also vary for different mics. Although two mics may have the same frequency response and dynamic range, one brand may sound more mellow, whereas the other sounds sharper. Choosing the right mic to enhance a given timbre is mostly a matter of trial and error and experience.

Duration

Another characteristic of sound is **duration**, the length of time that a particular sound lasts. Duration has three parts: attack, sustain, and decay. **Attack** is the amount of time it takes a sound to get from silence up to full volume; **sustain** is the amount of time the sound is at full volume; **decay** is the amount of time it takes sound to go from full loudness to silence. These three together add up to duration.

Clipped speech that occurs in certain dialects is largely the result of duration differences between that dialect and what we consider standard American speech. Much of the difference between the sound of a violin when it is plucked and when it is bowed is due to changes in duration. A note played in staccato on the piano has a shorter duration than one played while pushing the sustain pedal.

Velocity

Velocity refers to the speed of sound. This speed is 750 miles per hour, but it is relatively slow. It is certainly much slower than the speed of light, as anyone who has experienced thunder and lightning can attest.

Three-to-One Method

a

Head-to-Head Method

b

Figure 8.3

The two main methods of preventing multiple microphone interference. The three-to-one method (a) shows how to place the mics so that they are at least three times as far apart from each other as they are from the subject. The head-to-head method (b) shows the placement of mics facing each other.

This relatively slow speed can cause **phase** problems. If two microphones pick up the same sound at slightly different times, they can create a signal that is out of phase; one of the mics is receiving the sound when the wave is going up, and the other is receiving the sound when the wave is going down. The result is that some or all of the sound is canceled, and little or nothing is heard.

One way to avoid the phase problem is to follow the **three-to-one rule.** No two microphones should be closer together than three times the distance between them and the subject. In other words, if one mic is 6 inches from a person, the second mic must be at least 18 inches from the first mic. In this way the mics will pick up very little of each other's sound. Another way to avoid phase problems is to place the mics head to head so that they receive the sound at exactly the same time.[2] Figure 8.3 illustrates the three-to-one rule and head-to-head mic placement.

equidistant

Incorrect Placement

a

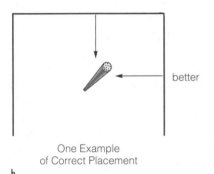

better

One Example
of Correct Placement

b

Figure 8.4

This placement of the microphone (a) is likely to cause phase problems because the mic is parallel to the walls and the same distance from all of them. Position b would be preferable because the mic is at an angle and slightly closer to one wall than to the other.

Phase problems can also occur when only one mic is used. If that mic is placed in the middle of a room that has perfectly parallel walls, the sound will bounce in such a way that some sound waves cancel each other out. This can be avoided by placing the mic so that it is at an angle to the walls and is not equidistant from the walls. One way to do this is to place the mic on a diagonal of the room, slightly off center. Figure 8.4 shows correct and incorrect placement of a single mic to avoid phase problems.

Microphones

In addition to differing in frequency response, dynamic range, and timbre-producing qualities, microphones have particular characteristics that relate to their directionality, construction, impedance, and positioning.[3]

Directionality

Directionality in a microphone involves its **pickup pattern**. The main pickup patterns likely to be used in moviemaking are **cardioid**

cardioid
or
unidirectional

omnidirectional

ultracardioid

Figure 8.5

The most common pickup patterns.

(picking up mainly from one side in a heart-shaped pattern) and **omnidirectional** (picking up from all sides).

If only one or two people are speaking and background noise is not desirable, a cardioid mic is appropriate. These mics are the workhorses in film because their pattern picks up sound from the front, where the talent is located, and not from the rear, where the camera and other equipment are operating.

Omnidirectional mics are best for picking up a large number of people and are excellent for gathering background noise. Because of their broad pickup pattern they do not pick up distant sounds well. Usually, an omnidirectional mic must be closer to talent than a cardioid mic in order to achieve the same volume as the cardioid.

Sometimes sound for a movie must be picked up from a great distance in order to keep the mic out of the picture. In these circumstances, more extreme cardioid mics, referred to as **supercardioid, hypercardioid,** and **ultracardioid,** are used. Their patterns are longer and narrower than those of the regular cardioid. (Figure 8.5 shows various pickup patterns.)

Stereo recording requires at least two microphones or specially designed stereo mics that have several different pickup elements within them. One approach to stereo recording is called **M-S (midside) miking.** This uses **bidirectional** (picking up from two sides) and supercardioid microphones (see Figure 8.6a). The

Figure 8.6

Two methods used for stereo recording. The M-S method (a) uses a bidirectional and a supercardioid mic. The X-Y method (b) uses two cardioid mics.

M–S Method

a

X–Y Method

b

a

Figure 8.7

Microphones for stereo recording. Photo a shows how two cardioid mics might be set up on one stand to record both left and right channels. Photo b is Audio-Technica's OnePoint™ X/Y Stereo microphone. This single microphone contains the elements necessary for X-Y miking. (Photo a courtesy of Shure Brothers, Inc.; photo b courtesy of Audio-Technica)

b

bidirectional mic picks up sound to the left and the right, and the supercardioid mic picks up sound to the front. The output of both mics is fed through a complicated circuit that makes use of their phase differences to produce left and right channels. You could set up two separate microphones, but it is more common to use one mic with both the bidirectional and supercardioid elements in it. Sometimes a switch on such a mic will disengage the bidirectional element so that the mic can be used to record monaural sound.

Another method of stereo recording is called **X-Y miking.** Two cardioid mics are placed next to each other. One angles to the left at a 45-degree angle, and the other angles to the right at 45 degrees (see Figure 8.6b). This way, both mics pick up sound from the center, and sounds for each side are picked up primarily by one mic or the other. When the recording is played back through stereo speakers, it yields left and right channels—one reproducing what was picked up by the right mic and the other reproducing what the left mic picked up. Once again, you can use either two mics or one mic with stereo elements. Figure 8.7a shows how to set up two mics on one stand to record left and right channels, and Figure 8.7b shows a single mic that can record stereo.

M-S is used more frequently than X-Y, in part because it is more compatible with monaural. In other words, a program recorded with M-S stereo will sound better through a monaural speaker than one recorded with X-Y pickup. Also, M-S recording reproduces the sound coming from the center with more sharpness than does the X-Y technique, and it can be manipulated more easily in postproduction.[4]

Quadraphonic and **surround sound** can also be recorded using a variety of pickup patterns. Quadraphonic mics can record four channels of sound, or four different mics can be placed in the scene to pick up the sound. Surround sound, which can encompass up to 360 degrees, is usually recorded with a number of cardioid and/or supercardioid mics, each pointed at a different spot around the circumference of the circle.

Most microphones have a set pickup pattern, often written on the mic or the box it comes in because it is not easy to discern the mic's pickup pattern simply by looking at it. Some microphones have interchangeable elements so that the mic can be changed from one form to another: for example, from cardioid to omnidirectional. In other instances, mics have a switch to change directionality, perhaps from cardioid to supercardioid. A more complicated variation is the **zoom mic.** It can be changed gradually from cardioid to ultracardioid so that sounds at different distances can be heard clearly.

Construction

The two main types of microphones used for electronic moviemaking, based on their construction, are dynamic and condenser.

A **dynamic mic** uses a diaphragm, magnet, and coils of wire wrapped around a magnet (see Figure 8.8a) to generate sound signals. The diaphragm moves in response to the pressure of sound and creates a disturbance in the magnetic field that induces a small electrical current in the coils of wire.

A **condenser mic** (Figure 8.8b) has an electronic component called a **capacitor** that responds to sound. A diaphragm moving in response to sound waves changes the capacitance in a backplate, which then creates a small electrical charge. Because charging the backplate requires a power supply, many condenser mics have batteries or some other external power source. Other mics, called **electret condenser mics,** have permanently charged backplates.

Dynamic mics and condenser mics are fairly rugged and have wide frequency responses. However, the dynamic mic is slightly more rugged because its sound element is more sturdy than that in a condenser mic. The condenser mic, on the other hand, has slightly better frequency response. Dynamic microphones do not work well with some individuals because the mics have a tendency to exaggerate plosives and sibilance. In other words, *p*'s will pop and *s*'s will hiss.[5]

Impedance

Microphones are also classified as either high or low **impedance.** Impedance is a characteristic, measured in **ohms,** that refers to the opposition to the flow of alternating current (AC).

Internal Construction of a Dynamic Mic

output   magnet

diaphragm   coils

a

Internal Construction of a Condenser Mic

output   backplate

diaphragm

b

Figure 8.8
The construction of the two most common types of microphones, the dynamic mic (a) and the condenser mic (b).

High-impedance mics can go as high as 10,000 ohms. One thousand ohms is usually considered the upper end of low-impedance mics, but most low-impedance mics are in the 150- to 350-ohm range. Professionals usually use low-impedance mics because they perform better. For one thing, low-impedance mics can be hooked up with long lengths of cable without the sound degrading, whereas high-impedance mics lose sound quality after several feet of cable. This is because the signal encounters less opposition if the impedance is low. Low-impedance mics are also less likely to pick up electrical noises, such as static from vacuum cleaners or fluorescent lights. Impedance should be consistent throughout a system. Low-impedance mics should be plugged into low-impedance tape recorders, and high-impedance mics should be connected to high-impedance tape recorders. Mixing low and high impedance yields distorted sound or degrades frequency response. Some low-impedance mics can be plugged into high-impedance equipment with only a slight degradation, but plugging high-impedance mics into low-impedance equipment can cause severe distortion. Specially made converters can correct an impedance mismatch by changing high-impedance mics to low and vice versa.[6]

Figure 8.9
A fishpole in its collapsed (unextended) position. (Photo courtesy of Beyer Dynamics)

Figure 8.10
A mic on a table stand. (Photo courtesy of Shure Brothers, Inc.)

Positioning

You can use many devices to position mics. The most common in moviemaking is the **boom**, a long pole with the mic on the end of it. It positions the mic above the actors and is moved as each person speaks. Sometimes these booms are elaborate devices with wheels, gears, and hydraulic lifts. Sometimes they consist of a simple pole (called a **fishpole**) held by the mic operator

(see Figure 8.9). Often they have a **shock mount** on the end to isolate the mic from vibrations. One advantage of a boom is that it can follow moving talent.

Stands can also hold mics, but because these stands will show in the picture, they are appropriate only when a mic would naturally be present—a singer in front of a **floor stand** or a radio commentator sitting by a **table stand** such as that shown in Figure 8.10. Sometimes people simply hold microphones. This is common for news and documentaries, but for dramas such an obvious show of the mic must be motivated.

You can also hide microphones on the set in props such as flower vases and figurines. You must hide mics carefully, in part so they won't show and in part so their pickup is adequate. **Hidden mics** are not desirable if people in the scene move a great deal because their voices will fade in and out as they move close to and away from the mics.

Mics can also be built into cameras or tape recorders, but **camera mics** are not advisable for moviemaking because they are usually too far from the actors to pick up their sound well. What they do pick up well is the noise of the equipment, which is definitely undesirable in a narrative movie. Mics mounted on cameras can prove satisfactory for news and documentary work, however. For example, a mic mounted on a camera is often best for an uncontrolled situation in which people are not willing or able to take the time to talk into a properly set-up microphone.

Very small microphones called **lavalieres** (see Figure 8.11) attach to clothing. Although lavs show in the picture, they usually will not be noticed because they are so small. They can be made to look like a tie clasp on a man or jewelry on a woman. However, most require a cable, which limits the actor's movement. Also, although you can hide the cable under clothes, it is likely to show in a long shot that includes the set. The sound from a lav may be inadequate when clothes rustle and when people turn their heads to one side or the other.

Some microphones—be they lavaliere or stand mics—do not have cables. They are called **wireless mics** and operate on FM frequencies. The mic has a small antenna attached to it or to a transmitter pack that can be hidden in a

Figure 8.11
A lavaliere microphone is often clipped to a tie. (Photo courtesy of Audio-Technica)

a

b

Figure 8.13
(a) A microphone case, a windscreen, a shotgun mic, and a shock mount. (b) A heavy-duty windscreen for a shotgun mic. (Photo a courtesy of Shure Brothers, Inc.; photo b courtesy of Light Wave Systems)

Figure 8.12
A wireless microphone system. A lav (bottom center) is attached to a small body pack (left). This unit transmits the audio signal to the receiving unit (right), which can be located at some distance. (Photo courtesy of Panasonic)

pocket (see Figure 8.12). This pack sends the audio signal to a receiver that can be located a considerable distance from the mic and attached to recording equipment such as an audio recorder or VCR. Because the mics do not have cables, the actors can move about freely and quickly, and cables do not need to be hidden on the set.[7]

Another way to pick up distant sound for a movie is to use a **shotgun mic** (see Figure 8.13a). This mic has a very long but narrow pickup pattern, usually super-, hyper-, or ultra-cardioid. It can pick up from a distance but must be pointed carefully and repointed if the sound source moves because of its narrow pickup. Unfortunately, this narrow area can include sounds reflected from an object, such as a building. Shotgun mics have been known to pick up the noise of a trash truck not in the immediate area; the sound had bounced off a building in the background that was in the microphone's path. A shotgun mic also tends to pick up some sounds to its rear, so its rear portion should be pointed toward something that is silent.

Shotgun mics are almost always covered with a **windscreen,** a metal or foam cover that cuts down on small noises such as wind (see Figure 8.13b). Other mics often have built-in or added-on windscreens, especially if the recording is being made outdoors.

Cables and Connectors

Most microphones (wireless excluded) use cables and connectors to carry the electrical impulses from the mic to other equipment. These

PHONE CONNECTORS

Male Plug   Female Jack

sleeve   tip

a

MINIPHONE CONNECTORS

Male Plug   Female Jack

sleeve   tip

b

RCA CONNECTORS

Male Plug   Female Jack

center prong

outer covering

c

XLR CONNECTORS

outer covering   Male Plug

slot for guide pin

prongs

Female Jack

guide pin

connector lock

d

Figure 8.14
Commonly used audio connectors.

Balanced and Unbalanced Cables

Cables consist of wires protected by a shielding, usually made of plastic. These cables are referred to as **balanced** or **unbalanced**. A balanced cable has three wires—one for the positive, one for the negative, and one for ground. Unbalanced cable has two wires, one for the positive and one that acts as both the negative and the ground.

Balanced cables are better because a separate ground wire means they are less susceptible to extraneous interference. Unbalanced lines are usually used for consumer-grade equipment because they are cheaper, but professional equipment uses balanced lines. Always take care to avoid placing audio cables (balanced or unbalanced) parallel to power cables because this can induce hum.

Connector Types

A variety of connectors attach mics to recorders. A **phone plug** is a long, slender connector with a sleeve and tip, and the **miniphone plug** is a smaller version of the phone plug. The **RCA plug** (also called the **phono plug**) has a short prong and outer covering. The **XLR connector** has three prongs and an outer covering. It also has a guide pin and lock so that it remains firmly in place. All of these connectors have male plugs and female jacks (see Figure 8.14). Usually, the male connector is at the end of the mic cable and plugs into the female connector built into the recorder.

Phone and miniphone connectors can be either **monaural (mono)** or **stereo** (see Figure 8.15). Monaural versions have one ring, and stereo versions have two. RCA and XLR connectors are always monaural. If you want stereo, you need two connectors, one to the left channel and one to the right channel.

The XLR is the professional standard because its three prongs accommodate the three wires of a balanced line. Its locking mechanism also makes it more reliable.

Other connectors are available, but they are not common. Sometimes manufacturers make unusual connectors, hoping that people will buy only their brand of equipment. This policy usually backfires, especially in the professional world where different situations call for different mics.

are actually the elements most likely to prove troublesome during recording sessions. Connectors that are not soldered properly and cables that contain broken wires are common causes of audio failure.

Figure 8.15
The connector at the bottom is stereo, as distinguished by its two rings. The connector at the top is mono.

Adapters are available to convert the more common connectors from one form to another (see Figure 8.16). For example, an adapter fitted on the end of an RCA plug can change it to a miniphone. This adapter consists of a female RCA jack and a male miniphone plug. Most production facilities have a variety of these adapters on hand because the connectors needed usually change as microphones and recorders are changed.

In general, professional high-quality equipment uses low-impedance mics, balanced lines, and XLR connectors. When cost is a factor, the combination is likely to be high-impedance mics, unbalanced lines, and miniphone connectors.

Figure 8.16
An array of adapters.

Recorders

Sound travels from a microphone through cable and connectors to recording equipment, which stores it on audiotape, videotape, disc, or computer drive. Tapes are plastic bases coated with metal oxide. High-quality tape should always be used for production; it will usually have less hiss than low-quality tape. **Hiss** is built-in noise at the high frequencies that can greatly detract from the clarity of the recording. Because high-quality tape can record a higher signal-to-noise ratio, it reduces the amount of hiss in relation to the desired signal. High-quality tape will also have fewer dropouts, a loss of signal because the oxide has fallen off the base. Reel-to-reel audiotape should be at least 1.5 millimeters thick, and 60-minute rather than 90-minute audiocassettes should be used so that the tape is thick enough. Thick tape is less likely to stretch and is less susceptible to **print-through,** the transfer during storage of sound from one layer of tape to the layer above or below it.

If possible, previously used tapes should be erased with a **degausser** before they are used again (see Figure 8.17). A degausser is a separate piece of electromagnetic equipment that lines up all the metal oxide particles so that the tape appears to be blank. Although the tape recorder itself erases the tape right before it is recorded, a safer procedure is to degauss an entire tape before you use it. In this way there will not be stray sounds on a tape if it is stopped and then started in a slightly different place.

Figure 8.17
A powerful tape degausser especially designed for the new metal particle audio and videotapes. (Photo courtesy of Garner Industries)

Discs, such as recordable CDs, are starting to be used to record sounds. Sound can also be recorded on computer hard drives but this is not yet practical for feature film recording because of the great quantity of computer storage space such recording would require.

Figure 8.18
A four-channel Nagra-D digital audio recorder. (Photo courtesy of Nagra Kudelski S.A./Switzerland)

Double System and Single System Sound Recording

Double system sound records the picture on one piece of equipment and the sound on another. **Single system** sound records both within the same piece of equipment.

Double system sound recording has its roots in film production, which has traditionally recorded sound on a **reel-to-reel** audiotape recorder, totally separate from the film. The picture is recorded within the camera, and the sound is recorded by the **audiotape recorder (ATR)**. The ATRs designed for recording film sound, such as the Nagra (see Figure 8.18), are of very high quality and usually have at least two channels. They accept low-impedance, balanced XLR connections, and they have excellent frequency response, signal-to-noise ratio, and dynamic range.

One reason film has traditionally used double system recording has to do with editing—film was physically cut when edited. This means the sound for each frame would have had to be adjacent to it if the cut were to be made properly. But placing the sound at the same point as its accompanying picture is impossible because taking a picture is an intermittent process. The film stops in the camera momentarily to be exposed. If sound were recorded intermittently, it

would be unacceptable. As a result, if sound is recorded in a camera, it is usually ahead of the picture by at least 18 frames so that the film has time to run at a more uniform pace.

Sometimes, single system recording was done with film, particularly in nonprofessional settings such as those involving Super 8 home movies. This method required a film camera with a sound head and film with a magnetic audio stripe along one edge. The quality of this sound was not as good as that recorded on a Nagra, and it was difficult to edit. If the edit was made to accommodate the picture, some of the sound needed was lost. If the edit was made to accommodate the sound, too much picture showed.

Video sound is generally recorded single system: that is, both the picture and sound are recorded on videotape. The audio and video heads of a VCR cannot be at the same place either, but because video editing involves dubbing rather than cutting, the sound and picture can be kept together.

Video can also be recorded double system. When the sound is recorded away from the camera, the sound operator can have more control over it. Also audio recorders often yield higher-quality sound than the sound track on VCRs. If the sound-recording capabilities of the VCR are limited, you may opt to record the sound separately on a high-quality audiotape recorder.

Of course, when the dialogue and picture are recorded separately, they will need to be put in **sync** at some time in the future. With single system film or video this is no problem because the two ride together. With double system film a cable was often used to connect the film camera to the audiotape recorder and send a pulse to the tape recorder as each frame passed through the film camera. In effect, this created electronic sprocket holes on the audiotape. If the camera ran at slightly less than 24 frames per second, a record of that was on the audiotape and could be corrected later. Another method of maintaining film-sound sync was to equip both the camera and tape recorder with a special crystal sync control unit that governed the speed of both units so accurately that sync problems did not occur.

With double system video, you can keep the VCR and ATR in sync by using **SMPTE time code**. Recording this code requires a special component or piece of equipment called a **time code generator** (see Figure 8.19a). It places a

a

b

Figure 8.19

(a) A time code generator. (b) A time code reader. (Photos courtesy of Gray Engineering Laboratories)

signal on both the ATR and the VCR that designates each frame. In other words, a signal that will translate to 2 minutes, 5 seconds, and 15 frames (00:02: 05:15) is recorded on the audiotape at exactly the same time it is recorded on the videotape. When both tapes are played back in conjunction with a **time code reader** (see Figure 8.19b), the frame numbers of each will appear on a TV screen or the time code reader's screen. This information is used, under computer control, to keep picture and sound in sync during the editing process.

Today, most film productions employ time code. This way, the film can be transferred to videotape that has the same SMPTE time code reference as the sound, and the two can be matched up during editing. This is discussed in more detail in Chapter 12.[8]

Analog and Digital

Much audio recording for film and video is **analog,** but **digital** recording is becoming more and more common. In fact, some people have described what's going on now as **digital creep.** Moviemakers, musicians, and others are gradually switching from analog to digital as old equipment wears out or as money becomes available to purchase new equipment.

For the analog process, the recorder produces a continuously variable electrical signal with a shape defined by the sound wave it is representing. Each time the analog signal is recorded or processed, it is subject to degradation because the signal changes shape slightly. Digital recording converts the audio information into an electrical signal composed of a series of on and off pulses. These do not degrade when they are rerecorded. Sound kept in digital form can be dubbed numerous times without losing quality. Because of this and other inherent characteristics of the digital process, digital sound is superior to analog.

Manufacturers have introduced several different digital recording formats, and it is difficult to know which one or ones will be accepted by moviemakers (or consumers). One of the first was **DAT (digital audiotape),** a cassette format marketed in Japan by Sony starting in the late 1980s (see Figure 8.20). Its quality was so good that American record companies feared it would cut into their business severely. They envisioned someone buying a CD, recording multiple copies on DAT, and giving those copies to friends who, of course, would not need to buy the CD. As a result, the record companies were able to delay the introduction of DAT in the United States while they pursued copyright considerations.[9]

While DAT was on hold, Philips developed a different format, **DCC (digital compact cassette).** Its main advantage over DAT was that it

Figure 8.20
Digital audio recording tape. (Photo courtesy of Maxell Corporation of America)

Figure 8.21
Tape first passes the erase head, then the record head, then the playback head.

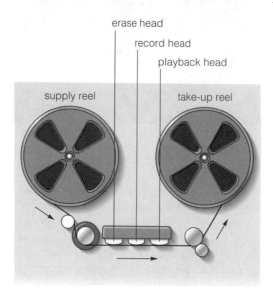

Features of Sound Recorders

The videotape recorders and the audiotape recorders used for moviemaking have the same function controls as most recorders—play, record, stop, pause, fast forward, rewind. Some allow you to hear the sound as it is rewinding or fast forwarding so that you can cue it easily. Most recorders have three audio heads—erase, record, and play (see Figure 8.21). The erase head lines up the iron particles in a straight manner that contains no audio impulses. The record head rearranges the particles to form representations of the sound. For that reason the erase head is always before the record head. The play head picks up the sound recorded by the record head and reproduces it. Some recorders have only two heads, one to erase and one that operates as both the play head and the record head.

Audiotape and videotape recorders usually have two types of inputs—mic and line. **Mic inputs** are for microphones, and **line inputs** are for other equipment, such as tape recorders and turntables. The difference between mic and line inputs is the amount of **amplification** that the signal is given. Tape recorders and similar equipment usually have some means of amplifying the audio signal. Microphones do not, so they need the extra amplification provided by the tape recorder. Therefore, you should always make sure the mic is plugged into a mic input, not into a line input. If you make a mistake, the sound will not record at a level high enough to be useful.

High-quality tape recorders have a **VU (volume unit) meter,** a device that shows how loudly the sound is being recorded. Sometimes this is an actual scale that has a red area at one end where the needle indicating the **volume** level should not linger. In other cases, the VU meter is a bar of flashing diodes that change color from green to red when the signal is too high. In either case, **peaking in the red** (also called **overmodulation**) for any length of time is undesirable because the recording will be distorted. On the other hand, sound that regularly rides at the low end of the meter (**riding in the mud**) will not be loud enough. See Figure 8.22 for examples. Ideally, audio should ride between 20 and 100 percent on the VU meter.

was compatible with the older analog cassette recorders. In other words, a DCC recorder could play standard cassettes as well as digital ones, while DAT could only play its digital tapes.[10]

Sony, meanwhile, developed the **Mini Disc,** a disc format that can record and play back.[11] Some moviemakers have experimented with recording double system dialogue with these formats, but more applications for digital recording have surfaced in the arena of film postproduction.

To add to the race, Nagra (*the* name in film audio for many years) has developed a recorder that looks and operates like the traditional Nagra ¼-inch machine, except that it records digitally instead of by analog.[12]

Some VCRs record and play back digital sound. For example, Sony's Hi-8 and Panasonic's M-II formats use **PCM (pulse code modulation)** as one way of recording audio. PCM converts microphone signals into the ons and offs needed for digital encoding.

Figure 8.22
The needle on the left VU meter is riding in the mud. The needle on the right VU meter is peaking in the red.

To help keep levels consistent throughout recording, some tape recorders are equipped with a **tone generator.** This sends out a constant 1 kilohertz sound that can be used to set the various volume controls. The controls should be set so that the **tone** registers at 100 percent on all the VU meters that are part of the audio system. That way, the operator can judge the relative loudness of different signals. For example, if a recorder has two channels, 1 and 2, and the volume controls for both are set at 100 percent, the operator can be sure that sound on both channels that registers at 60 percent will be the same volume. It is a good idea to record a minute of 100 percent tone at the beginning of a tape so that when the tape is played back, the playback recorder's controls can be configured properly. That way, the sound being played back will be at the same volume as when it was recorded.

Another feature often found on higher-end recorders is **equalization.** This function enables you to cut out or emphasize certain frequencies, such as treble or bass. Sometimes, unwanted noises in the high frequencies, such as whining from the equipment, can be filtered out through equalization so that they are not recorded. Of course, anything else at that frequency range will be filtered out, too. You definitely should not use equalization to get rid of frequencies in the voice area when you are recording dialogue.

Some recorders have **automatic gain controls (AGCs).** When this control is on, the gain is automatically adjusted so that the recording is neither too soft nor too loud. If the control is not on, an operator must adjust the volume control manually to change the degree of loudness.

The counter on a recorder can be valuable for finding your place. Many counters measure revolutions of the tape, but more sophisticated ones display the minutes and seconds into the recording. They can be reset to zero so that new counting can begin whenever you want.

A connection for earphones, a headset, or a speaker is also necessary. The only way you can really tell whether you are recording the sound properly is by listening to it as it is being recorded and/or afterward.[13]

Some recorders, especially camcorders, have very little in the way of audio recording features. Not only do they not have features such as a tone generator or equalization, but they don't even have a meter or a jack for a headset, making it extremely difficult to know whether the sound is being recorded. Before using (or preferably before purchasing) a video system for moviemaking, consider carefully the audio features available. Many users (and salespeople) become so enamored with the video features of a recording system that they forget about audio and end up with something that is unacceptable and difficult to edit.

Recording on Different Tracks

With many audio and video systems you can record sound on several tracks of the tape. For example, two people at opposite ends of a room can each be recorded on different mics, one fed into channel 1 and one into channel 2. This method permits you to control each person's volume separately.[14] Or the two tracks can be used for the left and right channels of stereo.

On analog ATRs the sound records horizontally along the tape. This is often referred to as **linear audio** recording. If the tape recorder is single track, the whole audiotape records that one sequence of sounds. If the recorder is two track, the top of the tape records one signal and the bottom records the other. If the tape is stereo, both signals go in the same direction. Multitrack configurations simply add to the number of separate signals that can be recorded (see Figure 8.23).

The positioning of the audio signal on videotape varies from format to format, to the point of confusion. For example, ¾-inch U-Matic

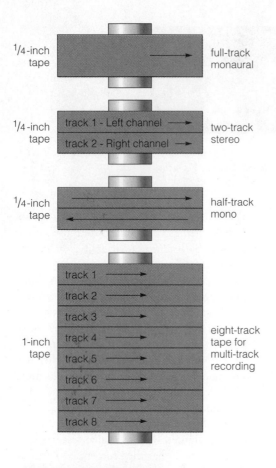

Figure 8.23
Tape can be recorded on in a variety of ways. This illustration shows four different track configurations.

1/4-inch tape — full-track monaural

1/4-inch tape — track 1 - Left channel / track 2 - Right channel — two-track stereo

1/4-inch tape — half-track mono

1-inch tape — track 1, track 2, track 3, track 4, track 5, track 6, track 7, track 8 — eight-track tape for multi-track recording

Figure 8.24
The positioning of the sound signals for the U-Matic format.

control track
— video tracks
— channel 2 audio
— channel 1 audio

3/4-inch U-Matic Configuration

AFM Audio Recording
— video track
— hi-fi audio track

PCM Audio Recording
— video track
— DATA area (time code, etc.)
— PCM audio track

Figure 8.25
Representations of AFM and PCM recording. The AFM audio track cannot be separated from the video for editing purposes, but the PCM audio can.

video also being erased or recorded over. PCM is separate from the video; it has its own "real estate" on the tape (see Figure 8.25). PCM and AFM audio recording allow for much higher-quality sound than does linear recording on videotape. For example, the frequency range for most linear tracks is 50 to 12,000 Hz, and for AFM it is 20 to 20,000 Hz. Likewise, dynamic range is 50 dB for linear and 80 dB for AFM, and signal-to-noise ratio is 45:1 for linear and 70:1 for AFM.[15]

Care of Audio Equipment

Although most audio equipment is manufactured to hold up under fairly rugged recording conditions, it should be treated as gently as possible. Microphones should always be carried in their cases, most of which are foam lined. Carrying mics in their cases also helps prevent the loss of accessories such as clips and batteries. You should never blow into a microphone to test it; such puffs of air can damage the sound element.

Always telescope mic stands down to their smallest size for carrying. If they have cases, use them for carrying and storing the stands.

Never pull cables out of their sockets by tugging on the wire; remove the connector gently with your hand. Some connectors require that you push a lever to release them. Always do so; don't just yank. Be sure to coil the cable properly. One way, called the *over-under method*, involves making repeated circles with the cable (see Figure 8.26). Another way is to lay the cable on the floor in a figure *8* and then double the top half of the 8 over the bottom half. Then put

VCRs record two linear tracks side by side below the video portion of the tape (see Figure 8.24). Audio 1 is at the bottom of the tape, and audio 2 is above it. If you need to record only one audio track, you should use audio 2 because it is less subject to tape damage than audio 1, which is placed at the edge of the tape.

The Video-8 and Hi-8 formats do not record linear audio tracks. Rather, they record sound diagonally, just as they record the video signal. These formats record two different types of sound, **AFM (audio frequency modulation)** (referred to as **hi-fi** in the VHS formats) and PCM (digital). AFM rides with the video signal, so it cannot be played back separately. It also cannot be erased or recorded over without the

a   b   c   d

tape or specially made cable holders over the wire so that it stays in place. Treat cable gently because the small wires inside the cable break easily. The breaks are difficult to find and difficult to repair. Also, cable that is not coiled becomes snarled, and the next time you try to use it you will find yourself spending precious time untangling it.

Handle recorders carefully so that their internal electronics do not become damaged. Clean video heads and audio heads frequently with special head cleaners.

Notes

1. For several other approaches to the nature of sound, see Stanley R. Alten, *Audio in Media,* (Belmont, CA: Wadsworth, 1990); Francis Rumsey and Tim McCormick, *Sound and Recording* (Stoneham, MA: Focal Press, 1994); Lenny Lipton, *Independent Filmmaking* (New York: Simon & Schuster, 1983); John Watkinson, *An Introduction to Digital Audio* (Stoneham, MA: Focal Press, 1994); and Herbert Zettl, *Sight-Sound-Motion: Applied Media Aesthetics* (Belmont, CA: Wadsworth, 1990).

2. Another method for minimizing phase problems is referred to as the 8 and 8 method. The mics should be placed either closer together than 8 inches or farther apart than 8 feet.

3. A good way to study microphone characteristics is to look over the specification sheets provided by manufacturers. Some of the major microphone manufacturers from which these may be obtained are Electro-Voice, 600 Cecil St., Buchanan, MI 49107; Sennheiser Electric Corp., 6 Vista Drive, Old Lyme, CT 06271; Shure Brothers, Inc., 222 Hartrey Ave., Evanston, IL 60202; Audio-Technica, 50 Barnes Park Road North, Wellingford, CT 06492. Books that discuss microphone characteristics include Michael Gayford, *Microphone Engineering Handbook* (Stoneham, MA: Focal Press, 1994);

and John Borwick, *Microphones* (Stoneham, MA: Focal Press, 1990).

4. "Stereo Sound Yields High Impact Video," *TV Technology,* February 1992, p. 33; and Bruce Bartlett, *Stereo Microphone Techniques* (Stoneham, MA: Focal Press, 1991).

5. Dick Reizner and Rick Lehtinen, "Of Mics and Men: Getting Great Audio in the Field," *AV Video,* March 1994, pp. 98–105.

6. Cecil Smith, "Questions from the Seminar Floor," *AV Video,* September 1990, pp. 125–127.

7. "Loose Cannon: Wireless Mikes Battle It Out," *AV Video,* September 1995, pp. 59–66.

8. Timothy Liebe, "Double-System Sound, A Shooting Secret You Can Share," *Video,* February 1995, p. 24.

9. "DAT Players Arrive; Opponents Vow Suit," *Variety,* 25 June 1990, p. 1; and John Watkinson, *R-DAT* (Stoneham, MA: Focal Press, 1991).

10. "Long-Awaited DCC Dominates CES," *Variety,* 13 January 1992, p. 3.

11. Ken C. Pohlmann, "Mini Disc Technology," *Mix,* November 1992, pp. 20–25.

12. "Audio Technologies for Film," *Mix,* January 1993, pp. 141–144.

13. "Say, What Do You Hear?" *Videography,* October 1991, pp. 20–25; and John Borwick, *Loudspeaker and Headphone Handbook* (Stoneham, MA: Focal Press, 1995).

14. The best way to record two people is to route the sound through a portable mixer with XLR inputs and outputs and then route it to a camcorder XLR input. The mixer allows for greater control and flexibility of the sound.

15. For more about the recording process, see Bruce Bartlett, *Introduction to Professional Recording Techniques* (Indianapolis, IN: Howard W. Sams, 1987); Blair K. Benson and Jerry C. Whitaker, *Television and Audio Handbook* (New York: McGraw-Hill, 1990); Ty Ford, *Audio Production Techniques,* (Stoneham, MA: Focal Press, 1993); and "One Hand Clapping," *Scientific American,* June 1989, pp. 35–37.

Figure 8.26

To coil cable using the over-under method, make a natural loop for the first coil (a). Then twist the cable for the second loop (b) and place it next to the first loop (c). The third coil is a natural loop (d), the fourth is a twisted loop, and so on until the cable is neatly coiled.

chapter nine
Approaches to Sound Recording

Sound recording is much more important in video than it used to be, partly because of listeners' increased sophistication and partly because of TV set improvements. For many years television sound came from a monaural speaker that was often no larger than three inches in diameter and incapable of reproducing quality sound.

But through the years listeners became enamored with high fidelity and stereo sound on records, cassette tapes, and radio. TV set manufacturers recognized this and began manufacturing sets with higher-quality sound systems. They correctly believed that a generation raised on quality radio sound would be willing to pay a little more for quality TV sound. Better speakers led to better recording techniques, which led to even better speakers.

Most TV sets manufactured today can receive several sound channels, which means the user can listen to stereo and/or a secondary audio program, such as a foreign language translation. This means that video production companies must take greater care with recording because TV speakers pick up even minor sound discrepancies. Listeners could barely perceive such problems as a change in background noise with the older small receivers, but now they can hear such aberrations.

Sound must be recorded properly during the production process so that it can be mixed and rerecorded during postproduction. In early television, technicians often just placed a mic close enough to pick up sound. Now, as in many other facets of electronic moviemaking, they are adopting more sophisticated techniques, most of which come from film.

Elements of Microphone Pickup

Central to all sound recording is the microphone. How it picks up the sound determines the quality and utility of the sound. Some elements of microphone placement are common to all recording, be it dialogue, narration, music, sound effects, or background noises. These elements include the need for presence, perspective, balance, and continuity.

Presence

Sound **presence** refers to the reality of the sound. It must appear to be coming from the picture. This means that it must have the quality that people expect when they are in a location similar to that shown on the screen. For example, sound in a gymnasium will be very different from sound in a living room with thick carpets and heavy drapes. Therefore, sound recorded to accompany a gymnasium scene should have the echo characteristics people expect of that environment.

One of the main elements of sound presence is how *live* or *dead* the room sounds. A gymnasium is quite live (bouncy), and a living room with carpets and drapes is dead (absorbing). One reason is the size; all else being equal, large rooms are more live than small rooms. But an even more important difference involves the surfaces in the room. Hard surfaces such as wood and concrete create live sound, and soft surfaces such as carpets and drapes deaden sound. Hard surfaces tend to bounce the sound from side to side, whereas soft surfaces absorb it. In other words, live sound has a great deal of **echo** and **reverberation,** and dead sound does not.

Echo and reverberation have slightly different technical definitions, but they create the same kind of effect. With echo the sound bounces once, and with reverberation it bounces a number of times. Sound that does not bounce is usually referred to as **direct sound**, which is generally dead. (Figure 9.1 depicts echo, reverberation, and direct sound.)

Neither live locations nor dead locations are wrong. The amount of deadness or liveness depends on the type of presence you are trying to create. But sound with a high degree of echo or reverberation often sounds muddled. In particular, the high frequencies tend to blend into each other and become indistinguishable. For that reason sound technicians often try to deaden a room so that the sound can be understood. The easiest way to do this is to hang blankets slightly in front of the walls, place carpet on the floor, put drapes over windows, and/or place cloths

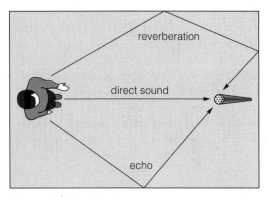

Figure 9.1
Direct sound goes to the source without bouncing off any surfaces, echo bounces off one surface, and reverberation bounces off two or more surfaces.

over hard tables. Moving the mic closer to the subject also makes for deader sound, whereas moving the mic farther away has the opposite effect. Removing carpets, drapes, and other cloth can enliven the sound.[1]

Of course, most of this must be done in relation to the picture. Closed drapes that show in the picture probably are not a problem because the drapes will also make the presence of the sound match that of the picture. But blankets hung in front of walls would look strange.

Sometimes compromises need to be made in the perception of the deadness or liveness of the scene so that the sound can be adequately understood. In general, though, the audience will perceive a setting with many hard surfaces as producing live presence and a setting with soft surfaces as dead.

Perspective

Sound **perspective** is related to distance. The voice of a person in the distance should sound different than the voice of that person when shown in a close-up. In this way the viewers will feel closer to or farther from the person, reinforcing what they see on the screen. Similarly, the sound of a bell ringing in the distance should be different from the sound of a bell ringing in the foreground.

The easiest way to achieve proper perspective is to move a boom mic farther from the person or object for a long shot than for a tight shot. This usually needs to be done anyway to produce a proper picture because a mic close to the talent will show up in a long shot.

Achieving proper perspective is more difficult, if not impossible, with a lavaliere (lav) or table mic. The lav mic is attached to the person and moves as he or she does. A person wearing a wireless lav mic is never going to sound farther away. A table mic must look like it is in front of the person, so it too is essentially unmovable.

Mics hidden in the scenery can provide perspective if the picture relates to where the mic is placed. In these cases, the person moves away from the mic rather than the mic moving away from the person. However, if the camera follows a person with a close-up as that person is moving away from the hidden mic, the perspective will be wrong. The camera should show a medium or long shot as the person is walking away from the mic.

The need for proper perspective is one of the main reasons filmmakers have traditionally used boom mics. They are by far the best for creating the proper perspective.

Balance

Balance refers to the relative volume of sounds. Important sounds should be louder than unimportant sounds. The human ear can listen to sounds selectively, but the microphone cannot. You can be talking to a friend in a noisy area, yet you hear your friend over the other noises because you concentrate on doing so. If you record your friend on a microphone, you will not be able to pick out his or her voice nearly as well as you can in person. Try placing a microphone in the middle of a table when several people are having several conversations. When you play back the tape, it will be a garble. Yet, if you are at the table, you can hear one particular conversation.

The need for balance is one reason microphones have been designed with directionality. A cardioid mic can act a little more like the selective ear than can an omnidirectional mic.

The best way to achieve proper balance is to record every important element **flat** and then adjust relative volumes in postproduction. You try to make the volume of every scene, every person, and every sound effect more or less the same.

This assumes, however, that you have access to sophisticated sound postproduction facilities that can mix various sounds and alter them in a variety of ways. If this is not the case, you will want to take sound balance into account during the recording process. You may, for example, want to have one person appear to have a booming voice, or you may want the sound of a waterfall to partially drown out a conversation. In those cases, you would record sound that is not totally flat.

Continuity

Continuity of sound refers to a sameness from shot to shot. It is as necessary as visual continuity. The script supervisor, who keeps track of continuity of visual elements, should also keep track of continuity of aural elements. If a water spigot is dripping during the man's close-ups, it should also be dripping during the woman's close-ups if you are going to intercut the two shots.

Elements that affect presence and perspective should also maintain continuity. If drapes were hanging over windows for long shots, they should also be there for close-ups, even though they won't be seen in the picture. Removing them will make the room sound more live and create a discrepancy in tone between the long shots and the close-ups.

The script supervisor also should note how far a mic was from a person if shooting is going to stop for the day and the same scene is going to be continued the next day. Knowing this distance is also advantageous when different angles of the same scene are being shot. If the mic is 3 feet from the man during his close-ups and 5 feet from the woman during her close-ups, the shots may not intercut well.

Using the same microphone for the same person throughout a production also helps to maintain continuity because the sound will be similar. If you are using different mics, they should match as much as possible in terms of frequency response, dynamic range, and timbre characteristics.

Keeping track of sound continuity can distinguish a professional production from an amateur one. It is fairly easy to do but is often neglected.

Eliminating Unwanted Noises

When shooting a movie, the recording equipment often will pick up noises that have no relation to the scene being recorded. One is the sound of the equipment itself. This is more of a problem with film than video because film cameras usually have motors. Placing various devices, such as soft foamy cases called **barneys** and hard cases called **blimps,** over film cameras muffles motor noise. Most of the noise created by video cameras comes from electronic circuits or from the equipment being moved around the set. For this reason microphones should be positioned as close to talent and as far away from equipment as possible. This is easy when equipment and talent are naturally far apart, but when they are close, you will have to compromise. One possibility is to move the camera farther from the talent and use a longer lens.

Another disturbing noise is wind. You may not hear the wind with your ears, but it often blows against the microphone sound element, making a low-frequency huffing sound. Placing a **windscreen** on the mic will help to eliminate wind noise.

The recording system may also pick up the hum of fluorescent lights. The best solution for this may be to turn off all fluorescent lights.

Recording equipment with mechanisms for **equalization,** can sometimes be used to eliminate unwanted sounds at certain frequencies. This is often better done in postproduction, when you have more time and control. Most equalizers have one position that cuts out high frequencies and another that eliminates low frequencies. If you are trying to tape birds chirping and the low hum of a motor clutters the audio, you can use the equalizer to cut out the low frequencies.

Conversely, the bird chirpings can be cut out when recording the rumble of a train. The problem arises when the sounds you want to record are at about the same frequencies as the sounds you do not want to record. In these cases, and in many others, equalization is not the answer.

A better solution may be to increase the directionality of the mics so that only the desired sounds are picked up. However, highly directional mics, such as the ultracardioid, can pose problems because they lose the signal if the subject moves slightly. In general, the more directional the mic is, the harder it is to control the small area it picks up.

Often the best time to solve sound problems caused by the surroundings is during preproduction. If someone checks out the area before recording begins, plans can be made to remove the offending sounds or choose a different location.

During production you can assign someone to keep pedestrians and, if possible, automobiles away from the production area. This minimizes the likelihood of unwanted sounds on the set.

Both the sound engineer and the continuity person should listen carefully for distracting sounds during shooting. If the sound will hurt the overall effect of the movie, you can retape.[2]

The principles of presence, perspective, balance, continuity, and unwanted noise apply to almost all field recording. Certain specific approaches apply to particular types of recording such as dialogue, voice-overs, sound effects, ambient sounds, and music.

Miking Dialogue

Dialogue is the most important sound element to record properly during production. You can create most other sounds during postproduction if necessary, but rerecording synchronous dialogue after the fact is a difficult, time-consuming, and sometimes impossible task.

Selecting the Mic

The first step in miking is to select the proper microphone according to the directionality, construction, impedance, and positioning characteristics discussed in Chapter 8. The **cardioid mic** is the most commonly used for moviemaking, but an **omnidirectional mic** will pick up broader sound such as that of a crowd scene, and a **supercardioid mic** will pick up narrow sound. Using a supercardioid mic is tricky because it picks up sounds close to the rear of the mic as well as sounds that are distant from the front of the mic. It should not be positioned where loud noises, such as honking horns, are right behind it. Also this type of mic telescopes the sound to the front of it in much the same way that a telephoto lens compresses distance. As a result, background noises may rise to an undesirable level.

You can use either a **condenser mic** or a **dynamic mic;** the condenser gives slightly better fidelity and the dynamic mic scores slightly higher on ruggedness. You should try to use low

Figure 9.2
Proper placement of a mic on a fishpole.

impedance, unless, of course, the recording equipment is high **impedance.** The **fishpole** is the device most used for mic positioning, mainly because it can handle changes in perspective well.[3] However, stand mics might fit naturally into the scene, and **hidden** or **lavaliere mics** solve the problem of the boom showing. **Wireless mics** are appropriate if a person is going to move a great deal, and **shotgun mics** are useful when sound must be picked up from afar. On-camera mics usually do not pick up dialogue very well, but sometimes they are all that is available.

For optimum pickup of voice frequencies, select a mic with a **speech bump.** To emphasize a particular male voice, choose a mic that creates a **proximity effect.** Check out the difference in timbre created by various brands of mics.

Sometimes you may want to use two different microphones to record the same sound. For example, using a boom and a lav, record the boom in channel 1 and the lav in channel 2. Then decide later which sound you want to use. Although miking this way allows for postproduction flexibility, it usually slows production because of the extra time required to set and operate the two mics.[4]

Setting Up the Mics

Ideally, a boom should be positioned above a person's head, pointed toward the mouth (see Figure 9.2). It should be *rotated* as the person moves so that it always points at the mouth. The best distance for a cardioid is 1 to 4 feet in front of the mouth and 1 to 3 feet above it; an omni should be slightly closer. However, the boom or fishpole should not show in the picture nor should its shadow.

Accomplishing all this is often difficult and requires compromises. The cinematographer may have to change the lighting slightly to get rid of the boom shadow, or the audio person may have to move the mic slightly away from its

Figure 9.3
Keeping the boom out of this shot may require holding it farther away. Note the miniature Nagra audio recorder on the boom operator's belt. (Photo courtesy of Ryder Sound Services)

Figure 9.4
In this shot five people are talking, so the movement of the boom becomes important.

optimal position. If the mic position must be changed, the audio operator should experiment by placing the mic in various sites and then selecting the one that sounds best (see Figures 9.3 and 9.4). Sometimes this position may be rather unorthodox, such as close to the floor pointing up. Some boom operators place a strip of white tape on the tip of the mic windscreen so the camera operator can readily see the mic if it dips into the shot.[5]

Position hidden mics with care. They should

not be in, on, or near something that will be moved during shooting. A lav should be attached 8 to 10 inches from the mouth but not where it is likely to pick up the sound of rustling clothes. You also need to be careful in positioning shotgun mics and monitor them constantly so that they pick up the dialogue. If the talent moves, the mics also must move.

For recording in a room, it is best to place the mic so that it is not equidistant from any two walls. Also, it should be at an angle to the walls rather than perpendicular. This lessens the chances of **phase** problems. If a person has a sibilant voice, place the mic slightly to the side of the mouth. This helps get rid of the high frequencies.

Special Dialogue Situations

Miking two or more people requires adherence to many of the principles already discussed and a few others. When using only one microphone, you'll have to move it often so that it picks up the person talking. The boom is a favorite of moviemakers because it is easy to move. Difficulties arise with one mic, however, if the various people speak at different volumes. If one person has a booming voice and another is soft-spoken, an equitable balance is hard to achieve. You could ask the two people to try to speak at more similar levels or move the person with the stronger voice farther from the mic than the person with the weaker voice. Another solution might be to record two takes of the scene, one recording the first person and the other recording the second person. With two takes, you'll need to pay attention to continuity so that the shots will edit together well.

Using two mics means each person's level can be set separately. This works best if the mics are attached to a portable mixer that can be used to set the separate volumes (see Figure 9.5), although it can also be done through two different audio channels on the VCR. Recording one voice at a higher level than the other will compensate for any differences in volume. However, the mics need careful placement so that they do not cause a phase problem and cancel each other out.[6] Some types of miking depend more on multiple mics than other types. When using wireless lav mics, there must be one for each person. One lav cannot pick up several people equally unless they are very close together. There will also need to be several hidden mics if any cast members are going to move. These mics cannot be moved during shooting, and their pickup radius is limited.

Under some circumstances proper dialogue pickup is impossible. If a scene must be shot in a noisy factory or on a busy airstrip, the sound will not be intelligible to the audience. In these cases the actors record their dialogue in a sound-proof studio during postproduction, and it is mixed with ambient sounds (such as that of the factory or the airport) at a low level. However, this dialogue must be synched to the characters' lips. Therefore, you'll have to record a cue track of dialogue during production so that the talent can hear what they have said and then rerecord it (see Chapter 13). In these situations selecting and positioning mics does not require a great deal of care. The sound must simply be clear enough to be used as a reference during rerecording.

Achieving high-quality dialogue sound requires time and patience because well over half the information conveyed in most movies is through the spoken words.

Miking Voice-Overs

Voice-overs (VO) are easier to record than dialogue because they do not involve synched sound. Usually, they serve such purposes as explaining complicated processes, indicating what a person is thinking, or representing someone's conscience. The person doing the talking is off camera, so all the problems related to keeping the mic out of the picture are absent.

A cardioid mic usually handles voice-overs. The best positioning devices are the table stand, floor stand, or boom. When putting a stand on an ordinary table, you might want to put a cloth over the table so that the mic and stand will not vibrate. People can also hold mics to record voice-overs, provided they do not need their hands for holding a script.

In fact, the positioning of the script is one of the primary concerns in regard to voice-overs. Actors must handle the script carefully so that it does not interfere with sound pickup. For example, they must never hold a script in such a way that it covers all or part of the microphone. Pages should not be stapled together because

Figure 9.5
A portable mixer being used during a shoot.

they may make a shuffling noise that is picked up by the mic when they are turned; rather, the actors should have loose script pages that they can carefully lift off and place to the side. The person reading should not have to turn his or her head away from the mic in order to see the script. The distance between the mic and the person's mouth should be constant, unless, of course, the voice-over is to sound as though it is fading off into the distance. Each page of the script should end with a complete sentence so that the actors do not have to turn pages in mid thought. Also, putting the script pages in plastic sheaths cuts down on rustle.[7]

Miking Sound Effects

Moviemakers add many **sound effects** during postproduction but record some during production, especially the **hard effects**—those that need to be in sync with the picture. The sound of a cowbell needs to coincide with the shaking of the bell; a door slam needs to sound as the door actually slams. These are noises best recorded during production; in fact, it is almost impossible not to record them while the dialogue is being recorded.

Hard effects that are an integral part of the dialogue should be recorded as realistically as possible because they cannot easily be removed from the track. In other words, if the cowbell is shown in close-up at the front of the scene, it should sound close. If the mic is far from the cowbell, taping talent at the rear of the scene, the bell's perspective will be incorrect. Sometimes this means recording the effect with a separate mic.

In other instances, sound effects are not actually recorded—someone verbally indicates that the effect is needed. For example, if a phone is to ring, one of the crew members might say "ring, ring" at the point in the script where the phone rings. This tells the people who add sound effects in postproduction that they need a ringing phone at that point.

Sound effects that need not be synchronous can be recorded separately from the picture. Several crew members might go to a waterfall to record its sound, which will be mixed with the dialogue or narration during postproduction.

Either omnidirectional or cardioid mics are good for recording sound effects because they pick up in a broad pattern. Just about any positioning device will do for asynchronous sounds because there's no problem with the mic appearing in the picture.

Miking Ambient Sounds

Ambient sounds are asynchronous noises that are mixed in during postproduction to give a scene authenticity. Sometimes they are called **wild sounds** because they can be recorded separately from the picture. One type of ambient sound is **room tone.** This is simply a recording of the general ambiance of the place where the dialogue is being recorded. When taping room tone, everyone should be quiet, but all the overall sounds of the room should be just as they have been during the production. In other words, if an air conditioner was running when the dialogue was taped, it should be running when the room tone is taped. All the equipment and set pieces used during production should be in place so that reverberation does not change.

During postproduction room tone smooths cuts from one shot to another (see Chapter 13). In the hectic pace of production people often forget to record room tone. However, it is a very simple process that should be done for all productions, professional or student. A sudden absence of room tone on the audio track calls attention to itself.

Another type of ambient sound is **atmosphere sound.** This adds a certain feeling to a scene. For example, the sound of a bubbling brook enhances the bucolic feeling of a serene country scene. The hustling, bustling mood of a street scene, which is actually shot in a studio, needs traffic noises. Factory sounds might be taped during a busy time because the factory was not operating when the scene was shot. As with room tone, these atmosphere sounds are mixed into the sound track during postproduction.

A third type of ambient sound is **walla walla.** This is the recording of people's voices so that the actual words they are saying cannot be understood. In fact, the term gets its name because sometimes the people talking say "walla walla" over and over at different speeds and with different emphasis. Walla walla might be needed if only a few characters are in a bar scene shot in the studio, but the illusion is that the bar is filled with people. Or many people appear in the bar scene, but they only pretend to talk while the principals are saying their lines. A crew would go to an actual bar and tape the general noises, which would then be mixed into the sound track or actors could be hired to "walla walla." All kinds of scenes—people walking through a museum, people at a party—need walla walla.

The distinctions among these various types of ambient sound are often muddy. Factory noise could be room tone, atmosphere sound, or even walla walla if factory workers are talking to each other. Sometimes ambient sounds and sound effects are one and the same. A dog barking could be considered a sound effect or an atmosphere sound. The definition is not important; what is important is recording the sounds so that they are available for later use.

Mic placement is not overly crucial for ambient sounds because you are trying to pick up general noises. This is one situation in which an on-camera mic may suffice. In general, record the ambient sounds with whichever mic you use for dialogue. Usually only a few minutes of ambient sound are needed, so it can be recorded at any time, as long as cast and crew are quiet.

Miking Music

Postproduction is the usual time for adding mood music to a movie (see Chapters 13 and 14). However, music inherent to the plot, such as a rock group's performance, usually needs to be recorded during production.

If the music can be taken from a prerecorded CD, it must at least be lip-synced during production. This requires some sort of playback setup so that the group or individual can hear the music. Playback can be something simple, such as a cassette recorder on the set, or it can be something more elaborate, such as a public address system. Somehow, picture and sound must be in sync. For this reason moviemakers usually rerecord the CD on the audio track of the videotape or on a separate audio recorder (reel-to-reel, cassette, computer workstation) while the actors are lip-syncing. Time code can aid in making sure sync will be maintained through the entire postproduction process.

There are several methods for recording music during production. You can record the whole musical group on one track or tape individual instruments and mix them later. When recording the whole musical sound at once, great care must be taken in placing the mics so that the recorded sound achieves the best balance possible. A mic placed above the string section of the orchestra, for example, will produce a recording in which the strings dominate the brass and percussion.

Individually miking a large group such as an orchestra is usually not practical. This technique is used more for small groups or individuals. You can mix the recordings from various mics as the recording session is taking place, or you can record each mic on a separate track and mix them later.

If sounds are mixed live, each mic feeds into a different input of an **audio mixer.** Technicians raise and lower the volume of each mic so the instruments are recorded at an appropriate level. Then they feed the mixed music to a single track (or two tracks if the sound is to be stereo) of an audio recorder. The disadvantage of this method is that the mixing must be done in real time. If one of the technicians makes a mistake, it cannot be corrected. However, for something simple, such as a singer accompanied by a guitar, this type of recording works quite well. The singer could be recorded with a mic placed about 6 inches from his or her mouth, and the guitar could be recorded with a mic placed by its sound hole. You can decide on the appropriate mix of guitar to voice, and then record the whole song at those volume levels through a mixer and into an audiotape recorder.

If the music is going to be mixed later, each mic must feed to a different track on a **multitrack recorder** or computer workstation. The sounds may go through an audio mixer to be recorded, but there is no need to adjust their levels because each sound is going on a *separate* track and can be isolated later. The audio technicians can send each track back through the mixer, adjust the volume of each track, and send it to one track of another audiotape recorder. This can be done in a fairly leisurely manner. The technicians can listen to the music, practice different levels, and make notes about what the levels should be at various places. They can also add reverberation or in other ways improve the sound. They can correct mistakes because the original multitrack recording can be played over again.

Another method of recording multitrack is to record different instruments at different times, each on a separate track of the tape or computer drive. This is the usual method when one musician wants to play several instruments. He or she might first play the guitar melody of the song. Then, while listening to what has just been recorded, the musician could sing the words to the accompaniment of the guitar. The guitar would be *playing back* from one track, and the singing would be *recording* on another track of the same recorder. After that, the musician might listen to guitar and singing and add drums on another track. All three tracks are played back through an audio mixer and recorded on a single track of another recorder. In the process, technicians can change the volumes of the guitar, voice, and drums so that they blend with each other properly.

The method of recording used usually depends on the complexity of the music and the size of the budget.

Recording Techniques

You should always carefully monitor the sound you are recording—dialogue, voice-over, sound effects, ambient sounds, or music—to ensure the best quality possible. If at all possible, monitoring should involve looking at a meter and listening through headphones. Headphones are not always reliable because they often have volume controls. With the headset volume cranked up all the way, you may think you are recording properly when in fact you are **riding in the mud.** The meter often shows what is going into the recorder but not what is coming out. The headset gives you the result and assures that you have, indeed, recorded. **Over-modulation** is the problem that occurs most often during recording. Sound recorded at too high a level causes distortion.

One of the best ways to prevent overmodulation and other field audio problems is to use a tone generator to set the reference level at 100 percent. Not all portable mixers or tape recorders have **tone generators,** but if one is available, you should definitely use it to set the reference level at 100 percent. This way, you know that all other inputs that register near the 100 percent level will be recorded properly.[8]

Most recorders have an **automatic gain control (AGC).** This circuitry prevents the signal from being recorded at too low or too high a level. If the sound is low, the AGC automatically boosts it; if it is high, it lowers it. However, AGC is not always appropriate. For one thing, most AGCs do not handle silence well. If there is a pause between lines of dialogue, the AGC will boost the gain, increasing the ambient noise. This can be quite disturbing if silence was really what was wanted. AGCs also try to compensate for changes in perspective. A distant sound should sound lower than a close sound, but AGC will try to boost the distant sound. This means that you may often want to put the sound gain on manual rather than on automatic so that you are the one making the decisions about the relative volume levels. This approach is similar to that of overriding automatic focus and automatic iris on the camera.[9]

Sometimes you'll be recording sound directly into the recorder on one or more tracks of the audiotape or videotape. Other times you will send it through a portable mixer where various sounds are mixed and sent to one track of the recorder. Neither method is right or wrong; the determining factor is the production situation. Obviously, a mixer is not needed to simply record one person's voice-over with one mic. However, to record a musical group and dialogue working at once, you will probably need more inputs than the recorder can handle. Taking along a mixer adds to the bulk of what you carry to the field and usually adds to the setup time. If there is access to elaborate postproduction fa-

cilities, it is best to record sounds separately so that the postproduction people have the ultimate number of options. If postproduction facilities are limited, you are better off mixing as much as possible in the field. In other words, the equipment used often makes the decision for you. Some tape recorders can record only one track, whereas others have multiple tracks. Some of the newer camcorders allow for recording on **hi-fi, PCM,** and/or **linear tracks.**[10] If you record on the hi-fi track, remember that you cannot separate the audio from the video. You also need to consider the equipment on which the movie will be played back. You do not want to record on PCM if the playback machine is not capable of playing that track.

Whenever you are recording sound of any sort, you should listen to at least part of it in the field to make sure it is acceptable. Recording it over is fairly easy during production. Fixing it later ranges from difficult to impossible.

Notes

1. Nick Batzdorf, "Micing and Mixing in the Field," *AV Video,* November 1991, p. 142.
2. Doug Schwartz, "Audio Mechanics Uses Sonic Solutions to Solve the Mystery of the Misdirected Mike," *Computer Video,* January/February 1995, p. 32.
3. Fred Ginsberg, "About Selecting Microphones for Fishpole and Boom Application," *Digest of the University Film and Video Association,* January 1989, n.p.
4. Nick Batzdorf, "A Guide to Micing and Mixing in the Field," *AV Video,* May 1991, p. 48.
5. Fred Ginsberg, "Tips on Your Boom Pole," *Equipment Emporium,* 1994, pp. 2–3.
6. Michael S. Pettersen, "The World's First Portable Automatic Mixer," *The Production Sound Report,* Summer 1991, p. 1.
7. Mike Sohol, "Create the Narrative that Shouts Quality," *Computer Video,* July/August 1995, p. 20.
8. Rick Shaw, "Sound Check: 20 Questions," *AV Video,* September 1990, p. 54.
9. Thomas D. Burrows, Lynne S. Gross, and Donald N. Wood, *Television Production: Disciplines and Techniques* (Dubuque, IA: Wm. C. Brown, 1995), p. 232.
10. Rick Shaw, "Audio and the New VTRs," *AV Video,* June 1990, p. 51.

part three
Postproduction

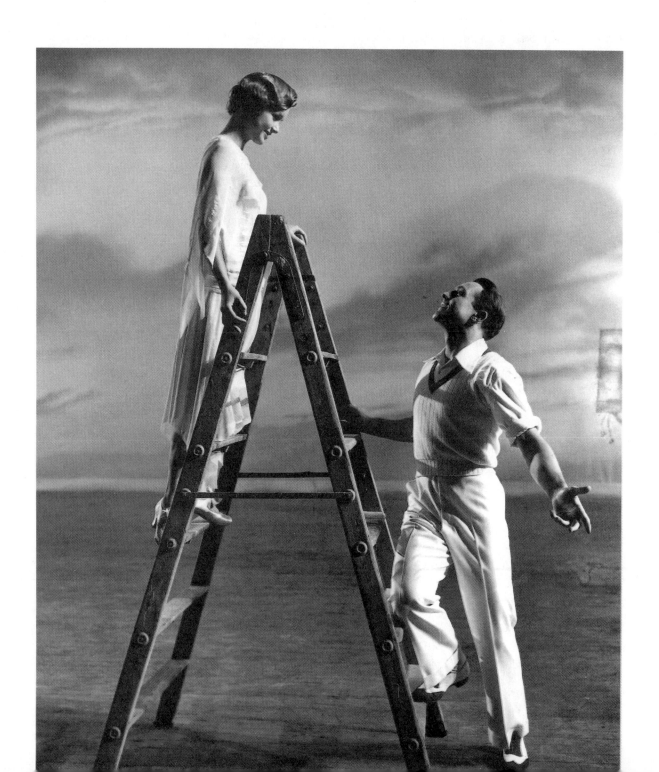

chapter ten
The Process of Postproduction

In recent times, postproduction has undergone enormous changes. Distinctions between preproduction, production, and postproduction used to be clearer. Postproduction encompassed all the things that occurred after the production phase had been completed. For a motion picture intended for theatrical distribution, this entailed selecting and editing the pictures and sound, adding music and sound effects and mixing them together, and creating titles and special effects. Once that was done, celluloid prints were made and sent to motion picture theaters. For a TV showing, original material was shot on film or tape and then edited on videotape. The video editing process involved rerecording. The material shot during the production phase was copied in a **linear** fashion, shot by shot, from an original tape onto another tape that could then be shown to a TV audience.

For some motion picture and TV productions today, these older processes still suffice. Increasingly, however, **digital** technologies are providing not only new tools for postproduction, but new ways of thinking about and organizing the entire postproduction process. Today most films destined for movie theaters encounter electrons somewhere along the way. A new method of editing called **nonlinear** has taken the main advantages of film and tape editing and combined them. More importantly, new technological advances are giving postproduction more importance and expanding its role into other areas of production.

Within this chapter we will overview various activities and methods undertaken in postproduction. In the remaining chapters in this postproduction section we will concentrate on the procedures most likely to be encountered by students while they are in school and when they first enter the workforce.

We will begin with a discussion of film editing, now a methodology that is clearly in tran-

sition. However, it is still in use and, more importantly, the underlying principles related to it are what have been used to develop the more modern forms of postproduction. Many schools start students out with this form of editing, using it as a base to teach principles. Not surprisingly, many of the terms developed over nearly a century of film editing are still being used in the digital age.

We will then briefly discuss videotape editing, comparing linear and nonlinear editing. This subject will be covered in much more detail in the following chapter. After that is a discussion of the people who are needed to accomplish the various postproduction duties. The chapter then concludes with a section examining the impact of digital technologies on the entire field of postproduction.

Film Editing

The need for editing was apparent, even in the early days of the moving image. The first films were short vignettes shot continuously, but filmmakers soon felt the need to show different scenes. At first they did this by turning the camera off after one shot, then repositioning and turning it back on for the next shot. The film was processed and then projected with all the scenes in the same order in which they had been shot. This was a very crude form of production, however. Real editing began when they turned the camera off and on several times in one reel, processed the film, and then cut the shots apart and glued material back together in a shorter form or different order.

Workprints

After the film has been exposed in the camera, it is taken or sent to the laboratory for processing. At this point most filmmakers order a print of the original camera footage, called a **workprint,** to be used for editing purposes. It is possible, of course, to cut the processed film that came out of the camera, but **negative** film (the professional standard) requires a print if you want to view it. Cutting the camera original avoids the extra cost of a workprint. This is a common practice in schools, where students

Figure 10.1

*Three types of film splicers. From left to right, a Rivas tape splicer, which uses sprock-
eted splicing tape; a cement splicer (hot splicer), which uses liquid cement and has a
heated element to speed up the drying time for splices; and a guillotine tape splicer,
which punches out (or clears) the splicing tape from the sprocket holes when the handle
is pressed down.*

typically work with Super 8mm or 16mm **reversal** film that produces a **positive** image after
processing. Choosing to edit without a workprint probably means that prints will not be
made of the finished film. It is almost impossible
to view, mark, and edit film without scratching
it. If you are going to cut your camera original,
keep the cutting room clean, and protect the
footage as much as possible during editing.

Normally, however, a workprint is used for
the intrinsically damaging editing process, and
the original negative is stored in a clean cool
place, usually at the laboratory. If damage does
occur to the workprint during editing, it is always possible to go back to the original material
and make another editing copy. That way the
original film that came out of the camera remains in pristine condition, untouched until all
of the editing decisions have been made on the
workprint.

Film Editing Equipment

A **film splicer** is used to physically cut and join
together two pieces of film. One type of splicer,
called a **cement splicer** (or **hot splicer** if it has a
heating element to speed the drying process),
joins shots with a special type of glue. The other

basic type of splicer, called a **tape splicer,** joins
shots together with a piece of clear mylar tape.
Figure 10.1 shows a cement splicer and two different types of tape splicers.

In addition to the splicer, a typical film editing bench would contain a film **viewer,** a piece
of equipment that allows the editor to scan back
and forth across the material to be edited, and
two **rewinds** that hold the reel of feed material
and the take-up reel. Scissors, grease pencils (for
marking the film), extra reels, and masking tape
are also common on any editing bench. See Figure 10.2 for a simple film editing setup.

Film dialogue requires some special equipment. Because this dialogue is usually recorded
on a separate audio recorder (¼-inch reel to reel,
or digital audio cassette recorder), it must be
transferred (copied) to sprocketed magnetic audiotape called **magnetic film stock** so that it can
be lined up with the film during the editing
process. This magnetic stock is the same width
(16mm or 35mm) as the film and has the same
number of **sprocket holes,** so it can move
through the editing equipment exactly as the
film does. In order to keep the dialogue synchronous with the picture, the tape must be recorded on a machine capable of recording a sync
signal that is derived either from the camera or

Figure 10.2

A typical editing bench for editing Super 8 sound film. The bench contains a set of rewinds, a sync block, a picture viewer, a sound reader plugged into an amplifier, and a small tape splicer (lower right-hand corner). (Photo courtesy of Super 8 Sound)

Figure 10.3

A four-gang synchronizer (or sync block) with a sound head. The magnetic film stock is in the first gang, and the workprint is in the second gang. A small footage counter is located on the bottom left side of the sync block.

heads into a single unit. In a vertical configuration they are called **upright** editing machines (see Figure 10.4a). Laid out horizontally, they are called **flatbed** editing machines (see Figure 10.4b). Such editing machines produce a bright, stable picture, and more important for sound work, they can run at a constant speed, something that is difficult to achieve when handcranking film through a viewer and sync block.

Film Editing Stages

In a film with lip-sync dialogue the sound is so intrinsically related to the image that editing decisions cannot be made until the editor has synced up the workprint and principal dialogue track. This process, called *syncing up* dailies (because this job is performed each day as new footage and sound come back from the lab and transfer service) is often done by an assistant editor. It involves marking the **slate clap** on the sound track and then finding the corresponding frame of the picture in which the slate just closes. Once the picture and sound track are locked into the sync block or editing machine at those marks, the image and sound should be in sync. Syncing up dailies is not really editing. It is simply getting sync-sound material into a form from which intelligent editing decisions can be made.[1]

The first real stage in film editing should be to **log** all the footage (sound and silent). Logging involves writing down each shot, what it contains, where it is located, and any other pertinent notes about the shot that will be useful during the editing process. After this tedious task has been completed, the editor begins to break down the workprint, cutting apart all the shots on the reel. Each shot is numbered with a

from a highly accurate **crystal** control unit built into the camera and recorder. This sync signal functions like electronic sprocket holes. The tape is transferred to magnetic film stock with a special **resolving unit** that reads the sync signal and adjusts the new recording so that it, too, will be in sync with the picture.

The sprocketed magnetic film stock is cut and spliced together just like the picture. A device called a **sync block** is used to lock the separate reels of picture and sound in a consistent relationship during editing (see Figure 10.3). A sync block may have multiple **gangs,** which give it the ability to hold in sync two, four, or six rolls of film and/or magnetic stock at once. A magnetic sound **head** and amplifier can be attached to any of the gangs so that the sound can be monitored.

Electrically powered editing machines combine feed and take-up reels, a viewer, and sound

a

b

Figure 10.4

(a) An upright editing machine with two sound heads and one picture head (note the viewing screen on the right side); (b) a flatbed editing machine, also with two sound heads and one picture head. (Photo b courtesy of W. Steenbeck and Co.)

grease pencil and then hung up in a **film bin** or placed on a plastic core along with its sound track if it has sound.

Using the logging sheets and script as a reference, the editor then begins to map out a plan for assembling the material, making preliminary decisions about which shots to use in what order.

The next step is to put together a loose assemblage, in order, of all the footage (picture and sound if there is dialogue) to be used in a particular scene or sequence. This is sometimes called a **string-out.** At this stage the entire shot, including material on the head or tail that is obviously not going to be in the final film, is left intact. Shots that are not going to be used, called **outtakes,** are labeled and stored away. It is normal to change your mind later and decide you need a particular shot.

The next editing stage, called a **rough cut,** consists of trimming the shots together more closely. The string-out simply places shots loosely in the proper order, one shot after another. This enables the editor to pull the two shots that are going to be cut together through the viewer, carefully weighing different in-points and out-points as potential cutting places. Once a decision has been made, the cutting point is marked with a grease pencil. Then the shots are taken out of the viewer, cut, and joined together with the tape splicer. A close-up

may be added or a few frames taken out to soften an edit, but a rough cut is considered rough because it is like the first draft of a paper. Many changes are still likely to occur, and most editors save every trim, no matter how small, aware that it may be needed later. As the editing proceeds, each successive cut refines the previous cut, moving closer and closer to a polished **final cut.**

Once the editing has been completed with the workprint, it is used as a guide for **conforming** or matching the camera original material. The key to this process is the **edge numbers** along the side of the film. These numbers are a uniform number of frames apart (twenty for 16mm and sixteen for 35mm) and are called *latent* edge numbers because they are exposed on the stock during the manufacture and do not appear until the film is processed. Once editing decisions have been finalized with the workprint, the edge numbers enable a negative cutter to find the same place on the uncut negative that had been stored away. Thus, the negative cutter can duplicate the editing decisions made on the workprint to the exact frame.[2]

Eastman Kodak's **Keykode**—a bar code system similar to that used at grocery store checkout stands—is available on all of its film stocks (see Figure 10.5). If the film is transferred to videotape for editing, special equipment reads the bar codes and, through a computer program

Figure. 10.5
A diagram of 16mm film with latent edge numbers and Kodak's machine-readable Keykode™ numbers.

Figure 10.6
Hardware and software for reading Kodak's Keykode™ numbers. (Photo courtesy of The Adelaide Works, Inc.)

(see Figure 10.6), relates them to time code.[3] After electronic editing decisions are made, the time code numbers can be translated to the edge numbers so that the original negative film can be conformed properly.

Because the negative is so easily damaged (any mark on the original negative will show forever in the prints made from it), it is conformed in a **clean room,** a spotlessly clean editing room with air filtered to remove the dust. Negative cutters wear gloves to keep the oil from their fingers from leaving marks on the film. Before prints are made, most laboratories use an ultrasonic process to remove any dirt or dust that the negative may have picked up during the cutting process.

The Role of the Laboratory in Film Postproduction

The motion picture laboratory does more than process the film and make workprints. It is also responsible for producing the final **composite release print,** a single strip of film that holds both the picture and the sound tracks. This is the print that runs through the projector in a movie theater.

Once the negative is conformed, it is sent to the lab for printing. With it is the final mixdown of the sound—dialogue, music, sound effects, and so on—on magnetic film stock. (The procedure for putting all the sound together is discussed in Chapters 13 and 14.)

The negative and magnetic stock go through a number of stages in order to make the release print. The key to this process is the film printer. Film laboratories use two basic types: **contact printers** and **optical printers.** A contact printer is used to run the negative and the new, unexposed print stock past a light source. The light passes through the negative and exposes the emulsion on the print, which is then processed and developed into a positive. Contact printers are very fast, efficient, and relatively inexpensive to operate.

With an optical printer the negative is projected onto the print stock. The two pieces of film do not come in contact with each other; the process is more akin to using a camera to take a picture of the image that a projector is showing. For this reason the image size can be manipulated. For example, something that takes up a full frame on the negative can be projected so that it takes up only the right-hand corner on the print stock. Optical printing is used to transfer 16mm film to 35mm, to place credits over film footage, to execute dissolves, and to build a variety of effects such as **wipes** and **freeze-frames.** Optical printers run more slowly and require more care and therefore are more expensive for printmaking than contact printers.

Figure 10.7

A-B rolls alternate successive shots in a checkerboard pattern from one roll to the next, filling the space between the shots with opaque black leader. When the A roll is printed, the section of black leader between shots 1 and 3 will leave an unexposed portion of film. The print is exposed a second time when the B roll passes through the printer. Shot 2 on the B roll is then printed into the unexposed area created by the black leader on the A roll.

To understand fully the laboratory's role in film postproduction we need to go back to the end of the film editing phase—to the point at which the negative cutter is conforming the original footage to the workprint. At that stage the negative cutter is actually preparing the negative for printing. Decisions about shot fades and other shot transitions, superimpositions, and title placement have already been made by the editor and are marked on the workprint.

If the negative is in the 16mm format, the negative cutter will prepare **A-B rolls** (see Figure 10.7). This requires the creation of two different printing rolls—the A roll and the B roll. The A roll contains the first shot, and the B roll contains the second. This pattern of alternating shots continues throughout the A-B rolls. When the A roll is completed, it will contain half the shots in the film, with each shot separated by a length of black leader exactly the length of each shot on the B roll.

When the A roll is run through the printer, the first shot is printed on the print stock, but when the printer light hits the black leader (which is so opaque that the printer light cannot pass through it), it leaves a section of the print stock unexposed. After the A roll is printed, the partially exposed print stock is wound back to the beginning, and the B roll is then printed into the unexposed spaces left when the A roll passed through the printer. Having multiple printing rolls not only hides the splices but also allows the editor to set up a number of printing effects.

All printers can be cued to open up or shut off their light source at a point specified by the editor, creating a **fade**-in or fade-out. A **dissolve**, however, is created by fading one shot out while another shot fades in. At one point in the middle of a dissolve the two shots are actually **superimposed**. If two shots are to appear in the print at the same time, multiple printing rolls are required. Thus, A-B rolls are needed to place a title over the opening shot of a film or to create other overlapping transitions, such as wipes and dissolves.

This same multiple printing technique is the basis for numerous special effects. Many of the motion picture space epics or other effects-oriented films such as *Raiders of the Lost Ark* or *Indiana Jones and the Temple of Doom* rely on a computer-controlled optical printer to build up

elaborate "process" shots. Individual elements of the shot are created layer by layer using multiple passes of the printer to create the **composite** shot. Many of these effects employ **blue-screen photography** to create a **traveling matte**. In this process an actor or object (such as a space ship) is photographed against a blue background.[4] The moving outline of the actor is matted out of the desired background in laboratory printing. Then, after additional lab work, the image of the actor is printed back into the moving (hence the term *traveling*) blank area created in the background footage, a technique that enables Superman to fly through Metropolis with the background and foreground elements married invisibly together. With each pass of the film through the optical printer, different areas of the image are matted out (leaving unexposed holes), while other areas are filled in with new elements of the composition. A special effects shot of this kind might require A, B, C, and D (or more) printing rolls, with each roll containing one layer (or element) of the final printed composite image.

After the printing rolls are prepared by the negative cutter and given to the laboratory, they are turned over to a **timer**, a person who evaluates each scene for correct exposure and color balance. For example, if a scene in the original footage is underexposed, the timer can increase exposure by instructing the computer that controls the printer to open up the printing light to a higher intensity. Similarly, the timer can help control color shifts by varying the amount of red, blue, or green light used in the printing process. The timer cannot correct huge errors in color or exposure, but a carefully timed print will appear much more even and balanced than an untimed print.

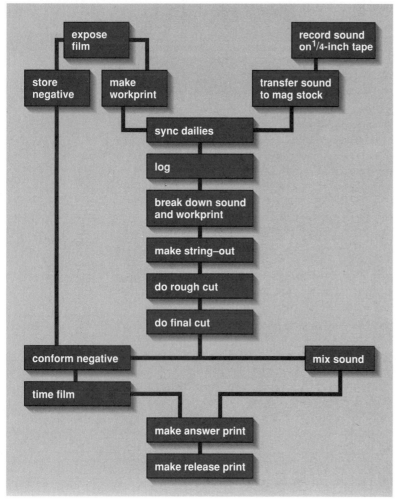

Figure 10.8

A flowchart illustrating the progression of the film image from camera original to release print.

Video Editing

When video editing first began, it, too, started with physical cutting and splicing of the tape. But this mode was abandoned largely because it was impractical. The human eye cannot see individual frames of video on tape, and the equipment designed to enable a human to see the end of one frame and the beginning of another was tedious and unreliable. What developed instead was an electronic process dependent on rerecording desired material from one tape to another (see the next chapter for a more detailed discussion of video editing).

Today a great deal of television programming is shot on celluloid and then edited and distributed electronically. An increasing number of movies destined for theatrical release are shot on film and then transferred to videotape, which is used to make editing decisions; after the decisions are made on tape, the final editing is completed on film.

Although the equipment used for both film editing and video editing has changed and is continuing to change, the concept is still the same. Material filmed or taped is rearranged to convey the essence of the idea—to create a syntax.

Transferring Film to Video

As previously mentioned, many narrative productions today are shot on film and edited electronically. When this is the case, the film must be processed and cleaned and then transferred to some electronic storage medium, most commonly videotape. This transfer is accomplished with a **telecine** using either a **flying spot scanner** or a **linear CCD array**. These devices can transfer the original film negative without damaging it (see Figure 10.9). They do not pull the film down one frame at a time as regular film projectors do. Rather, they electronically scan each frame as it flows from a feed reel to a take-up reel. While the negative is being transferred, the polarity of the picture is reversed so that the image recorded on tape is a positive. As digital technologies have begun to play a greater role in editing, a new type of telecine called a **Media Record Telecine (MRT)** has been introduced.

The first print obtained from the timed A-B rolls is called the **answer print**. The director and timer usually view it in a screening room at the lab, discussing and evaluating the timer's decisions on exposure, color balance, or effects timing. Frequently, filmmakers will go through several answer prints before a satisfactory print is finally obtained.

Finally, the film is ready for its final printing. If a large number of **release prints** are going to be made, which is normal for theatrical films appearing simultaneously in hundreds of theaters across the country, several additional generations of printing may be required. This is done to protect the original footage from wear and tear in the printer.[5] (The flowchart in Figure 10.8 illustrates the progression of the film image from camera original to release print.)

It converts the film into digital information during transfer.[6]

If the film is Keykoded, a special device attached to the telecine can be used to place information concerning the bar code on the tape signal's **vertical blanking interval.** In addition, **time code,** the video equivalent of film edge numbers, is usually added as the transfer takes place.[7]

One of the problems inherent in transferring film to video involves film speed. American TV operates at 30 frames per second, and most film is shot at 24 frames per second. To compensate for this difference a **three-two pulldown** method has been devised. Generally, the odd-numbered frames of the film are placed on two fields of the TV signal while the even-numbered film frames occupy three TV fields (see Figure 10.10). Over the course of 24 frames, 6 extra film frames are added to equal the 30 frames per second rate of video.

Once the film has been transferred to an electronic storage device, it can be edited with any of the various video editing systems. At this point there really is no difference between editing something shot on film and something recorded on tape. At the end of the electronic editing process the "film" can be displayed electronically on tape or the Keykode numbers can be used to conform the film negative. In the latter example, the only time the film itself is actually cut is when the negative is edited to create the celluloid release prints that are shown in motion picture theaters.

Linear and Nonlinear Editing

Originally, all video editing consisted of rerecording shots one after another from the beginning of the program to the end in a linear fashion. If someone finished editing an entire production and then decided that the second edit should be two seconds shorter, there was no easy way to fix the problem. The editor could either edit everything all over again from the second edit on, or he or she could rerecord the first two edits to another tape, shortening the second edit and then dub (edit) the rest of the material onto that same tape. The problem with this process is that the overall product suffers from **generation loss** because signal information

Figure 10.9

A flying spot scanner used to transfer film to video. (Photo courtesy of Rank Cintel)

Figure 10.10

The three-two pulldown method, which compensates for the speed difference between film (24 frames per second) and video (30 frames per second). Film frames are alternately scanned with two fields (one video frame) and then three fields (in effect, 1½ frames) so that 24 film frames equal 30 frames (60 fields) of video.

is lost or contaminated when material is dubbed from one analog tape to another.

Linear editing is often compared to writing a term paper with a typewriter. If you finish the entire paper and decide you want to remove a paragraph on page 2, you must retype the entire paper from page 2 on.

In the late 1980s the first nonlinear, **random-access** digital editing systems began to appear (see the section at the end of the next chapter that deals with nonlinear editing). The image (whether generated on film or video) is **digitized** (converted into digital information) and stored on large hard drives or some other digital storage medium in the editing system's computer. With the image converted to digital form, it can be stored, recalled, manipulated, and played back instantaneously and in any order. Nonlinear editing is like typing a term paper with a computer word-processing program. If you decide to move a paragraph from page 2 to page 15, a few keystrokes will accomplish the task. Likewise, in nonlinear editing, scenes can be trimmed and moved quickly and easily in a totally **nondestructive editing** process.

The continuing evolution of nonlinear, random-access editing systems is a crucial step in the merging of film and video postproduction. Today an editor working on a series TV show shot on film ("NYPD Blue" or "The X-Files"), a series TV show shot on tape ("Home Improvement"), or a feature film, might well do the editing on the same basic type of digital editing system (such as an Avid Media Composer). This does not mean that film editing has disappeared. Motion pictures are still being edited from beginning to end on celluloid, but the movement toward digital nonlinear, random-access editing is readily apparent. At the highest level of editing equipment, nonlinear systems from companies such as Avid and Lightworks are making strong inroads into traditional film editing, a trend that seems likely to intensify as digital technologies continue to improve and the cost of such systems continues to decline.

Postproduction Responsibilities

Postproduction does not require as many people as production. Many of the functions of this stage can be handled by one person working alone. Even when large numbers of people (such as an orchestra) are brought together, they interact for only a short time.

This does not mean, however, that postproduction is less hectic than production. Sometimes the time allowed for postproduction is insufficient, especially if production fell behind schedule and the movie has a set air date or theatrical release date.

A typical two-hour TV movie of the week has a twelve-week schedule—four weeks for production and eight weeks for postproduction. Of those eight weeks, the first three weeks are devoted to editing the picture and dialogue (see Chapter 11). In the subsequent three-week period the postproduction team composes the music and decides where to place it, rerecords and replaces poorly recorded location dialogue, and records and edits **sound effects** and **ambient sounds;** graphics and credits are also built. The seventh week is devoted to music recording and the final sound mix. The last week is for **timing, layback,** and **dubbing** (see Chapter 13).[8]

Student projects have a different schedule— they must be based on the availability of equipment, the length of the semester or quarter, and the number of student projects that must all be edited at the same time. Rarely do students leave enough time for postproduction, making for a hectic end-of-semester crunch.

The two major tasks of postproduction are editing the picture and structuring the sound. Different aspects of these two tasks take place both serially and simultaneously. Little can be done until picture and dialogue have been edited, but then a large number of tasks are attacked all at once. Someone must oversee the whole process so that all the individual parts add up to a unified whole.

General Overseeing

The **director** has the responsibility for seeing that the movie is edited properly. Some directors handle this responsibility by becoming involved in most details of postproduction. They decide all the edit points, indicate where the music goes, determine the type of sound effects that should be added, and generally make all the technical and creative decisions. Other directors convey general ideas to the people involved with picture and sound editing but delegate the specifics, such as which take to use, where to bring in sound effects, and whether to add **reverberation** to dialogue. Regardless of how involved or uninvolved directors are, they always view the edited versions of the picture and the dialogue and make suggestions, a process known as the **director's cut.**

The **producer** also oversees the entire postproduction process. The degree of involvement depends a great deal on the person, the structure established during preproduction and production, and the number of problems associated with the project. If the movie is coming in over budget, the producer will need to be very involved. But if the project is progressing well, financially and artistically, and the producer trusts the director, he or she will rarely appear. Usually, but not always, there is a **producer's cut** of the picture and dialogue.

For commercials or corporate videos the client usually has a definite say in the editing. Because these people are paying for the production, their opinions count.

Picture Editing

The picture editor (usually referred to simply as the **editor**) is the main person charged with putting together the material shot during production. This person is part technician and part artist. Editors must know how to operate the equipment and they must be firmly versed in the aesthetics of editing (see Chapter 12).

The director can overrule any editing decision. Ideally, the director and the editor are of the same mind about the film; otherwise, the editing will be slowed by arguments and misunderstandings. But if there is conflict, the director prevails.

An editor might work alone, perhaps with the director looking over his or her shoulder, or there might be **assistant editors** to handle such tasks as organizing and filing trims and outtakes and taping the splices together. In video, an assistant might digitize tapes into a nonlinear editing system and log and write shot descriptions with the computer.

More than one editor may work on a particular movie, especially if it has a tight deadline. Different people edit different parts of the movie so that it can be finished more quickly. One person may be called the editor and the others called assistant editors, but they all do essentially the same job. The editor will be responsible for making sure the editing style is consistent among all of them. In other configurations, one person does the initial editing on a less expensive **off-line** editing system, and another completes the final edit on a more advanced and more expensive **on-line** editing system.

Produced as group projects, student productions sometimes run into difficulty because only one person is needed for editing. It is easy to find significant jobs for ten students during production and preproduction. They do individual jobs but see and learn from what their classmates do. Editing, however, requires only one or two people. Ten people in an editing suite, all expressing their opinions, can lead to bedlam. Yet if the extra students are kept from the editing suite, they do not learn the ins and outs of editing. One solution, if there is sufficient equipment, is to make several copies of the production footage, break the large group of ten into several subgroups, and allow each subgroup to edit its own version of the project. This gives more people editing experience and can demonstrate that there are many ways to edit a production because, in all likelihood, the groups' end products will be quite different.

Postproduction also involves technicians and artists. If the footage was shot on film, someone must transfer the film to tape. Other people will need to design and create graphics, titles, and credits. A **timer** will adjust the color of the end product before it is dubbed to the master. But the intensive part of editing—piecing together the essential material that will make up the final movie—is the editor's domain.

The rapid development of digital technologies is creating new jobs and new responsibilities, putting editing and all of postproduction in a state of flux. In one setting, a single editor might do all of the editing alone; in another, multiple editors might divide the work based on special needs or talents. A feature film editor, for example, might have a more computer-literate assistant to help with the nonlinear editing system, but there would no longer be a need for an assistant to file trims and outtakes.

Sound Building

Putting together the elements of the final sound track usually involves a number of people. However, because these tasks are completed independently, most of them can be done by one person, even the person responsible for the picture editing. In the film business, the people who build sound are called **sound editors,** and the people who mix it are called **sound mixers.** In TV, anyone who works with sound is usually referred to as an **audio technician** or audio op-

a

b

Figure 10.11

An Emc² video editing machine (a) is an IBM-compatible random-access system. The Emc² laptop computer version (b) allows an editor to work on a brief scene even while traveling. (Photos courtesy of Editing Machines Corporation)

erator, although the term *sound editor* is being used increasingly.

The sound people decide what music, sound effects, and ambient sounds are needed and where they must be placed in relationship to the picture. They gather and record and edit sound effects and ambient sounds, rerecord and replace poorly recorded dialogue, add synchronous background sounds such as footsteps and rustling clothes, and mix music. They also do the final mix, during which all sounds are joined together. In large studios or postproduction houses people are specialists. For example, one person will engineer dialogue replacement sessions day after day for however many movies or TV series are being postproduced at that facility, while another gathers, records, and edits sound effects for the same group of films. In smaller facilities or for shorter movies (such as student productions), people have multiple duties.[9]

Completing the sound requires more people yet. The music requires a composer and sometimes a conductor and a number of musicians. Actors must be brought back to rerecord dialogue that then must be edited. Sound effects editors edit sound effects. The most valuable people in postproduction are those who have learned their craft well through a multitude of experiences.

Digital Moviemaking

More than in any other area of moviemaking, film and video are merging in postproduction. As we have already seen, the development of digital nonlinear, random-access editing systems (see Figure 10.11) provides an alternative to traditional film editing. As the quality of nonlinear editing systems has improved, it has become possible to digitize a tape (or film copied to tape) into the editing system at broadcast quality and after the editing has been completed to output (**print to tape**) the edited show at broadcast quality.[10] For a television production shot on film there is no need to actually edit the original film. Either the output from the nonlinear editing system or a reedit from the telecine tape master (using the nonlinear cut as a guide) produces the final version of the tape. Used this way, film is simply a means of gathering the image. After it has been transferred to video, it is treated as if it *were* video throughout the rest of the postproduction process. For a feature film, however, a cut done on a nonlinear editing system functions only as a workprint, a means of generating a list of editing decisions that are ultimately converted back to film via Keykode and edge numbers.

The incredibly high **resolution** of 35mm film is the basis for these differences. Obviously a telecine can create a copy of a film suitable for television broadcast, but the image it creates does not have the quality to be copied back to a film intended for large-screen theatrical exhibition. There is simply more information in the 35mm film frame than a traditional telecine can capture.

For this reason, it was initially easier to use some of the emerging new digital technologies in video than in film. The comparatively low resolution of video allowed a computer to combine film, video, and **computer-generated imagery (CGI)** in revolutionary new ways, and at a quality suitable for broadcast.[11] The convergence of these media was first exploited in music videos and television commercials (remember the Diet Coke commercials that seamlessly combined pop stars Elton John and Paula Abdul with old feature film footage of Humphrey Bogart, James Cagney, Carey Grant and Louis Armstrong).[12] The introduction of high-resolution digital film systems provided a bridge between the analog world of the theatrical film image and the digital world of the computer.

Digital Film

Many different companies were responsible for the development of high-quality digital film systems: Industrial Light & Magic, EFILM Digital Film Lab, Management Graphics, Quantel, and Kodak to name a few. The key to this new technology was developing a film scanner that could digitize film at full resolution, software that could manipulate that material, and a recorder that could copy that information back to film at full film quality (see Figure 10.12). For example, operating at only a quarter of its resolution capability, Kodak's *Cineon* film scanner (see Fig-

Figure 10.12

This Cineon Digital Film System *developed by Kodak includes a scanner that uses CCDs to digitize each film frame into approximately 3,000 lines of 4,000 pixels each, a high-resolution video workstation with which digital special effects can be manipulated, and a film recorder that uses red, blue, and green laser beams to place the images created in the workstation back onto film. (Photo courtesy of Eastman Kodak Company)*

Figure 10.13

The Cineon Digital Film Scanner. (Photo courtesy of Eastman Kodak Company)

ure 10.13) and recorder can digitize and record material that exceeds the standards for broadcast television. At half resolution the image quality exceeds the proposed standards for **high-definition television**[13] (see Figure 10.14). At full resolution the system equals film resolution. In other words, a system of this kind enables filmmakers to take advantage of all the various image enhancements and visual effects available in the

Figure 10.14
The TV screen for a high-definition television system. (Photo courtesy of General Instrument)

digital domain and then record them back to film with no loss of image quality.

Special Effects

The kind of special visual effects that astounded movie audiences in *Star Wars* and *Close Encounters of the Third Kind* did use microprocessors to control the animation cameras and printers, but the spaceships and death stars were still created on film using the traveling mattes, blue-screen photography, and optical printers discussed earlier in this chapter. By the late 1980s and early 1990s, however, companies such as Industrial Light & Magic had begun to exploit the power of the new high-resolution digital imaging systems to create effects for feature films.

Morphing, a computer process in which one object gradually changes into another, made one of its first appearances in the waterpod scene in James Cameron's *The Abyss*. This technique was significantly refined in *Terminator 2: Judgment Day.* Throughout the film, the Terminator constantly changes shapes, morphing from a patch of linoleum floor into a prison guard, growing a sword out of his arm, turning from a policeman into a housewife.[14]

Morphing uses the computer's ability to make subtle changes from frame to frame. For example, a computer can be programmed to change a square into a circle over a period of two seconds. Frame 1 would be a perfect square; in frame 3 the corners of the square might be slightly rounded; by frame 10, the square's sides would start to bulge; by frame 31, the corners would be totally rounded; by frame 45, the edges would be more round than square; and by frame 60, the figure would be a circle. Similarly, one man's face could change into that of another man. Among other things, the eyes might gradually change from blue to hazel to brown. An

automobile with the right kind of gasoline might morph into a charging tiger (see Figure 10.15).

Digital Compositing

Morphing is just one kind of special effect possible with the new digital imaging systems. **Digital compositing** refers to the combining of different elements that were shot separately, using digital matting techniques and the computer to converge different layers of the image. This technique is what enabled the computer-generated dinosaurs in *Jurassic Park* to be combined seamlessly with live-action footage, complete with digital shadows and texture enhancement.

Blue-screen effects are easier to do in the digital domain because lighting can be more easily corrected. When Meg Ryan rides the train in *French Kiss,* she is actually sitting on a train set with a blue-screen background. The French countryside moving by outside the train window is a different layer of the digital composite. When Jamie Lee Curtis is lifted through the sunroof of a moving car to a helicopter hovering above her in *True Lies,* you are watching another composite blue-screen effect. In *Judge Dredd,* live-action footage is combined with computer-generated imagery. To make the effects more believable, the exact pattern of the film grain is added to the CGI elements.[15] A small group of extras in *Coneheads* is multiplied digitally and placed around a large arena where they appear to do the wave in unison. In *Batman Returns* a Gotham intersection is flooded with penguins. These penguins were created digitally, as were the bats that floated over another scene.[16] In the film *In the Line of Fire,* an actor's head is composited on George Bush's body in footage of an actual campaign rally, and a real Secret Service agent is replaced by actor Clint Eastwood.[17] All of these examples illustrate the power of digital film systems to manipulate the image by seamlessly integrating multiple layers of image elements.

Touch-Up and Repair

The principles of digital compositing can be applied in many other ways. Once an image is digitized into the computer, scratches, dust, and

Figure 10.15

Three frames from a gasoline commercial that used computer morphing technology. (Photos of car transformation to tiger, compliments of Exxon Company, U.S.A. © Exxon Corporation 1991)

glare can be removed from the film, and shots can be color-corrected and reregistered. Several classic films like *Snow White* and *Ben Hur* have already been restored using high-resolution digital imaging systems and the same process has been used to repair contemporary footage that was shot poorly or damaged in the camera.

In the digital domain it is possible to correct just part of the image without affecting all of it. This is precisely what cinematographer Allen Daviau did in *Fearless* when he had a close-up of an actor's face where the ears were a different skin tone than the rest of the actor's face. He fixed the problem digitally, a procedure that would have been nearly impossible with an optical printer. Similarly, the prosthetic heads worn by the actors in *Coneheads* were color-corrected to match the actors' skin tone; wrinkles were removed to make them look more believable. In *So I Married an Ax Murderer* the director darkened the clouds and digitally painted out the sun to make a scene have the proper mood. In *Wrestling with Hemingway* a sequence where Shirley MacLaine and Richard Harris are looking at each other out of windows was salvaged by digitally matching the natural lighting conditions that had changed over several days of shooting.[18]

In films such as *Cliffhanger* and *The Super Mario Brothers* the wires used to support stuntmen were removed and replaced with appropriate backgrounds. Similarly, rigging or other unwanted objects can be digitally removed from a shot. It is also possible to add to a shot. A digitally created snowstorm was added to a scene in *Cobb* when the lack of a heavy snowfall could have caused a delay in the shooting. In *My Father, the Hero,* a young girl's skimpy thong-bikini was digitally enlarged to provide more coverage and help the producers avoid an R rating.[19]

The Postproduction Process in the Digital Age

Commenting on the impact of digital technologies in postproduction, director James Cameron said: "From the standpoint of the filmmaker, we're going to reach a point in a few years where we're going to think of postproduction in a different way. We're going to think in terms of image capture, which is the photography, and we're going to think in terms of the manipulation of the image—not just editing, but changing the components of what we've shot and recombining them in different ways, almost like an image mix in the same way that we mix sound."[20]

The new way of thinking about postproduction that Cameron is describing goes beyond image manipulation and digital compositing. The digital revolution is bleeding postproduction into new areas, making it more difficult to define a particular activity as something that takes place solely in preproduction, production, or postproduction.

Take, for example, the act of *building* sets. This has traditionally been a preproduction activity. Today it might take place during postproduction. Sets can be created digitally in a computer and added to a scene *after* the actors have been filmed. The ability to seamlessly integrate different layers of the image makes it possible to think of sets in an entirely new manner.

Editing has always been considered one of the basic elements of postproduction, but this too may be changing. **On-set editing** using the images obtained via the **video assist** system and a portable nonlinear editing system was used by filmmakers on films such as *Cutthroat Island,*

The Flintstones, and *Forrest Gump.* Footage was digitized into the editing system as it was being shot and then immediately assembled into a rough cut on the set. This process could be likened to a sort of digital **script supervisor,** a high-tech way of helping directors see quickly if they had shot enough coverage of a scene. If not, the on-the-set rough cut lets the directors know exactly what they need to shoot to make the scene work.[21]

The digital revolution in postproduction is just beginning. The techniques and terminology growing out of these technologies are moving so quickly that some of what has been written in this book will be out of date before it is printed. The equipment used for electronic moviemaking and the methods for combining film, video, and digital imagery are changing daily. These changes will be evident in professional production and in the academic world that is preparing students to enter professional production and postproduction.

In a time of rapid technological change, in a period when film, video, audio, graphics, photography, and other production forms are merging, blending, and intertwining in a variety of new ways, the only certainty is change. Learning to adapt may be the most important lesson for students to learn.

Clearly, high-end digital postproduction technologies are beyond the reach of most students. The most important issue in moviemaking is not the equipment, but how the equipment is used to accomplish an objective. Something is written, shot, and edited. Whether this is done electronically, photochemically, or digitally is less important, now and in the future, than how well an idea is brought to life.

Notes

1. At the professional level, editors usually send the synced dailies back to the lab. A coding machine prints a sequential series of numbers on the edge of both the picture and the sound, making it easier for the editor to maintain or reestablish sync throughout the editing process.

2. Sometimes the same numbers are put on the sound and the picture to keep them in sync after the slate is removed.

3. Three of the computer systems that correlate Key-kode and time code are *OSC/R* from Adelaide Works, 445 Adelaide St. West, Toronto, Ontario M5V 1T1; *Edge-Writer* from Film/Video Systems, Suite C, 8 School St. Plaza, Fairfax, CA 94930; and *Skycode* from Skyview, 541 North Fairbanks, Chicago, IL 60611.

Camera manufacturers such as Aaton and Arriflex provide another way of establishing a relationship between film images and video images. Both have introduced cameras that can generate and imprint time code right onto each film frame during shooting. See Claudia Kienzle, "The Best of Both Worlds: The Benefits of 16mm—Shooting on 16mm for Bigger Profits." In *Motion Film & Video Production Magazine* (Rochester, NY: Eastman Kodak, 1994), pp. 16–17.

4. Other colors in the spectrum, green in particular, can also be used to create a *blue-screen* effect. In television the process is far easier to execute. It is called chroma key or more recently Ultimatte (based on the name of a manufacturer).

5. For more on film editing, see Bruce Mamer, *Film Production Technique: Creating the Accomplished Image* (Belmont, CA: Wadsworth Publishing Company, 1995); Jerry Bloedow, *Filmmaking Foundations* (Boston: Focal Press, 1991); Norman Hollyn, *The Film Editing Room Handbook* (Los Angeles: Lone Eagle, 1990); Edward Dmytryk, *On Film Editing* (Boston: Focal Press, 1984); and John Burder, *The Technique of Editing 16mm Films* (Stoneham, MA: Focal Press, 1988).

6. Frequently the MRT is used to scan and digitize the film directly to removable hard drives that can then be used immediately in a nonlinear, random-access digital editing system.

7. Don Ver Ploeg, "New Tools from Kodak Aid Postproduction," *In Camera,* Summer 1995, p. 12; "Keykode Number Emmy Earned Through a Collaborative Effect," *Eastman Images,* Fall 1994, p. 7; "Keykode Establishing Film-Video Link in Post," *Post,* October 1991, pp. 34–36.

8. Material presented by Rob Wieland, vice president of ABC Circle Films Post Production, at the Academy of Television Arts and Sciences Video Tape Post Production Seminar "The New Frontier," April 30, 1988, Los Angeles, California.

9. Ken Hahn, "The Audio Mixer's Effect on Post," *TV Technology,* March 1991, p. 47; and Jeremy Hoenack, "Improving the Sound Track," *American Cinemeditor,* Summer 1991, p. 32.

10. For the moment at least, outputting directly from the nonlinear system to tape would be unusual for an episodic, dramatic television show. This type of program still tends to use the nonlinear system for off-lining and then goes back to the video master, increasingly on Digital Betacam, for an on-line ses-

sion. The kinds of television shows that are outputting directly to tape for broadcast are currently magazine shows or *reality* shows. Clearly the improving quality of nonlinear output is making great inroads at the level of corporate videos and commercials. It is certainly possible that more programming will move in this direction as time passes. See the next chapter for a more detailed discussion of nonlinear editing and current practices.

11. Because of the relatively low resolution of broadcast television, even a fairly well-equipped personal computer can do work at this level. As you will see in the next chapter, storage requirements add greatly to the expense of such systems, and slow rendering times encourage users to add enormous amounts of RAM and the fastest processor they can afford.

12. Debra Kaufman, "Video, Film, and CGI Converge in 'Nightclub,'" *Videography,* January 1992, pp. 79–80.

13. An improvement in the overall quality of the television picture has been "just around the corner" for more than twenty years. The original system developed by the Japanese in the early 1970s scanned 1,125 lines at 30 frames per second, had a 5:2 aspect ratio, and greatly improved color quality. However, the Europeans, and eventually the Americans, balked at adopting the Japanese system, and different parts of the world went their different ways.

   The system developed in the United States in the past few years is digital, whereas the older systems are analog. The proposed American system also uses compression that permits efficient transmission of the large amount of information inherent in a scanning process that at least doubles the lines of resolution. Currently, the Federal Communications Commission (FCC) is testing the digital HDTV system from the so-called Grand Alliance (AT&T, General Instrument, MIT, Phillips, Sarnoff Research Center, Thomson, and Zenith). It is expected to be approved sometime in 1996.

14. "Morph Mania!" *Videography,* December 1991, pp. 103–106.

15. "Cineon's International Success Is No Illusion," *In Camera,* Autumn 1995, p. 17.

16. "Expo Sings Praises of Digital Revolution," *Variety,* 22 June 1992, p. 8.

17. See D. R. Martin and Susan Wichmann, "The Digital Toolbox," *The Big Frame,* Fall 1994, pp. 29, 33–34, 37.

18. Bob Fisher, "Cinesite Marks First Anniversary: From Digital Experiment . . . to Industry Innovator," *On Production and Post-Production,* October 1993, pp. 41–43; Christine Bunish, "Digital Film," *Post,* 17 March 1994, pp. 38–41.

19. Bob Fisher, "Digital Snowstorm Makes Hollywood Dream Come True," *Silicon Graphics World,* January 1995, np; Bob Fisher, "Depicting Ty Cobb's Turbulent Journey," *On Production and Post-Production,* February 1995, pp. 38–39; Christine Bunish, "Wire Removal Usage Grows," *On Production and Post-Production,* November 1994, pp. 50–55.

20. Quoted in *Cineon: The Sea of Truth* (Rochester, NY: Eastman Kodak Company, 1992), videotape.

21. Debra Kaufman, "*Cutthroat Island:* A New Adventure in On-Set Editing," *American Cinematographer,* September 1995, pp. 24–28.

chapter eleven
Picture and Dialogue Editing

The most basic step of postproduction involves putting the picture and dialogue in proper order. However, the kind of equipment available determines how you do this. As you have already seen, technical advances in electronic editing have been numerous and rapid. Editing systems are available in every conceivable configuration and price range, and new editing systems seem to appear almost daily. Not only does the equipment seem to be constantly changing, but the terms and concepts used to describe picture and dialogue editing techniques become obsolete or shift in meaning as new equipment is introduced.

Any editing system, however, from the most simple to the most advanced, can help you learn the role editing plays in effective storytelling. Therefore, we will start by discussing the type of editing systems still used in many colleges and universities—the **linear** editing systems that essentially rerecord shots from one tape to another. We will divide these into simple cuts-only systems and the more advanced editing systems that use a greater array of equipment. We will then discuss **computer-assisted editing** systems and **nonlinear, random-access** digital editing systems.

Cuts-Only Linear Editing

A **cuts-only** linear editing system can butt one video image and its dialogue against another; it cannot be used to show two pictures at a time. In other words, a cuts-only system cannot execute a **dissolve** because doing so would involve overlapping two shots for a brief period of time. By the same token, it cannot be used for **wipes** and other special effects. A cuts-only system is the simplest, most basic editing system. The two primary methods of editing used with cuts-only systems are control track editing and time code editing.

Control Track Editing

Control track editing, as its name implies, involves using the video **control track.** This track, which has much the same function as **sprocket holes** in film, is present on all recorded videotapes. It helps to maintain picture steadiness, in part because it contains an electronic pulse for each frame. An **edit controller** that can count those pulses is connected between two VCRs. An operator uses the controller to mark the **edit-in** and **edit-out points** on the tape. Then the controller backs up both machines an equal amount (usually five seconds) so that they can get up to speed, starts them forward with the frames running in sync, counts control pulses to the edit-in points, and then starts the edit. This type of video editing involves rerecording each shot from the original tape onto another tape. In effect, the edit-in point is simply a command to begin recording, and the edit-out point is a command to stop recording.

The main drawback of control track editing is that the pulses are not numbered on the tape. There is no way to keep track of edit points so that they can be planned at one session and executed at another. And sometimes edits are not accurate because the tape stretches or edit points slip in the VCR after they have been marked on the tape counter.

Time Code Editing

The solution to these problems is **SMPTE time code.** It identifies each **frame** with a specific number that always stays with that frame. In this way it is similar to film **edge numbers.** Time code is a digital numerical address that includes the hour, minute, second, and frame number for each frame (see Figure 11.1). For example, one frame might have the address 03:45:27:08 (3 hours, 45 minutes, 27 seconds, and 8 frames). The next frame would have the address 03:45:27:09. The use of time code editing requires a **time code generator** that writes the code on the

Figure 11.1
SMPTE time code displayed on a monitor. From left to right are hours, minutes, seconds, and frames. (Photo courtesy of Gray Engineering Laboratories)

tape, a **time code reader** that decodes it from the tape, and an edit controller that can read time code. This, of course, makes time code editing more expensive than control track editing, which uses pulses that are already part of any videotape recording.

Time code can be recorded on the tape in any of several places.[1] It can be on a **linear audio track**, in which case it is referred to as **longitudinal time code.** Of course, if this track is used for time code, it cannot be used for audio. With formats that only have two audio tracks, this loss can be a major problem. Another disadvantage of longitudinal time code is that it cannot be read when the videotape recorder is in pause or is moving very slowly. This is because it is read by an audio head and not by the rotating video heads.

The time code can also be placed in the vertical interval. This is the retrace area where the **scanning** stops at the bottom of the frame and returns to the top of the frame. If time code is placed here, it is referred to as **vertical interval time code,** or VITC. VITC can be read at slow speeds or in pause because it is riding with the video information and is read by the same rotating heads that enable the picture to stand still. The main disadvantage of VITC time code is that it must be placed on the tape at the same time that the picture is being recorded. Longitudinal time code can be recorded on the audio track as an audio dub after the picture has been taped. But because VITC rides along with the video, the only way to add it after the fact is to

make a **dub** (another recording), which takes the material down a generation. Increasingly, new formats are providing a track specifically dedicated to time code so that it is not necessary to use either an audio track or the retrace area.

Some portable tape recorders or camcorders have time code generators in them or have provisions for attaching a separate time code generator to them. In these circumstances the time code can be placed on the tape during the original recording. This is preferable to making a dub, but it adds to the cost of the portable recorder setup; therefore, laying down time code is frequently a postproduction activity.

Because of various technical difficulties when color video was developed in the late 1950s, the frame rate was slowed fractionally by one-tenth of 1 percent in order to produce color that was compatible with black-and-white receivers. This causes problems when using time code. The actual frame rate for material recorded and played back in color is 29.97 frames, or 59.94 fields, per second. This is 0.003 frames per second slower than the 30-frame black-and-white system. When time code is used to time a tape, this results in a discrepancy between the time code numbers and the actual running time. The actual clock time and the time code display do not agree. A one-hour program measured by the time code frame count actually runs 3.6 seconds (or 108 video frames) longer than an hour. To correct for this accumulating timing error the TV industry developed **drop-frame time code,** a system that corrects the time code frame counter by systematically dropping (actually not counting) just enough frames to match the clock time and the time code address numbers. Thus, the old type of continuous time code (without any kind of counting adjustment) is called **non-drop-frame time code.**

Time code allows for editing that is **frame accurate** because it creates an address for each frame. If an edit is to be made at 00:02:34:12, it will occur precisely at that point, with no tape slippage. Editing equipment can store the time code numbers that indicate the edit-in and edit-out points. Once these editing addresses are in the computer's memory, they can be recalled at any time in order to undertake the edit. This means that editing decisions can be made one

a

b

Figure 11.2

(a) A basic video editing system consisting of two monitors, a source deck, an edit deck, and an edit controller; (b) Sony's EVO-9700 Hi-8 editing machine has the source and editing decks in a single unit. This system uses a single monitor (not shown) for both the source and edit machines and includes a titling keyboard. (Photo a courtesy of The Winsted Corporation; photo b courtesy of Sony Corporation)

day, and actual editing can occur a different day.[2]

Equipment

Cuts-only video editing involves two videotape recorders, one or two monitors, and an edit controller. (Figure 11.2 shows two simple editing systems.) One videotape recorder, called the

source deck, contains the original camera footage that is to be rerecorded. The other recorder, called the **edit deck** (or the **record deck**), is the machine onto which selected materials from the source deck are edited. One monitor shows the output of the source deck; the other shows the output of the edit deck (with some editing systems, both the source and edit outputs appear on the same TV monitor). The edit controller is used to mark the editing points and cue the decks to execute the editing decisions.

The source machine has all the regular functions of most videocassette recorders, such as play, stop, fast forward, rewind, and pause. It does not necessarily need to have a record function because it is used only to play back. One control on the source machine that is particularly important for the editing function is the **tracking** control. This positions the head for playback as it was when the tape was recorded.[3] If the head is not positioned properly, the image quality will suffer. Tracking can be adjusted by turning the tracking knob and looking at the video meter. The best tracking position is where the needle peaks at its highest point.

Obviously, the edit deck can record. In addition, it has special extra electronics that allow it to accept signals related to the editing procedure.

The edit controller, such as that shown in Figure 11.3, is usually a separate unit, but some edit decks can be programmed to mark editing points and do not need an external edit controller. Consumer editing systems sometimes include edit controller functions within the VCR's remote control. But most cuts-only controllers are separate units that are brand and/or format specific. In other words, a Sony controller probably will not work with Panasonic recorders, and a controller made for a VHS system will not work with a Hi-8 recorder. However, a number of independent companies manufacture controllers that are made to work with almost any recorder or format.[4]

Controllers can usually undertake all the regular videotape recorder functions—play, fast forward, rewind, pause, stop—for both machines through remote control buttons. Look carefully at Figure 11.4 and refer to it frequently as you read this section. They also have a **search dial** that allows the operator to move the tape of either machine at varying speeds in order to find exact locations. The edit controller is used to set the edit-in point on the source machine where you want the shot to begin and on the edit deck at the point where you want to start recording the edit. You can also use the controller to set the edit-out point on the source machine, or you can end the edit manually after it is completed by pushing the **edit stop** button. On some systems the edit-out point automatically becomes the next edit-in point; with this type of system you can save a step if you mark the actual edit-out point.

Once you have set the edit-in points on both machines with the controller, you can preview the edit; that is, you can see exactly what it will look like without transferring any signal. In other words, you can see what the edit will look like on the monitor, but the edit deck will not actually record it. When you are satisfied that the edit will work properly, you press the edit button on the controller to execute the edit. Both the source deck and the edit deck **preroll** (back up) five seconds to get up to speed.[5] This is why you must have enough time on the source tape *before* your edit-in point to execute the preroll. If not, most editing systems will abort the edit. If you do have enough material on the head of the shot to encompass the preroll, both the source deck and edit deck will back up and then go forward. When they reach the edit-in points, the controller will place the edit deck in record so that the edit begins. You can review the edit by rewinding the tape or by pushing the review button on the edit controller.

A **frame counter** on the controller also helps to find locations. If a tape has time code, the frame counter will display the hour, minute, second, and frame address assigned to each frame. If the tape does not have time code, the frame counter will still display hours, minutes, seconds, and frames, and it will advance one frame each time the tape does. But the numbers will be more arbitrary; the operator can set the counter to zero at any point and count frames from that point. If the counter stops at any point and the tape continues to move forward, the tape does not have control track. Control track is essential for editing, so any lack of counter movement should be noted carefully.

Edit controllers also have ways of marking beginning and ending points for edits without

Figure 11.3
An edit controller. In addition to controlling the source and edit machines, this piece of equipment has a built-in character generator. (Photo courtesy of Sony Corporation and Geltzer and Company, Inc.)

Figure 11.4
The controls on a typical edit controller.

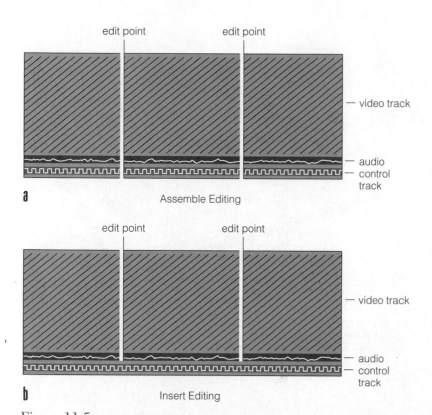

Figure 11.5

The first panel (a) depicts assemble editing. A new control track is recorded along with the audio and video signals. In insert editing (panel b), the audio and video signals are inserted on an existing control track. Thus, the control track must be on the master tape before an editor can insert edit.

the operator having to enter all the points for both tapes. For example, if the operator marks one edit-in and two edit-out points, the controller does the math to figure out the other edit-in point. Also, as mentioned before, some editors automatically use the last edit-out point on the record tape as the edit-in point for the next edit. Most controllers have a **trim** function so that frames can be added to or subtracted from the edit point without resetting the edit. In addition, they allow you to choose the elements you wish to edit—audio, video, or both audio and video—and also allow you to select the type of editing you desire, assemble, or insert.

Insert and Assemble Modes

Assemble editing and **insert** editing are two different ways of laying down segments of material in linear editing (see Figure 11.5). The key to understanding the difference between them is knowing what happens to the control track. For assemble editing, the control track information used to accomplish the edit is taken from the

material on the source tape. As the edit is made, audio, video, *and* control track are transferred from the source machine to the record machine. At the point at which the edit stops, the picture will break up and the frame counter will stop because there is no more control track.

For insert editing, the control track information is already on the edit tape. When the edit is made, only the video and/or audio material from the source deck is transferred. This material is inserted onto the control track that exists on the tape in the edit deck.

Because a blank videotape does not automatically have control track on it, the control track must be laid down on the edit tape before the editing session is to begin. This is usually called **blacking** the tape. The tape is placed in a record machine that is connected to a video signal, and it is run through from beginning to end in the record mode. The video signal material that is recorded is black, usually obtained from a studio switcher. In other words, there is no picture. Theoretically, a picture could be recorded on the tape because it, too, would give the tape an unbroken control track, but black is usually preferred because it is less likely to show a disrupting image if an edit slips a few frames.

An analogy of a train and its track may help explain the difference between insert and assemble editing. For assemble editing, both the train (the video and audio) and the track (the control track) are brought from the source to the edit tape. For insert editing the track is already on the edit tape, and only the train is brought over from the source tape.

A number of reasons exist for these two systems of editing. Assemble editing is quicker because it does not require time to black the tape. However, because the audio and video are tied to the same control track, they cannot be separated during the editing process. For example, if you have music laid down on the edit tape and you wish to edit pictures to the music, you cannot do this in the assemble mode without erasing the music. Each time you lay down a picture from the source machine, you will also lay down the control track and audio from the source machine—even if the audio consists of silence. This new audio will erase the audio on the edit tape. Likewise, if you are using the dialogue from a shot of character A and want to insert a cutaway of character B, you cannot do so in the assemble mode.

Assemble editing is used primarily when you have a series of shots that you want to lay down (assemble) in succession without changing the audio or video. The insert mode is used when you want to lay down audio and video separately. Most edit controllers have buttons that allow you to select audio only, video only, or both audio and video when you are in the insert mode. In most instances you have a choice of several audio tracks; you can choose to edit onto audio channel 1 or audio channel 2 or both. The insert mode can also be used to edit a series of shots without changing the audio or video. You can black a tape and then insert one shot in succession after another. Someone looking at the finished product usually cannot tell whether it was completed in the insert mode or in the assemble mode.

As its name implies, insert editing is also used to insert material after a basic tape has been built. For example, you might edit a scene with a man and a woman talking, cutting to both picture and dialogue of each person as he or she speaks. Later you would go back and insert the reaction shots of the man into the woman's dialogue and vice versa. You could not do this in the assemble mode, in part because the dialogue would be erased, and in part because you would lose the control track at the end of the edit. Because assemble editing brings a new control track with each edit, the picture breaks up at the end of the edit when the control track stops. This is not true of insert editing; the picture remains stable because it attaches to a control track that is continuing on the edit tape.

The breakup occurs during normal assemble editing, but it is not a problem because you are laying down one edit after another. When you put down the first piece of audio and video, you will have breakup after the end of the edit. But after you mark your second edit, the edit controller will back up both decks by five seconds from the edit point and will read the sync pulses on the source tape and the sync pulses that were laid down on the edit tape during the first edit. The controller will then make sure the two control tracks are matched when the second edit is made. In that way the control track of the second edit will be a continuation of the control track of the first edit, and there will no longer be breakup after the end of the first edit. Of course, after the end of the second edit the picture will break up, but that can be rectified by the third edit.

The end of the program needs to have an unobtrusive ending, such as a fade to black, so that the very last edit does not show the breakup. Although a stable control track is built during the assemble process, this track is usually not as stable as the track that exists in insert editing, simply because the control track of the insert process never has any interruptions, even of a temporary nature. This stability is another advantage of insert editing over assemble editing.

More Advanced Linear Editing

As we have already mentioned, a simple cuts-only system can do no more than butt two images together. It cannot dissolve, fade, or wipe from one picture to another, hold an image still, or add graphics or lettering to the image. It also cannot correct minor color errors or losses of video information that become magnified during the editing process. Although nothing can eliminate this generation loss, many "black boxes" have been designed to keep picture quality as high as possible.

Because of all the limitations of a cuts-only system, people interested in making high-quality videos usually do not use one for their final editing. Rather they use an expanded editing system that includes equipment for special effects, control and measurement of signal quality, and the addition of graphics.

Equipment for Effects

In order to **fade-in** (gradually go from black to an image) or **fade-out** (gradually go from an image to black), you need some means of generating black and some means of making the transition from the image to black. The most common way to achieve this is to run the image of the source machine through a **switcher** (see Figure 11.6) to the edit machine. The source machine is punched up on one **bus** of the switcher, and black is on the other bus. A lever

Figure 11.6

A video switcher. (Photo courtesy of Grass Valley Group)

Figure 11.7

A time-base corrector. (Photo courtesy of Nova Systems, Inc.)

regulates the strength of the signal of each bus, gradually taking the image to black or vice versa.

In order to execute a dissolve (the temporary overlapping of one image over another), you must have two source machines so that the two images can be recorded on the edit tape at the same time. The same is true if you wish to wipe one picture into another or do any other special effects that require two inputs to appear on the screen at the same time. Using two sources to supply one edit machine is referred to as **A-B roll,** a term that was obviously adopted from film editing.

The two sources cannot simply be fed into the edit machine, however. They, too, must be routed through a switcher or **special-effects generator (SEG)** so that an operator (or a computer) can manipulate a lever or knob to make one picture gradually replace the other.

In addition, these various effects require that the output of each source machine be routed through a **time-base corrector (TBC)** (see Figure 11.7) to synchronize the machines to each other and to the rest of the system. Using digital storage techniques, the TBCs place the pictures from the machines in temporary storage and read the pictures back out so that the timing of all machines is the same. Sometimes the TBC is built in to the VCR.[6]

Some complicated digital effects require a **frame store**. This piece of equipment stores a whole frame of video at one time. (Many time-base correctors store only several lines of a frame at one time. Expensive TBCs store whole frames, which means they are a combination time-base corrector and frame store.) Frame stores permit the editor to add various effects, including **still frame** (the process that makes a picture freeze).

Equipment for Control and Measurement

Many pieces of equipment have been designed to maintain the quality of audio/video signals during the editing stage. For example, a **color corrector** (sometimes called a **timer** because it serves the same function as the timing that occurs before film is printed) can make subtle color changes. It separates the color signal into its primary red, green, and blue elements in such a way that each color can be increased or decreased separately. Unlike the film timing process, some sophisticated digital video color correctors can change one part of the frame and leave other parts as is; this is done by digitally isolating a particular portion of the frame, such as the upper corner, and color correcting only that portion. Color correctors can also be computer controlled. Once the desired color settings for a particular scene are set, they can be stored in the computer and used every time that scene appears.

A vast array of other equipment is available to enhance the picture during the postproduction process. Many of these will become obsolete as digital recording becomes commonplace. But with an analog recording an **image enhancer** can be used to correct for the loss of sharpness and smearing of color that result when a picture is taken apart and recorded. A **dropout compensator** fills in gaps created when the head loses contact with the information on the tape. Many dropout compensators do this by filling in information missing from one scan line with information from the scan line below it.

Some of what these pieces of equipment do can be seen with the naked eye by looking at a

Figure 11.8
(a) A waveform monitor display and (b) a vectorscope display. (Photos courtesy of Tektronics, Inc.)

monitor. However, this is not an accurate way of deciding proper changes because color and brightness can vary greatly from one monitor to another. A better way is to use test equipment that is calibrated to remain consistent.

The two pieces of equipment used most frequently during the editing process for measuring the video signal are the **waveform monitor** and the **vectorscope** (see Figure 11.8). The waveform monitor measures the brightness of the video signal, and the vectorscope measures its color parameters. Both also measure signals as they come from other pieces of equipment—a color corrector, a TBC, a VCR, or a camera.

Figure 11.9

A sophisticated computer graphics generator that can be used to create, store, and retrieve graphics and titles. (Photo courtesy of Quantel Inc.)

In general, the brightest point in a scene should be adjusted so that it peaks at 100 percent on the waveform monitor, and the darkest blacks should register at 7.5 percent. This will give the best all-around picture. If a source tape is played through a TBC or other piece of equipment, and much of the scene is pushing against or exceeding 100 percent on the waveform monitor, the **gain** control on the TBC (or other equipment) should be turned down so that the picture is less bright. Similarly, the **pedestal** control can be raised or lowered to place the darkest part of the scene above or below 7.5 percent.

The vectorscope makes use of the color bars recorded on the source tape. As the tape is displaying the color bars, the colors—red, blue, green, cyan, magenta, and yellow—should be put in proper balance. To give the truest color, vector lines on the vectorscope should be in appropriate boxes. If the red vector line is to the left of the red box, all reds coming from the tape will look somewhat orange. If any of the lines fall short of the boxes, the colors will be undersaturated; if the lines go beyond the boxes, the colors will be oversaturated. For example, a red

line that is short of the box will make reds look somewhat pink.

Each scene should be set up using the color bars recorded on the day the scene was shot because color bars recorded by different cameras, VCRs, and videotapes can vary. This is one of the reasons for recording color bars on every tape during the production process. If the color bars are set for each scene, the scenes should come close to matching; the shade of green in the sweater an actor wore during the taping in a restaurant on Monday should appear to be the same shade of green in the scene that was taped in the living room on Tuesday.[7]

Equipment for Graphics

The area of electronically created graphics has come very far very fast. **Character generators,** which can be used to type letters on the screen electronically and then store them for future use, appeared in the early 1980s. This relieved television stations of having to draw their titles and credits with pen and ink. Today, the humble character generator has evolved into a digital **computer graphics generator** (see Figure 11.9), which can be used to create charts and designs, embellish photographs, combine real people with animated characters, draw background settings, and gradually transform a human being into an animal. The line between graphics and special effects is blurring.

Character/graphics generators are still used to type words for credits for narrative pieces, multimedia productions, documentaries, and corporate videos. During the editing session, the letters can be routed through a switcher. If you are building an opening sequence that includes a video image of buildings and the opening credits, the switcher can be used to place the credits on top of the buildings.

However, one important caution is that, in the analog realm, you cannot add words to the picture after the fact without going down a generation. In other words, you cannot lay down the video of the buildings, finish the rest of your editing, and then come back and add the credits over the buildings. If you do an insert edit to add the credits, you will erase the buildings. Unlike audio, there is only one channel of video on a tape, so two images cannot be recorded at the same time unless they are mixed through some sort of switching device. The only way to lay credits after the entire tape is built is to put the edited master in the source machine and run it through the switcher to the edit machine. As the buildings appear from the source machine, you can add the credits by routing them through the switcher. The finished tape with credits that is recorded on the edit machine will be a new generation and will have a certain degree of picture degeneration beyond what was on the source tape. For this reason, adding credits during the initial editing phase is the much preferred method.

Beyond titles, graphics generators can be used to create pleasing and informative pictures. They are ideal for developing charts and graphs for commercials, documentaries, and corporate or educational works. They can be used to create, shrink, expand, repeat, paint, and shade images. Photographs or frames of video can be digitized and altered. For example, a photograph of an automobile can be scanned into the graphics generator, its color can be changed, its headlights can be made to look textured, and its bumper can be duplicated at the top of the screen. Such artistic uses of computer graphics are seen frequently in music videos and commercials.[8]

Obviously, using equipment for effects, measurement and control, and graphics adds to the cost of the editing process. Minimizing the amount of time that all this equipment needs to be used can significantly reduce the budget of any production, especially if an editing facility is being rented by the hour. One way to save time is to use the added equipment only for those segments of the movie that need it—those that involve effects, graphics, and multiple images. The rest can be done on a cheaper cuts-only system. Another way is to be thoroughly prepared before you enter the editing room so that you do not waste time making rudimentary decisions or searching for some specific tape segment.

Preliminaries

Regardless of how sophisticated or unsophisticated a linear editing system is, there are several things that need to be done before editing can begin.[9]

Blacking the Tape

If you plan to insert edit, you must black the master edit tape with an uninterrupted video signal. Your final product should not have any areas without a control track. If the counter on the edit controller stops once, even for a second or two, you have lost the control track. That means the picture will break up when the tape plays that area back.

It is important to remember that you cannot switch back and forth between insert and assemble modes when you are laying down one piece of video and audio after another. If you plan to edit audio only or video only, you must use the insert mode. Do not use the assemble mode to insert any material (audio only, video only, or video and audio) into a tape that has already been edited. Switching from insert to the assemble mode causes many problems. More than one student's entire production has been ruined because as a final touch he or she laid down music on one of the audio channels in the assemble mode. Laying down the music this way erased all the picture and dialogue editing that the student had slaved over for days.

The safest and most professional way to edit with a linear editing system is in the insert mode. That means you must black the tape to provide the continuous, uninterrupted control track that you will need to edit.

Laying Time Code

Depending on the configuration of your editing system, you may need to lay time code on your original tape if it was not recorded in the field. Again, editing systems and tape formats vary considerably in their ability to handle time code. If you were working with an industrial grade S-VHS system for example, you might consider laying time code on one of the hi-fi channels so that the two linear tracks would be open for audio. There is a problem with this, however. Because the hi-fi channel is inseparable from the video signal, the only way to do this is to make a dub of the video. And that would take the original material down a generation. Laying vertical interval time code (VITC) also would require another generation. One option might be to lay longitudinal time code on one of the linear audio channels, the one that does not contain the dialogue recorded in the field. You can do this by activating the time code generator and recording only on one audio channel, leaving the video and the dialogue unchanged. If the tape format and/or editing system provides a separate address track (an area of the tape specifically available for time code), then laying time code is obviously much easier.

Organizing Your Footage

If the production people kept an accurate **log** and slated well, you should have little trouble finding the shots you want to consider. If not, you will need to log the footage prior to editing. You might want to make a time code **window dub,** a copy of the original tape with time code superimposed on it. You can use this window dub copy (perhaps on a regular **VHS** tape) to make your initial editing decisions. This can be done away from the edit bay, anyplace where there is a VCR and monitor. Before you start viewing your tape, you may want to consult your log and check off the various shots you think you might want to use. You do not need to look at shots that you know are unsatisfactory, such as out-of-focus material or shots in which actors muffed the lines.

As you look at the tape, you may need to shuttle back and forth quite a bit to make a list of the shots you want to use in the order you want to use them. This preliminary editing list includes the reel number, the scene and take number, the time code in- and out-points (from your window dub), and a description of the shot (see Figure 11.10). You may want to give yourself some options because the shots you really want to use may not always work when they are placed next to each other. Any decisions you can make at this stage on paper can really help speed up the editing process.

Making Leaders

Before you actually start editing you need to build a **leader** at the beginning of the tape. This provides technical and identifying information and also prevents the placing of program material at the head of the tape where it is most likely to be subject to damage. The standard leader for the beginning of a tape consists of **color bars,** **tone,** a **slate,** and a **countdown.** Color bars are usually one of the outputs of the switcher, and tone is an output of the audio board. They are recorded together at the very beginning of the tape for about one minute. The tone should be set so it reads 100 percent on the audio board **volume unit (VU) meter** and 100 percent on the VCR audio meter. That way, everything recorded through the board to the VCR will be at the appropriate level. Color bars and tone are important when someone is playing the tape back on some other system. An engineer can use the vectorscope and bars to make appropriate adjustments in color so that the colors recorded are the colors that are played back. He or she also makes sure the tone is at 100 percent so that audio will play back as it was recorded.

The slate identifies the program and usually contains such information as the program title, the director's name, the date the program was edited, and the program's length. You can create it with the graphics generator, and it is usually laid on the master tape for about twenty seconds. Someone playing back the tape uses this information to make sure the right program is, indeed, being shown.

The countdown gives the number of seconds before the program material will appear; countdown numbers usually go from 10 to a single frame of 2, followed by two seconds of black. Countdowns stop at the number 2 so that two seconds of black can play before the program's image appears. The countdown is usually on a separate videotape kept at the editing facility, although you could create it (tediously) with the graphics generator. It is used to cue up the program material.

You can record all these items on the tape in succession through the switcher, or you can edit them onto the tape, each in its turn. One thing you must consider while building the leader is the need for continuous control track. If the tape has already been blacked, you will want to edit the various leader elements in the insert mode. If you simply record them, or if you edit them in the assemble mode, you will lose control track at the end of the last edit. Another approach is to record all the leader material on an unblacked tape and then punch up black on the switcher after the countdown and black the rest of the tape at that point.

EDIT DECISION LIST

Reel	Scene	Take	In-Point	Out-Point	Description	Comments
2	1	2	00:02:15:12	00:03:05:17	neighborhood	put credits over do silent — add music later
1	2	1	00:07:10:04	00:08:15:28	establishing shot of children	
1	2A	1	00:11:52:20	00:15:19:17	MS of David and Eddie	begin picture before sound
1	2B	3	00:19:29:12	00:19:33:00	CU of David	use as react shot
3	2D	2	00:02:22:14	00:03:15:04	LS of children and Mrs. Oliver	use shot 2F if this doesn't work
1	2C	1	00:19:33:00	00:20:02:15	CU of Eddie	

Figure 11.10

An example of what a paper version of an edit decision list might include.

Many different methods will work for building a leader, but when you have finished, you should have a tape with the necessary technical and identifying material on the front of it. Figure 11.11 shows the positioning of the various leader information. For this diagram remember that the tape is running from left to right, so the items to the far right are the first items on it.

video	countdown	slate	color bars
audio			tone

Figure 11.11

The elements that should be placed on a typical video-tape leader and the order in which they should appear.

Computer-Assisted Editing

Powerful personal computers have changed the world of editing. Of course even the humblest of cuts-only editing systems uses digital computer technology to keep track of edit points and execute the edits in the right order, but these systems are proprietary in that the editing controller (which is really a specialized computer) cannot be used for other tasks, such as word processing, calculating a budget, or playing solitaire.

The low cost of personal computers and the development of computer-assisted editing has enabled nonprofessionals to use many of the techniques previously reserved for professionals. Desktop computers can, of course, be used to execute cuts-only editing, but their real value is that they can do much more for very little added cost.

The computer's ability to keep an accurate and comprehensive record of editing decisions leads to another way of describing editing systems—as either **off-line** or **on-line.** Off-line video editing is often compared to film editing that uses a **workprint.** In fact, the tapes used for off-line editing are sometimes referred to as workprints.

Historically, off-line editing was done on a less expensive, less sophisticated editing system, usually employing a lower-quality tape format. For example, a program shot in the **Betacam SP** format might be edited off-line on a ¾-inch **U-Matic** editing system.

On-line editing is analogous to cutting the film **negative.** The original tapes, not copies, are what is edited. On-line editing systems are usually more expensive because they can produce the highest quality master tape. In addition, on-line editing systems typically incorporate more powerful tools to enhance the image, add graphics, and manipulate the sound.

The key to off-line editing is time code. Right after tapes are shot, they are dubbed (with their time code) to workprint tapes that are used to make all the editing decisions. The original tapes are temporarily filed away, much as the negative of the film is. As the edit points are marked with the off-line system, their time code numbers are stored in the computer to make what is called an **edit decision list** (EDL), a step-by-step listing of each edit that contains such information as the edit number, the original tape number, the type of edit that is to take place (for example, video only, audio only), the type of transition between edits (for example, cut, dissolve, wipe), the duration of the transition, and the in and out time code numbers (see Figure 11.12). This EDL is then exported to a floppy disk and taken to an on-line system, which also has a computer. The original tapes are loaded into recorders, the floppy disk is inserted in the on-line system's computer, and editing takes place. The computer cues the source and edit tapes at the edit-in point and then executes the edit, stopping at the edit-out point. The source tape is then shuttled to the next edit-in points as designated by the EDL, and additional edits take place.

The problem today with the concept of *off-line* and *on-line* editing is that the level of sophistication between systems can vary greatly, and the type of equipment used for off-line on one project (such as a movie-of-the-week or a situation comedy) might be on-line equipment for another project (such as a student production). In other words, *your* off-line system might well be *my* on-line system.

Technological advances have added to the confusion. Off-line systems were once considered useful for cuts-only editing. They could not handle dissolves or special effects. Those were the domain of the on-line system. However, off-line systems are now available that can do switching and special effects, which can also be programmed into the computer, further cutting down on the time and tape shuttling needed during the on-line editing session. And, as you will see later in this chapter, nonlinear editing systems have blurred the distinctions between off-line and on-line editing systems even more.

Nevertheless, there are some facilities that do

```
                         EDIT DECISION LIST

     Edit    Reel    Edit   Tran-   Dura-    Play         Play         Record       Record
     Number  Number  Mode   sition  tion     In           Out          In           Out

     001     5       B      F       0:15     00:09:01:20  00:10:03:29  00:00:00:00  00:01:02:09

     002     3       V      C       0:00     00:14:15:15  00:14:20:18  00:01:02:09  00:01:07:12

     003     3       B      C       0:00     00:15:10:21  00:15:21:23  00:01:07:12  00:01:18:14

     004     6       A      C       0:00     00:23:07:02  00:23:10:05  00:01:08:10  00:01:11:12

     005     4       B      D       0:30     00:12:07:01  00:13:22:16  00:01:10:18  00:02:14:15

     006     3       B      C       0:00     00:20:14:10  00:21:14:09  00:02:14:15  00:03:14:14

     007     2       B      C       0:00     00:05:30:12  00:06:33:16  00:03:14:14  00:04:17:18
```

Figure 11.12

A typical edit decision list. Reading from left to right, the EDL shows the number of each edit, the tape that contains the shot, the edit mode (Video, Audio, or Both), the type of transition (Cut, Dissolve, Fade), the duration of the transition, and the time code addresses, in and out, for the playback and the record machines.

not have both off-line and on-line systems. In these cases, off-line and on-line are one and the same.

The Hardware

Computer-assisted editing systems, like other editing configurations already discussed, need at least one source machine and a record machine. The computer becomes the controller, and the computer screen can become the monitor for both the source and record pictures. A mouse (or keyboard) is used to fast-forward and rewind tapes, mark edit points, and execute edits. The video material goes from a source tape to an edit tape, just as it does with any editing system. The video information remains on the source and edit tapes; it is not stored within the computer as it would be in a nonlinear editing system. Only the list of editing decisions is stored in the computer.

The Software

Any number of companies have entered the computer-assisted video software business.[10] Some have come and gone rather rapidly; all are regularly modifying their products; some are written primarily for one computer platform (such as the Macintosh), and some are written for both the Mac and IBM (and compatible) machines based on the Intel x86 chip series.[11] Some specialize in picture and dialogue editing programs, while others branch out to include graphics, special effects, and audio mixing. In short, the world of computer-assisted editing software is far from stable.

Most software programs actually require some type of hardware add-ons—a board or boards that fit into the computer (see Figure 11.13). These boards may contain, among other things, the connections (ports) that allow you to attach the source and edit VCRs.[12] They may also enhance the computer's graphics capabilities, or provide some other function. Sometimes the regular computer ports are used for video equipment. For example, the printer port can be adapted to send signals to the record machine.

Software programs vary in their complexity and capability, but in general they all build some sort of time code-based edit decision list that can be easily manipulated. Some regular cuts-only systems can also build edit decision lists, but they are not as flexible as those that are PC-based. Using a word-processing analogy, EDL software allows for easier insertion and deletion of edits than a cuts-only system. If, after planning ten edits, the editor decides to lengthen edit 3 by ten frames, the edit decision list in the computer will **ripple**—the positioning of all

Figure 11.13

A computer-assisted editing system that requires five boards. (Photo courtesy of Matrox)

the following edits will change by ten frames. If the editor decides that edit 12 should actually be edit 4, a few keystrokes or mouse clicks will do the job. Because the computer is managing all of the edits, changes can be made in the EDL, and a new final product can be easily produced.

Depending on the type of source and edit decks it is controlling, and the peripheral equipment attached, a computer-assisted editing system can be either on-line or off-line. Increasingly, software and/or hardware has been developed to incorporate a variety of additional functions into the computer. Most common are graphics programs that eliminate the need for a specialized graphics generator, but some systems also include switchers that can perform transitions (see Figure 11.14), others include add-in boards or software-based time base correctors, waveform monitors, or vectorscopes. The continuing evolution of computer-assisted editing seems to be bringing these systems ever closer to the newer nonlinear editing systems, bridging, if you will, the gap between analog, linear editing, and true digital nonlinear editing.[13]

Nonlinear Editing

The development of nonlinear, random-access, digital editing systems is totally reshaping the entire field of video editing. Such systems rep-

resent nothing less than a revolution in postproduction. Compared to the editing systems previously discussed in this chapter, nonlinear editing offers many advantages. Shots and scenes do not need to be laid down one after the other. Someone can begin editing the last scene of a movie before the first scene is even shot. Late-arriving footage can be incorporated with ease.

Random access refers to the means by which the source materials are brought up. Any particular shot can be accessed immediately in any order; there is no wait while tapes are rewinding or fast-forwarding, no shuttling from the first shot on the tape to the twenty-fifth. In addition, most nonlinear editing systems have hardware and/or software that provides a variety of other functions: shot **transitions** (wipes, dissolves, fades, and more), titling, graphics, special effects, sound mixing, **image layering**, animations, and a number of control tools (time base correctors, vectorscopes, waveform monitors).

At the most basic level, what differentiates a nonlinear editing system from a computer-assisted editing system is how the video and audio are stored and accessed. With a computer-assisted editing system, the computer controls the source deck and the edit deck. The video and audio are still stored on tape. With a nonlinear editing system, the video and audio are converted into digital information and stored on hard drives (or other digital storage media) that are in (or attached to) the computer.

As already noted, the field of nonlinear editing is changing daily. New systems are introduced, new standards evolve, and new hardware and software are developed at breakneck speed. In this respect nonlinear editing is as volatile as any computer-based technology. Most of us have had the experience of buying a new personal computer. Within a few weeks, or months, or years, our investment begins slipping toward obsolescence. New computers using a faster processing chip begin to appear; our double-speed CD-ROM is eclipsed by one that is four or six or eight times faster; our operating system software is upgraded to version 8.0, then 9.0, or 10. Nonlinear editing systems are no different. Companies come and go. New breakthroughs lead to new hardware and software, and new terms are developed to describe them. Undoubtedly, at least some of what is written here will be out of date even before this book is even printed.

Today the cost of a nonlinear editing system (including the computer and monitors) might range from $6,000 to $10,000 for a system suitable primarily for multimedia authoring to well over a $100,000 for the kind of system used to edit an episodic television show or feature film. There are many, many systems that fall somewhere between those figures. Like most computer products, the cost of nonlinear editing systems seems to be declining even as the quality and available features improve. In general, what you are paying for when you buy a more expensive nonlinear editing system is improved image quality, faster processing, greater video and audio storage capacity, and a larger number of high-quality postproduction accessories (for titling, graphics, special effects, sound editing, mixing, and so on).

The number and possible configurations of nonlinear editing systems are seemingly endless. Still, at a very basic level, nonlinear editing involves a number of common steps.

1. Digitize. The sound and images recorded during production must be loaded into the computer for editing. Essentially this means an analog videotape (or film transferred to videotape) undergoes an analog to digital conversion.[14] This is done with a digital **capture card** or cards (and accompanying software) and is what enables the digitized audio and video to be stored on the computer's hard drives for editing.[15] In effect, the hard drive or drives in a nonlinear editing system take the place of the source and edit machines in a linear editing system.

The cost, quality, and performance of digitizing hardware (boards or chips) and software varies considerably. Although there are many possible variations, a typical nonlinear system might include a capture card, a card to compress the digitized information, a playback card, a computer with a large amount of **RAM**, a large hard drive, a monitor, and editing software. **Compression** hardware (and software) is vital to preserving space on the hard drive, and it is also an important variable in overall image quality.[16] Increasingly many of these functions are bundled together on a single card or chip.

a

b

Figure 11.14

The Video Toaster (a) is used today primarily for its titling and digital effects; (b) a close-up of the Toaster's control panel shows some of the many transitions available. (Photos courtesy of NewTek)

Different systems support different levels of video and audio input and output, ranging from VHS, S-VHS, or Hi-8 quality to **component** Betacam, D-1 or D-2. Most systems support two to four input/output channels for audio and some can digitize audio at levels approaching CD quality.[17]

Even with compression, nonlinear editing systems require enormous amounts of hard disk

Figure 11.15

(a) A window in Fast Electronic's Video Machine used for editing effects, graphics, and titles; (b) the effect editing mode window in an Avid Media Composer. (Photo a courtesy of Fast Electronic; photo b courtesy of Avid Technology, Inc.)

storage. Depending on the level of compression, video can consume hard disk space at the rate of 150 kilobytes per frame or more.[18] **Disk arrays** or **RAID (redundant array of independent disks)** devices set up two or more hard drives with the data split among them, greatly increasing the potential storage capacity and allowing

the highest rate of data throughput. Large hard drives are fairly commonplace today in nonlinear editing systems, and multiple drives can be chained together to create the enormous amounts of storage required for the highest-quality nonlinear editing.[19] Disk arrays are also available in modular units called **RMAGS**, a configuration that allows the entire drive (and the data on it) to be removed from an external chassis and carried to another machine. It is important to note that some nonlinear editing systems require the audio to be stored on separate drives from the video.

Most nonlinear systems can control external videotape decks. The best video digitizing software incorporates on-screen waveform monitors, vectorscopes, and input level meters for adjusting sound levels and picture (**hue, saturation, brightness**) as material is being put into the computer.

2. Organize. Nonlinear editing software typically provides a variety of tools for organizing, logging, and undertaking database management. Digitized video and audio clips are stored in bins, file folders, or lists. Each video, audio, or graphic element or titling sequence can be identified and catalogued in various modes, depending on the conventions of that particular editing system. Some nonlinear editing software allows logging information to be added as each clip is being digitized, others after the raw source material has been captured.

Clip databases are viewed in windows or some other type of viewer. Spreadsheet-style clip lists often contain such basic data as the clip title, reel name and number, a free-form shot description, image/sound quality information, and time code in and out points. Most systems also allow for the capture of a selectable and sizable head and/or tail frame, sometimes called a **keyframe** or **picon (picture icon)**, to identify each clip. Again, depending on the software, these databases can be searched, sorted, grouped, and organized in any number of ways.

3. Edit. After the material has been logged and organized, the real editing process can begin. Most nonlinear software offers a number of different editing modes or views (see Figure 11.15). They are usually displayed on the screen as a window, and depending on the system, it may be possible to overlay multiple windows on a single screen or to toggle between different editing views on the same screen. Some systems employ a single computer monitor and others display video clips on an additional attached video monitor. Different editing programs use different names for their editing windows, but a typical system might have modes for **timeline** editing (see Figure 11.16), clip editing, transitions, graphics, timecode, color and motion effects, and audio editing and mixing (see Figure 11.17).

The timeline (sometimes called a **storyboard**) has become one of the conventions of nonlinear editing (see Figure 11.18). It presents a graphical representation of the program's various video and audio elements laid out in tracks across and down a viewing window. Using a mouse or keystrokes, you can drag a clip from the storage bin and drop it onto one of the video channels on the timeline. Similarly, you can drag shot transitions, often represented as icons, to the timeline. Most systems include a variety of built-in transitions (dissolves, wipes, flips, fades), and many can provide motion-controllable effects. You can also add audio elements, superimposition tracks, graphics, and titles to timeline tracks in the same way.

To facilitate trimming, a clip editing window might show one or two monitors (like the source and edit monitors in a traditional editing system). In the clip editing window you can jog a shot back and forth, mark in and out points, check transitions, and preview the edit. Depending on the editing system, you may even be able to drag the marked shot from the source clip window to the timeline window where it can be dropped in the proper place.

In order to see the way titles, effects, and transitions will actually look in the program, they must be **rendered.** Only the most powerful (and most expensive) nonlinear editing systems can play effects (or some of them) in real time. The time it takes to render an effect is typically stated as a multiple of real time. Many nonlinear systems offer upgrade options to "accelerate" effects rendering.

4. Review and Refine. As with any editing system, the process of editing on a nonlinear editing system is one of trial and error. From the first rough assembly to the final cut, editing decisions are made and reviewed, then readjusted and reviewed again.

Figure 11.16

The main editing screen of Matrox Video's Personal Producer *system includes timelines that illustrate the placement, duration, and transitions for audio, video, and graphics. The software and hardware for this system are IBM-compatible. (Photo courtesy of Matrox)*

Figure 11.17

Note the audio controls (the VU meters and gain control) to the left of the picture window built into this video clip editor. (Photo courtesy of Matrox)

Figure 11.18

The Avid Media Composer™ is a Macintosh-based, nonlinear, random-access editing system. Note the "picture icons" (a frame grabbed from each shot) on the right-hand monitor and the timeline with source and editor windows on the center monitor. (Photo courtesy of Avid Technology, Inc.)

The best nonlinear editing software makes it easy to make changes. Pull-down menus and various control buttons provide many options for viewing, marking, trimming, and fine-tuning editing decisions, and for navigating and manipulating video and audio clips on the timeline. Video and audio elements can be inserted (rippled), overwritten, or replaced. Some systems provide multiple undo/redo levels; others offer video and audio **scrubbing** (using the mouse to slowly play a recording in order to find a precise point for trimming or adjusting).

When all editing decisions have been finalized, they are saved in a file containing not only the edit-in and edit-out points (and timecode numbers), but information about transitions, audio synchronization, video overlays, video and audio level settings, titles, special effects, and other appropriate data.

5. Output. The final output from a nonlinear editing system can take many forms. Many systems can produce an edit decision list in one of the standard EDL formats.[20] This is absolutely required if the nonlinear system is being used off-line and the final assembly will take place in

an on-line editing suite. Other systems can output media files at a level suitable for CD-ROMS or multimedia applications. Many systems can print directly to videotape at widely varying qualities, ranging from VHS, S-VHS, or Hi-8 to Betacam or D-1 levels.

Different hardware and software provide radically different output resolutions, compression and decompression schemes,[21] and data transfer rates. In general, the most powerful and expensive nonlinear systems can both input and output the highest-quality video and audio.

As noted earlier, nonlinear editing systems have begun to totally blur the distinctions between off-line and on-line editing. Obviously, a feature film edited on a nonlinear system is off-line. The EDL generated on the nonlinear editing system is translated back to the film via the **Keykode** numbers on the film negative and is used to assemble the final product—the cut film.

The first generation of nonlinear random-access editing systems could only output an edited program to videotape at something like VHS quality. For a television program recorded originally on Betacam SP, such a system was by definition off-line. Editing decisions were made in low resolution using the nonlinear editing system, an EDL was generated and copied to floppy disk, and that disk was used to control the on-line editing system that actually assembled the master tape (using the Betacam originals).

As nonlinear editing systems have continued to improve, the situation has become more confusing. Today nonlinear systems are sold as off-line and/or on-line; the same system might be able to function as both. Material can be edited in the off-line mode with a higher compression ratio (and lower picture quality) to conserve precious hard drive space. The EDL generated in this mode can then be used to redigitize the material at a lower compression ratio (yielding a higher image quality) and then guide the auto-assembly of the production in the on-line mode.

Already some magazine-style television programs or "reality" shows have begun outputting their final product directly from the nonlinear editing system to tape, but at the moment most dramatic, episodic television series are still edited off-line. As you will see in the next section, this may be due as much to the incredible specialization of different postproduction areas as to the technology. The revolution in editing created by nonlinear editing systems is still in the early stages. The first nonlinear systems were not introduced until the late 1980s and they have improved at a dramatic rate. Clearly, as the speed and image quality of nonlinear editing systems continues to develop, and as other functions (particularly audio editing and mixing, special effects, and titling) progress to a higher level, one-stop editing will become more commonplace.

There are so many different types of nonlinear editing systems, using different computer platforms and software, that there is no way to describe every possible feature, option, or configuration. You will need to study the instruction manual and learn the conventions of the particular nonlinear editing system that you plan to use. What is certain is that future editing will increasingly revolve around the computer.

A Nonlinear Example

In order to provide an overview of professional editing, we have included a current example of off-line editing using a nonlinear editing system.

The flow chart (see Figure 11.19) shows the postproduction stages for an episodic television series—"Chicago Hope."[22] This is only one example, and in the rapidly changing field of postproduction other models, as you will see in subsequent chapters, are quickly evolving.

"Chicago Hope" is shot on 35mm film and the sound is recorded on a reel-to-reel Nagra audio tape recorder with SMPTE timecode. The show, however, is distributed on videotape for broadcast. Once the film has been transferred to video for editing, it is, in effect, treated like videotape throughout the rest of the editing process. As a result, this model is also applicable to television shows shot originally on tape.

Transferring Picture and Sound

After the original 35mm film negative has been shot and processed, it is transferred to video with a **telecine**.[23] At the time of the transfer, the audio is synched with the image. A video master is produced in the Digital Betacam format and set aside for future use. At this stage, the Digital Betacam master is not color corrected. Simultaneously, ¾-inch U-Matic SP cassettes are made with the telecine for use in the Avid nonlinear editing system.

Off-Line Editing

The off-line editor digitizes the ¾-inch cassettes into the nonlinear editing system and begins editing the picture and principal dialogue tracks. The lower image quality of the ¾-inch format is perfectly adequate for making off-line editing decisions. In addition, the lower resolution of the ¾-inch format conserves hard disk space and makes it easier (and faster) for the nonlinear system to render transitions.

When the editor has finally completed a cut of the picture and principal dialogue tracks, the show is turned over to the director for approval. If the show is on schedule (and things are not backed up), the director has four days to make changes. After the editor has incorporated the director's changes into the nonlinear editing system, the show is turned over to the producer for approval. If the show is still on schedule, the producer may have as long as two weeks to look at the cut and make new suggestions. Again, the

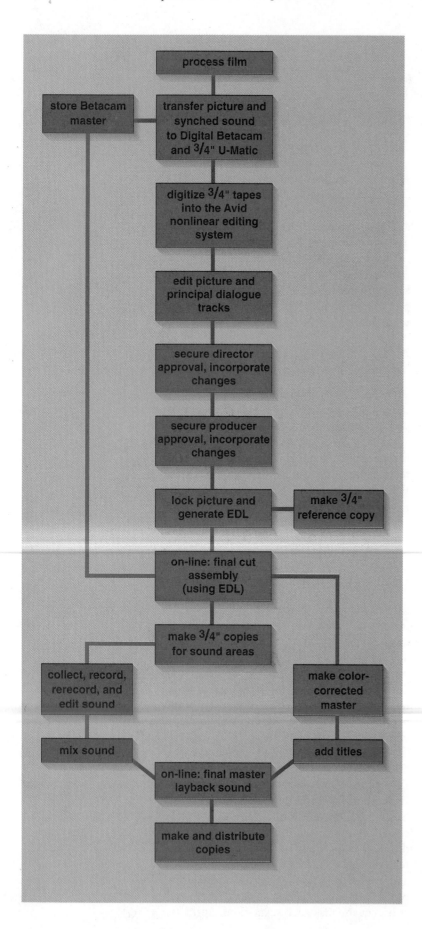

Figure 11.19
A flowchart summarizing a professional nonlinear off-line editing model.

editor makes any changes the producer wants in the nonlinear editing system.

Lock Down and Final Cut Assembly

Once all of the editing changes have been made and approval secured, the picture is locked. This means that the editing of the picture and principal dialogue tracks is finished and no further changes (except in usual circumstances) will be made. Only at this point does the editor generate an edit decision list. A ¾-inch reference copy is printed out of the computer as a means of back-checking the EDL, but it is seldom used. The EDL is copied out to floppy disk.

With the EDL in hand, the entire show moves to an on-line editing suite. There a final cut is assembled using the raw original Digital Betacam master tapes that were produced with the telecine. There is almost no generation loss when making copies in a digital tape format. The copying process is virtually "transparent" for many, many generations. When the on-line cut is finally assembled, ¾-inch copies are struck from it and distributed to the various sound areas. Then while the sound tracks are being built, a color-corrected version of the final cut is produced, again in the Digital Betacam format. Finally that color-corrected version of the tape is used to produce another version of the tape with the titles added.[24]

Sound Building

While the color correction and titling for "Chicago Hope" are taking place, the sound editing begins. Sound is collected, recorded, rerecorded, and edited using a variety of equipment and audio formats. (See Chapter 13 for a complete discussion of the sound building process.) The ¾-inch copies of the locked picture are used as a visual reference as the various sound elements (dialogue, music, and sound effects) are being constructed.

After the sound editing has taken place, all of the different sound elements are brought together for a **sound mix**. In the sound mixing facility the image is projected with a video projector and the various sound tracks (music, effects, and so on) are routed into a sound mixing board. All the audio and video equipment is locked together with time code to maintain synchronization. The mixing session involves adjusting and equalizing the sound levels of all the individual sound elements in relation to the picture and to each other. The final result of the sound mix is three tracks of clean, balanced, equalized sound, one each for the dialogue, music, and sound effects.

Layback

The final step in our "Chicago Hope" example is the **layback,** the placing of the final mixed audio on the master videotape. At this point, you will remember, the video master has been color corrected and titles have been added. The Digital Betacam tape format has four discrete audio tracks. Tracks 1 and 2 are used for a stereo mix containing all the program's sound elements. Tracks 3 and 4 are used primarily as a backup. Track 3 contains the dialogue only, Track 4 all the music and sound effects. Keeping the dialogue separate from the other sound elements makes it easier to fix the sound if some problem arises. And if the tape is used in a foreign country, a dubbed version of the dialogue can be recorded and then mixed with the music and sound effects on Track 4.

Once the picture and sound have been married, the completed master tape is ready for duplication and distribution. "Chicago Hope" is distributed on Digital Betacam tapes and a copy in the D-2 format is made for archival purposes.

It is important to remember that the flowchart in Figure 11.19 presents only one model of nonlinear, random-access editing. There are many ways to execute postproduction. This model seems to have evolved from a film editing model: the film and principal dialogue tracks are cut first, and once they are locked, other postproduction activities can begin. In the digital age new possibilities abound. A **Media Record Telecine (MRT)** can transfer material directly to hard drives for immediate use in a nonlinear editing system. And once images and sound are converted into digital form, they can be stored in a central location and accessed from a network of digital editing systems. The linear step-by-step progression shown in the flowchart is likely to look far different in the future.

Notes

1. Some camcorders can lay time code on audio tracks other than the linear audio tracks. For example, machines that can record hi-fi audio can place time code on that track. This, like VITC, must be laid down during recording because the hi-fi track rides with the video. Recorders with PCM can place time code in that area, but the disadvantage of this is that the time code is then occupying the highest quality, most flexible audio track.

2. *Time Code Handbook* (Frederick, MD: Cipher Digital, 1987). For a discussion of how timecode works on consumer-grade equipment, see Glenn Calderone, "Time Code," *Videomaker,* April 1995, pp. 88–93.

3. What the tracking control actually does is vary the delay between the control track and the head servo loop control so that the heads play back down the center of the recorded track.

4. For more on controllers, see "The Cutting Edge," *Video,* April 1990, pp. 63–65, and "Editing Controllers Tap Small Formats," *TV Technology,* February 1991, p. 1.

5. Some editing systems back up tape as little as three seconds, and others back it up as much as seven seconds. Others are adjustable, so you or an engineer can determine the number of seconds of preroll.

6. Matt Drabick, "The ABCs of TBCs," *AV Video,* September 1994, pp. 42–45.

7. Victoria Bushnell, "The New Heroes of Post," *Film and Video,* October 1991, pp. 58–68.

8. For more on graphics, see George Maestri, "Pro-Animator: Animating the Face," *Digital Video Magazine,* January 1996, pp. 54–55; Michael Murie, "3-D Software for the PC," *NewMedia,* 29 January 1996, pp. 62–69; Jeff Burger, "Alpha Channels UnMasked," *NewMedia,* 29 January 1996, pp. 70–71; George Maestri, "Playing with Power, Animation's Big Three: Alias, Softimage, and Wavefront," *Digital Video Magazine,* September 1995, pp. 40–48; Frank McMahon, "Best Buys in 3-D Animation," *Digital Video Magazine,* March 1996, pp. 48–56; Lynda Weinman, "2-D Animation's Not Just for Mickey Mouse," *NewMedia,* July 1995, pp. 41–46; and Bob Gillman, "Video in a Window: Picturing the Future," *AV Video,* May 1992, pp. 50–57.

9. Several good books on linear editing are Arthur Schneider, *Electronic Post-Production and Videotape Editing* (Boston: Focal Press, 1989); Steven E.

Browne, *Videotape Editing* (Boston: Focal Press, 1989); and Gary Anderson, *Video Editing and Post-Production: A Professional Guide* (White Plains, NY: Knowledge Industry Publications, 1986).

10. A trip to your local computer superstore is the only way to find the latest versions of computer-assisted editing software.

11. Many of these systems are tied closely to the computer's own operating software (Macintosh 7.5, or Windows 3.1, 95, or NT); others are more proprietary programs. There are, of course, editing systems based on the Amiga platform as well. The second edition of this text devoted an entire section to the Video Toaster and the Amiga. Although the Toaster is still being used in many schools (primarily for character generation and graphics), it is clear that the Macintosh and Intel x86-based machines have won the day, at least for now, in the marketplace.

12. The software used to control consumer-level editing systems usually comes bundled with cables and/or other adapters that allow a computer to interface with home VCRs and camcorders.

13. So-called hybrid editing systems actually combine the principles of both nonlinear and computer-assisted editing. Such systems employ less expensive (lower resolution) nonlinear editing to generate an EDL, and then provide a linear edit control system to complete the editing process the old-fashioned way, using the computer to control the tapes and VCRs.

14. Even this seemingly basic step seems subject to change. The new Digital Betacam records digital images and sounds as do the new consumer-level DVC (digital video cassette) camcorders. Another method for eliminating digitizing might be the CamCutter, a camera introduced by Avid/Ikegami. This camera replaces the videotape deck with a field pack that holds two large hard disks for direct digital recording. These hard drives can be inserted right into an Avid nonlinear editing system for instant editing.

15. See, for example, Jan Ozer, "Digital Video, Shot By Shot," *PC Magazine,* 11 April 1995, pp. 104–148; Daniel Greenberg, "PC Video Capture Cards," *Digital Video Magazine,* September 1995, pp. 71–82; Bob Turner, "How to Buy It: A Nonlinear Editing System," *Videography,* January 1966, pp. 63–65; and Steve Mullen, "The Nuts and Bolts of Nonlinear," *AV Video,* January 1966, pp. 71–78.

16. There are a number of interrelated elements that affect image quality. Among them are low compression rates (the less the image is compressed, the more data per frame it will contain), the qual-

ity of the image put into the system, and the hardware and chips used for processing that information. The amount of data and the speed at which that data can be moved to and from the hard disk also affects image quality. Most systems use a SCSI connector (small computer systems interface) for data transfer (SCSI-2, Fast SCSI-2, or Fast and Wide SCSI-2), allowing the greatest throughput of the highest-quality video (30 frames per second, 60 fields with no dropped frames, 640-by-480 capture in 24-bit color or higher).

Even higher capture rates such as 720-by-486 (this is the actual specification for a frame of video based on the CCIR-601 standard), or even higher, are possible depending on the capture board. See Ozer, pp. 104–106; Bob Doyle, "Mac Still King of Non Linear Video," *NewMedia,* July 1995, pp. 61–68; Tim Tully, "Nonlinear Desktop Video Editing Systems," *NewMedia Tool Guide: A Special Edition,* 1995, pp. 31–45.

17. Virtually all systems can digitize audio at sampling rates of 22 kHz (roughly AM-radio quality); and most at 44.1 kHz (CD quality). A few systems can digitize audio at an even higher rate—48 kHz (DAT-quality). See Craig Anderton, "Digital Audio Software for Multimedia," *NewMedia,* 29 January 1996, pp. 55–61.

18. Motion-JPEG (M-JPEG) is the most common compression technology used in digital editing systems today. The JPEG (Joint Photographic Experts Group) standard produces a stream of compressed individual frames that, for the moment at least, makes it easier to use for video editing than the MPEG 1 (Motion Picture Experts Group) and MPEG 2 video compression standards.

M-JPEG, which was developed for still image compression, is completely scalable. Compression rates are typically expressed as ratios: 1:1 is uncompressed; 5:1 might equal Betacam SP video quality; 10:1 Professional S-VHS video quality; 30:1 regular VHS video quality. JPEG compression does not visibly degrade the image at rates below 10:1. Most high-end capture cards employ JPEG compression technology, and JPEG chips can also be used to accelerate video playback.

There are so many variables involved in compression that it might be better to provide compression ratios for a specific system—Fast Electronic's Video Machine. Fast lists the following compression ratios, approximate video quality, and the number of minutes of video that can be stored per gigabyte. At a 2:1 compression ratio (roughly Digital Betacam quality), 1:37 of video could be stored per GB; at 5:1 (Betacam SP), 4:00 of video per GB; at 10:1 (Pro S-VHS), 8:00

of video per GB; at 30:1 (VHS), 24:00 per GB; at 60:1 (low quality off-line), 48:00 per GB. See Stewart Sweetow, "Fast Electronic's DP/R: Can It Compete in the Marketplace?" *Video Pro,* August 1995, pp. 34–37. See also Daniel Greenberg, "DV by the Dollar," *Digital Video Magazine,* October 1995, pp. 28–38; Bob Turner, "Avid Does Windows," *Videography,* January 1996, pp. 75–80; Bob Doyle, "Data Translation's Media 100," *New Media,* February 1996, pp. 59–60.

19. See Chris Straghalis, "Sizing Up the Storage Issue," *Videography,* November 1995, pp. 138–142; Kennedy Gray, "Inside Storage," *Video Pro,* August 1995, pp. 43–45; Craig Lyn, "Beyond Tomorrow: The Future of Storage," *Digital Video Magazine,* September 1995, pp. 30–38; and Jiri Weiss, "RAIDing Storage," *NewMedia,* February 1996, pp. 34–38.

20. The standard EDL formats include Sony, CMX, GVG, or SMPTE.

21. Another element that plays a role in choosing an appropriate output option is the choice of an appropriate software codec, the particular compression/decompression algorithm used in the system. For a full discussion of codecs, see Jan Ozer, "Software Video Codecs: The Search for Quality," *NewMedia,* 29 January 1996, pp. 46–52.

22. Based on telephone interviews with "Chicago Hope" editor, Mark Baldwin, February 8 and 11, 1996.

23. Some dramatic, episodic television shows have begun moving from the 35mm film format to the Super-16mm film format as a cost-saving measure. Like 35mm, Super-16 preserves the 16-by-9 widescreen aspect ratio and will make it easier to convert the show to high-definition television when that new video format finally arrives.

24. Even at this next-to-last stage, dirt and dust removal, also known as "dust-busting," might take place. This can be done at the same time as the titles are being added.

chapter twelve
Editing Approaches

Some stories about editing have been told so often that they have become clichés: the actor whose great performance was left on the editing room floor, the producer or director who "saved" a film during the editing, the psychologist who blames the fast cuts of music videos for the three-second attention span of the American teenager. These are all exaggerations, of course, but they contain just enough insight into the power and purpose of editing to have a semblance of credibility. Editing is important. As much as any one area of moviemaking, editing can intensify the mood and place the audience within the action.

Examples of powerful and effective editing abound: the shift of rhythm in *Psycho* in the scene in which Norman cleans up after "Mother" has made a mess in Cabin 1, the scene in *The Wild Bunch* in which ninety-eight different shots are held together by the drumbeat of the steam engine as Angel separates the train cars to steal the weapons, the interrogation scene in *Bladerunner* that builds to the breaking point as the android grapples with the word *tortoise*.

In one way editing is relatively simple. The physical act of joining one shot to another is not difficult to accomplish in film or video. On the other hand, choosing which shot to use, where it goes, and how to cut it can be far more complicated. Fortunately, editing decisions are not irrevocable. Edits can be remade. Shots can be edited so that they are shorter or longer. The editor can try an entire group of shots in one position, move it to another, and then return it to its original position without permanently damaging the footage. The editing process is one of trial and error, of testing and retesting. Cuts are made, reviewed, then made again. Ultimately, someone—the director or the producer—must decide that a particular cut is the final cut. Otherwise, given the almost limitless number of editing patterns possible, the process might never end.

The editor is responsible for selecting and arranging shots according to the director's over-all plan for the movie. Some directors totally control the editing process. Others convey their ideas to the editor and allow the editor to work in relative freedom, reviewing the work as it is completed. In theatrical filmmaking the script is the guide to the movie's basic structure, but the editor can play a major role in determining its rhythm, mood, and pace. Individual shots (and the principal dialogue track) are selected or rejected for a variety of reasons: the quality of the acting performance, the effectiveness of a particular camera angle or movement, the emphasis a shot gives to a scene, or the elimination of technical errors in the shot. Once these decisions have been made, the real job of editing can begin—establishing relationships between the individual shots in both time and space.

Conventional Hollywood Patterns

The classic style of Hollywood editing is so dominant worldwide that it is virtually the standard editing pattern for theatrical filmmaking, the norm against which other styles of editing are measured and evaluated. Even as a point of departure for less traditional editing, it is simply too pervasive to ignore.

Editing in the Service of the Story

In the hands of the early film pioneers, particularly D. W. Griffith in the United States, editing quickly became one of the most important tools for motion picture storytelling. This kind of narrative editing was honed to perfection in the Hollywood studios of the 1920s and 1930s. In the classic Hollywood editing system the editing is almost totally subservient to the dramatic needs of the story.

One of the key elements in this approach is **continuity editing,** the attempt to make the cut from one shot to the next flow as smoothly and unobtrusively as possible. This is most apparent within the **scene,** the basic building block in conventional motion pictures. The scene, as you will recall from our discussion in Chapter 1, can be defined as unified action, usually occurring in a single time and place. It may be composed of a single shot, but in most cases a scene is made up of a number of shots. In the typical

Hollywood film the story unfolds scene by scene. In most cases the scenes are organized in chronological order, showing only those events that advance the story or provide some piece of information significant to the plot. The story may move from one time period to another or from location to location, but within each individual scene the editing usually creates the illusion of continuous time and place.

Take, for example, a group of scenes from Steven Spielberg's *Indiana Jones and the Last Crusade*:

Scene 6   Aboard a freighter during a violent storm, Indiana Jones and Fedora fight over the Cross of Coronada. Indy gets the cross and jumps ship.

Scene 7   Indy lectures to a class of admiring archeology students.

Scene 8   Indy gives Brody the Cross of Coronada.

Scene 9   Indy enters his office, wading through a horde of anxious students. He flees out his office window.

Scene 10   Indy meets Donovan, who convinces him to go after the Holy Grail. Indy learns his father is missing.

Scene 11   Indy and Brody find that someone has broken into the father's house. Indy recalls the package he received—his dad's Grail diary.

Scene 12   Donovan says goodbye to Indy and Brody.

Scene 13   Indy flies to Venice.

Scene 14   Indy and Brody arrive in Venice and meet Elsa.

Scene 15   Indy, Brody, and Elsa walk to the church that has been converted to a library.

These ten scenes illustrate some basic patterns of conventional Hollywood storytelling. The story moves forward in time, skipping extraneous events. We do not see how Indy gets from the ship to his classroom or how he moves from his meeting with Donovan to his father's house. Those periods of time are insignificant. In fact, it is impossible to determine exactly how much time passes from the moment Indy jumps ship until we see him in the classroom. It may have been a few days, a week, or a month. In the context of the film it does not matter. Similarly, the locations vary according to the needs of the plot. Within these ten scenes are seven locations (the ship, the classroom, Indy's office, Donovan's house, Indy's father's house, the plane flying to Venice, the Venetian library-church) and fragments from at least three different days. Obviously, the editing can organize the story events freely in time and space. But within each individual scene, such as Indy's lecture to the classroom of lovestruck coeds, a series of shots edited together presents a continuous piece of action in a single time and place.

In the single-camera shooting method a scene is shot from a variety of angles and perspectives. To ensure a continuous and clear flow between these different shots, Hollywood filmmakers developed an elaborate system that encompassed a number of editing techniques and procedures for shooting the scene. One basic goal of this system is to mask the cuts, to make them less apparent, an approach that is sometimes referred to as **hidden editing** or **invisible editing**.

What makes this system even more effective is that each successive shot is psychologically correct from the audience's point of view. Film theorist André Bazin has compared this to a stage play, where the viewer's attention shifts naturally from one character to another according to the logic of the drama, the dialogue, and the movements or gestures in the scene.[1] For example, a shot of a character who suddenly turns and looks off-screen is naturally followed by a shot of what the character is looking at. When two people are carrying on a conversation and one stops talking, we expect a cut to the other as he replies. This does not mean that the editor must always cut to the shot the viewer expects. In fact, cutting against the natural flow of the action and against the audience's expectations often heightens the drama. Nevertheless, in traditional filmmaking cutting to a shot that is totally unrelated to the basic action in the scene would be inappropriate.

At its core Hollywood-style continuity editing is self-effacing: it does not call attention to itself. It avoids disconcerting shifts in time or space and encourages anything that makes the shots in the scene flow together smoothly and

a

b

Figure 12.1

Cutting from shot (a) to (b) might maintain perfect continuity in terms of time and space, but the cut will appear to "jump" because the shots are so similar in size and angle.

unobtrusively. The editing is supposed to serve the story, organizing scenes and the different shots within individual scenes in a clear, logical, and convincing manner. From the point of view of the Hollywood editor, if the audience is unaware of the editing, its attention is focused where it should be—on the actors and the story.

The Continuity System

The continuity system creates the illusion of continuous action by carefully coordinating every element of the **mise-en-scène**, the cinematography, and the editing. The way a scene is staged for the camera can also break continuity: the prop that appears in one shot and disappears in the next, the lighting that changes direction or color on the cut, the tie that changes patterns or the cigarette that suddenly becomes shorter, the actor who abruptly reverses screen direction.

The script supervisor helps to guard against continuity violations during production, and the editor tries to hide them in the editing. To discuss continuity editing without referring to how the scene is shot and staged for the camera is impossible.[2]

Technically, a single **shot**, no matter how complex, will always maintain continuity. Problems arise when we try to edit a group of shots together seamlessly, with no sense of break, jump, or discontinuity in the action. To make it easier for the editor to hold continuity among these different shots directors frequently use a technique called **overlapping action.** The director makes sure that action in one shot is repeated, at least in part, in the shot that may follow it. In other words, a character opening a door in one shot repeats that movement exactly when shot from a different angle. This provides the editor with a number of possible places at which to make a **match cut,** a cut in which the character's movement and position are perfectly aligned in time and space from one shot to the next. Failure to do this results in what is commonly called a **jump cut,** an obvious and jarring break in continuity from one shot to the next. A similarly abrupt jump occurs if part of the action is repeated in successive shots. This is sometimes called *double action.*

Hollywood filmmakers also recognized a related problem. Even when two shots match perfectly in time and space, a jump can appear to occur if the camera angles or the size of objects in the shots are *too similar.* Correcting for this requires emphasis of the difference between two shots by changing their angle and size. Judging how much the shots should vary is not always easy. If the change between the shots is too great, the edited footage can be disconcerting; if the change is too small, their similarity will make the cut seem to jump.[3] (Figure 12.1 illustrates shots that are too similar.)

The Master Scene Shooting Method

Hollywood filmmakers developed a method of shooting that provided the editor with shots that could be edited together seamlessly and continuously. It involves analyzing and breaking the action in the scene down into its logical components. The first step in this method is to

SCENE 11

EXT. MRS. OLIVER'S HOUSE - NIGHT

David and Scottie pass by Mrs. Oliver's house. The
lights are off. The dark old house looms in front of
them like an old haunted mansion. An owl hoots from a
nearby tree. A cat screeches in the distance.

                    SCOTTIE
    1   I wonder if the old witch is home
    2   tonight.

                    DAVID
    3   I bet she is. She just doesn't
    4   want to give out any candy.
    5   (Pause) Hey, look at this.

They bend down. David draws a picture of an old witch
on the sidewalk with a chunk of chalk.

                    DAVID
    6   This is what Oliver looks like.

                    SCOTTIE
    7   Hey, that's great! Put a wart on
    8   the end of her nose.

David adds the wart and then writes in big letters, OLD
MOTHER WITCH, and draws an arrow pointing toward Mrs.
Oliver's house. The boys laugh. Then Scottie gives
David a shove toward the house.

                    SCOTTIE
    9   Ring Oliver's bell!

They start scuffling and shoving each other.

                    DAVID
    10   Hey! Not me! Come on. Let's go
    11   to the Bridwell's.

Figure 12.2
Scene from Old Mother Witch. *The numbers in color are added for reference.*

shoot a **master scene shot.** This is usually a wide shot or long shot that covers all the action and dialogue in the scene or portion of the scene. The master scene shot has the effect of locking continuity for all other shots. It establishes the lighting, the costumes, the props, the setting, and the spatial relationships of the actors. Once set, shooting additional shots from different angles and perspectives breaks the scene down further.

A brief scene from *Old Mother Witch,* shown in Figure 12.2, provides an example of how this might work. Note that the numbers next to the dialogue are for reference only.

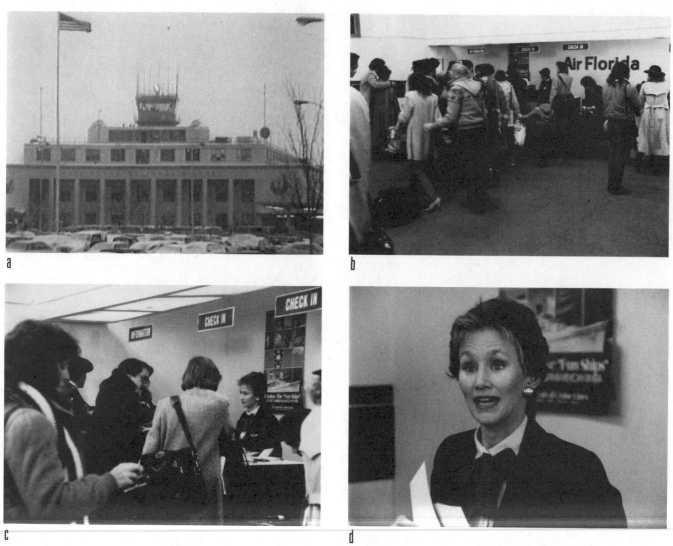

a

b

c

d

Figure 12.3

The traditional exposition pattern—moving closer and closer within the scene. A scene from the made-for-television movie Flight 90 *begins with (a) an establishing shot to set up the airport location, followed by (b) a long shot inside the terminal, cutting to (c) a medium shot in the ticket line, and to (d) a close-up of the ticket agent. (Photos courtesy of Finnegan-Pinchuk)*

Neither of the actors playing Scottie or David is enough of an artist to draw the witch on the sidewalk. A close-up of the real artist's hand reaching into the frame to do the drawing covers that action. Because the scene has this natural break, the master scene shot breaks into two different shots: one is a wide shot covering all the dialogue and action from line 1 to just beyond line 5, where the boys bend down to begin drawing the picture, and the other is a wide shot providing coverage of the dialogue and action from line 6 to line 11 (the actor playing David

can draw a wart on the nose and add the lettering and arrow).

The first master scene shot functions as an **establishing shot** for this scene, orienting the audience to the location and providing information vital to the action (Mrs. Oliver's house in the background). Establishing shots are the traditional way of beginning each new scene in narrative moviemaking. In fact, the traditional editing pattern of establishing shot–long shot–medium shot–close-up (see Figure 12.3) developed for much the same reason—to establish

Figure 12.4

Reversing the traditional pattern. Isolated close-ups of (a) the man, (b) the dog, and (c) the woman in a scene from Flight 90 *creates questions in the audience's mind about what the action is and where it is taking place. These questions are eventually answered by the last shot in the sequence (d), which brings the three together in the same shot. (Photos courtesy of Finnegan-Pinchuk)*

the location before moving in to focus on important details within the scene. Sometimes a scene will have, in effect, two establishing shots. For example, we might see an exterior shot of an office building and then cut to the scene inside (a space that will also have to be established). Reversing this pattern—starting with a close-up of some detail within the scene—can build anticipation, making viewers wonder where they are (see Figure 12.4). These questions are answered as subsequent shots reveal and establish the space in which the scene is taking place.

The master scene shooting method mirrors the logic of the traditional establishing shot–long shot–medium shot–close-up pattern. Once the master scene shots are completed, the scene

is broken down into increasingly greater detail. For example, we might shoot close-ups of David and Scottie delivering their lines. This will enable the editor to establish the familiar **shot/reverse shot** pattern (see Figure 12.5) by cutting from a shot of David talking to a shot of Scottie talking. In framing, these shots will mirror each other. The shot/reverse shot pattern often uses **over-the-shoulder shots.**

The scene breakdown might include **reaction shots**, shots of David or Scottie reacting to something the other has said or to something else in the scene—the drawing on the sidewalk or Mrs. Oliver's foreboding house. The **shot/reaction shot** pattern (see Figure 12.6) gives the editor the option of focusing the audience's attention on the character responding to the dia-

a

b

Figure 12.5

A shot and a reverse shot in Flight 90 *mirror each other in composition and subject size. (Photos courtesy of Finnegan-Pinchuk)*

a

b

c

Figure 12.6

The young boy's reaction shot (b) is cut between shots of his mother talking on the telephone (a and c) in a scene from Flight 90. *(Photos courtesy of Finnegan-Pinchuk)*

logue or action, rather than on the person speaking or the action itself. Alfred Hitchcock, a director who felt that the event was usually less interesting than a character's reaction to it, frequently exploited the power of the reaction shot.[4]

For shot/reverse shots and shot/reaction shots the editor will need to be highly conscious of **eyeline match** (see Figure 12.7). Because these shots may isolate David or Scottie in the frame, the directions in which they are looking offscreen (toward each other) and their angles of view must match precisely. If Scottie is taller, his eyes will need to angle slightly down to where David is supposed to be standing. In effect, the direction established by Scottie's eyes creates a target area that the editor must match in the shot that follows.

Finally, to complete our breakdown we will probably shoot close-ups of significant details within the scene, such as the chalk drawing of

Figure 12.7

The eyeline established by the woman in shot (a) must be matched by the man's eyes in shot (b). (Photos courtesy of Finnegan-Pinchuk)

the witch (or even a small part of the drawing). The editor will use some of these close-ups for **cut-ins** and some for **cutaways.** A cut-in focuses on some element that appeared in the previous shot (see Figure 12.8). A cutaway is a shot of something that did not appear in the previous shot (see Figure 12.9). For example, if the shot for lines 7 to 8 was a long shot that included Scottie, David, and the witch, a cut to the drawing of the wart would be a cut-in. If the shot for

Figure 12.8

In this series of pictures the close-up of the baby (b) is used as a cut-in between shots (a) and (c). If you look closely, you can see a continuity problem with the baby's arm and the man's hand. (Photos courtesy of Finnegan-Pinchuk)

Figure 12.9

In this sequence from Flight 90 *shot (b) functions as a cutaway between shots (a) and (c). Because neither pilot appears in the cutaway, continuity can be dropped momentarily and then be picked up again when we return to the pilots in shot (c). (Photos courtesy of Finnegan-Pinchuk)*

lines 7 and 8 was a close-up of Scottie's face,' the cut to the wart would be a cutaway. Cut-ins must maintain continuity. If David's foot was on the witch's mouth in the long shot, it must be there on the cut-in. Cutaways do not need to maintain continuity; the position of David's foot is not crucial.

In reality, the director probably would not shoot such extensive coverage for a scene this simple. To do so would take too much time and be too costly. Some decisions about how the scene will be edited will be made *before* the shooting, allowing the director to shoot fewer shots. Nevertheless, even without such comprehensive coverage the editor will still have countless options for structuring the scene.

Ensuring a Consistent Screen Direction

Obviously, it is not easy for the editor to maintain continuity when the scene is broken down into different shots this way. It was for precisely this reason that the so-called **180-degree rule** evolved. This system of shooting, as you will recall from Chapter 5, is used to ensure a continuous and unconfusing space from one shot to the next. The placement of David and Scottie in the shot establishes an **axis of action,** or *line*. As long as all shots are taken on one side of that line (within the 180 degrees), the space presented in those shots will be consistent when they are edited together. Crossing the axis will make the characters' positions shift drastically. This principle is also helpful in preserving a constant screen direction when the shot contains movement. Once a character begins moving in one direction, the next shot must maintain that direction. Again, crossing the imaginary 180-degree line can cause confusion, making the character appear to reverse direction abruptly on the cut. When a character enters or leaves the frame, that too sets up anticipation of direction for the next shot. If David walks out of the frame by moving from left to right, we expect him to enter the next shot from the left side. A shot directly down the axis of a character coming toward or away from the camera is neutral, allowing the editor to establish a new screen direction in subsequent shots (see Figure 12.10).

By maintaining consistent direction and systematically covering the scene with the master scene shooting method, the director provides the editor with material that can be edited together to create the illusion of continuous action. The editor uses the individual shots to build the scene according to the logic of the drama, the dialogue, and the actor's movements or gestures. With such comprehensive coverage the editor can also develop a sense of off-screen space, building expectations that can be used to motivate and drive the film forward.

Finding the Cutting Point

By looking carefully at two shots in succession, the editor can select the appropriate cutting point at the end of the first shot and the beginning of the next. This is often a difficult task that involves looking for continuity details. Hands, arms, feet, and other elements must be in similar positions from shot to shot. This is much easier if the director has provided many cutting places by overlapping action during shooting. One technique for making two shots flow together more smoothly is **cutting-on-action.** Rather than letting the actor complete an action in one shot and cutting to the next, the action *begins* in the first shot and ends in the second. Continuing the same movement across two shots draws the viewer's eye naturally to the next shot, helping to mask the cut and make it less obvious.

Often the editor will find it necessary to drop continuity and then pick it up again. This is where cutaways and reaction shots are especially handy because they do not include elements present in the previous shot. They allow the editor to momentarily drop continuity, either for aesthetic reasons or to hide continuity problems that occurred during shooting.

Other Editing Concerns

The editor also is responsible for controlling the rhythm or tempo for each scene and for the movie as a whole. Each shot has its own pace or rhythm, determined by the speed of the dialogue or the movement of the camera or actor in the shot. But the editor can control or alter

a

b

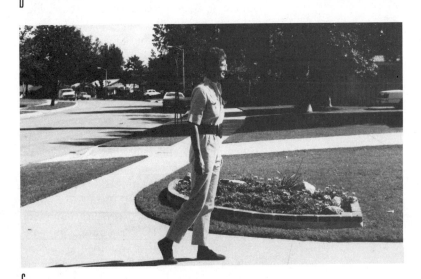

c

Figure 12.10

Shooting right down the axis (b) allows the screen direction to be reversed from shot (a) to shot (c).

a   b

Figure 12.11

Compressing time by eliminating unimportant material is a common editing practice. Here a shot of an airplane that has just landed on the runway (a) is followed by a shot of the airplane as it docks at the terminal (b). Eliminating a portion of time in this manner is seldom confusing to the viewer. (Photos courtesy of Finnegan-Pinchuk)

that pace by varying the length and number of shots in the scene. The shorter each shot is, the faster the tempo becomes. Long, uninterrupted shots slow the tempo. Similarly, the time it takes for a scene to unfold can be expanded by inserting in the main action a series of extra shots, such as cutaways, reactions, and different angles. The editor can compress time by cutting shots shorter and by using cutaways or reverse shots that eliminate some part of the action while maintaining a semblance of continuity (see Figure 12.11). For example, the first shot of a person going to bed might be of the person starting up the stairs. The next shot is that person opening the door, taken from an angle within the bedroom. Time compression is commonplace in theatrical films. It enables the editor to control the tempo and eliminate extraneous material while moving the story forward.

A completely different kind of time-space manipulation occurs in **parallel editing** or **cross-cutting.** By alternating shots from one line of action to another, the editor can imply that the two actions are occurring simultaneously (see Figure 12.12). This would seem to be a complete violation of continuity, but in conventional filmmaking what holds the different actions together is their relationship in the story and the implication that they are occurring at the same time. We have all seen the old melo-

drama in which the black-caped villain is tying the heroine to the railroad tracks. This traditionally is cross-cut with scenes of a steam engine roaring down the track and the hero riding furiously to the rescue on his white horse. When these scenes are intercut, usually at a faster and faster pace to build suspense, we all understand their conventional meaning—the hero is trying to reach the heroine before the train does. Although the individual scenes are unrelated in space and time, the cross-cutting unifies them in the context of the story. Cross-cutting need not be so melodramatic, however. It can be used to comment on, or compare, different lines of action, or it can be used to expand time in the scene.

An editor might also choose to **flash back** or **flash forward** to a scene or sequence that portrays events in the past or future. In traditional moviemaking a line of dialogue or some other device (pages flipping on the calendar or hands spinning on a clock) cues the viewer to a jump to the past or future. A **flash cut,** a shot just a few frames long, can present a brief image from the past or future that is almost subliminal—*Magnum, P.I.* flashing back to some moment in Vietnam or forward in anticipation of some event. A less traditional filmmaker, such as Alain Resnais in *Last Year in Marienbad,* uses this kind of time shifting to disorient the viewer.

a

b

c

d

e

Figure 12.12

Parallel editing. The film Flight 90 *relies heavily on parallel editing to develop the narrative. The preparation of the airplane (b, d) is intercut with scenes of many characters (a, c, e) as they prepare to board the ill-fated flight. (Photos courtesy of Finnegan-Pinchuk)*

The editing process can also enhance an actor's performance. By **overlap cutting** the sound track the editor can allow an actor's lines to be heard while we see something else. With a judicious use of cutaways and reaction shots, the editor may be able to strengthen an actor's performance. By eliminating bad takes and by taking parts of lines from other takes the editor can sometimes create a better reading. **Point-of-view shots** can add a subjective feeling that a scene needs, and intercutting just the right close-up or reaction shot can build a dramatic moment that did not actually exist in the original performance.

Other Transitions

Thus far we have been concerned only with **straight cuts,** a transition in which one shot instantaneously replaces the next. This is not the only kind of transition that the editor has at his or her disposal. Fades, dissolves, wipes, and a whole arsenal of digital effects provide other ways to join shots together.

A **fade-in** is a gradual transition from black to a full view of the image. A **fade-out** is the reverse, a transition from the image to black. The editor can also choose how quickly or slowly these transitions occur (a fast fade-in, a slow fade-out). Most movies and television shows begin with a fade-in and end with a fade-out. Using a fade-out to end a scene or sequence *within* the movie usually implies a stronger degree of closure, a more final conclusion to the scene than a straight cut. To use a punctuation analogy, a straight cut between two scenes is like a comma, whereas a fade-out is like a period. Furthermore, because a scene ending with a fade-out is usually followed by a fade-in to the next scene, the fades suggest a greater passage of time between the two scenes than does a regular cut. This sensation is heightened if the fades are executed more slowly.

A **dissolve** is a much softer transition than a fade or a cut. It entails the gentle fading of one shot *into* the next. Actually, as the first shot fades out, it overlaps with the second shot as it fades in. For a brief time in the middle of the dissolve the two shots are superimposed. This is much more visible in a long, slow dissolve than in a short, quick one. Like a fade, a dissolve suggests the passage of time, although possibly with less emphasis. Editors often use dissolves to hide problems (such as a reversal in screen direction) or as a transitional device when some part of an action is omitted. Because dissolves visibly (albeit briefly) combine shots, they suggest a relationship between them that can be exploited effectively. In a flashback, for example, the editor might select a dissolve to amplify the link between the present and the past. Similarly, dissolves can suggest a link between images because of their common shapes, colors, movements, or subject matter.

While a dissolve is a soft, unifying transition, a **wipe** is generally a hard, abrupt, and obvious one. In a wipe the second image pushes across or into the first image, replacing it on the screen. The two images are not superimposed as in a dissolve; rather, the cutting edge of the second image has a visible pattern or shape (vertical, diamond shaped, circular, rectangular) as it gradually replaces the first image. A wipe suggests the passage of time or a change of location in the same time. Its use as a transition is somewhat different in film than in video. In theatrical moviemaking a wipe is somewhat archaic, a familiar transition in the era of movie serials and melodramas. Sometimes wipes were used to add a touch of humor to the transition between two scenes. In comparison, wipes are a fairly common transition in video. They often appear in televised sports events, commercials, and TV magazine shows.

Digital video effects provide another type of transition. Once an electronic signal is converted into digital form, an editor can manipulate its shape, size, and movement to create almost any transition imaginable. Such effects (spins, twirls, flips, page turns) are obvious, of course, and not as useful in conventional Hollywood-style storytelling where the objective is usually to make transitions as invisible as possible.

These various transitions—fades, dissolves, wipes, and digital effects—imply the passage of time. In the appropriate place they can be just the transition the editor needs to punctuate a scene, to shift tempo, or to link a series of shots. Student moviemakers often overuse these transitions, however. Unless there is a good reason in the context of the story for using a fade, dissolve, wipe, or digital effect, the cleanest and most efficient transition is still a straight cut. Using transitional effects too often lessens their impact when you really need them.

Alternatives in Time and Space

Every cut, as we have already seen, is a cut in both space and time. Although there are many time-space relationships, conventional Hollywood editing tends to limit itself to a handful of possibilities.[5] In a traditional Hollywood motion picture the editing typically organizes events in chronological order. The story moves forward, omitting unimportant segments of time. Time reversals of any kind are not the usual way of advancing the story. Movies use flashbacks occasionally, of course, but they are a relatively rare and unusual transition, often set apart in quotation marks by flipping calendar pages, spinning clock hands, or a dazed look in the character's eyes. Cuts forward in time are even more rare. Similarly, the classic style consciously avoids any time-space relationship that creates a jump in time or space.

Obviously, there are many alternatives to this conventional pattern. Imagine, for example, a music video that shows a dancer repeatedly performing the same dance step. Each shot, in effect, repeats the action of the previous shot. Yet the space (or background) in each shot might be totally different (at the seashore, in the snow, in a forest). This kind of editing would be totally unacceptable in conventional Hollywood filmmaking but is rather commonplace in music videos. Freed of the constraints of narrative editing, the editor can explore many more time-space relationships, cutting to the beat of a very different drummer.

While the goal of conventional narrative editing is to maintain continuity and make the edits as invisible as possible, a less traditional editor may want the cuts to be abrupt, discontinuous, and extremely obvious. The editor may select cutting points in order to create a particular rhythm or beat. The tempo of the music,

not the natural rhythm of the shot, might govern those decisions. An editor may match shots according to some shape, form, movement, or color in successive shots, a rationale that has nothing to do with consistent screen direction or smooth, continuous action.

Such cutting is relatively common in nonnarrative productions such as abstract films and videos, commercials, music videos, and some of the newer multimedia productions. But many modern directors, such as Robert Bresson, Michaelangelo Antonioni, Nicholas Roeg, Jean-Luc Godard, and Bob Fosse, have consciously broken or extended the rules of the classic continuity system in their own narrative films. Their work suggests that classic Hollywood-style editing is only one of many approaches. It is simply the *conventional* way of editing, not the only way.

Montage Editing

Perhaps the best-known alternative editing system is called **montage editing.** This term has been applied to so many different types of editing that it can be confusing. Montage is simply the French word for editing, but it implies a more comprehensive building up or assembly of the total film.

Several Russian filmmakers and theorists extended this concept in the 1920s.[6] V. I. Pudovkin, for example, developed a theory of montage based on what he called relational editing—a process that emphasized the different relationships that could be established among a series of shots by using contrast, similarity, symbolism, or repetition. Pudovkin felt that a scene could be constructed simply by adding significant detail to significant detail and that this kind of "linkage" could be done unobtrusively, masked by the logic of the editing and power of the drama. Film director Sergei Eisenstein, Pudovkin's contemporary and the author of numerous essays on editing, developed an opposing theory based on the violent "collision" of images.[7] Eisenstein believed that an entirely new meaning could be created by blatantly and obviously cutting from one shot to another; the meaning was not contained in either shot alone but was produced exclusively by their juxtaposition.

Today, the one place where such concepts are most consistently applied is television commercials. Think about the typical cold drink or beer commercial. The sequence of shots might go something like this:

1. Shot of beautiful suntanned teenagers playing volleyball on the beach.
2. Close-up of a beautiful smiling blonde in a tiny bikini.
3. Medium shot of a grinning lifeguard with sunglasses. Drops of sweat are rolling down his handsome bronzed face.
4. Extreme slow-motion close-up of a hand reaching into an ice-filled container. The hand slowly pulls out a can of Brand X soft drink or beer—icy water runs down the side of the can in tiny rivulets.
5. Shot of a dog catching a Frisbee in the surf.
6. Shots of happy beautiful teenagers on beach blankets. The boys and girls are just beginning to talk in the hot sand.
7. Another dreamy close-up of a bottle of Brand X being extracted from the ice chest. (And so on . . .)

You have seen this pattern enough times to finish it in your own mind. Juxtaposing the shots of the happy beachgoers with the sweating bottle of Brand X creates a meaning that is not contained in the shots of the beachgoers or soft drink bottle alone. Of course, to make sure you don't miss the connection between Brand X and the active beautiful people (who are obviously successful with the opposite sex), most advertisers would probably insert shots of the teenagers and Brand X together as the commercial progresses.

It was precisely the power of editing to suggest new relationships that most interested Pudovkin and Eisenstein. From their perspective, editing need not always be focused on maintaining continuity. A shot of a spinning tire might be cut to a spinning roulette wheel because of the similar shape and movement in the two shots. An editor might make a cut for metaphoric purposes: a shot of a Cossack swinging his sword at a peasant cut against a shot of helpless animals being butchered in a slaughterhouse.

Ironically, Hollywood filmmakers also tried their hands at montage. Many films in the 1930s and 1940s contained a *montage sequence,* often credited to special montage editors such as Slavko Vorkapich and Jack Killifer. Hollywood montage, however, tended to adopt the Russian methods in a unique way—it created a discrete sequence designed either to establish a particular mood or to condense a long and complicated action in a brief on-screen time period. The bicycle ride (cut to the tune of "Raindrops Keep Falling on My Head") in *Butch Cassidy and the Sundance Kid* and the tribute to Beethoven cut to his Ninth Symphony in *Immortal Beloved* are typical of Hollywood mood montages.

Just as common are the time-compression montages. We have all seen the montage shorthand for "the election campaign": shots of speech making, baby kissing, spinning newspaper headlines, more speech making, pages of the calendar turning, more speech making. Together this series of shots equals The Long Election Campaign. Many series TV shows open with a montage that condenses the backstory. "The Nanny" starts with a series of cartoons cut to music that show how the main character moved from working in a bridal shop to selling cosmetics to being taken in as a nanny. The opening of "Fresh Prince of Bel-Air" condenses the story of how a ghetto kid came to live with rich relatives, all set to rap music.

Although this technique clearly uses many of the Russian montage principles, it is basically a special device that Hollywood editors use to abridge time without confusing the audience. In effect, conventional Hollywood filmmaking uses montage in exactly the same way that it uses every other editing technique—in the service of the story.

Notes

1. André Bazin, *What Is Cinema?* trans. by Hugh Gray (Berkeley: University of California Press, 1972), pp. 31–32.
2. Jay Ankeney, "Editing with an Eye for Style," *TV Technology,* September 1995, p. 73.
3. The so-called 30-degree rule (discussed in Chapter 5) evolved to respond to this problem.
4. See, for example, François Truffaut, *Hitchcock* (New York: Simon & Schuster, 1967); David Ster-

ritt, *The Films of Alfred Hitchcock* (Cambridge: Cambridge University Press, 1992): and Robert E. Kapfis, *Hitchcock: The Making of a Reputation* (Chicago: University of Chicago Press, 1992).

5. For a systematic classification of time-space relationships and an excellent discussion of traditional narrative editing and alternative approaches, see Noel Burch, *Theory of Film Practice,* trans. by Helen R. Lane (New York: Praeger, 1973), pp. 3–15.

6. See, for example, V. I. Pudovkin, *Film Technique and Film Acting* (New York: Grove, 1970), and *Kuleshov on Film: Writings of Leo Kuleshov,* trans. and

ed. by Ronald Levaco (Berkeley: University of California Press, 1974). For a general discussion of the Russian montage experiments, see David Bordwell and Kristin Thompson, *Film Art: An Introduction* (New York: McGraw-Hill, 1993), Chapter 7, and Gerald Mast, *A Short History of the Movies* (New York: Macmillan, 1986), Chapter 8.

7. Eisenstein's combined essays are contained in two volumes: Sergei Eisenstein, *Film Form* (New York: Harcourt, Brace & World, 1949), and *Film Sense* (New York: Harcourt, Brace & World, 1947).

chapter thirteen
Structuring Sound

Structuring sound refers to creating, editing, and mixing different sounds—dialogue, music, and various forms of sound effects. All sounds are manipulated so that they are distinguishable and so that each contributes to the reality and emotion of the movie. Sometimes the process of working with postproduction sound is called sound **sweetening**.[1] Originally, *sweetening* referred to improving sound recorded during production by adding **reverb**, using **equalization**, or in some other way manipulating the sound. However, as time progressed, the meaning of sweetening broadened to include the myriad processes that have become available for sound postproduction. In fact, 85 to 90 percent of what you hear in a movie is added after the movie is shot.

In recent years sound postproduction processes have been changing rapidly, thanks mostly to digital technology. The various production facilities have been experimenting to try to find the most efficient and creative ways to utilize the new technologies. As a recent article in *Mix* magazine states, "Perhaps the most exciting change brought on by the technical revolution in sound-for-film is that there are no more established rules for putting together effects, music, and dialogue elements of a rerecording session."[2]

Variations in Structuring Sound

The number of variations for editing and mixing sound have become almost infinite. In recent years the innovations in this field have been as great as those for video editing, if not greater. In a few instances, sound for motion pictures is still edited the "old-fashioned" film way, but more often the sound, like the picture, is manipulated on tape or within a computer.

Magnetic Film Stock Systems

Because some theatrical motion pictures are still edited using **flatbeds** (see Chapter 10), some elements of sound, especially dialogue, are reproduced in a form that can be used on a flatbed. This process involves the use of **magnetic film stock**. As you may remember (see Chapter 8), film is shot **double system**; the picture is in the camera and the dialogue is recorded on an audiotape recorder such as a Nagra. If the picture is going to be edited on a flatbed, the dialogue (and any other synchronous on-location sound) is transferred to magnetic film stock (often shortened to "mag stock"), a recording material that is the same gauge as the film (16mm or 35mm) and has **sprocket holes** down the side so that it can be edited in an exact frame-for-frame relationship with the picture (see Figure 13.1). The piece of equipment that is used to transfer the audiotape to mag stock is a sound dubber that contains a **resolving unit** (see Figure 13.2). It locks onto the special sync signal recorded in the field, enabling the mag stock to be synched frame for frame with the picture.

The mag stock is then placed on the flatbed on platters that are right below the platters that hold the picture (see Figure 10.4). The platters can be **interlocked** so that picture and sound are in sync. In this way the film **workprint** and sound are edited together; if ten frames are taken out of the picture, the same length of material is removed from the sound track.

In the past, other elements of sound (music, sound effects, narration) would also be recorded on mag stock and these too would be synched to the picture. Then all of the reels of mag stock would be taken to a sound mixing facility and loaded on a bank of magnetic stock players (see Figure 13.3) that could be synched to each other and to a projector that displayed the picture. The outputs of these mag players would be sent to an **audio board** where one or more technicians, while watching the picture, would adjust the levels so that they best suited the movie. The output of the audio board was then recorded onto another reel of magnetic film stock that was taken to the lab with the **conformed** nega-

Figure 13.1
A roll of 35mm magnetic film stock. (Photo courtesy of GCI Group, Inc.)

Figure 13.3
A bank of mag players at a sound mixing facility. (Photo courtesy of Ryder Sound Services)

Figure 13.2
A sound transfer unit. The ¼-inch tape goes on the top reels and the mag stock on the bottom reels.

tive of the picture. Picture and sound were then placed together on the **release print**.[3]

Mag stock, although it is still used to edit dialogue and other synchronous on-location sounds, is rapidly becoming a thing of the past.

Magnetic Tape Systems

Sound is now likely to be created, edited, and mixed using equipment that incorporates magnetic audiotape and/or videotape or some form of computer-assisted system. Some postproduction facilities (especially in universities) are quite limited in terms of what they can accomplish in the way of sound building. They have no audio equipment other than the controls that are part of the videotape recorders. Sound can be manipulated only slightly, by dubbing it from the source machine to the edit machine. The volume can be changed a bit by raising or lowering the record control on the edit machine, but little else can be done. If the editing equipment incorporates an audio board and some other equipment such as a CD player and an audio cassette machine, more options are possible. But videotapes have a limited number of audio tracks (usually only two to four), so complicated sound building is at best difficult.

More effective are audio editing facilities where sound can be edited and mixed on a **multitrack audiotape recorder** that is separate from the VCR and that, as its name implies, can hold many tracks of audio—8, 16, 24, or more. A VCR is still needed in such a configuration. It is used to display the picture so that the audio technicians can use the video as a reference while they make their decisions. These multitrack facilities vary in their sophistication, but at the very least they contain a professional audio board with multiple inputs and outputs, a number of pieces of **outboard equipment** (CD players, cart machines, DAT cassette players, music synthesizers), and the multitrack audiotape recorder (either **analog** or **digital**) that can record what comes out of the board. Various sounds (music, dialogue, sound effects) are

Figure 13.4

A typical multitrack sound mixing setup. The picture is projected onto a large screen, and several people operate the audio board so that they can mix the various sources properly. (Photo courtesy of Digital Sound and Picture)

placed on different tracks of the tape and can then be mixed onto yet another track of the tape. (See Figure 13.4.)

This configuration works best if the multitrack recorder, the VCR, and at least some of the outboard equipment can operate in sync. This is most easily accomplished if all the inputs and outputs are tied to **SMPTE time code** and if a special machine that reads the time code and keeps all the machines running together is part of the system. This machine serves as the "sprocket holes" of the system. Many of these facilities also have equipment that can improve or alter the sound by varying **frequency, timbre, duration,** and other audio characteristics. And they often have special rooms for creating sound in a controlled environment.[4]

Computer Systems

The newest concept in audio postproduction involves digital computer-based sound equipment. Sometimes what is used for structuring sound are the audio tracks of a **nonlinear** video editing system, such as the Avid. Although they are continuing to improve, many of these sys-

tems are somewhat limited because they cannot accommodate a large number of tracks. For this reason, stand-alone computerized audio systems, often referred to as **digital audio workstations (DAWs)**, have been developed (see Figure 13.5). As with many other pieces of equipment, these vary in capacity, complexity—and price. Some can hold over a hundred channels of audio; others are designed for twenty-four.

With DAWs or video editing systems, all sounds are fed into some sort of a computer hard drive where they can be stored and manipulated in nonlinear, **random-access** fashion. Characteristics of each individual sound (loudness, pitch, hisses) can be altered and shaped. Dialogue, music, and effects can be edited to accompany the picture, and the sounds can be mixed together, all within the computer. Because the sound is kept in digital form throughout, it does not degrade.

Some less sophisticated computer-assisted audio systems do not actually store the sounds within the computer. They are essentially computer programs that allow a personal computer and various forms of conventional audio equipment to speak to each other. The computer

Figure 13.5
A digital audio workstation. (Photo courtesy of Digidesign)

stores commands that trigger the equipment to play at the proper time and with the proper pitch, loudness, tonal quality, and other characteristics. Some of the personal computer programs can be used to store limited amounts of actual audio, such as sound effects and short musical phrases.

DAWs, video nonlinear editors, and personal computers are now used extensively in the creation, recording, and manipulation of sounds used in movies.[5] In the remainder of this chapter we will discuss the different types of sounds that might be present in any movie and tell how they might be handled using different types of equipment. We will then cover the mixing function, showing, in detail, how it is undertaken with the various forms of sound structuring.

Dialogue

Dialogue is edited with the picture using methods and techniques discussed in Chapters 10, 11, and 12. However, in many situations the dialogue is copied onto a tape or disk that is separate from the picture to make sound editing and mixing easier. Rerecording dialogue in this manner is referred to as **laydown.**

If tape is used, it is usually a ¾-inch, ½-inch, or 8mm videocassette tape that is used solely for audio. In other words, no picture is recorded on the tape; the whole tape is used for the audio and its accompanying time code. This, plus the fact that the audio is recorded digitally and diagonally using the **pulse code modulation (PCM)** method, makes for high-quality sound.

If a nonlinear editing system or digital audio workstation is being used, the dialogue is copied to a computer disk that stores it until it needs to be edited, mixed, or sweetened in some other way. Sometimes this sound is stored on the hard drive within the computer and sometimes it is stored on a removable hard drive called an **RMAG** (see Figure 13.6). Storing it on an RMAG has the advantage that the sound from one movie can be removed from the computer and the sound for another movie can be loaded onto it. In this way several movies can use the

Figure 13.6
An RMAG. (Photo of Removable Microdisk *courtesy of StreamLogic Corporation)*

same computer system, each being edited at different hours of the day.[6]

At some point all the dialogue that was recorded during production but is not being used for the final movie must be eliminated. When mag film stock was the primary sound postproduction medium, the extra dialogue was cut out, rolled up, and stored in boxes in case it was needed later. If a multitrack recorder is being used for the audio mix, all the audio takes that are going to be needed can be transferred from the ¾-inch (½-inch, 8mm) tape to one track of the multitrack tape, along with the appropriate time code. This will then be synced to the picture when the final mix takes place. The sound that was recorded during production but is not going to be used is simply left on the ¾-inch tape, where it can be retrieved if needed. With computer-based editing, the dialogue that is not being used can be deleted from the drive, or the dialogue may not be placed on the drive until the picture has been edited. Then only the dialogue from the takes to be used will be transferred from the original source to the computer.

Of course, not all sound mixing systems are as sophisticated as the multitrack and DAW. Often, such as during student productions, the sound from the master is used throughout the sound editing process. This is all the more reason that audio should be recorded properly in the first place.

Automatic Dialogue Replacement

If dialogue recorded during the filming or taping process is of such poor quality that it cannot be used, then it must be rerecorded. Today, this rerecording process is called **automatic dialogue replacement,** or **ADR,** sometimes referred to as **looping.**

On occasion, scenes are shot with the idea that ADR will be used. For example, a certain camera angle might make it impossible to place the microphone properly in the shot, or very fast movements by the actors might make them sound unnecessarily out of breath. In these instances, everyone knows the dialogue must be recorded later.

In other instances, ADR is needed because of mistakes that were not caught at the time of shooting—an airplane flying overhead during a Civil War movie or the university chimes ringing during the master shot but not during the close-ups that are to be intercut with it.

After the movie is shot, someone needs to **spot** for ADR. This involves looking at and listening to (on a high-quality speaker) all the footage, logging places where ADR will be needed. Of course, if the shots with bad audio are not going to be used in the final version of the movie, there is no reason to redo them. Also, sometimes the person who is spotting can find good audio of the same dialogue on a **take** that is not being used in the final movie but that can work with the scene that is going to be used.

ADR is an expensive, time-consuming process, so the less of it that needs to be done the better. It requires bringing the actors back for a session in a special soundproof room where they watch short segments of themselves on a screen and listen through earphones to the audio that needs to be changed. They rehearse the lines until they feel they can deliver them in sync with their lips as seen on the screen. When they are ready, they record the lines into a microphone. Then they go on to the next few lines and rehearse and record. This goes on until all the necessary dialogue replacement is completed. (Figure 13.7 shows an ADR session.)

This process used to be referred to as looping because individual loops of magnetic stock had to be cut for small segments of sound, usually a sentence. These loops would be played back, and the actors would rerecord one loop at a time. Then these loops had to be spliced back together in sync with the picture. As magnetic sound recorders improved and as audiotape recorders began to be used for rerecording dialogue, these individual loops were no longer needed, and longer segments could be dealt with at one time. At this point, the term *automatic* was devised to describe the dialogue replacement, although a great deal of tedious manual work still goes into ADR. In truth, there is nothing very automatic about automatic dialogue replacement. Some computer postproduction audio programs make it possible to create "loops" easily because the computer can be used to mark beginning and ending points of what needs to be replaced, can repeat the material over and over, and then can record and delete as often as needed. But still, the actor has to get it right.

Once ADR is complete, the new dialogue is substituted in the sound track for the poor dialogue. This can be done by recording the new dialogue over the old on the master, the workprint, the separate audiotape made during laydown, and/or the computer disk. However, the dialogue recorded by ADR often sounds different from the other dialogue because it was recorded in a soundproof studio and the other dialogue was recorded in the field. So somewhere during the mixing process, field sounds need to be mixed with the new dialogue. For that reason, ADR often is not actually laid over the original but is kept separate so that it can be manipulated later in the mixing process. Its position within the movie is carefully logged so that it is easy to find when it is needed.

Some actors are better at rerecording dialogue than others, but all actors should be brought back for these sessions as soon as possible after shooting is completed. Their memory of the production experience will still be fairly fresh, and they are less likely to be off somewhere shooting another movie.

The voices for dubs into foreign languages are usually done as though they were ADR. The people doing these must, of necessity, become adept at the process.

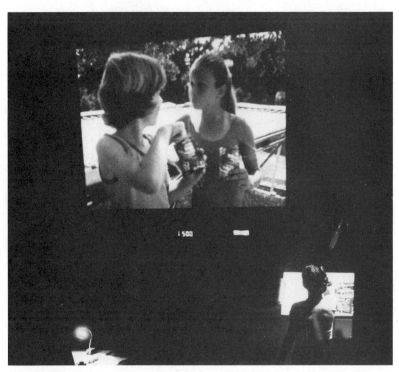

Figure 13.7

An automatic dialogue replacement session. The woman by the podium is rerecording some dialogue. (Photo courtesy of Ryder Sound Services)

Students rarely have the luxury of replacing dialogue. Most colleges do not have facilities for ADR, so the solution, once again, is to record the sound properly in the first place.

Voice-Over

Voice-over (VO) also involves adding words after the fact, but because it does not involve lip sync, it is a much simpler process than ADR—and one that students can usually accomplish fairly easily. Voice-over can be used for any number of reasons—someone's conscience talking, someone's thoughts. The most common use, however, is narration—commenting on what is occurring in the picture.

Once a movie is edited, VO can be recorded in the same facility as ADR, or it can use any soundproof room where the picture can be shown on a monitor. The performer watches the picture and reads the narration or other form of VO at a pace that matches what is on the screen. When what is being conveyed through words is the dominant element, the voice-over sometimes is recorded before editing, and the picture is then edited to the narration. In this case, the recording can be done just about anywhere because there is no need to play back a picture.

Narration can be recorded directly onto a master videotape simply by plugging a mic into one of the input channels of the VCR. This has certain disadvantages, however. If the talent stumbles over a word or makes some other mistake, the recording has to be stopped. The recording can be started over again from the beginning, or an edit can be made. The former can be a time-consuming process, especially if the error is near the end of the recording. The latter is difficult to do smoothly because the pace of the narration is likely to change, or a word may sound cut off. Also, if music, dialogue, or other sound elements are to be mixed with the voice-over, the relative levels may be hard to control if the recording has been done on the master tape.

A better way to undertake voice-over is to record it on a separate audiotape that can be mixed and added later. If a multitrack recorder is going to be used, the voice-over can be recorded on one of the tracks. Likewise, a VO can be recorded directly to computer disk for desktop audio applications. One of the advantages of recording it on a computer is that if minor changes are needed when picture and narration are joined together, they are easy to accomplish. For example, if the narration runs a second longer than the picture, small portions of the silence between words can be deleted so that the narration becomes the right length.

Another possibility, especially if a facility has **control track** rather than time code editing or if time code cannot be generated on the audio equipment, is to record the narration on a separate videotape. In this way, the narration can be on a source tape that is edited onto the master tape in the audio-only mode. If errors occurred and the narration was recorded in segments, these segments can be previewed before they are joined together. If need be, they can be trimmed so that the pacing is smooth on the final edited version.

Of course, voice-over could also be recorded on magnetic film stock, but it rarely is anymore. Compared to ADR, voice-over is usually a fairly simple process, but as with all other aspects of sound, it must be carefully monitored so that it is completed properly. Mistakes should be corrected during the recording session, before the talent has left.

Sound Effects

Some **sound effects** are taped or filmed during production, and others are found and added after production. Both need to be handled during the postproduction stage. First, someone needs to verify the usability of the sound effects taped on location. Does the car's backfire actually sound like a backfire, or does it sound more like a cannon? Often, sound effects taped on location need to be replaced or at least improved. Those that are of good quality and that are intrinsic to the action can be left on the dialogue track and edited along with the picture and dialogue.

Once picture and dialogue (and limited sound effects) are edited, someone needs to look at the entire movie and spot all the places where additional sound effects are needed. This person makes up a **spotting sheet** that indicates at what point in the movie the effects should be placed (see Figure 13.8). Often, a note will also be made of whether or not the sound needs to be synchronous. The sound effect of a dog barking off-screen is much easier to execute than a dog barking on-screen because the off-screen barks do not need to be in sync with the dog's mouth.

After all the sound effects are listed, they need to be found. Some of this hunting can start as early as preproduction because the script will indicate many of the effects that are needed. The best source is sound-effects tapes and CDs. These are available in audio stores, but most production companies and many universities have libraries that include not only commercially available sound effects but also effects that have been specially taped for previous productions.

If some unusual effect cannot be found or if the effect on a CD just won't sync with something on-screen, a crew may need to go out and tape that particular effect. If these needs can be anticipated during production rather than left for the postproduction stage, the sounds can be taped while principal photography is being completed. This saves time and money.

Some facilities, especially those using computer-based audio, can create sound effects from

SPOTTING SHEET

Project Title ___The Event_____   Page Number ___4___

Spotter ___Al Marcino_____   Date Prepared ___10/21___

Item	Sync/ Nonsync	In Time	Out Time	Description
1	NS	01:42:15:10	01:43:12:09	Airplanes taking off
2	NS	01:45:26:29	01:46:15:12	Muddled voices
3	S	01:49:52:12		Door slam
4	NS	01:49:52:12	01:53:05:05	Traffic noises
5	NS	01:54:03:27	01:56:22:17	Restaurant noises
6	S	01:56:13:25		Gunshot
7	NS	02:03:14:23	02:04:03:10	Phone ringing
8	NS	02:10:52:12	02:11:01:24	Glass breaking
9	NS	02:11:27:03	02:12:04:19	Dog barking
10	S	02:12:46:18		Glass breaking
11	NS	02:15:33:16		Thunder
12	NS	02:16:12:15	02:19:22:04	Rain, wind, and thunder
13	S	02:21:45:23		Car backfire
14	NS	02:21:50:20	02:23:47:04	Children playing
15	NS	02:23:47:04	02:26:33:12	Ocean waves
16	NS	02:24:55:23		Thunder
17	NS	02:26:10:10		Thunder
18	S	02:30:12:14		Hit glass
19	NS	02:33:05:06	02:34:55:07	Dogs barking
20	NS	02:35:12:14		Door slam
21	S	02:36:36:11		Door slam

Figure 13.8
A spotting sheet used to list various sound effects that will be needed for a movie sound track.

digital samplers. These consist of recordings of various sounds that can be changed to sound like something else. By manipulating such characteristics as pitch, volume, and timbre, a door slam can become an explosion or raindrops can become machine-gun fire. A dog's bark could also be slowed down or speeded up to fit with the action of the scene. There are also CD-ROMs available that contain sound effects that can be easily imported into the computer.

Once the sounds are found on tapes, CDs, digital samplers, CD-ROMs, or in the field,

Figure 13.9
Waveforms of the audio tracks are visible on the computer screen and make it easier to edit the sound. (Photo Courtesy of Editing Machines Corporation)

random-access capability of the computer allows quick access to it. Sound effects are so easy to do on a computer that sometimes they are added to the **rough cut** of the dialogue and picture so that the director (producer, client, and so on) can have an idea of how they will be incorporated in the final version of the movie.

If the picture calls for a large number of effects to occur simultaneously, several sound-effects reels will be made (or several tracks on a multitrack tape will be used). If the number of reels or tracks becomes excessive, a **premix** is often undertaken to combine some of the effects before the final mix.

The person in charge of sound effects should keep close track of where they came from and how they are going to be used. This is essential information, especially if something doesn't work during the final mix.

they must be recorded so that they can be used during the sound mix. Often, a tape sound-effects reel is built, a process that is similar to that used in the past for magnetic film stock editing. The sound effects will be placed on a separate audiotape in the order needed. Then they can be dubbed onto one of the tracks of the master videotape, or they can be recorded on a source videotape so they can be previewed and edited onto the master videotape (the process that was described for voice-overs).

If multitracking is being used for the mix, the sound effects can be placed on one track of the tape, positioned in such a way that they will sync with the video. Time code is essential for this process. With computer-based audio, the sound effects can be recorded on the computer disk in any order. Then they can be brought in as needed—a gunshot to accompany the pulling of a trigger, a door slam as a person exits. The beauty of doing sound effects with computer programs is that the effects can be manipulated very easily. The computer screen displays waveforms that show exactly when each portion of an effect occurs. (See Figure 13.9.) If the effect comes in a little too soon, it can be moved slightly with a few clicks of the mouse. Some computer audio programs include a sound-effects library that can be stored in the computer. When some particular effect is needed, the

Foley

Foley work involves a special type of sound-effects recording. The person spotting a movie for sound effects usually also spots for Foley. An unusual sound effect, such as a hyena laughing, that cannot be found on a CD can be created in a Foley room, but the word *Foley* is more often thought of in terms of background sounds such as footsteps, clothes rustling, and branches waving in the wind.

The Foley process is named after Jack Foley, the man who designed the room in which Foley activities take place. This room contains a large screen, several mics, a number of sound-effects devices, and many walking surfaces—gravel, sand, dirt, cement, carpet, hardwood floor (see Figure 13.10). A Foley room often contains a variety of cloth that can be rustled to simulate people walking past furniture, water to be poured from one container to another, twigs and branches to be snapped, dishes and utensils to be jiggled, and a variety of other articles.

People called **Foley walkers** watch the movie being projected onto the large screen and perform the acts needed to provide synchronous sound for the actors' movements, recording them all through properly positioned microphones. For example, if the movie shows an

Figure 13.10
A Foley room setup. The two Foley walkers are using the various pits and equipment to
perform, in sync, the sounds that should emanate from the picture on the screen. (Photo
courtesy of Ryder Sound Services)

overweight man walking on dirt in tennis shoes, the Foley walker will put on tennis shoes, place the mic by his feet, and walk heavily in the dirt pit in step with the man on the screen.

In addition, Foley walkers clap their hands, scream in terror, slap faces, or fall for fight scenes. Most Foley walkers are very graceful; in fact, many of them are dancers or ex-dancers.

Someone (usually the person in charge of sound effects) prepares a Foley setup sheet for the Foley walkers. This lists all the actions they need to perform for the movie (see Figure 13.11). Foley walkers use it to determine whether they have all the supplies they need. For example, if the setup sheet calls for wind chimes, they might need to purchase or request some.

Foley walkers sometimes work in pairs—a man imitating men's movements and a woman imitating women's movements—but sometimes they work alone and do the actions of each character in the scene in turn. A technician usually sits in an adjoining room and records all the sounds on an audiotape that is synced with the picture. This later becomes the Foley reel used

in the final mix. Or the sounds can be recorded on a computer disk.

Computer-based audio lends itself very well to Foley. The sound of one footstep can be placed in a computer, and the audio characteristics of that footstep can be manipulated so that it can take on just about any sound—an overweight man walking on dirt in tennis shoes, a woman in high heels on a pavement, a horse galloping through a field. What's more, the step can always be placed in perfect sync. Computerized Foley is usually created by someone hitting a key on a piano keyboard that is attached to the computer. The sound (for example, the click of a woman's high heel) is created and programmed to occur whenever someone pushes middle C on the keyboard. A person watches the movie and plays middle C each time the woman's shoe hits the pavement. The harder the key is hit, the heavier the sound will be. If the person misses and gets one or two of the steps out of sync, he or she can later correct this mistake by looking at the computer screen waveform and moving the step to the right position.

Figure 13.11

A Foley setup sheet to indicate what sounds should be made at which points in the movie and to list the materials needed to make those sounds.

FOLEY SET UP AND LOG

Program _The Top_   Date _11/4_

Foley Walkers _Susan O'Donnel   Jack Washington_

Time Code	Track 1	Track 2	Track 3
00:20:03:40	Maribel walking (red shoes, concrete)	Jim walking (tennis shoes concrete)	
00:25:00:00	Maribel's dress rustles (silk)	glasses clink (white plastic glasses) / dishes move (fork and plate)	candle is lit (match)
00:30:00:00	waitress walks (brown shoes, carpet)		customer knocks on door (screen door)
00:35:00:00		coffee is poured (water, pitcher, cup)	

A number of Foley effects can be created at once. A man's footstep on dirt could be programmed into A above middle C; the clink of a glass could be accessed from G-sharp. Someone "playing a keyboard" can create as many effects as hand-eye coordination will allow. In fact, sometimes creating effects is like playing the piano. Glass clinks that are low-pitched could be programmed into the bottom of the keyboard and could become progressively higher pitched with each note that progresses toward the top end of the keyboard. The person creating effects plays the various keys depending on the size and shape of the glasses being clinked.

Traditionally, student productions have incorporated very little Foley work because of the complexity of the setup, but the little touches provided by Foley are often what differentiate, at a subconscious level, a professional motion picture from a nonprofessional one.

Ambient Sounds

Ambient sounds also differentiate professional movies from nonprofessional student ones. However, in this case, students can easily add ambient sounds if they take the time to record them in the field.

Room tone and/or **walla walla** are often mixed into the final audio so that there will be a consistent background sound for all shots from one location (see Chapter 9). A master scene may be shot in a building on a hot day when the air-conditioning is operating, and the close-ups may be shot on a cool day when the air-conditioning is off. When cuts are made from master shot to close-ups, the lack of the air-conditioner sound will be noticed. If room tone was recorded on the first day, the air-conditioning sound can be added to the close-ups. Likewise, walla walla of voices in a restaurant could be used to cover the sterile background sound that might occur from taping in that restaurant when it was closed. Room tone and walla walla are invaluable when dialogue is replaced. The background noise level of the soundproofed ADR room will be very different from the inherent sound of the location.

Ambient sounds can also add to the atmosphere of a particular location. A brook flowing near a field will probably not record very loudly on the dialogue track, but if it is recorded by itself, it can be mixed in at a louder level, giving a more bucolic feeling to a scene. In fact, even if there is no brook flowing near the field, the illusion of one can be achieved by adding a brook sound taped somewhere else.

Ambient sounds are often recorded onto a continuous loop of tape (or mag stock) so that they can be brought in at any time during the mix. If they are part of a computer audio system, they can also be repeated endlessly. They are

never synchronous, so they do not need to be timed and placed as carefully as other sounds. They do need to be listened to carefully, however, to make sure they do not contain some recurring noise. A ten-second loop of outdoor sounds that contains several recognizable bird chirps can become humorously distracting if it is played over and over during a two-minute scene.

Sometimes these atmosphere sounds are found in sound-effects libraries, and sometimes they are specially recorded. Of course, someone must spot the film to determine where they are needed. Usually, one person can spot for sound effects, Foley, and ambient sounds.

Music

Music for theatrical movies, corporate videos, multimedia productions, or documentaries can be obtained a number of different ways. Professional moviemakers usually hire a composer to write music specially for the various scenes of the movie. However, music that has been recorded previously can also be used. Sometimes this is popular music that needs copyright clearance, sometimes it is music that is so old it is in public domain, and sometimes it is stock music that comes from special libraries of copyright-cleared compositions.

Original Music

When a composer is to write music for a picture, the first chore is spotting the movie to determine where music is needed. This spotting should not be done at the same time as spotting for sound effects, Foley, ADR, and/or ambient sounds. Spotting for music involves a very different process that generally has nothing to do with the quality of the previously recorded sound.

The picture and dialogue almost always are totally edited before anyone begins to consider the music. There is little sense in planning music at the raw footage stage because the music must fit precisely with the action as it appears in the final edited version. One of the problems inherent in this process is that the composer is usually under intense time pressure. The movie

Figure 13.12

An example of a timing sheet, which goes to a composer as an aid for writing the music. The actions taking place and their durations are specified so that the composer can work (at least some of the time) without actually watching the movie.

```
                    TIMING SHEET

TITLE: Up in Arms

DATE: November 4, 1990                    START: 00:50:03:21


CODE              TIME                  DESCRIPTION

                                Max and Oliver enter the room and
                                glare at Maggie.

00:50:03:21      :00:00:00      Music starts as Maggie moves toward
                                the sofa.  The camera follows her
                                as she sits and stares at the two
                                men.

00:50:10:23      00:07:02       CUT to MS of Oliver.

00:50:12:21      00:09:00       Oliver: You don't seem to be
                                showing no respect.

00:50:13:24      00:10:03       Cut to CU of Maggie.  Maggie: Why
                                should I?

00:50:14:25      00:11:04       Cut to CU of Max glowering.

00:50:15:22      00:12:01       Max: That really ain't a smart way
                                to talk to two nice gents like us.

00:50:17:02      00:13:40       Music swells as a LS reveals Oliver
                                and Max moving in closer to Maggie,
                                who is still sitting on the sofa.

00:50:27:00      00:23:38       CU of Maggie looking frightened.

00:50:29:04      00:25:42       MS of Max and Oliver.  Music stops
                                abruptly.  Max and Oliver laugh an
                                evil laugh.  Max: That's all for
                                this time, babe, but next time you
                                don't get off so easy.
```

has been edited, and people are almost ready to begin the sound mix, but this cannot be accomplished until the music is finished. The composer is the last person in the postproduction process.

Usually, music spotting is a joint project of the director and the composer. However, this is not always the case. The director or someone else can determine where music should be placed and then send that information to the composer, who determines the actual notes, rhythm, melody, and other musical elements.

Traditionally in film a composer was given a copy of the edited workprint to use as a guide for composing. The spots where music was to start and stop were marked on the workprint with a diagonal pen line called a **streamer.** Obviously, videotape cannot be physically marked, but a computer program has been developed that ties a videotape workprint to computer graphics and places a computer-generated streamer at the beginning and end of each section of the movie in which music will be required. Many composers use their VCRs to watch the tape while composing at home.

Composers also used a **click book** as an aid to writing music for movies. This helped a composer figure out how many measures to compose for a certain length of movie according to the tempo of the music. In other words, if a section of the picture needing music was two minutes long, the click book told the composer how many measures to write if the music was in 3/4 time at a slow rate of 60 beats per minute or if it was at some other rate, such as 4/4 time, at 150 beats per minute. This book has now been superseded by computer programs that calculate and display this information easily.

Once the music is spotted, the composer can begin to create the music. Whether this spotting is completed by the composer or by someone else, the spotter usually prepares a **timing sheet** to aid in the composition process (see Figure 13.12). This sheet gives **time code numbers** for the places where music is to be heard, tells the length the music is to run, and gives a description of what is happening in the scene. The composer uses this as a guide for completing the job, making sure all music is the right length and conveys the mood of the visual material.

Sometimes, composers both write and record the music. This is especially true if the music can be played with a synthesizer, drum machine, and other electronic equipment. Since 1983 musicians have been using **musical instrument digital interface (MIDI)**, a technical standard that allows electronic instruments to interact with each other. For example, a musician playing a melody on an electronic keyboard can use MIDI to coordinate, select, start, and stop the rhythm that is coming from a drum machine. In the late 1980s MIDI met SMPTE time code, and now MIDI-based music can easily be incorporated in videos. The MIDI commands coordinate (*shake hands* in computer terminology) well with computer audio systems (see Figure 13.13).[7]

A fair number of computer programs exist to help composers create music.[8] (See Figure 13.14 and color plate 10.) For some of these the music is stored on the computer hard drive. For others only the commands that activate the electronic instruments are stored within the computer; these **triggers** store and convey information such as pitch, volume, and timbre. Other computer programs are designed to store triggers and samples of digitally recorded instruments or voices. The main difference is that some programs are made to be used with digital audio

Figure 13.13

A digital audio editing suite with a synthesizer and DAW. (Photo courtesy of Digital Sound and Picture)

Figure 13.14

A screen from the computer program Cakewalk, which can be used to assist people who are composing music. (Photo courtesy of Cakewalk Music Software)

workstations that have very large storage capacity while others are designed as programs to run on personal computers with more limited capacity. For example, storing the triggers for a snare drum for a three-minute piece of music might take about 15 kilobytes whereas putting the snare drum itself on the hard drive would use up about 15 megabytes—a thousand times more space.[9]

The MIDI-SMPTE-computer liaison has simplified much of the movie music composition process. For some TV shows and movies the music is spotted in Hollywood by a person with musical training, and the timing sheet and a VCR copy of the entire movie (or just the parts that need music) are sent to a composer in another state. The composer writes and performs the music and sends it back to Hollywood on an audiotape or disk or over a high-quality phone line. This material then is used for the audio mix.

At other times a composer writes the music, and an orchestra or other musical group performs it. In these cases the composer must know how much is budgeted for the music so that he or she does not write for more musicians than the picture can afford. When the music is recorded, the musicians gather in a recording studio that has a large screen onto which the movie can be projected. A conductor (often the composer) leads the orchestra while watching the movie on the screen. This ensures that all the passages will be the right length. Technicians in a control room record all the music. The miking and recording techniques used for recording are similar to those used for miking and recording live musicians during the production phase of moviemaking. Mics can be set up for **monaural, stereo,** or **surround sound.** The whole orchestra can be recorded at one time, but more often multitrack recording is used so that the instruments can be balanced later (see Chapter 9).

Overall, composing and recording music is a complicated job that involves many stages. However, audiences have come to expect music in movies, and it contributes to the overall effect of the picture.

Previously Composed Music

To lessen the hassle (and sometimes the cost) of having music specially composed and recorded for a movie, musical selections that have already been written and recorded can be used. These include popular songs of the day (or yesteryear). Sometimes these are needed because they help establish a particular time or place. A scene set in the 1960s might be enhanced by a Beatles song of that era. Jazz could help establish a New Orleans nightclub. More often, though, such music is used because it matches the mood of the movie.

Most previously composed music needs copyright clearance. This is often a time-consuming and expensive process. Music that is old enough to be in **public domain** does not need copyright clearance, but often special arrangements of it are not in public domain. In these cases, the arrangements need copyright clearance.

Because of the difficulties involved both in composing original music and using already composed popular music, a number of libraries offer copyright-cleared music for a nominal fee.[10] Anyone choosing to use this music can be assured that it does not need copyright clearance or payment; either it has been specially written and recorded for the library or it is in public domain. These libraries often also categorize the music—chase music, romance music, dinner music. The problem with many of these music libraries is that much of their music is uninspired; it all sounds more or less the same. One of the difficulties with using any type of prerecorded music is fitting it into the allotted time. Because it was not specially composed to fit a certain set of actions, it will not necessarily end when the action ends. Sometimes it is more difficult to try to find music that fits a scene, both in terms of time and mood, than it would be to have it specially composed.

Students often find it easier to use prerecorded music because they do not have elaborate recording facilities at their disposal. However, with MIDI-based electronic equipment readily available and with music departments on most campuses, specially composed music is becoming more prevalent.

Mixing

After all the various elements—dialogue, voiceover, ADR, sound effects, Foley, ambient sounds, and music—are found and recorded, they must be mixed together. The process of doing this varies according to the type of postproduction equipment being used. Multitrack recording has more steps (and more flexibility) than VCR-to-VCR recording. The computer-based editing systems are not perfect but show promise of having the greatest flexibility for the least cost.

Limited Mixing

The least flexible of all sound editing involves transferring sound from the source VCR to the edit VCR. About the only type of sound manipulation that can take place is varying the volume. Usually, this procedure does not really qualify as "mixing" because only one source of sound (usually dialogue) is transferred. Although this VCR-to-VCR process is common (and appropriate) for news and talk shows, it generally proves unsatisfying for narrative forms because there is little possibility for music and sound effects.

VCR-to-VCR flexibility can be improved slightly if the dialogue from the source VCR is sent to one channel of the edit VCR and the output from a cassette recorder is sent to another channel. In this manner, music and voice can be mixed together. However, determining the relative volume of the two sources can be quite difficult. It is all too easy to mix in such a way that the music totally overpowers the dialogue.

One step better is to route various audio sources through an audio board to the VCR. Dialogue from the source machine, music from a cassette, sound effects from a CD, ambient sound from a cartridge loop—each can be wired to a separate channel of an audio board. Then they can be raised to the proper volume level and mixed together as the master VCR tape is being edited. However, bringing in the right elements at the right time can be quite difficult. Sound effects of a door slamming must occur as the door closes. If the audio operator does not hit the play button on the CD at the precise moment, the effect will be out of sync. However, movie sound that is not overly complicated can be mixed successfully with a little practice.

To make the process a little less harrowing, sounds can be mixed onto a separate videotape instead of the master. This tape can then be used to edit the sounds onto the master in the audio-only edit mode. This allows for more control because edit-in and edit-out points can be set; a proper edit is not dependent on someone cuing up a CD or bringing in an audiotape at the right time. Often, this level of sound mixing is undertaken for student productions because colleges do not have the more sophisticated equipment. Thorough preparation and patience can yield acceptable results.

One definite limiting factor of dealing with VCR audio tracks is that most videotape formats have only two or three tracks. Even Betacam has only four audio tracks. If something is to be mixed in stereo, track flexibility is very limited. Surround sound, which usually has at least six outputs, is, of course, impossible.[11]

Professional-Level Multitrack Mixing

Movies, music videos, multimedia productions, corporate videos, and other professional-level productions use audio mixing facilities that allow for greater control and accuracy than those discussed previously.

They often use a number of audio players (one for music, one for sound effects, one for ambient sound, and so on), an audio board, and the master videotape. But all the tapes will contain time code, and all will be locked together by synchronizing machines that read the time code.[12] This is similar to the process long used for films—the one that involved many reels of magnetic film stock being mixed down to one. However, instead of being governed by sprocket holes, the tapes are governed by time code. When the master VCR advances five seconds, each audio player also advances five seconds.

Other times, all sound will have been recorded on one multitrack tape, with each sound occupying a different track and the all-important time code placed on a separate track. These sounds could have come from a wide variety of sources—mag stock for dialogue, DAT for music, CD for sound effects, audio cart for walla walla, DAW for Foley.

Originally these multitrack recorders were analog, but now many of them are digital—a definite advantage because the sound will not degrade as it is rerecorded. A wide variety of brands and types exist; some use 2-inch tape while others use ½-inch or 8-millimeter tape. The most common analog ones have twenty-four tracks; digital recorders tend to have fewer tracks because the sounds can be combined a number of times without losing quality[13] (see Figure 13.15).

a

b

Figure 13.15

(a) A twenty-four-track analog multitrack recorder that uses 2-inch tape and (b) an Emmy-award winning digital cassette recorder (Photos courtesy of TASCAM, TEAC Professional Division)

Usually the first step in this professional-level multisource mixing process, be it multitrack or separate sources, involves playing back the picture and sounds without regard to the relative volume of sounds. This allows someone to make sure that all the sound elements can be brought in at the right time and are the right length. This process is referred to as **interlock** or **lock-up**.

Before mixing occurs, a **cue sheet** is prepared. This lists all the different sources of sound and indicates when each should be brought in and taken out of the sound mix (see Figure 13.16). This is really a compilation of all the spotting sheets that have been prepared.

One of the main purposes of the mix is to rerecord all the material so that each sound is at the right relative volume. In order to undertake this mix, each sound source is routed to a different input on an audio mixing console. The mixed sound can be fed from the board to a master videotape or, more commonly, to a multitrack audiotape. Time code is laid down on the multitrack tape for synchronizing the various elements. Usually, time code is placed on the bottom track, and the track above it is left blank because time code has a tendency to bleed over into the tracks near it.

In multitrack recording, how the output tape is actually handled varies from situation to situation. Sometimes each sound is rerecorded on a separate track of the multitrack tape. (Figure 13.17 shows the various sounds that might appear on a twenty-four-track multitrack tape.)

The only major difference between the input and the output is that the volume of each sound has been adjusted so that it meshes correctly with volumes of other sounds. At other times various sound elements are mixed together so that the multitrack tape contains only three or four tracks, perhaps one for dialogue, one for music, and another for everything else.

Several technicians sit at the audio console working with the various sounds as indicated on the cue sheet. They work cooperatively so that the overall sound is balanced properly. If the music is overpowering the dialogue, they may lower the music, raise the dialogue, or do a little of each. Many sound technicians prefer that all sound be recorded originally at approximately the same volume level so that they know what to expect and can plan changes more easily. Modern boards have memory so that the levels of the different inputs can be stored and called up again. In this way, the engineers can try one combination, store it, try another combination, store it, and then compare the two and select the one that sounds best.

Depending on the equipment available in the recording facility, technicians may also enhance the sound. For example, if scratchy sounds are evident in a sound effect taped from a record, they can use an equalizer to help remove the frequencies where the scratches occur. If the dialogue sounds lifeless, a reverb unit can be used to give it some bounce. Some recording facilities include **room simulators.** These can be

CUE SHEET

Production: *Away with Time*   Date: *9/17*   Editor: *Peterson*

Track No. 1 Dialogue		Track No. 3 Music A		Track No. 4 Music B		Track No. 6 Effects A		Track No. 7 Effects B	
		2:15 <				2:15 fire, crackles in fireplace			
2:31 Peter: Try									
								2:41 glass breaks in fireplace	
2:47 (last word) think.									
2:49 Susan: No									
3:15 (last word) today									
		3:21 ——→		3:21		3:21 wind		3:21 rain	
		4:45 ←——		4:45		4:45		4:45	
4:47 Peter: Someday									
5:06 (last word) gun		5:06				5:06 gun shot			

< = fade in   > = fade out   ⇄ = segue (dissolve)

used to create room tone of various-sized rooms, which is helpful if proper room tone was not recorded originally.[14]

The whole mixing procedure depends on the complexity of the movie and to some extent on the philosophy of the director and those charged with obtaining proper sound. Some people like to split dialogue onto several tracks—perhaps one for master scenes and another for close-ups or one for the male lead and another for the female lead. They do this because they feel those types of sounds need different treatment in terms of such factors as equalization and reverb. Others keep all dialogue on one track in order to simplify the mixing process. Some like to have all the original dialogue available, not just the dialogue that was used in the edited version. That way, they can go back to the original if

some of the processed sound is not to their liking.

Sometimes several sound effects tracks are needed because various effects are heard at the same time. Some people like to do a premix of sound effects so that they are already mixed at the proper relative levels for the mixdown. If **cross-fades** from one music source to another occur, several music tracks will be needed, unless, of course, these cross-fades have been premixed. In general, some people think that the more tracks there are, the easier it will be to mix, whereas others think just the opposite.

Multitrack mixes are usually done in stereo or surround sound rather than in monaural. In these cases, various tracks can be assigned different sounds that will eventually be heard on different speakers. Usually effects are recorded so

Figure 13.16
A cue sheet used during the mixing session. It indicates when each sound should be taken in and out.

Figure 13.17
Sounds that might appear on a twenty-four-track tape.

Track	Sounds
1	Original production dialogue
2	Foley 1
3	Foley 2
4	Edited dialogue 1
5	Edited dialogue 2
6	ADR 1
7	ADR 2
8	Ambient sounds 1
9	Ambient sounds 2
10	Walla walla
11	Sound effects 1
12	Sound effects 2
13	Sound effects 3
14	Music 1
15	Music 2
16	Music 3
17	Dialogue mix—right channel
18	Dialogue mix—left channel
19	Music mix—right channel
20	Music mix—left channel
21	Effects mix—right channel
22	Effects mix—left channel
23	Blank
24	Time code

they will appear to come from the left and/or right. Dialogue is made to sound as though it is coming from the center because people who are talking are generally center screen. Music can be right and left channel, according to how the music was recorded. For surround sound the ambient sounds are usually the ones recorded on tracks that will play back through the speakers positioned around the room.

In the mixing session short segments of the movie are rehearsed over and over until all the technicians agree that they have the proper levels and enhancements. Then that section is recorded, and another section is rehearsed. Eventually, all the sound is transferred from the various audio inputs to the single tape on which the mix appears.[15]

Computer-Based Mixing

Much of the sound mixing that occurs in the computer-based realm is with digital audio workstations, although more and more use is being made of the audio tracks that come with the nonlinear editing systems. Mixing that uses audio software on personal computers can be utilized for short pieces, such as PSAs or student projects. The reason that DAWs are favored at present is storage capacity and **random-access memory (RAM)** capacity. Mixing audio, by nature, involves dealing with a number of sounds. These sounds must be stored in such a way that they can be intermingled, and that uses up a great deal of disc space and memory.

Some of the personal computer programs provide for limited mixing wherein several seconds or several minutes of sounds can be mixed together, but that is inadequate for a feature-length movie where the same piece of music may continue for several minutes. Trying to piece that together several seconds at a time would be tedious, to say the least. These programs are much more likely to be used for manipulation of one sound at a time (moving a Foley step several frames, bringing in a thunder sound effect, creating a snare drum track) than they are for actual mixing. These programs are relatively inexpensive, however, and are good for students who want to learn the basics of computer-based mixing.[16]

The random-access, nonlinear, digital editing systems are used extensively for editing picture and dialogue. Those two elements use a great deal of storage space, sometimes leaving little room for other forms of sound. As computer memory and storage grow by leaps and bounds, however, the picture editing systems are providing capacity for other sources of sound. Some of them have four audio tracks, which means dialogue, music, and effects can be mixed together and placed on the fourth track. That is good enough for some TV material (magazine programs, reality shows) that does not place a great deal of emphasis on sound, but it is not adequate for an action movie that might have six different sound effects going at once. Such works are more likely to use DAWs or multitrack recorders. More and more the nonlinear editing systems are used for placing at least some of the sound effects on a rough cut of a movie so that the director can hear how they will work. As technology improves, so will the sound capabilities of these systems.

Figure 13.18
A stand-alone digital audio workstation that can be used in the creation, manipulation, and mixing of sound. (Photo courtesy of WaveFrame Corporation)

Digital audio workstations, with their computer storage space devoted entirely to audio, have at least twenty-four tracks. Some of the companies that manufacture nonlinear editing systems also make digital audio workstations that can easily be integrated with their editing systems.[17] In this way, one technician can be working on sound editing while another is undertaking picture editing, but anytime the two want to compare notes, the machines can easily be hooked together. Most DAWs, however, are manufactured by companies that have a fairly long history in the audio equipment business.[18]

DAWs are generally capable of holding all the sound for an entire movie, either on the hard drive or within RMAGs that are inserted into the system. As previously mentioned, these sounds can be created, edited, and manipulated before they are mixed. DAWs often contain entire sound effects libraries, any effect of which can be brought up immediately. They are also often connected to synthesizers used for the composition of music. In fact, even if a DAW is not used for the final mix, one is often involved

within the mix process, feeding various sounds to the multitrack tape (see Figure 13.18).

The mixing procedures for DAW-based audio are largely a function of the computer program of the particular machine. In an attempt to be user friendly, some computer programs include a graphic of an audio board. The person doing the mixing can use a mouse to raise and lower fader bars for the various sounds coming into this "mixer" (see Figure 13.19). Other programs look more like a visualization of a multitrack tape. The waveform of the sound on each track is shown, and the operator can fade the sounds in and out as desired. The results can be previewed easily. Clicking the mouse on a particular area will play that particular sound back immediately. If the results are unacceptable, changes can be made easily. For example, if a musical bridge comes in a little too soon, the mouse can be used to build a box around the waveform of the bridge and move the whole thing forward slightly.

For flawless audio accuracy the video image and its time code can be consulted. The time code of the frame at which the music is to start

a

b

Figure 13.19

The board on the left (a) is a real audio mixer such as might be used in a multitrack mixing session. The "board" on the right (b) is actually a Macintosh computer screen that simulates a mixing board. (Photo a courtesy of Digital Sound and Picture; photo b courtesy of New England Digital)

can be noted, and the music can be started at that exact frame. If a computer audio operator makes a mistake and brings in a dog bark rather than the music, most programs have an "undo" function that comes to the rescue and eliminates the unwanted sound.

Sounds can be changed while they are being mixed. Reverb can be added, and frequencies can be filtered, provided those functions are included in the computer program. Sounds can be made to go faster without the accompanying change to a higher pitch that occurs when taped sounds are speeded up. If a fifteen-minute piece of music is two seconds too long for a particular sequence, the music can be slowed down very slightly throughout so that it covers two seconds less without any perceptible change in tempo. If an actor made a mistake and said *walks* instead of *walk*, the ess sound on the end of walks can be eliminated by using the mouse control to trim the very end of the waveform.

Because DAWs are digital, the sound quality does not degrade, and because they are nonlinear, sound for the end of the movie can be

mixed before sound for the beginning. This audio technology has come a long ways in a short time and promises to proceed even further.[19]

Laybacks and Dubs

Once all the sounds are mixed together, this final mix must be rerecorded on a master copy of the movie, a process known as **layback.** For a videotape master the multitrack audiotape or DAW output is dubbed onto the master along with the picture. At the professional level this tape might be in one of the digital formats, but the master tape could be in any of a variety of forms—U-Matic, Betacam SP. The master could also be a laser disk or a CD-ROM.

Time code is an important element of this layback process. At this point the final sound mix on the multitrack audiotape or DAW has the same time code as the video on the workprint; therefore, as long as the machines are all set up properly, picture and sound should stay in sync. For most professional TV programs sounds are edited and mixed in stereo, so two tracks of the master videotape are used.

Student productions often do not have this luxury and are recorded in a monaural fashion. If such is the case, all sound should be on one track. In other words, the dialogue should not be on one track and the music on another. The best procedure is to place the entire movie audio on all available tracks. In that way, the sound will be heard regardless what tracks are played back.

After the master tape is made, copies can be dubbed from it. At the professional level this is done so that the product can be distributed. At the student level it is often done so that all the students involved in the project can have a copy. Audio should be carefully monitored during the dubbing process. Sometimes people forget to check the levels on both the master copy and the **dub** and wind up with dubs that have unsatisfactory sound.

For movies that are going to be dubbed into a foreign language, the dialogue track must at some point be kept separate from all other tracks, usually at the final mix stage. Then new dialogue in a foreign language can be recorded and mixed with all the other premixed sounds, saving time and money. Even sound effects such as doors slamming should be on some track other than the dialogue track. Because these synchronous sounds are often recorded with the dialogue, the sound effects and Foley people often have extra work to do for a foreign dub. They must go through the movie noting the effects that are recorded with the dialogue and then recreate them so they can be recorded on the effects track.

The layback process for a movie that is going to be shown theatrically is more complicated. Theaters often have digital surround sound, so the final mix consists of six or so tracks that can be sent to separate speakers throughout the theater. For example, in the drawing of Figure 13.20, one set of sounds would go to the left speaker, one to the subwoofer, one to the center speaker, one to the right speaker, one to all the right surround speakers, and one to all the left surround speakers. These six channels of sound, recorded on a multitrack tape or computer disc,

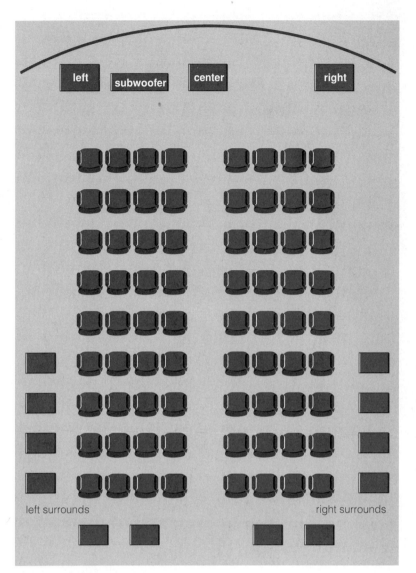

Figure 13.20
Speaker placement in a surround sound theater.

would be sent to the film laboratory where they would be joined with the picture on the film itself. In recent years, there have been many different, incompatible systems developed for surround sound projection. One uses a compact disc that is synched to the picture, one uses space between the sprocket holes, one uses the edge of the film next to the picture. A single motion picture usually provides for all these forms of sound so that it can be shown in all theaters, regardless of the type of equipment they have opted for. Of course, the sound must also be recorded in the old-fashioned, analog, stereo format for theaters that have not con-

35mm

digital sound track

optical sound tracks

Figure 13.21
This frame shows optical sound and one form of digital sound.

verted to digital. That audio is on an **optical sound track** that rides next to the picture, where it has been since the early days of sound[20] (see Figure 13.21).

The Digital Depot

Some postproduction facilities are taking the digital domain one step further and placing all picture and sound elements for a movie on a **local area network (LAN).**[21] What this means is that many people can access any part of a movie at any time. A person at one workstation in the building can be editing the music while a person at another workstation is mixing a dog bark with a fire engine siren, still another person is composing the music for a chase scene, and the Foley walkers are creating the swishing sounds to go with a ballroom dance scene. All of these sounds are fed onto the LAN and each person has access to what anyone else has done. The LAN becomes the "depot" where everything congregates, but any signal can go out in one or many directions.

If the movie is shot on film, the film is transferred at the telecine directly onto the LAN. The dialogue, which may have been recorded on DAT, also goes direct to LAN. The LAN can store a large sound effects library as well as a copyright-cleared music library. Once the movie is finished, it can be sent from the LAN to whatever film, tape, or disc media is desired.

This type of operation has the potential to revolutionize the postproduction procedure. Now picture and dialogue are usually edited before any other sounds are added. With a digital depot configuration, however, one person can be creating the dog barks for a shot that has not yet been edited into the film but probably will be. When the picture editor gets around to editing that shot, he or she can use it with the barks included. If, because of the way the picture is edited, the barks do not fit exactly, they can be moved slightly with the computer program tools that are available. There really is no need to lock the picture. It can be changed right up to deadline so that it works more effectively with the sound. This type of procedure could lead to more emphasis on sound because, under the present system, the sound is almost always edited to match the picture. With everything happening simultaneously, the picture can become, at least in part, the servant of the sound.

With high-quality phone lines, the digital depot can send and receive signals throughout a city, the country, or the world. Theoretically, Foley walkers at Fox studios in Hollywood, ADR actors at a facility in North Carolina, and a composer in Malaysia could all place their work on a network and it could then be edited in Australia.

The entire sound-structuring process is crucial to the understandability of a movie. Whether the sound is postproduced with simple equipment or whether it is part of a LAN experiment, care should be taken to ensure the best sound quality possible is achieved.

Notes

1. "Terms of End-EAR-ment," *AV Video,* April 1991, p. 57.
2. Tom Kenny, "Assembling the Soundtrack for Martin Scorsese's *Casino,*" *Mix,* January 1996, pp. 82–83.
3. For more on magnetic film stock, see Eastman Kodak, *The Moving Image* (Rochester, NY: Eastman Kodak, 1990), pp. 19, 23; Lenny Lipton, *Independent Filmmaking* (New York: Simon & Schuster, 1983), pp. 304–340; David Cheshire, *The Book of Movie Photography* (New York: Alfred A. Knopf, 1984), pp. 231–248; and Norman Hollyn, *The Film Editing Room Handbook* (Los Angeles: Lone Eagle Press, 1990).
4. Nick Batzdorf, "Audio Editing Choices," *AV Video,* February 1991, pp. 48–50; and Don Rushkin, "Five Decades of Magnetic Tape in Broadcasting," *College Broadcasting,* April-May 1990, pp. 30–31.

5. Mike Sokol, "DAWs Stay on the Right Track," *TV Technology,* NAB Extra 1995, p. 98; and Ken Hahn, "Audio Workstations Take Center Stage," *TV Technology,* NAB Extra 1993, p. 20.

6. Sometimes dailies are shown electronically using a nonlinear editor. At the media record telecine (MRT), the picture will be loaded onto one RMAG and the sound will be loaded onto another. Both RMAGs are then inserted into an editing system such as the Avid or Lightworks, picture and sound are synced, and the day's work is viewed by the director and others. See Mel Lambert, "Audiotracks' Digital Dailies," *Mix,* January 1996, pp. 165–174.

7. Stephen R. Acker, "MIDI and Television," *Feedback,* Spring 1990, pp. 2–5; Jonathan Weber, "Computers Are Busy Setting Music on Its Ears," *Los Angeles Times,* 15 April 1992, p. D-1; and Francis Rumsey, *MIDI* (Stoneham, MA: Focal Press, 1990).

8. One of the most popular is "Cakewalk," from Twelve Tone Systems, Inc., P. O. Box 760, Watertown, MA 02272.

9. Sokol, p. 98.

10. Some of the music libraries are Audio Action (800–533–1293), Canary Productions (800–368–0033), DeWolfe Music Library (800–221–6713), FirstCom/Music House/Chappell (800–858–8880), Killer Tracks (800–877–0078), Metro Music (212–799–7600), The Music Bank (408–867–4756), and Sound Ideas (800–387–3030). For further detail, see "Sound Tracking," *AV Video,* September 1995, pp. 87–100.

11. Mike Sokol, "Keeping Track of Your Audio Decks," *TV Technology,* October 1995, p. 27.

12. Two brand names for these synchronizing machines are Lynx and Adams-Smith.

13. Two of the most popular digital multitrack recorders are the Alesis ADAT and the Tascam DA88. See Michael Groticelli, "Affordable Digital Multitrack Update," *Videography,* September 1995, pp. 88–89; and Daniel Kumin, "In the Digital Domain with ADAT: Crystal Clear Audio-for-Video," *AV Video,* July 1993, pp. 78–84.

14. Two videotapes available on this subject are "Shaping Your Sound with Equalizers, Compressors and Gates," and "Shaping Your Sound with Reverb and Delay." Both are available from Alan Gordon Enterprises, 1430 Cahuenga Blvd., Hollywood, CA 90028. This material is also discussed in Lynne Gross and David Reese, *Radio Production Worktext: Studio and Equipment* (Boston: Focal Press, 1990), pp. 108–119.

15. Ken Hahn, "Multitrack's Mighty Role," *TV Technology,* January 1992, p. 13.

16. Keith Hatschek and Brent Hurtig, "Affordable Desktop Audio Is a Reality," *AV Video,* February 1992, pp. 42–47; and David M. Rubin, "Strike Up the Band," *Presentations,* October 1995, pp. 30–36.

17. Avid makes Audio Station to go with its Media Composer and Lightworks makes Fader Box to go with its Heavyworks.

18. Some of the major DAW manufacturers are Fostex, Roland, Fairlight, and Yamaha.

19. Ken Hahn, "Disk-Based Systems Proliferating," TV Technology, April 1992, p. 40; and Mel Lambert "Fairlight MFX3," *Mix,* November 1995, p. 132.

20. Larry Blake, "Digital Sound in the Cinema," *Mix,* October 1995, pp. 116–129.

21. Tom Kenny, "Digital Sound and Picture," *Mix,* January 1996, pp. 165–170.

chapter fourteen
Approaches to Structuring Sound

The French theoretician Christian Metz describes five channels of information in motion pictures: the image, written language and other graphics on the screen, speech (dialogue and narration), music, and noise (sound effects and ambient sounds).[1] In this analysis there are more possibilities for communicating information through sound than through picture. Metz makes an even stronger point when he discusses how we look at an image versus how we hear sound. We must redirect our attention in order to read words on the screen or look at the picture, whereas sound washes over us.

Many writers stress the image when discussing film and television. They consider the two to be visual media. But as Metz's analysis (and common observation) demonstrates, film and TV are really audiovisual media. The sound we hear influences the way we look at the picture. The same series of pictures projected with different sound tracks can have radically different meanings.

The Evolution of Sound

The early filmmakers recognized the importance of sound almost from the beginning. In fact, Thomas Edison and William Dickson, who have been credited with inventing the motion picture in America, were really trying to create pictures to accompany Edison's phonograph.

Even though early movies were silent, they were usually accompanied by music when shown in a theater. At first piano players improvised as they watched the film—fast music for chase scenes, minor chords for grief. Eventually, magnificent organs and even full orchestras accompanied the showing of films. Much of the power of the silent era, which is usually considered to have lasted until the 1927 showing of *The Jazz Singer,* was the overwhelmingly powerful live music that accompanied the moving image.

When sound on film arrived, many moviemakers felt it would destroy the art of the image. Cameras had to be locked down in soundproof booths so that the microphone would not pick up their whirring. Actors could barely move because they had to stay within pickup distance of the mic, which was usually hidden in a flowerpot.

But the audience loved sound, so the moviemakers could not dismiss it. In 1926 only a few movies had any type of recorded sound, and most of that was bits and pieces of music. By 1929 almost all movies were shot with synchronous sound.

The Hollywood community eventually learned to manipulate the sound equipment so that sound did not hinder the picture. Someone thought of placing the mic on the end of a pole (**boom**) so that it could be moved around, and housings were built to silence cameras so that they too could move. Perhaps most important was the development of postproduction sound techniques that meant sound could be built into the movie after it was shot. Car chases, for example, could be shot silently and all the crash noises, screeches, and chase music could be added later. All of this made sound an important aspect of the movie business; today some films often have dozens of sounds playing at one time.[2]

Television, of course, was never silent. But in the early days of TV, audio received little emphasis, mainly because engineers were struggling to produce a viewable image. Today sound on videotape is approaching the same importance and sophistication that sound in film has acquired. In both media, postproduction of sound greatly enhances the movie's impact on the audience.[3]

The Relationship of Sound to Image

Despite its importance, the sound in motion pictures does not stand alone like the music on compact disk. Movies by definition involve the juxtaposition of sound and image. In fact, one of the editor's primary concerns in postproduction is establishing or creating effective relationships between the picture and the various elements of the sound track—the dialogue, sound effects, and music.

The spoken words and ambient sounds recorded with the image during production are usually referred to as **synchronous sound.** In **double system** film production the editor must actually sync up the picture and sound, but regardless of how this relationship is created, it is essentially a relationship in time. In other words, we consider the sound and picture to jibe in sync if the sound we hear is perfectly matched in time to the person or object creating that sound on the screen. Conversely, sound is out of sync if a person talking or a hand knocking on a door is not timed precisely with the sound of the words or door knock.

In the first stages of editing the editor usually cuts the picture and synchronous dialogue track together. But as the cutting proceeds, the editor can begin to establish entirely different relationships between the picture and its matching sound. By using cutaways, reaction shots, or close-ups of isolated details within the scene, the editor may juxtapose the synchronous sound from one shot with images that are entirely different. Furthermore, the editor can make the sound from one scene overlap the following or preceding scene, foreshadowing the scene we are about to see or recalling the scene that has just ended.

Because the editor can cut the sound track at any point, it is possible to establish a variety of relationships with the image. The editor can use sound to create a **sound flashback** or **sound flashforward.** We might, for example, hear sounds from a character's past while seeing an image of the character in the present. This kind of sound-image juxtaposition is also possible with sound effects and music.

In their book *Film Art: An Introduction,* David Bordwell and Kristin Thompson examine a variety of sound-image relationships.[4] They differentiate between sound that is **diegetic** (from within the story space) and sound that is **nondiegetic** (outside the story space). When we see the image of characters talking and also hear their words, the sound is diegetic. The same would be true of sound effects or music that emanate from sources on the screen, such as a door slam or jukebox. All these sounds might occur on-screen, but they would still be diegetic sounds if they took place off-screen—provided that they came from the story space.

Nondiegetic sound comes from outside the story space. The most common kind of nondiegetic sound is the musical score that typically accompanies a motion picture. Unless the director is making some kind of joke, we do not expect to see a shot of John Williams and the British Philharmonic Orchestra as the film reaches a dramatic climax; the musical score by convention is not part of the story space.

Similarly, an omniscient narrator might provide a voice-over introduction to a motion picture, setting the stage for the action to follow. This kind of narration would be nondiegetic, but if it were provided by a character in the story it would be considered diegetic sound.

Whether it is diegetic or nondiegetic, narration can provide information about the past, present, or future that may not be contained in the image. Many directors have made extensive use of interior monologues, in which we hear what characters are thinking but do not see them moving their lips in the image on-screen. This kind of subjective narration is diegetic. A narrator who comments on the action from outside the story space would convey a completely different kind of information and set a different tone.

Such distinctions are helpful in demonstrating at least a few of the complex relationships the editor can develop while constructing the sound tracks. No sound is irreversibly locked to its matching image. The editor is free to build any number of sound-image relationships in space or time. Sounds may originate from within the story space or from outside it. Sounds may be on-screen or off-screen. They may present information about the past, present, or future. In the hands of a skillful and creative editor, sound-image relationships can make a significant contribution to the completed motion picture.

The Functions of Sound

The editors who spot for music and sound effects and who edit dialogue must be aware of the various purposes that sound can fulfill. They do not wantonly place cricket chirps, tire squeals, factory noises, soft romantic music, and lines of dialogue in the sound track. They go through a definite thought process, either consciously or subconsciously, to determine which sounds are needed and where they should go. Usually, the picture and dialogue cue the music and sound effects. That is why **spotting** is not done until *after* the picture and principal dialogue track have been edited. The people working with sound must consider the various possibilities for sound and incorporate them when and where they are appropriate. There is no set list of purposes for sound, but most sound can be thought of in terms of supplying information, enhancing reality or fantasy, establishing time, place, and character, creating mood and emotion, giving a sense of rhythm, and directing attention.

Supplying Information

In many instances sound, primarily the **dialogue**, conveys most of the information in a movie. Talking heads do not give much visual information beyond the emotion that actors can convey through their expressions. The essence of the information is in the words that they speak. For this reason, great care should be taken to ensure that the dialogue is understandable.

If you are spotting for **automatic dialogue replacement (ADR)**, the need to supply information must be uppermost in your mind. Any dialogue that is so muddled that it cannot be understood should be rerecorded. If you are editing, you should consider the clarity of the dialogue in selecting the takes to include in the master. The original dialogue should also undergo as little generation loss as possible so that it does not lose its information-giving ability.

Voice-over narration can also convey a great deal of information, but it must be planned and recorded properly so that its message is understood. In productions designed primarily to inform, voice-over is often the main source of information. In these cases, the director must decide whether the picture should be edited to the voice-over or the voice-over should be recorded to suit the needs of the image. Also, the picture and voice-over must be coordinated so that there are no duplications. If the words simply describe what is happening in the picture, they are superfluous and often give the impression that the narrator is talking down to the viewer. Another problem arises when a narrator reads words that appear on the screen. Most members of the audience will be able to read the words faster than the narrator can speak them, so the visual and aural information will interfere with each other. The best way to convey information through narration is to have the voice-over convey facts that relate to but also add to the picture.

When voice-overs are used in movies, they often appear at the beginning of a film to give information about what has preceded the action or to provide information about what is going to happen. An excellent example of this is the opening narration from *Bull Durham* by writer-director Ron Shelton (see Figure 14.1).[5] This voice-over, delivered by Annie Savoy (played by Susan Sarandon), succinctly covers much of the backstory. It also prepares the viewer for the story line of the movie.

Someone had to select the pictures to use with the voice-over. The picture could have shown Sarandon delivering the lines to the camera, but then the image would not have given much more information than the audio. The pictures could have illustrated the various "religions," but that would have repeated what the words were saying. What was selected—a few baseball photos and shots of Sarandon primping before the mirror and walking to the baseball stadium—conveyed additional information and moved the story toward the next scene.

Occasionally, voice-overs state what people are thinking or reiterate dialogue from earlier in the movie. This technique uses the dialogue and voice-over to link several parts of the film, doubling the impact of the information contained in the words.

Sound effects and **ambient sounds** can also convey information, albeit in a less straightforward manner than dialogue or narration. Dogs barking can mean someone is coming; the volume of an ambulance's siren is an indication of how soon help will arrive. Off-screen sound effects can tell us that the teenage son has crashed

Figure 14.1

```
         ANNIE SAVOY'S SOLILOQUY FROM BULL DURHAM
                     by Ron Shelton


I believe in the Church of Baseball.

I've tried all the major religions and most of the
minor ones--I've worshipped Buddha, Allah, Brahma,
Vishnu, Siva, trees, mushrooms, and Isadora Duncan.

I know things.  For instance--

There are 108 beads in a Catholic rosary. And--

There are 108 stitches in a baseball.

When I learned that, I gave Jesus a chance.

But it just didn't work out between us...The Lord laid
too much guilt on me.  I prefer metaphysics to
theology.

You see, there's no guilt in baseball...and it's never
boring.

Which makes it like sex.

There's never been a ballplayer slept with me who
didn't have the best year of his career.

Making love is like hitting a baseball--you just got to
relax and concentrate.

Besides, I'd never sleep with a player hitting under
.250 unless he had a lot of R.B.I.'s or was a great
glove man up the middle.

A woman's got to have standards.

The young players start off full of enthusiasm and
energy, but they don't realize that come July and
August when the weather is hot it's hard to perform at
your peak level.
```

(Continued)

the car into the garage even though we never see the crash and no one in the cast refers directly to it.

Supplying facts is not the primary power of music, but on occasion music can be informative. When lyrics comment on what is being presented, they add another layer of meaning. In fact, in musicals the lyrics often drive the story forward. For example, in *Singin' in the Rain*, the song "You Were Meant for Me" establishes the love interest between Gene Kelly and Debbie Reynolds that Kelly is supposedly un-

Figure 14.1
(Continued)

The veterans pace themselves better. They finish
stronger. They're great in September.

While I don't belive a woman needs a man to be
fulfilled, I do confess an interest in finding the
ultimate guy--he'd have that youthful exuberance but
the veteran's sense of timing...

Y'see there's a certain amount of "life-wisdom" I give
these boys.

I can expand their minds. Sometimes when I've got a
ballplayer alone I'll just read Emily Dickenson or Walt
Whitman to him. The guys are sweet--they always stay
and listen.

Of course a guy will listen to anything if he thinks
it's foreplay.

I make them feel confident. They make me feel safe.
And pretty.

'Course what I give them lasts a lifetime. What they
give me lasts 142 games. Sometimes it seems like a bad
trade--

--but bad trades are part of baseball--who can forget
Frank Robinson for Milt Pappas, for Godsakes!

It's a long season and you got to trust it.

I've tried 'em all...I really have...

...and the only church that truly feeds the soul--day
in, day out--is the Church of Baseball.

able to articulate (Figure 14.2 shows Gene Kelly singing "You Were Meant for Me"). Music can also foreshadow, giving information before the picture or dialogue do. For example, the music can become ominous before tragedy occurs. Music can also heighten the impact of information given by dialogue or narration. It can punctuate the words to give them added importance. In a few films music has been a source of information. The spaceship's musical refrain in *Close Encounters of the Third Kind* was part of a language that the people on Earth had to decode.

Sound can also *withhold* information. In *North by Northwest* Alfred Hitchcock uses the noise of an airplane to drown out part of a conversation between Cary Grant and a CIA agent.

Sometimes sound conveys information that is totally *opposite* to the picture. This can be used for comic effect. In *Singin' in the Rain* Gene Kelly's voice tells of his glorious rise in show business while the pictures are showing that he was really a flop. It can also be used for shock effect. Light, happy music accompanies the opening scene of *Natural Born Killers* that shows numerous people being murdered.

Supplying information is a primary power of sound, especially within the structure of corporate videos and conventional Hollywood narrative films. Most films are not intended to be abstract or ethereal. If they are to be successful, the audience must understand what is happening. If you are spotting a movie, you must make sure that some sound source will give the audience all the information you want them to have that is not conveyed in the picture.

Enhancing Reality and Fantasy

Adding reality cues is a major function of **Foley**, ambient sounds, and sound effects. These are the elements that make the viewer believe the mise-en-scène. An airport without airplane noises, a crowded waiting room without coughs and muffled voices, or silent footsteps on gravel would not be believable. For dialogue the main reality cue is **perspective**; a booming voice coming from someone who is far away does not sound real. Sound effects can employ perspective, too. In *Jurassic Park* the sound of the dinosaurs approaching from the rear of the theater gives an exceptionally realistic scariness to the movie.[6] In general, dialogue and voice-overs can set up reality, but the little noises that are always present in life are what give that reality substance.

John Edwards-Younger, who is in charge of effects for "NYPD Blue" has a definite thought process he goes through in order to make the series realistic. He places **walla walla** in each scene of each episode because there is always noise in bustling New York. The show has a

Figure 14.2
In this scene from Singin' in the Rain *the lyrics advance the story. (© 1952 Loew's Inc. Ren. 1979 Metro-Goldwyn-Mayer, Inc.)*

group of actors that have been named the SuperLoopers, who do all the different types of walla walla from very general cafe noises to cops in the background yelling out codes. Edwards-Younger also includes traffic noises in all scenes, be they indoor or outdoor, again because one can always hear traffic in New York, even in a quiet apartment. He then considers general off-screen elements—perhaps jackhammers or fire sirens if the scene is a busy street. Often these noises are used to fill holes where there is no dialogue, so Edwards-Younger will go through a scene and "paint" in sounds to enhance the aural canvas. He also considers off-screen needs of the story; if a helicopter is coming, it must be heard well before it is seen. Finally, he looks for on-screen needs. Often this requires knowledge of the story line. For example, if a woman officer answers the phone, he must know if she is waiting for the call and answers it quickly or if she is engaged in something more important and lets the phone ring several times before answering. Easier are on-screen **hard effects** such as door slams that give a very concrete sense of reality.[7]

Creating fantasy is another matter. Music is excellent for creating fantasy because most of us do not hear violins as you walk down the street. Sound effects are also excellent for creating fantasy. The sound that is made when one of the Three Stooges "gouges" someone's eyes does not approximate the actual sound that act would make. The sound lets you know that this action is not real. In fact, if the sound were authentic, the Three Stooges' movies might be truly offensive. Sounds that do not exist on Earth give such films as *Star Wars* a futuristic effect. Dialogue and voice-overs can also add to fantasy. Donald Duck's voice would never be mistaken for real, although it is diegetic.

Spotting for these elements is difficult. You must look at the entire scene carefully and determine what sounds would be appropriate. Would there be traffic noises coming in the open window? Will the clinging evening gown rustle as the woman moves? To what extent should the clinking glasses in the long shot of the bar carry over to the close-up of the two gangsters talking? Is the guitar playing in the background acoustic or electronic? What kind of noise might a laser gun make? Is the sound of an extra snapping his fingers in the back of the scene worth including? These are the types of details that spotters must consider.

Acquiring and recording the sounds is not easy either. Sound effects from CD libraries are often not quite right (and they are unlikely to contain futuristic sounds). Going to the actual source sometimes does not work. A real crackling fire doesn't sound very much like one when it is recorded. Wrinkling paper might create a more "realistic" crackle. **Digital samplers** and computers can help create unusual or specific sounds, but consulting an experienced sound editor is often the best way to find just the right effect.

Establishing Time, Place, and Character

Theoretically, the dialogue could establish everything the audience needs to know about when and where the scene is taking place and the type of people involved. However, using only dialogue to do so usually becomes tedious and stilted. ("I'm glad we're coming to visit Uncle Herman this bright May morning even though I know he is your father's grouchy bachelor uncle who lives on a rundown farm with his cows and pigs and never answers his telephone.")

For this reason, sound editors often use other elements to help identify time, place, and character. Voice-overs can do this even more blatantly than dialogue without seeming forced. For example, the narrator in Orson Welles's *The Magnificent Ambersons* opens the film by describing all the characters. People accept narration as expository and so do not find being bombarded with facts unnatural.

Music is excellent for establishing time, place, and character. A Gregorian chant bespeaks medieval times; oriental music sets a movie in China; jazz puts the audience in New Orleans; and "Here Comes the Bride" establishes a wedding. In *Forrest Gump* music from the various decades accompanies Forrest's life story. Character is a little more difficult to establish with music, but some films contain a **motif**, a particular group of notes that is played to herald the arrival of a particular character. For instance, in *Jaws* the same music always signals the appearance of the hungry shark. Music can also indicate character qualities. In old melodramas cellos playing in a minor key often denoted a villain, a sturdy brass march accompanied the hero, and soft violin passages signified the heroine.

Sometimes music is purposely composed to contrast with the picture. This can create a comedic effect—for example, pompous overblown music accompanying the antics of Bud Abbott and Lou Costello.

Sound editors also use sound effects and other noises to indicate time, place, and character. The cock crowing, the alarm ringing, and the clock striking midnight all indicate time.

Putting traffic noises in the background during a close-up of a woman tells us that she is in the city and can eliminate the need for an establishing shot. Similarly, cannon noise can save the cost of a mammoth battle scene and allow you to concentrate on several actors involved in battle. Sound effects can also signal a character's arrival. A particular snort or the sound of creaky shoes can announce that some well-established character is near. Surround sound can provide an unusual type of location cue. An editor can convey sense of space in a particular scene by delaying sound between the speakers in the back and those in the front.

One of the main considerations when spotting, editing, and mixing sounds that establish time, place, and character is not overdoing them. If the time is evident from the picture or the dialogue, there may be no need to add the crowing cock, which has become a cliché. Like sounds that supply information, sounds that establish time, place, and character should clarify what is happening.

Creating Mood and Emotion

Music is important for creating mood and emotion. Music can express just about any emotion—love, hate, fear, tension, serenity, anger, friendship. Music has its own cultural language in this regard. Soft, slow music is considered romantic, and music in the minor key denotes sadness. However, music is highly subjective. For this reason the director and the composer should be of the same mind about what the music is conveying or the postproduction process will grind to a halt as they argue over the appropriateness of a particular score.[8]

Theme music can provide a comfortable familiar mood, especially if it is associated with a popular production. Series TV makes great use of theme music over opening and closing credits. Just about anyone can hum the theme music from a favorite series—"Cheers," "Star Trek," or "Friends." Movies with sequels, such as the James Bond series, also use music to capitalize on past successes and familiarity. Theme music can be reassuring even within a movie. For ex-

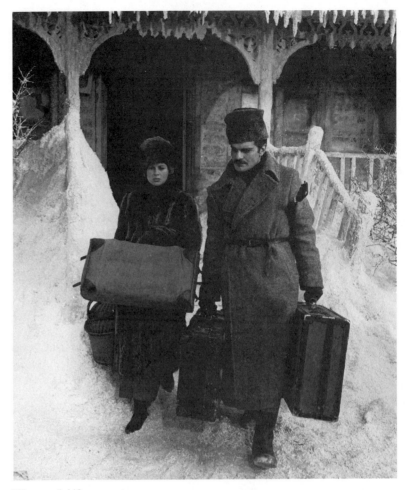

Figure 14.3
For many people any scene from Dr. Zhivago *will automatically conjure up the theme music. (© 1965 Metro-Goldwyn-Mayer, Inc.)*

ample, the theme for *Dr. Zhivago* (see Figure 14.3) repeats often throughout to reemphasize emotion.

A movie's opening music can set the mood for the entire motion picture. Specifically, it clues the audience to whether the movie is for laughing or for crying. Music within a movie can also create humor by punctuating a humorous event with an unusual musical sound. Or the music itself can be funny, as in the toy store piano-playing scene in *Big*. Tom Hanks using his feet to play "Chopsticks," a ditty just about everyone has heard or played, added to the humor of the scene.

Most film music is composed after the movie is completed so that it can fit the emotion and timing of the scene. Sometimes, however, the music comes first. *While You Were Sleeping* used familiar popular music from the past to heighten its emotion. Documentarian Ken Burns ("The Civil War," "Baseball") usually starts with music. As he puts it, "We do not 'score' a picture, which is the mathematical application of timed music once a film is done. When music is added to a film in this way, it can only be 'canned.' What we do instead is record the music of the period before we begin editing, giving ourselves a wide variety of music, which, more often than not, dictates the rhythm and the emotion of every scene before we begin to edit it. So in the case of the Civil War, we will hear the sounds of the music that the soldiers sang and played among themselves, and we will hear it on the authentic instruments that they themselves played. In addition, we isolate certain theme music which we feel can become a bridge to our twentieth-century audience, reminding them of music's incredible power to convey the most complicated emotional information."[9]

Although music is written or selected to enhance the script and visual aspects of the movie, it often takes on a life of its own. Many movie scores have become popular in their own right and have hit the top of the record charts, as did the scores from *Saturday Night Fever, The Bodyguard, Against All Odds,* and *Waiting to Exhale.*

Sound effects can also create mood and emotion. Waves lapping against the shore or birds chirping connote serenity. Squealing tires create tension. An ominous off-screen thud can raise anticipation. A siren signals danger. A coyote call denotes isolation. Sound effects are also excellent for creating humor. Many of Jim Carrey's antics in *The Mask* are made funnier by the sound effects that accompany them.

Voice elements in dialogue and voice-overs can also create emotion. The muffled voices of an argument add to tension. The tone and content of the voice-over at the beginning of *Bull Durham* say that this movie is not going to take itself too seriously.

One of the best devices for creating emotion is the absence of sound—silence. Because sound permeates most movies, a period of silence creates great tension. The first sound that follows silence greatly intensifies its impact. For exam-

ple, in *Platoon* a long period of silence ensues while the soldiers are watching for the enemy. Suddenly a twig snaps. The audience does not see danger but certainly feels it because of the sound.

Spotting for mood and emotion is probably the most difficult of all spotting because context clues are not obvious in the picture. There is no dress that needs to rustle or lightning that needs thunder. The person doing the spotting must feel the emotional needs and think of ways to fill them.

Giving a Sense of Rhythm

As much as picture editing, music can establish pace—long phrases and a limited number of notes per measure (perhaps a minuet) for slow-paced material and short phrases and a multitude of notes (perhaps heavy metal) for fast-paced material. The music's level of rhythmic energy greatly affects the energy level of a movie scene.

Music can also magnify the movie's climaxes—cymbals clashing just as the prizefighter floors his opponent. Making climaxes of music and picture coincide is fairly easy if the music is composed specifically for the movie. But if the music is acquired from a library or other source, creating this effect usually requires an editing technique known as **backtiming.** The editor lines up the climax of the music, which is on audiotape or on the source videotape, with the prizefighter's punch on the master videotape. Then using the edit controller, the editor backs up both machines an equal number of frames to the point at which the music begins. For example, the music climax might come at 00:05:30:00 on that tape, and the punch might be at 00:20:30:30 on the master videotape. If the music, from the beginning to the climax, lasts 1 minute and 30 seconds, the editor needs to rewind both machines by 1:30 to 00:04:00:00 and 00:19:00:30, respectively. Those two points become the edit-in points for the edit. The edit-out point would be at the end of the music, perhaps 30 seconds and 10 frames past the climax. The editor would set the edit-in points on the controller, the source and record machines would back up, and the music would be recorded on the master tape, starting at 00:19:00:30, climaxing at 00:20:30:30, and ending at 00:21:00:40 (see Figure 14.4). Backtiming can be undertaken with control track as well as time code and is frequently used for montages.

Handling this type of picture-music interrelationship is easier with computer editing. For example, Martin Scorsese's *Casino* used only 1970s and 1980s music that already existed. Before editing the picture, Scorsese laid most of the music tracks. He gave the editors directions about actions he wanted to occur at particular lyrics within the songs or at particular musical points. The editors then tried to cut the picture so that it matched the music and still made sense from a visual point of view. Sometimes this did not work out perfectly and the picture could not be made to hit the music cues exactly. However, because the music was on a digital audio workstation, the editors were able to expand or contract segments slightly so that it fit with the picture.[10]

For some types of editing, music dictates the pace and the picture supplements it. This is almost always true for music videos because the music exists before the pictures. The picture-editing decisions are based on the content, the rhythm, and the feel of the music. Usually with this type of editing, you want to make the video cuts on the music beat, although doing so throughout an entire selection can become boring. Music sets the rhythmic agenda for many commercials. Within narrative motion pictures music can be the driving force of montages. For example, at the beginning of *Wayne's World* a montage sequence is cut to the beat of Queen's "Bohemian Rhapsody."

Sound effects too can add to the rhythmic effect of the movie. Cartoons often use a barrage of effects, mixed with music, to punctuate chases, tumbles, and other antics that make up most of these high-energy minimovies.

Dialogue and voice-overs can set pace. Clipped speech delivered in a sarcastic tone is usually fast paced, and raised voices of an argument often build to a climax.

Generally, all the sound elements work together and with the picture to reinforce certain

Figure 14.4
By backtiming the music the sound editor can make the punch of the prizefighter and the clash of the cymbals occur at the same time.

rhythmic elements. But sometimes the sounds are in opposition to the picture, just as they are when they provide incorrect information.

The rhythmic function of sound is subtle. Sound editors and composers must be in accord with the director on the pace, energy, and climaxes of the movie and individual scenes. A high-energy picture with slow sound will lose energy.

Directing Attention

Sound also has the ability to direct the audience's attention. Ordinarily, the audience focuses its attention on the person who is talking, and that person is usually in the center of the screen. But if a door opens to the right, the audience will expect someone to enter from the right and will probably look in that direction. In this way sound expands the frame, defining off-screen space in such a way that it becomes almost as much a part of the story as the on-screen space. Directing attention with sound can also frighten the audience (à la Hitchcock). If the audience is looking to the right side of the frame because the main sound and action are occurring there, the director can bring in something unexpected from the left. The audience members may be caught unaware, and their fear will be heightened.

Sound can direct attention to particular elements of the frame that might not be noticed otherwise. A car that is backfiring often is just part of a traffic scene, in which case the backfire might not even be heard on the sound track. But if that car's presence in the scene in which the hero gives secret documents to a spy is important to the story, the editor can accentuate the backfiring noise in such a way that the audience becomes aware of it. Then when they

Figure 14.5

A sound mixing session. Note the cue sheet propped up on the console. (Photo courtesy of Ryder Sound Services)

again hear the car at the scene of the murder, the audience members who were aware of the backfire become privy to a special clue.

Even more extreme would be including the sound of a bomb ticking, which might not actually be audible in a particular circumstance, to focus the audience's attention on the possibility of an explosion. Sometimes the sound track even includes something totally inaudible, such as a beating heart.

Sound at the end of one scene can foreshadow the next to intensify the audience's reaction to the second scene. A siren wailing at the end of a bucolic scene can draw the audience

into the next scene, where a frantic rescue attempt is under way. When the fireplace shoots flames into the living room in *On Golden Pond,* we hear Katharine Hepburn's screams about the fire for several seconds (over a shot of Henry Fonda and the boy) before the cut shows Hepburn and the fire.

Using sound to direct the viewer's attention where the director wants it focused is a rather subtle art. Sound is not often used for this purpose and probably should not be. Using sound to direct attention should be reserved for especially appropriate circumstances. People who spot for music, sound effects, ambient sounds, Foley, and ADR usually do not consciously consider the various purposes of sound; indeed, these purposes could be identified in many different ways.[11] What is important is that sound is used to enhance the movie.

Layering Sound

Usually by the time the director and the editor are ready for the final sound mix, much of the decision making is over. The picture cut is locked down irrevocably. The postproduction team has spotted, gathered, and edited into place the various sound tracks in relation to the cut images. All that remains is the mix—the last creative task in the moviemaking process.[12]

The mixing cue sheet that the sound editor brings to the mixing session is a graphic illustration of the remaining creative decisions (see Figure 14.5). It is a map showing which sound elements the editor has made available and where they begin and end in relation to the picture. Still, even with this guide the sound mixer(s) must make a number of aesthetic judgments during the mixing session. Working by ear and with suggestions from the director or editor, the mixers must blend the various sound elements together to create the final sound track.

This is what sound **layering** is all about. Although motion pictures make occasional use of multiple images or superimpositions, we cannot really read a group of images if they appear simultaneously on the screen. In comparison, we are accustomed to hearing many sounds together and selecting what is most important to listen to. Therefore, it is appropriate to think of sound track building as a layering process, the construction of not just one sound element (such as dialogue) but of a variety of sounds (sound effects, ambient noise, and music) that may all be heard at the same time.

Our ears (and minds) hear sound selectively—we subconsciously shut out unimportant background sounds (the television, air conditioner, and refrigerator hum) to hear what we want to hear, such as someone talking to us. This does not automatically occur in a motion picture sound track, however. Even a relatively simple scene can easily contain five or six different sound elements (dialogue, background music, and three or four sound effects), all playing simultaneously. Unless certain sounds are given special emphasis during the mixing session, the finished sound track will be an unintelligible muddle of competing sounds.

Many of these decisions are fairly subjective. A mixing session proceeds by trial and error, providing an opportunity to test different choices. Essentially, the sound mix manipulates the various sound elements in three basic ways. The first involves volume levels. Generally, the louder the sound, the more emphasis it has. By raising the sound level for a particular sound effect, line of dialogue, or piece of music, the mixer(s) can separate it from the other sounds and give it special significance. In an exchange of dialogue one performer's lines may need to be punched up to a higher volume. At other times it may be more appropriate to drop a performer's lines into the background. The volume of music will vary according to whether dialogue must be heard over it or whether the music is the primary sound element. In a typical shoot-'em-up scene the music is often the most important (and loudest) sound, with the sound effects and throwaway dialogue playing a distinctly supporting role.

The second area of control concerns when and how to establish a sound in relation to the image. Music, for example, often fades in slowly and unobtrusively at some point in the scene, pushes to a higher level as the intensity of the drama increases, and gently fades out after the climax. In contrast, an explosion or door slam should be abrupt. Such sounds must begin immediately at full volume. A gentle fade-in would destroy the effect. Finally, because most sound elements are recorded flat (without equalization) they sometimes need equalization during the mix. This is often true for dialogue because the quality of location sound recordings tends to vary wildly. The high or low frequencies in a particular sound may need boosting or lowering. The mixers might have to use special effects (reverberation or filters) to simulate a telephone conversation or echo-filled cave. They may have to use noise reduction to reduce background hiss.

Admittedly, the director, editor, sound editors, and composer will have discussed and made many of these sound decisions before the mix. If the proper sound elements are not available in the appropriate places on the sound tracks or in the computer, they will not magically appear during the mixing session. Nevertheless, the best planning and intentions mean nothing until they are brought to life in the final sound track. The mixing session is the final chance to make adjustments, to see and hear how the various sound and picture elements work together. Quite simply, when the mix ends, the decision making ends with it.

Notes

1. Christian Metz, *Film Language: A Semiotics of the Cinema,* trans. by Michael Taylor (New York: Oxford University Press, 1974), pp. 39–91.

2. For more on the history of sound, see Douglas Gomery, *Movie History* (Belmont, CA: Wadsworth, 1990), pp. 163–168; Kristin Thompson and David Bordwell, *Film History: An Introduction* (New York: McGraw-Hill, 1994), pp. 213–220; and David A. Cook, *A History of Narrative Film* (New York: W. W. Norton, 1990): 253–266.

3. Frank Beacham, "Every Sound Tells a Story," *TV Technology,* November 1991, p. 16.

4. David Bordwell and Kristin Thompson, *Film Art: An Introduction,* 4th ed. (New York: McGraw-Hill, 1993), pp. 244–273.

5. *Bull Durham* (1988) is an Orion Pictures Release from A Mount Company Production. It stars Kevin Costner, Susan Sarandon, and Tim Robbins. The executive producer is David V. Lester, the producers are Thom Mount and Mark Burg, and the writer and director is Ron Shelton.

6. Tom Kenny, "Sound Design for Steven Speilberg's Dinosaur Epic," *Mix,* July 1993, pp. 128–134.

7. Maureen Droney, "A Sonic Week in the Life of *NYPD Blue,*" *Mix,* May 1995, pp. 148–155.

8. Mitch Coodley, "Secrets to Successful Collaboration with a Composer," *AV Video,* July 1992, pp. 52–57.

9. Ken Burns, *Making Film History* (Detroit: General Motors, n.d.), p. 5.

10. Tom Kenny, "Assembling the Soundtrack for Martin Scorsese's *Casino,*" *Mix,* January 1996, pp. 82–91.

11. For other approaches to this subject, see Lee R. Bobker, *Elements of Film* (New York: Harcourt Brace Jovanovich, 1974), pp. 82–107; and Herbert Zettl, *Sight-Sound-Motion: Applied Media Aesthetics,* 2nd ed. (Belmont, CA: Wadsworth, 1990), pp. 333–385.

12. Ken Hahn, "The Effects of an M&E Track," *TV Technology,* June 1995, p. 28; and Jeremy Hoenack, "Improving the Sound Track," *American Cinematographer,* Summer 1991, pp. 32–33.

Glossary

A-B roll A process that enables two pictures to overlap, either by printing two rolls of film or by taking two video signals through a switcher and time-base corrector; also, the reels of film or tape used when the pictures are A-B rolled.

above-the-line Refers to expenses for the many administrative, conceptual, and creative aspects of a specific motion picture, such as writing, producing, acting, and directing.

AC Alternating current; usually used to refer to the power found in homes and offices.

Academy ratio The standard of three vertical units to four horizontal units adopted by the Academy of Motion Picture Arts and Sciences as the aspect ratio for movies; also the current standard for the television aspect ratio.

ADR See *automatic dialogue replacement.*

AFM See *audio frequency modulation.*

AGC See *automatic gain control.*

alligator clamp A spring-loaded clamp that opens in such a way that it can secure a light almost anywhere; also called **gaffer grip**.

ambient sounds Background noise recorded asynchronously, either during production or at a different time for use during editing.

amp A unit of electrical current or rate of flow of electrons.

amplification The boosting of a signal by an apparatus that draws power from a source other than the input signal and then increases the essential features of the input.

amplitude The height of a sound wave.

analog A recording, circuit, or piece of equipment that produces an output that varies as a continuous function of the input. Analog recordings tend to degrade as material is transferred from one source to another.

anamorphic lens A lens that optically squeezes an image during filming and then unsqueezes it during projection to produce a widescreen aspect ratio.

answer print The first film print obtained from timed A-B rolls and magnetic stock; also known as a trial print.

aperture The variable opening in a lens that controls the amount of light passing through it.

arc Moving of a camera and its supporting device in a circular manner around an object.

art director A person who deals with the look of sets and other visual aspects of a movie.

ASA A rating system developed by the American Standards Association that refers to the sensitivity to light of different film stocks. See also *exposure index.*

aspect ratio The relationship of the height to the width of a picture; for example, TV screens are three units long for each four units wide, creating a 1:1.33 aspect ratio.

assemble An edit mode that transfers the control track of the source tape to the edit tape along with the image and sound during editing.

assistant director In film production, the person who does work delegated by the director, such as conducting rehearsals or directing a second unit. See also *associate director.*

assistant editor A person who helps a film editor by filing trims, taping splices together, and handling other duties.

associate director The TV production term for the person who assists the director. See also *assistant director.*

atmosphere sound General background noise recorded to add a certain feeling or sense of location to a scene.

ATR See *audiotape recorder.*

attack The amount of time it takes a sound to get from silence to full volume.

audio board A mixer used to combine various audio sources and then send them to other equipment.

audio engineer See *audio technician.*

audio frequency modulation An audio signal recorded diagonally on videotape along with the video signal so that it cannot be separated from the video; abbreviated **AFM**.

audio mixer A board used to combine various audio inputs and then send them to other equipment; a person who mixes sounds by using an audio board.

audio technician A video term for the person who records, edits, adjusts, and mixes sound; also called an **audio mixer**, or **audio engineer**.

audio tone See *tone.*

audiotape recorder A device that can be used to record, store, and play back sound; abbreviated **ATR**.

automatic dialogue replacement Rerecording dialogue that for one reason or another was not recorded properly during production; abbreviated **ADR**.

automatic focus A device that continuously alters the focus control of a lens to keep the picture sharp and clear.

automatic gain control A device that continuously alters the strength of a video or audio signal to produce the best possible picture or sound; abbreviated **AGC**.

automatic iris A device that continuously alters the diaphragm of a lens to create the best exposure possible.

axis of action The principle that places an imaginary line between two people talking or the screen direction established by a walking character or moving object. If the camera is placed on one side of this imaginary line anywhere within a 180-degree arc, spatial continuity will be maintained; if the camera is placed beyond 180 degrees, screen direction will change on the cut.

back light A spotlight placed above and behind a person or object to make it stand out from the background.

background light A light that illuminates the scenery, giving depth to the scene; also called **scenery light**.

backstory   Background material that the audience needs to know to understand the plot.

backtiming   Making the picture and sound end at the same point by timing a sound element (music or effects) so that it can be started at the right point to make a perfectly timed edit.

balance   The relative volume of different sounds or the relative weight of different portions of a picture.

balanced   Refers to cable that has three wires, one for positive, one for negative, and one for ground; also refers to a composition that has the same relative weight on both sides of the frame.

barndoor   Black metal flaps placed on a lamp or lamp housings to block part of the light beam.

barney   A soft, foamy case that dampens the noise of film cameras.

base   The part of film that serves as a support for the emulsion.

base plate   A light fixture that attaches to a flat surface to hold a light.

baselight level   The minimum amount of light needed to ensure proper exposure by a particular imaging system.

below-the-line   Refers to expenses, usually in the crafts areas, that could be associated with any movie, such as costumes, camera rental, set designers, camera operators, and transportation.

Betacam   Sony's ½-inch, professional-level video format.

Betacam SP   An improved, hence Superior Performance, version of the ½-inch, professional-level Betacam video format.

Betamax   The first ½-inch, consumer-grade video format, introduced by Sony.

bidirectional   A microphone that picks up sound from two directions.

bit players   Actors with five lines of dialogue or fewer in a movie.

black reference   Something in a scene that is at the lowest level of the brightness range the camera can reproduce.

blacking   Placing a control track on a videotape by feeding it a black signal from some source, such as a switcher or camera.

blimp   A hard camera cover that softens the noise of film cameras.

blocking   Placing actors and determining their movement within a particular shot.

blue-screen photography   A photographic process for creating different layers in a special-effects shot. An actor or object is filmed against a blue (or green) backdrop, and after lab work, cut out of the shot.

After additional lab work, the actor (or object) is inserted into a separately photographed background, producing a seamless marriage of the two image layers.

BNC connector   A bayonet-type video connector that uses a twist lock.

body brace   A device that attaches to a camera and a person's body, enabling the person to hold the camera steady.

boom   A long counterweighted pole that holds a microphone; moving a camera and what it is mounted on up and down.

boom arm   A device for mounting a lightweight light.

boom operator   The person who positions the boom microphone before and during production.

bounce light   Light reflected into a scene from a ceiling, wall, or reflector.

bracket   To shoot a scene at several different f-stops above and below what you think the actual f-stop should be.

brightness   How light or dark a particular color appears on a black-and-white television set or how much light a color reflects on a color television set.

broad   A rectangular floodlight that has an open-faced housing.

bus   One row of buttons on a switcher.

butterfly scrim   A large piece of translucent black fabric or stainless steel mesh suspended from a frame to reduce the intensity of sunlight.

call sheet   A list posted during production to let people know when and where they should report each day.

camcorder   A single unit that contains both a camera and a videocassette recorder.

camera assistant   The person assigned to help the camera operator.

camera light   A small battery-powered light mounted directly on the camera.

camera mics   Microphones built into or mounted on video cameras.

camera operator   The person who actually sets up and handles the film or video camera during production, doing such things as framing shots and focusing.

canted shot   Picture composition in which the framing is not level with the horizon.

capacitor   The element in a condenser mic that responds to sound.

capture card   A computer board used to convert an analog video signal into digital information that can be stored in the computer.

cardioid   A microphone that picks up sound in a heart-shaped pattern.

casting   Deciding who will act the various roles in a movie.

CCD   See *charge-coupled device.*

C-clamp   A clamp with a screw that locks against a pipe or other support in order to hold a light.

cement splicer   A piece of equipment that glues together two pieces of film.

center-weighted metering   A light-metering system that measures light for the entire frame but is biased toward a rather small area in the middle of the frame.

CGI   See *computer-generated imagery.*

character generator   A piece of equipment an operator uses to type letters onto a screen electronically and then store them so they can be added to video material whenever they are needed.

charge-coupled device   A solid-state imaging device (also called a chip) that translates an image into an electronic signal in a video camera; abbreviated **CCD.**

chrominance   The color characteristics of a video signal.

cinematographer   The person who has the overall responsibility of making sure all shots are properly lit and composed; also called the **director of photography** or **DP.**

clean room   A spotless room with filtered air used to cut the original negative of a film.

click book   A list or computer program that indicates to a composer how many measures of music to compose for a certain length of film and at what tempo.

close-up   A shot that isolates a subject in relation to the surroundings; abbreviated **CU.**

color balanced   Refers to the way a film stock is manufactured to produce the correct colors in different lighting conditions (such as daylight or tungsten light).

color bars   The colors red, green, blue, yellow, magenta, cyan, white, and black as shown on a monitor for test and setup purposes.

color circle   A graphic representation of which colors complement each other.

color conversion filter   A filter that converts daylight-balanced light for use with a tungsten-balanced film or electronic imaging system, or that converts tungsten-balanced light for use as daylight.

color corrector   A piece of equipment used to make subtle color changes in a video picture; sometimes called a **timer.**

color temperature   A measurement, expressed in degrees Kelvin (K), that provides color information about light. The lowest numbers are reddish, and the highest numbers are bluish.

color-compensating filter   A filter that compensates for subtle shifts in the color temperature of light.

completion guarantee   A type of insurance that covers expenses so a movie can be finished if its original funding is inadequate.

component   A video system that records luminance and chrominance information separately.

composite   A single video signal containing the picture information (chrominance and luminance) and sync information; a video recording system in which the luminance and chrominance are recorded together.

composite release print   A single strip of film holding picture and sound.

compression   A technique for placing more video and/or audio information in less space by including only elements that change from one frame or sound to another.

computer-assisted editing   An editing system that uses a computer to control the source and edit decks. Unlike a nonlinear editing system, video material is still stored on videotapes; the computer essentially takes on the role of the edit controller in a traditional linear editing system.

computer-generated imagery   Images created in the computer than can be combined with other film, video, or digitally produced images; abbreviated **CGI**.

computer graphics generator   Equipment used to manipulate lines and forms to draw graphs, alter photographs, create credits, and undertake a variety of other, art-related tasks.

concept   A brief written account of the basic idea for a story.

condenser mic   A microphone construction that is based on changes in which movement of a diaphragm results in changes in capacitance.

conform   To match the camera original of a movie to the workprint.

contact printer   A piece of equipment that prints film by running the negative and the unexposed print stock next to each other and past a light source so that the light passes through the negative and exposes the emulsion on the print stock.

continuity   Consistent and unobtrusive progression from shot to shot in terms of screen direction, lighting, props, and other production details.

continuity editing   A cutting method designed to maintain a smooth and continuous flow of time and space from one shot to the next.

contrast   The varying levels of brightness and darkness within a particular scene.

contrast range   The range of the brightest area in the scene to the darkest area in a scene.

contrast ratio   The ratio of the brightness of the key light plus the fill light to the fill light alone.

control track   Part of a videotape that contains the electronic timing impulses to keep the picture information stable.

copyright   The exclusive right to a publication or production.

costume designer   A person who plans and creates what people will wear in a movie.

countdown   Numbers (usually 10 to 2) on a tape or film just before the program material that are used for cuing.

crane   A large piece of equipment that holds the camera and its operator and moves in many directions, including up and down; moving the camera and its supporting device up or down.

cross-cutting   Editing back and forth from one location to another or one story line to another in order to imply that the two actions are taking place simultaneously; also called **parallel editing** or **intercutting**.

cross-fade   To gradually bring in one sound while another is gradually fading out.

crystal   The crystal-controlled timing element in film cameras and audiotape recorders that allows both to run at the same speed without a connecting cable.

CU   See *close-up*.

cue sheets   Vertical lists that indicate when each sound of a movie should be brought in and taken out during the mix.

cutaway   A shot of someone or something not directly visible in the previous shot. It is frequently used to show some related detail or reaction to the main action.

cut-in   A cut to a shot that isolates some element in the previous shot.

cuts-only   A form of editing that only places one piece of material after another. It cannot involve dissolves or other transitions.

cutting-on-action   Refers to shots edited so that action begins in the first shot and is completed in the second.

dailies   The unedited workprint of a film that comes from the lab each day, allowing the director and others to view their work before the next day's shooting.

daily production report   A report, usually on a standardized form, that tells what was accomplished during each day of production.

DAT   See *digital audiotape*.

DAW   See *digital audio workstation*.

day-for-night   Shooting during the day but making it look as though the footage were shot at night.

dB   Abbreviation for **decibel**.

DC   Direct current; usually used to refer to battery power.

DCC   See *digital compact cassette*.

decay   The time it takes a sound to go from full volume to silence.

decibel   A measurement of noise or loudness; abbreviated **dB**.

degausser   Electromagnetic equipment that erases tape by lining up all the iron particles.

depth of field   The area in which objects located at different distances from the camera remain in focus.

dialogue   Words spoken by characters in the movie.

diaphragm   The adjustable ring of a lens that opens and closes to allow more or less light to pass; an element in a microphone that vibrates to create electronic impulses in the form of sound.

dichroic filters   Blue filters that convert tungsten-balanced lamps to daylight balance.

dichroic mirror   A filterlike mirror that reflects certain colors and allows others to pass through; used in some cameras to separate the incoming light into its red, blue, and green components.

diegetic sound   Sound that comes from within the story space.

diffusion filter   A filter that scatters light, making for a softer, less detailed picture.

digital   Refers to a recording, circuit, or piece of equipment in which the output varies in discrete on-off steps so that it can be reproduced without generation loss.

digital audio workstation   Computer equipment that can be used to record, create, store, edit, and mix sounds, all in digital form; abbreviated **DAW**.

digital audiotape   A high-quality audiocassette format that records diagonally; abbreviated **DAT**.

digital compact cassette   A high-quality audiocassette format that is compatible with standard analog audiocassettes; abbreviated **DCC**.

digital composite   An image composed of different layers or elements that are combined together in the digital domain.

digital creep   The gradual switching, by individuals and companies, from analog equipment to digital equipment.

digital sampler   Equipment that manipulates sounds by varying such characteristics as speed and volume so that one sound can be made to sound like something else.

digitize   The process of converting a film or video image into digital form.

dimmer board   A device that reduces the intensity of light by varying the voltage supplied to the lighting instruments.

direct sound   Sound that does not bounce and therefore sounds dead.

directionality   A microphone's ability to pick up sound from a variety of locations.

director   The person responsible for the overall creative aspects of a motion picture.

director of photography   The person responsible for making sure all shots of a movie are properly lit and composed; abbreviated **DP**; also called **cinematographer.**

director's cut   The edited version of a film that includes the suggestions made by the director.

disk array   Several hard drives linked together to create a large storage medium. See also *redundant array of independent disks.*

dissolve   The gradual fading in of one picture while another is gradually fading out.

distortion   Muddy audio caused by recording a sound at a higher volume than the equipment can handle.

dolly   A wheeled cart used to move a camera during shooting; moving a camera and its supporting device forward or backward.

dot   A round piece of metal or cloth that can be placed between a light and a subject to create shadows or keep light from reaching certain surfaces.

double system   A method of recording the sound on one piece of equipment and the picture on another.

double-fog filter   A filter that scatters light from bright areas to shadow areas without reducing the sharpness of the picture.

DP   See *director of photography.*

drop-frame time code   A time code that is adjusted so that the frame rate of 29.97 per second reads out at 30 frames per second.

dropout compensator   A piece of equipment used to fill in bits of video signal where imperfections in the oxide leave small unrecorded portions on the audiotape or videotape.

dropouts   Areas where imperfections in the oxide leave small unrecorded portions on the audiotape or videotape.

dub   A copy of a videotape or audiotape; also the process used to make a copy of a tape.

duration   The length of time a particular sound lasts.

dusk-for-night   Shooting at twilight in order to create the effect of shooting at night.

dynamic mic   A microphone that creates an electrical current based on the motion of a diaphragm attached to a movable coil suspended in a magnetic field.

dynamic range   The degree of loudness and softness that a piece of equipment can accommodate.

echo   Sound that has bounced off a surface once.

edge numbers   Numbers along the side of film used to synchronize and to conform the workprint, camera original, and/or sound.

edit controller   The piece of equipment used to mark the editing points and cue the recorders used to execute the editing decisions.

edit decision list   A step-by-step list of each video edit (usually based on SMPTE time code) to be made, along with a description of the material, including the reel numbers involved, whether the edit is to be a cut or a dissolve, and the duration of the edit; abbreviated **EDL.**

edit deck   The VCR onto which material is recorded.

edit stop   A button on the edit controller that terminates an edit.

edit-in point   The precise location where an edit is to begin.

editor   The person who cuts together the picture and principal dialogue of a movie.

editor's script   A script prepared by the script supervisor for the editor that includes information about each shot as well as the changes made in the script during production.

edit-out point   The precise location where an edit is to end.

EDL   See *edit decision list.*

EI   See *exposure index.*

electret condenser mic   A type of condenser mic with a permanently charged backplate.

electromagnetic spectrum   The continuous frequency range of wavelengths that includes radio waves and light waves.

electron gun   The part of the TV tube that shoots electrons to the target, where they scan the information that becomes the video signal.

electronic image stabilization   A camera feature that makes for steadier shots by digitally magnifying part of an image and tracking it as the camera moves.

emulsion   The film layer containing the light-sensitive materials that record the image.

encoder   Part of a video system that recombines the red, green, and blue chrominance signals with the luminance signal.

equalization   Emphasizing, lessening, or eliminating certain audio frequencies.

establishing shot   A shot that orients the audience to a change in location or time.

executive producer   The person who oversees a number of different movie projects.

exposure index   A measure of the speed or light sensitivity of a film, like the ASA numbers; abbreviated **EI.**

extendable lighting pole   A device for mounting a lightweight light.

extras   People who are part of the atmosphere of a movie but do not have any distinguishable lines.

eyelight   A small focusable light placed near the camera to add sparkle to a person's eyes.

eyeline match   Matching two shots so that a person appears to be looking at the right person or in the right direction.

fade   To go gradually from a picture to black or from black to a picture; also, to go gradually from silence to sound or sound to silence.

fade-in   To go gradually from black to a picture; to go gradually from silence to sound.

fade-out   To go gradually from a picture to black; to go gradually from sound to silence.

fast film stock   Film that is very sensitive to light but does not record a particularly rich range of grays or a sharp image.

fast lens   A lens that can transmit a large amount of light. A fast lens requires less light than a slow lens.

field   Half of a frame that contains a scan of the odd-numbered lines or the even-numbered lines of the 525 lines of a TV image.

fill light   Light that reduces the shadows and high-contrast range created by the key light; a lighting instrument, typically open-faced, used for fill lighting.

film bin   A big container in which film shots are hung during editing.

film splicer   A piece of equipment used to cut and join together pieces of film.

film-style lighting   Setting up a new lighting scheme for virtually every shot.

filter   A glass or gelatin that alters light.

filter factor   The degree of light exposure compensation needed for a particular type of filter.

filter wheel   The part of a video camera that allows the operator to select the correct filter for different lighting conditions.

final cut   The last edited version of a film or videotape.

finger   A long thin piece of metal or opaque material that can be placed between a light and a subject to create shadows or keep the light from reaching certain surfaces.

fishpole   A type of mic boom that consists of a simple pole held by an operator.

fixed lens A lens of a single focal length, as opposed to a lens (such as a zoom lens) with a variable focal length; also called a **prime lens.**

flag A rectangular piece of metal or opaque material placed between a light and a subject to create shadows or keep the light from reaching certain surfaces.

flashback Portrayal of events that happened before events already shown.

flash cut A shot of just a few frames, the effect of which is almost subliminal, that can be used to present a brief image from the past or future.

flashforward A cut forward to portray events in the future before returning to the point in the movie at which the time shift began.

flashing A film process for reducing contrast that involves exposing the film to a low light level before it has been exposed in the camera or before it is processed.

flat In audio, term describes frequencies picked up equally well; in lighting, used to describe placement of lights so that there are very few shadows.

flatbed An electrically powered film editing machine that is in a horizontal configuration.

flood To adjust a variable focus lighting instrument to the position that allows it to cover a broad area.

floodlight A diffused light that covers a wide area.

floor stand A pole device that rests on the floor and is used to hold a microphone.

fluid head A mounting device on which a camera is placed that allows for smooth operation because it uses hydraulic resistance.

flying erase head A moving erase head located in front of a record head on a VCR for making a clean edit.

flying spot scanner A machine that produces a high-quality transfer of the film image to videotape and does not pull on the film.

focal length The distance from the optical center of the lens to the point in the camera where the image is in focus.

focus To make an image look sharp and clear.

fog filter A filter that scatters light from bright areas to areas with shadow, thereby lowering contrast and sharpness.

Foley The recording of sounds such as rustling dresses and footsteps in sync with the picture; the room where this activity takes place.

Foley walkers People who create the sounds in a Foley room.

footcandle The amount of light that is present 1 foot from a source of 1 candlepower.

forced development See *pushed processing.*

formats The specific size and/or characteristics of particular film or video systems (for example, 35mm, Super 8, VHS, U-Matic, Hi-8).

frame In film, a single picture within a motion picture; in TV, one complete scan, from top to bottom, of the 525 lines (composed of two fields) of video information.

frame accurate Refers to video editing systems that consistently execute an edit to the exact frame desired.

frame counter Part of an editing controller or VCR or other piece of equipment that displays the time code or control track numbers.

frame store A piece of equipment that stores a whole frame of video so that it can be manipulated digitally.

freeze-frame To stop (that is, freeze) the action on one frame of film or video. In video, this can be accomplished in a variety of ways, using digital video effects equipment or still-frame storage units. In film, a freeze-frame is created in the lab during printing.

frequency A measurement of wave movement expressed in cycles per second (hertz).

frequency curve A line indicating how well a particular piece of equipment picks up different sound frequencies.

frequency response The range of sound frequencies that a particular piece of electronic equipment is capable of reproducing.

Fresnel spotlight A light with a well-defined lens. The beam width is varied as the bulb is moved toward and away from the lens.

friction head A tripod head that uses a spring or sliding mechanism to control its movement.

front focus Focusing the elements of a zoom lens so that the image will stay in focus throughout the zoom range.

f-stops Numbers that indicate the setting of the lens aperture.

fundamental Refers to the main frequency of a particular sound.

gaffer A person who directs others on how to position and plug in lights on a set.

gaffer grip A spring-loaded clamp that can secure a light almost anywhere; also called an **alligator clamp.**

gaffer tape Strong adhesive tape used primarily for securing lighting equipment.

gain The amount of amplification an audio or video signal receives.

gangs Multiple tracks on a synchronizer that hold two to six rolls of film and/or magnetic stock in a constant relationship.

gelatin filter A filter made of gelatin that is placed over lenses, lights, or windows or in filter holders placed between the lens and the imaging device.

generation loss A deterioration of picture or sound caused by dubbing material from one tape to another.

glass filter A filter that has gel cemented between two pieces of glass, or dye laminated between two pieces of glass, or dyes added to the glass during manufacture.

graduated neutral density filter A filter that darkens only part of a frame, usually the top.

grips People who do physical labor on a shoot, such as carrying set pieces, pushing dollies, and handling cables.

hard effects Sound effects that are synchronous with the picture.

hard light Light that has a narrow angle of illumination and produces sharp, clearly defined shadows.

harmonics Pitches that are part of an overall sound and are exact multiples of the fundamental frequency of that sound.

haze filter A filter that eliminates the bluish cast on overcast days.

HDTV See *high-definition television.*

head A device placed between a tripod and a camera that allows the camera to pivot smoothly; magnetic elements that can erase, record, or play information on or from a videotape or audiotape.

headroom The amount of space above a character's head in a particular framing configuration.

hertz A frequency measurement of 1 cycle per second; abbreviated **Hz.**

hidden editing See *invisible editing.*

hidden mics Microphones placed in the set so they cannot be seen.

Hi-8 An improvement on the Sony Video-8 format that uses metal particle tape and a wider luminance band.

hi-fi A frequency modulated audio signal that is recorded diagonally on videotape along with the video signal in such a way that it cannot be separated from the video signal in editing.

high hat A camera mounting device that is close to the ground because it consists of a board on top of very short legs.

high-angle shot A shot taken from above, looking down on a scene.

high-definition television TV that scans more than 1,000 lines per frame and has an aspect ratio wider than 1:1.33; abbreviated **HDTV.**

high-key lighting Lighting that is generally bright and even, with a low key-to-fill ratio.

hiss A distracting high-frequency noise often inherent in low-quality audiotape.

HMI light   Hydrogen medium-arc-length iodide lamp that is daylight balanced and therefore used to supplement the sun as a light source.

horizontal blanking interval   The period of time during which the electron beam of a camera or receiver tube is turned off so that it can move from the right side of the screen to the left side of the screen to begin scanning another line.

horizontal resolution   The common way of describing a video camera's ability to distinguish fine detail in a picture; the number of vertical lines per millimeter that can be distinguished by a camera imaging device or a TV receiver.

hot splicer   A piece of equipment with a heating element that uses glue to join together two pieces of film. The heating element speeds drying.

hue   The specific tint of a color.

hypercardioid   Refers to a microphone that picks up in an extreme heart-shaped pattern.

Hz   The abbreviation for **hertz.**

image enhancer   A piece of equipment that corrects for the loss of sharpness and the smearing of color that result from a video image being taken apart and recorded.

image layering   Building up the final composite image element by element.

imaging device   The part of a camera on which the image gathered by the lens is focused.

impedance   A characteristic that refers to the opposition a sound signal encounters as it goes through a system.

incandescent light   A lamp that contains a tungsten filament sealed in a vacuum tube that heats up and produces light when an electric current is passed through it.

incident light meter   An instrument that measures the amount of light falling on the meter.

insert   A method of video editing in which the control track is laid down on the edit tape first and then audio and video information only (not control track) are laid down from the source deck; audio and video can be split during the editing process.

interactive media   Presentations in which the content can be controlled to some extent by the person using them; usually, the person can use a keyboard, mouse, or remote control to select the options.

intercutting   Editing back and forth from one location to another or one story line to another in order to imply that the two actions

are taking place simultaneously; also called **cross-cutting** or **parallel editing.**

interlaced scanning   Combining two video fields in one frame to reduce flicker.

interlock   The projection of a film or video workprint in sync with all its sound tracks so that all the sound elements can be checked to make sure they occur at the right points; also referred to as **lock-up.**

internal reflector spotlight   A bulb with a reflector unit and focusing lens built into it.

inverse square rule   The principle that states that light intensity decreases by the square of the distance from the subject.

invisible editing   A process that attempts to mask edits and make them unobtrusive; also called **hidden editing.**

iris   The adjustable metal diaphragm of a lens that can be opened and closed to allow more or less light to pass through.

jib-arm   A cranelike counterweighted mounting device for raising or lowering a camera.

jump cut   A distracting break in continuity caused by a mismatch in object position, screen direction, action, setting, or other production details.

Kelvin   The scale in degrees for measuring color temperature.

key light   The main source of light in a typical lighting setup, usually a spotlight set above the subject and to the front and side.

keyframe   A representative frame from a shot that can be captured in a nonlinear editing system and used in the editing process.

Keykode   Eastman Kodak's system for marking film so that the negative can be cut accurately; it identifies frames with a bar code that can be related to a time code for electronic editing purposes.

kicker light   A light placed low and behind a subject in order to provide more separation of the subject from the background.

LAN   See *local area network.*

latitude   The difference, expressed as an amount, between the brightest and darkest areas that can be faithfully reproduced by a particular film stock or video imaging system.

lavaliere   A small microphone, usually attached to a person's clothing.

layback   To place the final mixed audio on the master videotape.

laydown   To record production dialogue digitally on a ¾-inch tape so that it can be conformed to the picture later.

layering   Blending various sounds so that each is given its proper emphasis or deemphasis.

leader   Material that appears on a videotape before the program material; usually con-

sists of color bars, tone, a slate, and a countdown.

leadroom   The space to the side of the frame that is in front of someone or something that is moving.

lens   The part of the camera that gathers light and focuses the image.

lens hood   A cover built into or attached to a lens to keep stray light out.

light meter   An instrument used to measure the amount of light falling on or reflected from a subject.

light stand   A device that holds lights. It consists of a tripod base and a pole that can be telescoped.

light-balancing filter   A filter that makes a slight shift in the color temperature of light.

lighting crew   The people who set up and position lights in a TV studio or at a remote location.

lighting director   In TV, the person in charge of setting up the lights in a studio or at a remote location.

lighting plot   A diagram showing the camera position, the set, and the location, size, type, and direction of the lighting instruments.

lighting ratio   The ratio of key light plus fill to fill light alone.

line inputs   Jacks built into equipment for connecting tape recorders, turntables, and other pieces of equipment (but not microphones).

line producer   The person who represents the producer on the set and makes sure all is being accomplished on time and within budget.

linear   Refers to video material edited together in sequence from beginning to end.

linear audio   The track along the edge of the videotape on which sound can be recorded. Time code also can be recorded in this area.

linear CCD array   A film transfer device using two different sets of CCDs (one following another) to scan the image. The first device (with four separate sensors) scans only the luminance information; the second device contains three CCDs, one each for the red, green, and blue information. Together they produce a very high resolution image with an excellent signal-to-noise ratio.

linear track   The audio track on a videotape that runs horizontally near the bottom or top of the tape.

local area network   An interconnect for a group of computers (usually in one building) so they can all access and share the same information; abbreviated **LAN.**

lock-up   See *interlock.*

log   A list of all the shots, in the order they are taken, and a description of each shot.

long lens   A lens with a long focal length that magnifies a subject and foreshortens distances.

long shot   A shot that emphasizes the surroundings and the subject's placement in them; abbreviated **LS.**

longitudinal time code   Time code laid down on an audio channel.

look space   See *noseroom.*

looping   An old term for **automatic dialogue replacement.**

low-angle shot   A shot for which the camera is positioned low and angled up at the subject.

low-contrast filter   A filter that scatters light in a scene so that it brightens shadows but does not reduce sharpness.

low-key lighting   Lighting that is dark and shadowy with a high key-to-fill ratio.

low-light sensitivity   The ability of a camera to produce an acceptable image with minimal illumination.

LS   See *long shot.*

luminance   Pertaining to the brightness characteristics of a video signal.

lux   The amount of light 1 meter from a source of 1 candlepower; 1 lux is roughly one-tenth of 1 footcandle.

macro   A setting on a lens that allows it to focus on objects very close to the front element of the lens.

magazine   A lightproof device containing film that is placed on the camera.

magnetic film stock   A sprocketed audiotape used in film editing that has the same dimensions and moves at the same speed as the film.

master scene script   The final script for a movie, set up much as the script for a stage play, describing all the dialogue and action but without individual shot designations (as in a shooting script).

master scene shot   A shot that covers an entire scene from an angle wide enough to establish all the major elements.

match cut   A cut that provides a continuous sense of time and space between two shots.

matte box   An adjustable bellows that attaches to the front of the camera and extends beyond the lens to hold filters or mattes that cut off part of the image; also called a filter box.

Media Record Telecine   A special type of film transfer system designed to convert film material directly into digital information; abbreviated **MRT.**

medium shot   A shot that gives a sense of the subject and the subject's surroundings; abbreviated **MS.**

M-format   The professional-level ½-inch video format of JVC and other companies.

MIDI   See *musical instrument digital interface.*

M-II   An improvement on the ½-inch professional-level M-format video format.

midside miking   A stereo pickup method that combines bidirectional and supercardioid microphones. Also called **M-S miking.**

mic inputs   Jacks built into equipment for connecting microphones. See also *line inputs.*

Mini Disc   A recordable audio compact disk developed by Sony.

minicassettes   Small videocassettes used for field recording in some formats.

miniphone plug   A small audio connector most commonly found in consumer-level equipment.

mise-en-scène   A theatrical term that describes the placement of scenery and actors. In film and TV it refers to the director's control of such elements as lighting, sets, locations, props, makeup, costumes, and blocking and direction of actors; in other words, it refers to everything that can be controlled before the camera comes into play.

mix   See *sound mix.*

mixed lighting   Lighting that contains daylight and artificial light.

mixer   An audio board that combines audio from various sources and then sends it to other equipment; a person who mixes sounds by using an audio board.

modulate   To vary the amplitude, frequency, or phase of a wavelength by impressing it on another wavelength that has constant properties.

monaural   Single-channel audio.

monitor   A TV set that does not receive off-air signals but can receive line-level signals straight from a camera or a VCR.

mono   See *monaural.*

montage editing   Editing built on the relationships of the material being edited, such as size, theme, or symbolism, rather than its continuity.

morphing   Gradually changing one video or film form into another, such as a man into a beast.

motif   A particular musical refrain that follows a character or event throughout a movie.

MRT   See *media record telecine.*

MS   See *medium shot.*

M-S miking   See *midside miking.*

multimedia   Information combining at least two formats, such as still graphics and video, usually requiring the use of a computer.

multipin connector   A connector that carries a number of signals between a camera and a VCR or between a monitor and a VCR.

multitrack audiotape recorder   An audiotape recorder that can record and play back a large number (usually four, eight, sixteen, or twenty-four) of signals on separate channels.

musical instrument digital interface   A communication system that allows musical instruments and other electronic gear, such as digital audio workstations, to interact; abbreviated **MIDI.**

negative   A photographic image that reverses the light values; in color, every color is reproduced as its complement; in black and white, dark areas are recorded as light and light areas are recorded as dark.

neutral density filter   A filter that reduces the amount of light reaching the imaging device without affecting the color in any way.

neutral density gelatins   Large pieces of gelatin, usually hung over windows to reduce the strength of the light.

night-for-night   Shooting at night in order to create the look of night.

noise   Any type of unwanted audio or video interference.

nondestructive editing   Digital sound editing that does not physically alter or damage the original sound recording.

nondiegetic sound   Sound that is from outside the story space, such as the musical score.

non-drop-frame time code   Time code that reads thirty frames as thirty frames, without any counting adjustments.

nonlinear   Refers to video material that can be edited without having to lay one shot after another: the end can be edited before the beginning.

normal lens   A lens with a focal length that shows objects approximately as they appear to the eye.

noseroom   The space to the side of a frame at which a person is looking; sometimes called **look space.**

off-line   Video editing that uses workprints rather than original footage.

off-screen space   Areas beyond the edge of the screen and to the front and rear of the frame that can be used to imply that an action or a sound is coming from somewhere just beyond the visible picture area.

ohms   A measurement of impedance.

omnidirectional   A microphone that picks up from all sides.

180-degree rule   The principle that places an imaginary line between two people talking, or the screen direction established by a walking character or moving object. If the camera is placed to one side of this imaginary line and anywhere within a 180-degree arc, spatial continuity will be maintained; if the camera is placed beyond 180 degrees, screen direction will change.

on-line   Refers to editing that uses original material and actually puts all edits onto a finished master tape.

on-set editing   Using a portable nonlinear editing system during production to assemble a rough edit. This enables directors to see if they have shot adequate coverage and helps maintain continuity.

open casting   General auditions that anyone can come to in order to try to obtain a part in a movie.

optical center   The part of a lens where the image is turned upside down so that it can be sent to the imaging device.

optical printer   A piece of equipment that prints film by projecting the camera original onto unexposed film stock.

optical sound track   A visual representation of film sound that runs along the side of the film and depends on the modulation of a beam of light.

OS   See *over-the-shoulder shot.*

outboard equipment   Equipment such as CD players and tape recorders that feeds into an audio board.

outtakes   Material shot but not used in the final movie.

overlap cutting   Editing sound and dialogue so that the actor's lines are heard while something else appears on the screen.

overlapping action   A method of shooting film or tape in which some of the action in one shot is repeated when the next shot is recorded. The technique is used to provide the editor with options.

overmodulation   A signal recorded at a level higher than the system can handle, resulting in distorted sound.

over-the-shoulder shot   A shot that looks from behind the shoulder of one character toward another character or object; abbreviated **OS**.

overtones   Pitches that are part of an overall sound that may or may not be exact multiples of the fundamental frequency of that sound.

pan   Moving the camera left or right on a tripod or by hand.

PAR lights   Parabolic aluminized reflectors, which have a reflector unit and focusing lens built into the bulb.

parabolic reflector   A lamp housing that produces a concentrated beam of hard light.

parallel editing   Cutting back and forth from one location to another or one story line to another, usually to show that two actions are occurring simultaneously but sometimes to compare or contrast two actions; also called **cross-cutting** and **intercutting**.

PCM   Pulse code modulation; a digital audio signal that is recorded diagonally on videotape and is separate from the video.

peaking in the red   Recording sound at such a high volume that the needle of the volume unit meter is almost always in the red area.

pedestal   The control on a time-base corrector or other piece of video gear that sets the darkest level. Normally, this level is set to 7.5 percent on a waveform monitor.

perspective   The spatial relationships established in regard to some source (audio or visual) within the picture.

phase   The relationship of one sound wave to another, expressed in time; waves are *in phase* if they are at the same point in their cycles at the same time; they are *out of phase* if they are at different points.

phone plug   A long slender audio connector often used for microphones and headphones.

phono plug   A connector with a short prong and outer covering; also called an **RCA plug** or **RCA connector**.

photoflood   An inexpensive artificial light that uses bulbs that look somewhat like normal household bulbs.

pickup pattern   The particular directions from which a microphone gathers sound.

pickup tube   A vacuum tube that creates the image within a tube video camera.

picon (picture icon)   A selectable frame used to identify a shot in a nonlinear editing system. The frame is displayed as picture icon, and depending on the editing system, can be dragged to a timeline or brought onto the screen. See also *keyframe.*

pitch   How high or low a particular sound is in terms of frequency.

pixels   Light-sensitive picture elements.

point-of-view shot   A shot that shows a scene as a particular character in the movie would see it; abbreviated **POV**.

polarizing filter   A filter used to minimize reflections by influencing the angle of the light between the lens and a shiny surface.

positive   Film that produces an image with lights and shades corresponding to those of the subject.

postproduction   The stage of moviemaking that occurs after the shooting and that includes the editing and sound building.

POV   See *point-of-view shot.*

practical light   A light, such as a table lamp or lighting fixture, that is visible in a scene.

premix   Certain sounds, such as multiple sound effects, mixed together before the final sound mix is undertaken.

preproduction   The stage of moviemaking that involves making the decisions, plans, and budget for production and postproduction.

preroll   The time during which VCRs get up to a stable speed during the editing process.

presence   The authenticity of a sound in terms of perceived distance and fidelity.

prime lens   A single-focal-length lens; also called a **fixed lens**.

principal actors   The people who have the main speaking parts in a movie, usually the leads and the supporting cast.

print-through   When an audio signal on one layer of tape seeps through to the layer of tape above or below it.

print to tape   Copying the output of a nonlinear editing system directly to videotape.

prism block   A device in a camera that breaks incoming light down into the primary reds, blues, and greens present in a particular video image.

producer   The person who is in overall charge of a particular movie, especially the schedule and money.

producer's cut   The edited version of a film that includes the suggestions made by the producer.

production   The stage of moviemaking during which all picture and principal sound are shot.

production assistant   A person who performs a variety of general tasks during the production phase of moviemaking.

production designer   The person whose job it is to make sure the overall look of the film is consistent.

production manager   The person who breaks down a script and handles much of the scheduling and detail work of preproduction and production; also called the **unit manager** or **unit production manager**.

production schedule   A detailing of the lengths of time allocated for preproduction, production, and postproduction and what should occur during each phase.

props   Items that are necessary to the plot of a movie.

proximity effect   A phenomenon produced by certain microphones wherein low frequencies are boosted when someone speaks close to the mic.

public domain   The legal condition covering copyright that states that when material is a certain age, it can be used without having to obtain permission.

pulling focus   Manually changing the focus of a lens as a shot is in progress.

pulse code modulation   See *PCM*.

pushed processing   Increasing the developing time when film is processed so that underexposed film receives more exposure. The effect of forced development is to increase film speed; it is also called **forced development.**

quadraphonic   Sound that picks up and reproduces through four separate channels.

quartz lamp   See *tungsten-halogen lamp.*

quartz-halogen lamp   See *tungsten-halogen lamp.*

rack focus   To change focus from one object or area in a frame to another during the course of a shot.

radio frequency   The carrier wavelength on which audio and video signals are superimposed; abbreviated **RF.**

RAID   See *redundant array of independent disks.*

RAM   See *random-access memory.*

random access   The ability to bring up audio or video material instantly, in any order, such as from a disk, without having to wait for tapes to rewind.

random-access memory   Resident memory in a computer that can emulate a very fast temporary disk drive; commonly referred to as **RAM.**

RCA connector   See *phono plug.*

RCA plug   See *phono plug.*

reaction shot   A shot that shows someone responding or reacting to what someone else is saying or doing.

record deck   The VCR onto which material is edited after receiving the signal from the source deck.

redundant array of independent disks   A technique for linking two or more hard drives together to increase data storage capacity, reliability, and performance at the level required for multimedia applications, such as digital video; abbreviated **RAID.**

reel-to-reel   An audiotape recorder that requires the tape be threaded from one side to the other from open reels.

reflected light meter   An instrument that measures the amount of light bounced off a subject.

reflector   A light-colored surface used for bouncing light back into a scene; often used for fill lighting outdoors.

reframing   Slightly adjusting the composition of a shot as characters change position.

release print   The final print of a film, the one that is shown in movie theaters.

render   The often slow, CPU-intensive process of creating multilayered graphics, animations, transitions, or effects in the computer. Building-up video, audio, and/or graphic elements frame-by-frame can be very time consuming.

resolution   The degree to which fine detail in the image can be distinguished.

resolving unit   A piece of equipment that uses the sync pulses recorded on ¼-inch audiotape to transfer the sound to magnetic stock so that it can be edited in sync with the filmed picture.

reverb   See *reverberation.*

reverberation   Sound that has bounced a number of times or has been processed so that it sounds like it has bounced.

reversal   Camera film that produces a positive print when it is developed.

rewinds   Two arms that hold the feed and take-up reels of film while they are on the editing bench.

RF   See *radio frequency.*

RF connector   A connector used to play back both picture and sound through an ordinary TV set.

Richter   Shaky camera movement done on purpose.

riding in the mud   Recording sound at too low a level, one in which the needle of the volume unit meter is usually below 20 percent.

ripple   In an edit decision list, the effect produced by one change in an edit number, which automatically changes all the edit numbers that follow.

RMAG   A removable hard drive. Often used in conjunction with nonlinear editing systems, the hard drives storing the digital information are encased in a portable magazine that can be transported from machine to machine.

rock 'n' roll   Starting a scene with a series of long shots that move about a great deal as though someone was moving his or her head to see the whole area.

room simulators   Pieces of equipment that can imitate the room tone of rooms of various sizes.

room tone   The noise or the general ambience where a movie is being shot, recorded during production to be used as background during editing.

rough cut   A loose assemblage of the pictures and dialogue of what will eventually become the edited master of a movie.

rule of thirds   The principle that states that to make composition more dynamic, it is better to try to break a frame into thirds rather than halves.

saturation   The intensity or purity of a color.

scanning   The process by which the TV image is picked up and reproduced. It involves moving an electron beam very rapidly left to right and up and down on the TV screen.

scene   A shot or series of shots, usually presenting a unified action and occurring in a single place and time.

scene number   The number of a particular scene as shown on the master scene script; scene numbers often are followed by letters (*A, B, C*) labeling particular shots within a scene.

scene outline   A list in numerical order of all the scenes in a screenplay with a barebones description of what occurs in each scene.

scenery light   See *background light.*

scoop   A floodlight that contains a single bulb in a bowl-shaped metal reflector.

screen direction   The spatial relationship established by composition or movement within the frame.

screen test   The filming or taping of actors to see how they will come across in general or in particular roles.

scrim   A translucent black fabric or a stainless steel mesh used to reduce light intensity.

script breakdown   A list of all essential elements of each scene, such as whether it is interior or exterior, the time of day it is supposed to take place, and the actors and props needed.

script breakdown sheets   The forms on which script breakdowns are written.

script clerk   See *script supervisor.*

script supervisor   The person in charge of seeing that all parts of the script are actually shot and that continuity is maintained; sometimes called a **script clerk.**

scrubbing   A feature available in many nonlinear editing programs that allows the user to hear or see an audio or video file as the mouse drags through it.

search dial   The dial on an editing controller that allows the operator to find particular points on a tape by shuttling at various speeds.

second unit   A group of production people who shoot scenes that do not involve the principal actors while those actors are involved in the main production.

SEG   See *special-effects generator.*

separation light   A light that enhances the modeling and three-dimensional effect of the three-point lighting system.

sequence A group of scenes linked together or unified by some common theme, idea, or action.

set decorations Items that give an overall feel to a scene but are not essential to the plot.

set designer The person who plans and makes drawings that define the look and needs of any location areas built specially for a movie.

shock mount A device that keeps a mic stable, even if the pole it is on is moved.

shooting schedule A list of what is to be accomplished during each day of production.

shooting script The director's breakdown of a master scene script into individual shots with particular camera angles, movements, or positions.

short lens A lens with a short focal length that makes objects appear smaller and farther apart than they appear to the naked eye; also called a **wide-angle lens.**

shot An element of a movie that begins when the camera starts running during production and ends when it stops running.

shotgun mic A microphone with a long, narrow pickup pattern that is used to gather sound from a great distance.

shot/reaction shot An editing pattern that cuts from some action or event to a character's response to it.

shot/reverse shot An editing pattern in which shots in succession mirror the framing of each other.

shoulder mount A device attached to the camera so that it rides comfortably on a person's shoulder.

shutter speed The amount of time per frame during which light is allowed to reach the imaging device.

signal-to-noise ratio The amount of desired audio or video a piece of equipment picks up in relation to the amount of unwanted electronic disturbance it picks up; abbreviated **S/N.**

single system A method of recording sound and picture on the same medium.

sky filter A filter that blocks out haze for black-and-white photography.

slate A tablet that provides pertinent information about a shot. It is held in front of a camera and recorded just before a shot is started. Also, an identification on a tape that precedes program material, listing such information as the length of the program and the director's name.

slate clap The sound of a wooden flag hitting the top of the slate. It is recorded on the audio during filming and later is used to synchronize picture and sound.

slow film stock Film that is not very sensitive to light but reproduces a rich range of grays and a sharp image.

slow lens A lens that cannot transmit a large amount of light. A slow lens requires more light than a fast lens.

SMPTE time code Numbers recorded on tape that can be shown on a screen or displayed on the editor to indicate the particular address of the audio and the video in terms of hours, minutes, seconds, and frames.

S/N See *signal-to-noise ratio.*

snoot A metal funnel that restricts a light beam to a circular pattern.

soft light Gentle, diffused, shadowless lighting.

soft-contrast filter A filter that reduces contrast but preserves fairly dark shadows.

softlight reflector A lamp housing (reflector) that blocks the light coming directly from the lamp and bounces it back into and off the reflector's surface.

softlights Lighting instruments that produce diffused light.

sound editor A person who spots, acquires, and edits such sounds as sound effects and room tone.

sound effects Noises that accompany what is happening on the screen, either synchronously or asynchronously.

sound flashback The use of particular dialogue, music, or other sound to indicate within a movie something that happened in the past.

sound flashforward Particular dialogue, music, or other sound used to indicate within a movie something that happens in the future.

sound mix The final joining together in a single recording all the sound elements of a movie so that they relate properly and are at the correct volume.

sound mixer The person who records sounds, blending them together as appropriate.

source deck The VCR that supplies the video image and/or sound to the record deck during video editing.

source lighting Lighting that mimics the direction and source of the light that might actually be in the scene, such as sunlight that might be coming through a window or a streetlight in a dark alley.

special-effects generator A piece of digital equipment that generates such special effects as wipes and starbursts; abbreviated **SEG.**

speech bump The phenomenon that allows a microphone to pick up speech frequencies better than other frequencies.

split-page A type of script often used for nonnarrative movies that lists video elements in a column opposite another column of audio elements.

spot To determine where sound effects, ambient sounds, automatic dialogue replacement, Foley, or music should occur within a movie; focusing the rays of a lighting instrument to a narrower, more concentrated pattern.

spot meter A special type of reflected light meter that measures the light coming from a very narrow angle of view.

spotlight A concentrated light that covers a narrow area. It usually provides some means for varying the angle of the illumination by moving the bulb within the housing.

spotting The process of deciding where music, sound effects, and other sounds should go in the movie.

spotting sheet A paper compiled by a sound editor that indicates at what point in a movie sound effects, ambient sounds, automatic dialogue replacement, Foley, or music should occur.

sprocket holes Holes at the edge of film used to keep the film moving evenly through a camera, editing equipment, or projector.

standby A switch on a camera that allows the camera's circuitry and tube to preheat without using full power.

stand-ins People who replace principal actors in a scene when equipment needs to be set up or changed.

star filter A special type of diffusion filter that turns a bright point of light in a scene into a bright star pattern.

Steadicam A counterweighted camera mounting device that allows extremely smooth hand-held camera operation.

stereo Sound that picks up and reproduces through two separate channels to simulate the way the ears hear.

still frame A picture that looks frozen in that nothing in it moves.

storyboard Drawings that show the main actions of a movie; in video editing, the pictures on the computer edit screen that show a frame grabbed from each shot being used.

straight cut A transition in which one shot is instantaneously replaced by the next.

streamer A marking that shows where on film or videotape music is to begin and end.

strike To tear down and clean up after shooting.

string-out A loosely edited assembly of all the film and sound to be used in a particular scene or sequence.

stripboard A large board that summarizes the scenes, locations, and actors needed for each day of movie production.

sun gun A battery-powered light, typically hand-held, that provides flat, straight-on lighting for location shooting.

supercardioid A microphone that picks up in an extreme heart-shaped pattern.

superimpose To layer one image atop another in such a way that the images are seen through each other.

Super-VHS A ½-inch video format that was enough of an improvement on VHS that it could be used by the professionals and industry as well as by consumers. Also referred to as **S-VHS**.

surround sound A sound recording or processing technique that emphasizes spatial relationships, giving the audience a sense of the sound moving around them.

sustain The amount of time a sound is at full volume.

S-VHS See *Super-VHS*.

sweetening Improving or in other ways working with sound during post-production.

switcher A piece of equipment used to select and/or mix video inputs and send them to an output such as a VCR.

sync To coordinate two elements, such as audio and video, with each other; in video, the electronic timing pulses that coordinate the scanning process.

sync block A piece of equipment that locks film and magnetic stock together in a consistent relationship during editing.

synchronous sound Sounds, such as dialogue and some sound effects, recorded during production that need to be in sync with the picture.

table stand A device that rests on a table and holds a microphone.

take An indication of the number of times a certain shot is recorded; the first recording would be take 1, the second would be take 2.

tape splicer A piece of equipment that uses clear mylar tape to join together two pieces of film.

target The photoconductive area at the front end of a TV tube, or the CCD.

TBC See *time-base corrector*.

technical rehearsal A run-through of a shot or scene that is held mainly for the benefit of the technical crew rather than the actors.

telecine A device for transferring film to tape.

telephoto lens A long focal length lens that magnifies and foreshortens a subject.

30-degree rule The convention of changing the camera angle at least 30 degrees between two shots to minimize the apparent jump in size or volume when those shots are edited together.

three-point lighting A traditional approach to lighting that employs a key light, fill light, and back light.

three-to-one rule The principle that states that no two mics should be placed closer than three times the distance between them and the subject so that multiple mic interference will not occur.

three-two pulldown A process used when film is transferred to video to account for the fact that film runs at 24 frames per second and video scans at 30 frames per second; the odd film frames are transferred to two fields of video, and the even film frames are transferred to three fields of video.

threshold of pain The point at which sound hurts the ears, usually about 120 dB.

tilt Moving the camera up or down on a tripod or when hand-held.

tilted shot See *canted shot*.

timbre The particular sound that each musical instrument or voice has, involving such characteristics as mellowness, sharpness, and resonance.

time code See *SMPTE time code* or *vertical interval time code* or *longitudinal time code*.

time code generator A device that produces numbers indicating hours, minutes, seconds, and frames for recording on magnetic tape.

time code numbers Hours, minutes, seconds, and frame numbers embedded in videotape or audiotape that are used primarily to provide an accurate address for each frame to facilitate editing.

time code reader A device that displays on a monitor or other device the hour, minute, second, and frame numbers embedded in a tape.

time-base corrector A device that places a VCR video frame (or part of it) in temporary digital storage so that its scanning timing can match that of video coming from other VCRs; abbreviated **TBC**.

timeline A graphical editing interface common in nonlinear editing software in which thumbnail representations of video and audio clips are arranged along a display of the different tracks; sometimes called a *storyboard*.

timer A person who evaluates each scene of a film or tape and then corrects for exposure and color balance as needed; a piece of video equipment that can be used to make subtle color changes in the picture.

timing Making minor color corrections to a film or video image.

timing sheet A list that aids the music composer by providing the edge numbers or time code numbers for the places where music is to be heard, the length the music is to run, and a description of the scenes.

tonality The range of colors or black and white that a particular film stock reproduces well.

tone A high-pitched hum, usually coming from an audio board, that can be set at 100 percent in order to calibrate audio equipment; a control that can emphasize bass or treble frequencies.

tone generator The part of a tape recorder or audio board that sends out a constant 1 kilohertz sound that is used to set consistent volume levels on various pieces of equipment.

track Moving a camera and its supporting device left or right, parallel to the subject.

tracking A control on a VCR that can be adjusted to make sure that the tape head position for playback is similar to the position used for recording.

transitions Methods, such as dissolves and fades, used to get from one shot to the next.

traveling matte A laboratory process for printing a moving object in one shot into a background that was shot separately. See also *blue-screen photography*.

treatment Written prose that gives the story line for a proposed screenplay.

trigger Part of a computer program that stores information about such sound elements as pitch, duration, and volume and then recreates those, through MIDI, to activate electronic musical instruments.

trim A button on a video edit controller that allows the operator to change an edit point slightly without marking entirely new edit points.

tripod A three-legged device for supporting a camera.

trombone A light-mounting instrument shaped like the musical instrument.

truck Moving a camera and its supporting device left or right, parallel to the subject.

t-stop Lens stop, similar to the f-stop, based on the actual amount of light transmitted through a particular lens.

tube See *pickup tube*.

tungsten-halogen lamp A light that has a tungsten filament and quartz envelope (bulb) filled with halogen. It maintains color temperature and brightness longer than regular incandescent lamps.

TV receiver A TV set that is designed to display broadcast signals.

Type C   A 1-inch video format used professionally.

UHF connector   An ultra-high-frequency video connector that has a center pin and a barrel-like, threaded outer housing.

ultracardioid   A microphone that picks up in an extreme heart-shaped pattern.

ultraviolet filter   A filter that eliminates haze by blocking out ultraviolet rays; also called the **UV filter.**

U-Matic   The standard ¾-inch videotape format.

U-Matic SP   An improvement (superior performance) on the ¾-inch U-Matic video format.

umbrella reflector   Shiny material in umbrella shape that is attached to a light stand so that the lighting instrument can be turned into it and the light can be bounced off it, creating a diffused effect.

unbalanced   Refers to cable that has two wires, one for positive and one for negative and ground; also refers to a composition with more relative weight on one side of the frame than the other.

unit manager   See *production manager.*

unit production manager   See *production manager.*

universal clamp   A small metal clamp that attaches to a porcelain socket for holding photofloods.

upright   An electrically powered film editing machine in a vertical configuration.

utility person   A person who performs a variety of general tasks during the production phase of moviemaking.

UV filter   See *ultraviolet filter.*

variable focal length lens   A lens that can capture wide and narrow shots and everything in between; commonly referred to as a **zoom lens.**

variable shutter   On a film camera, the thin metal disk near the iris that can be adjusted to allow more or less light to hit the film; on a video camera, an electronic device that makes it possible to record extremely fast action without blurring.

VCR operator   The person who operates a videotape or videocassette recorder.

vectorscope   A piece of equipment that displays the color characteristics of the video signal.

velocity   The speed of sound.

vertical blanking interval   The period of time during which the electron beam of a camera or receiver tube is turned off so that it can move from the bottom to the top of the

picture in order to begin scanning another field.

vertical interval time code   Time code that is recorded in the space created during the scanning process while the beam is retracing from the bottom to the top of the picture tube; also referred to as **VITC.**

VHS   A ½-inch consumer-grade video format introduced by JVC that became very popular.

VHS-C   A small videocassette used in recording with the VHS format.

video assist   Using a video tap in conjunction with a film camera to provide immediate feedback about how a particular shot looks.

Video-8   A consumer-grade video format introduced by Sony that uses 8mm-wide tape.

videographer   The person in video production who has overall responsibility for making sure all shots are properly lit and composed.

viewer   A piece of equipment used by an editor to look at the footage during film editing.

viewfinder   The part of the camera that shows the picture that is being framed.

VITC   Vertical interval time code; time code laid down in the vertical interval of a video signal.

VO   See *voice-over.*

voice-over   Words spoken by an off-screen narrator or character; abbreviated **VO.**

volt   A unit of measure of electromotive force that equals the force required to produce a current of 1 amp through a resistance of 1 ohm.

volume   The relative intensity of a sound.

volume unit meter   A device, either with a meter and needle or a digital readout of lights, that shows how loudly a sound is being recorded or played back; also referred to as a **VU meter.**

VU meter   See *volume unit meter.*

wall plate   A light fixture with a flat surface that attaches to a wall in order to hold a light.

walla walla   A background sound that involves the recording of people's voices so that the actual words they are saying cannot be understood.

watt   A unit of electrical power that equals the power expended when 1 amp of current flows through 1 ohm of resistance.

waveform monitor   A piece of equipment that displays luminance information about a video signal.

wavelength   The distance between points of corresponding phases in electromagnetic waves.

white balance   To adjust the imaging system of a video camera so that it reproduces white (and therefore all other colors) correctly for a particular lighting situation.

white reference   Something in a scene that is at the highest level of the brightness range the camera can reproduce.

wide-angle lens   A lens with a broad angle of view that makes objects appear smaller and farther apart than they appear to the naked eye; also called a **short lens.**

widescreen   An aspect ratio wider than 1.33: 1, such as 1.85:1, 2.21:1, 2.35:1.

wild sounds   Asynchronous noise recorded separately from the picture and generally supplied during editing for background.

window dub   A copy of recorded material that shows time code numbers burned into a rectangular area somewhere in the picture area.

windscreen   A metal or foam cover for a microphone that cuts down on small disruptive noises.

wipe   Gradual replacement of one picture with another by having one picture push the other off-screen.

wireless mic   A microphone that operates on FM frequencies and has an antenna that transmits to a receiver. It does not require an audio cable.

workprint   A copy of the original film or tape footage used for editing so that the original does not become damaged.

writer   The person who creates the script for a movie.

XLR connector   A connector that has three prongs and an outer covering; also called a Cannon connector.

X-Y miking   A stereo pickup method that uses two cardioid mics placed next to each other.

zoom   To adjust the focal length of the shot on a variable focal length lens while the shot is being executed.

zoom lens   A complex lens with variable focal lengths, adjustable in a range from wide to telephoto.

zoom mic   A microphone, the pickup pattern of which can be changed gradually from cardioid to supercardioid so that it can pick up sounds at different distances.

Suggested Readings

Adams, Michael H. *Single-Camera Video.* Dubuque, IA: Wm. C. Brown, 1992.

Alten, Stanley R. *Audio in Media,* 4th ed. Belmont, CA: Wadsworth, 1994.

Amyes, Tim. *The Technique of Audio Post-Production in Video and Film.* Newton, MA: Focal Press, 1990.

Armer, Alan A. *Directing Television and Film,* 2nd ed. Belmont, CA: Wadsworth, 1990.

———. *Writing the Screenplay: TV and Film,* 2nd ed. Belmont, CA: Wadsworth, 1993.

Arnold, Richard L. *Scene Technology.* Englewood Cliffs, NJ: Prentice-Hall, 1985.

Blum, Richard. *Television and Screen Writing.* Newton, MA: Focal Press, 1995.

Bordwell, David, and Kristin Thompson. *Film Art: An Introduction,* 4th ed. New York: McGraw-Hill, 1993.

Brown, Blain. *Motion Picture and Video Lighting.* Newton, MA: Focal Press, 1993.

Burch, Noel. *Theory of Film Practice,* trans. by Helen R. Lane. New York: Praeger, 1973.

Burder, John. *The Technique of Editing 16mm Films,* 5th ed. Newton, MA: Focal Press, 1988.

Burrows, Thomas D., Lynne S. Gross, and Donald N. Wood. *Television Production: Disciplines and Techniques,* 5th ed. Dubuque, IA: Wm. C. Brown, 1995.

Carlin, Dan, Sr. *Music in Film and Video Productions.* Newton, MA: Focal Press, 1991.

Cheshire, David. *The Book of Movie Photography.* New York: Alfred A. Knopf, 1984.

Cox, James Stevens. *Hairdressing and Wig Making.* London: Batsford Academic, 1984.

Darby, William, and Jack Du Bois. *American Film Music.* Jefferson, NC: McFarland, 1990.

Di Zazzo, Ray. *Corporate Scriptwriting.* Newton, MA: Focal Press, 1992.

Eargle, John M. *Music, Sound, and Technology.* New York: Van Nostrand Reinhold, 1995.

Egri, Lajos. *The Art of Dramatic Writing.* New York: Simon & Schuster, 1946.

Ferncase, Richard K. *Film and Video Lighting: Terms and Concepts.* Newton, MA: Focal Press, 1994.

Field, Syd. *Screenplay: The Foundations of Screenwriting.* New York: Dell, 1982.

Gates, Richard. *Production Management for Film and Video.* Newton, MA: Focal Press, 1995.

Goldman, William. *Adventures in the Screen Trade: A Personal View of Hollywood and Screenwriting.* New York: Warner Books, 1983.

Gomery, Douglas. *Movie History.* Belmont, CA: Wadsworth, 1990.

Gross, Lynne, and David E. Reese. *Radio Production Worktext: Studio and Equipment.* Newton, MA: Focal Press, 1993.

Hollyn, Norman. *The Film Editing Room Handbook.* Los Angeles: Lone Eagle, 1990.

Honthaner, Eve Light. *The Complete Film Production Handbook.* Los Angeles: Lone Eagle, 1992.

Huber, David Miles. *Audio Production Techniques in Video.* Indianapolis, IN: Howard W. Sams, 1987.

Ingham, Rosemary. *The Costumer's Handbook.* New York: Prentice-Hall, 1987.

Joyner, Harry M., Jr. *Roll 'Em! Action!* Jefferson, NC: McFarland, 1992.

Kehoe, Virginia. *The Techniques of the Professional Make-Up Artist.* Newton, MA: Focal Press, 1995.

Lipton, Lenny. *Independent Filmmaking.* New York: Simon & Schuster, 1983.

Lowell, Ross. *Matters of Light and Depth.* Philadelphia: Broad Street Books, 1992.

Madsen, Roy Paul. *Working Cinema: Learning from the Masters.* Belmont, CA: Wadsworth, 1990.

Maier, Robert G. *Location Scouting and Management Handbook.* Newton, MA: Focal Press, 1994.

Manner, Bruce. *Film Production Technique.* Belmont, CA: Wadsworth, 1996.

Mast, Gerald. *A Short History of the Movies,* 4th ed. New York: Macmillan, 1986.

Mathias, Harry, and Richard Patterson. *Electronic Cinematography.* Belmont, CA: Wadsworth, 1985.

Mehring, Margaret. *The Screenplay.* Newton, MA: Focal Press, 1990.

Millerson, Gerald. *Technique of Lighting for Television and Film,* 3rd ed. Newton, MA: Focal Press, 1991.

———. *TV Scenic Design Handbook.* Newton, MA: Focal Press, 1989.

Monaco, James. *How to Read a Film,* rev. ed. New York: Oxford University Press, 1981.

Morgan, Bradley J. and Joseph M. Palmisano. *Film and Video Career Directory.* Detroit: Visible Ink, 1994.

Nisbett, Alex. *The Use of Microphones,* 3rd ed. Newton, MA: Focal Press, 1989.

O'Donnell, Lewis B., Philip Benoit, and Carl Hausman. *Modern Radio Production,* 2nd ed. Belmont, CA: Wadsworth, 1990.

Olson, Robert. *Art Direction for Film and Video.* Newton, MA: Focal Press, 1993.

Richards, Ron. *Director's Method for Film and Television.* Newton, MA: Focal Press, 1992.

Rosenthal, Alan. *Writing Docudrama.* Newton, MA: Focal Press, 1994.

Rumsey, Francis. *MIDI Systems and Control.* Newton, MA: Focal Press, 1994.

Schneider, Arthur. *Electronic Post-Production and Videotape Editing.* Newton, MA: Focal Press, 1989.

Sterritt, David. *The Films of Alfred Hitchcock.* Cambridge: Cambridge University Press, 1993.

Tucker, Patrick. *How to Act for the Camera.* New York: Routledge Press, 1993.

Viera, Dave. *Lighting for Film and Electronic Cinematography.* Belmont, CA: Wadsworth, 1993.

Watkinson, John. *The Art of Digital Audio.* Newton, MA: Focal Press, 1994.

Whittaker, Ron. *Video Field Production,* 2nd ed. Mountain View, CA: Mayfield, 1996.

Wilson, Anton. *Cinema Workshop,* 3rd ed. Hollywood: ASC Holding Corp., 1983.

Wolff, Jurgen, and Kerry Cox. *Top Secrets: Screenwriting.* Los Angeles: Lone Eagle, 1992.

Zettl, Herbert. *Sight-Sound-Motion: Applied Media Aesthetics,* 2nd ed. Belmont, CA: Wadsworth, 1990.

———. *Television Production Handbook,* 6th ed. Belmont, CA: Wadsworth, 1997.

Index